PAS
REVOLUTION

JESUS
MARIA Y JOSE
VENCIT MUNDUM
CS ML
N D S + M D.
Cruzes Hoc patibulum si bire vutuiste et inimici concede nobis signaterumes super Lucem vultus tui + Domine +
Crusis Furgalo atte deposee tres cruzes erute Sunt
EST VICTORIA QUE VENCIT
JUSTA CRU
CRUCEM
Ascendit decite rignabit aligno ridemit
SANTAM subil qui in fernum con fregit nos
CRUZ EST ARBOR +
CRUZES
QUEM FACIEVAT QUIS
EGO SUM VIA BENIDICTUS VOBIS FACDAD PRIDEUM
Hom
Curpuris
HOC
N R L B S P M T

PASYON AND REVOLUTION

Popular Movements in the Philippines, 1840–1910

Reynaldo Clemeña Ileto

Ateneo de Manila University Press

ATENEO DE MANILA UNIVERSITY PRESS
Bellarmine Hall, Loyola Heights, Q.C.
P.O. Box 154, 1099 Manila, Philippines

First Printing 1979
Second Printing 1981
Third Printing 1989
Fourth Printing 1997
Fifth printing 1998

The cover illustration is an artist's composite based on a statue housed in the Santa Clara church (of the Philippine Independent Church) in Sampaloc, Manila, and on Aurelio Tolentino's story of a Katipunero's dream of the Virgin dressed in the Filipino *balintawak* and leading a handsome child in peasant garb who is armed with a glittering bolo. The illustration facing the title page is taken from a photograph of Macario Sakay's *anting-anting* found in the U.S. National Archives.

The National Library of the Philippines CIP Data

Recommended entry:

Ileto, Reynaldo C.
Pasyon and revolution : popular movements in the Philippines, 1840–1910 / Reynaldo Clemeña Ileto. – Quezon City : ADMU Press, c1997
296 p

1. Philippines – History – 1840–1910. I. Title.

DS675 959.902'3 1997 P971000001
ISBN 971-550-232-6 (pbk.)
ISBN 971-550-233-4 (n.p.)

Handog
kay Loolee
kina Mama at Papa
at sa lahat ng dumamay
sa lakarang ito

Abbreviations

ANL	Australian National Library, Canberra
APSR	Archivo de la Provincia del Santisímo Rosario, Quezon City
ARPC	Annual Reports of the Philippine Commission (variously titled), Washington, 1901–1910
BCTE	Beyer Collection, Tagalog Ethnography Series, ANL
BIA	Bureau of Insular Affairs, USNA, Washington, D.C.
BRPI	Blair and Robertson, *The Philippine Islands, 1493-1898*
MHC	Michigan Historical Collections, University of Michigan
PCR	Philippine Constabulary Records, H.H. Bandholtz Papers,
PIR	Philippine Insurgent Records, PNL
PIR-SD	Philippine Insurgent Records, Selected Documents (separate section of PIR)
PNA	Philippine National Archives, Manila
PNL	Philippine National Library, Manila
RENFIL	*Renacimiento Filipino*, a bi-monthly publication in Spanish and Tagalog, Manila, 1910–1912
USNA	United States National Archives, Washington, D.C.
WPC	Worcester Philippine Collection, University of Michigan Library, Ann Arbor

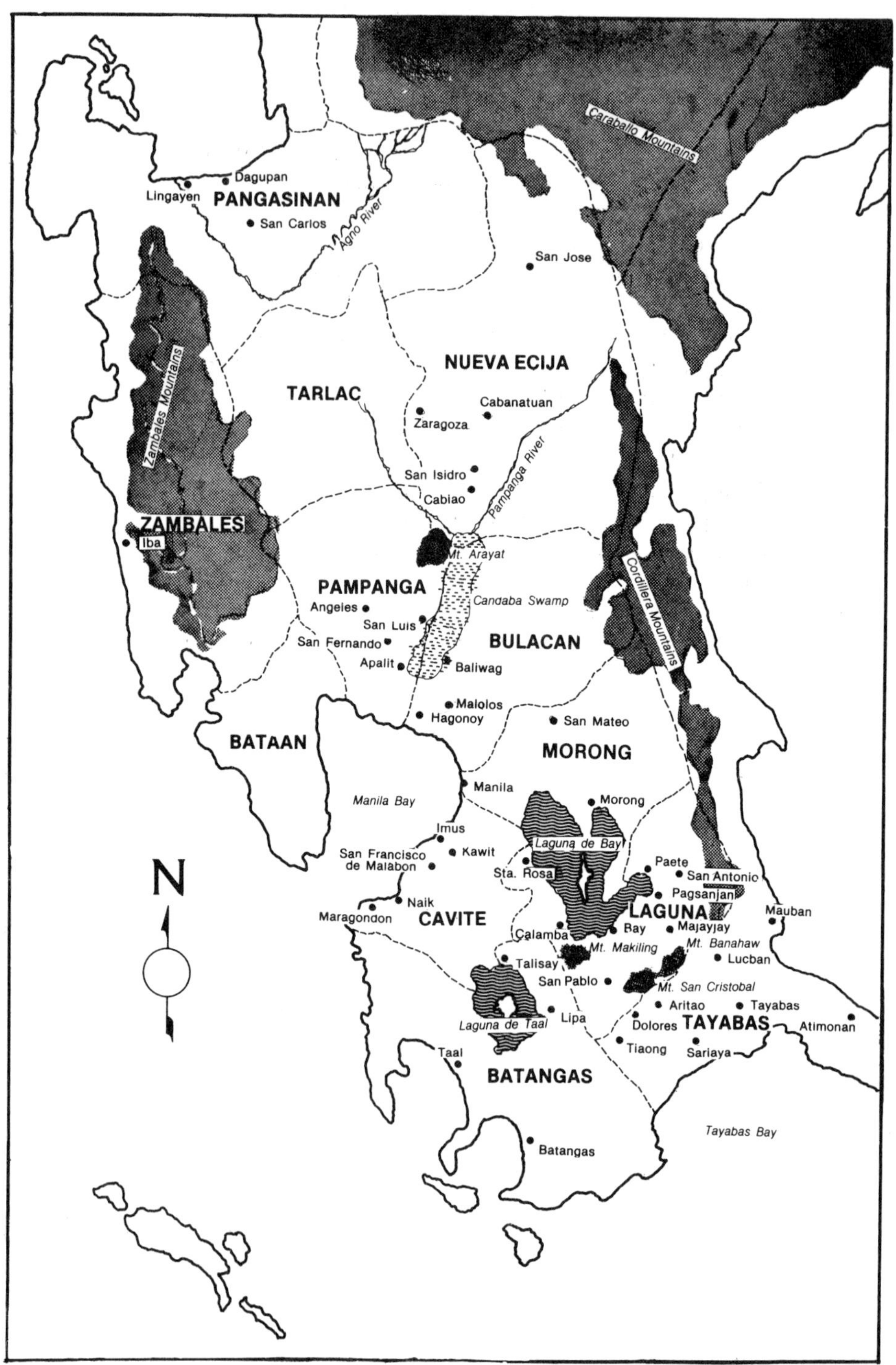

Central and Southern Luzon in the nineteenth century

Contents

Preface

My choice of subject matter was determined by much the same conditions that led the Filipino youth to question the nature of their society and politics during the late sixties and early seventies. The basic research for this book was done in the Philippines in 1971 and early 1972, the eve of Martial Law, a time of great outpouring of energy from many sectors of the populace. It was not just the libraries and archives that offered interesting material, but also the people around me who were asking similar questions about the relationship of the past to the present. Ultimately, a couple of apparently unrelated experiences in 1971 confirmed the direction of my thinking. One was hearing an activist priest named Fr. Ed de la Torre describe to a student audience the idiom of liberation that, he had discovered, Tagalog peasants best related to; it had to do with a certain understanding of Christ's passion, death, and resurrection. To the students steeped in Marx and Mao this was a revelation, but I thought I had felt the power of that very same language as I observed and participated in the rituals of the Watawat ng Lahi peasant society in rural Calamba and interviewed its late president, Jose Baricanosa.

The gap I perceived between student and peasant idioms of protest led me to the question of suppressed discourses in Philippine politics. The nationalist codification of history in linear and developmental terms had swept into the sidelines a discourse and a series of events that activists like Fr. Ed who took seriously the slogan "Learn from the people!" were beginning to rediscover. It seems to me, however, that the dominant ilustrado discourses emanating from the universities would have prevailed almost unsullied, had it not been for a period of reflection and self-criticism beginning in September 1972. This book was drafted during the first two years of Martial Law. How depressing it was to witness the regime's cooptation of nationalist symbols, its empty promises of a new and prosperous society, the grandiose claims of its Leader. And yet a rereading of history revealed that it had all happened before and, more importantly, that in Philippine culture itself could be found the elements of a critique of such empty externalities. True, the Filipino elite had learned to play the political power game, but from time to time individuals had crossed the scene with a different set of priorities for which they had often paid the price of their lives. *Pasyon and Revolution* looks into the conditions of the possibility of their emergence.

Looking back, it seems to me that a book of this sort would not have been possible without the introduction to French and German philosophy that I gained from Ramon Reyes and other professors at the Ateneo de Manila. Indeed, it took years of enduring the rigors and, at times, meaninglessness of

American social science, before I was able—through the construction of this book, in fact—to reconcile my gut intellectual concerns with the demands of modern historical research. I was fortunate in having mentors like Benedict Anderson, James Siegel, and Oliver Wolters who helped me rethink my earlier ideas and introduced me to new perspectives in the fields of anthropology, history, literary criticism, and politics. Their scholarship on Southeast Asia is reflected in the questions I raise here concerning the Philippines. Their perceptive comments on the manuscript were instrumental in getting this book into its present shape.

I am grateful to the many individuals who gave me much needed suggestions, encouragement, and inspiration at various stages of this project. My understanding of folk religion and religiopolitical associations owes much to Robert Love and Prospero Covar. I gained many new insights on the Philippines from discussions with Knight Biggerstaff about Chinese peasant uprisings. My distrust of behaviorism in the social sciences was reinforced by my wife Loolee Carandang's preoccupation with Piaget's theories. Aurora Roxas-Lim introduced me to the work of Teodoro Agoncillo and the wealth of Tagalog literature. John Larkin and David Sturtevant in 1971 gave me valuable advice as to how and where to start my investigations. Samuel Tan's research experience and companionship helped me tame the vast U.S. National Archives. And Cesar Majul convinced me, at the time that the anti-Martial Law movement was emerging in the U.S., that this book in the long run would be a more valuable contribution to the Filipino cause than anything else I did.

In the painful process of reworking the manuscript I was helped by the comments and suggestions for improvement provided by Leonard and Barbara Andaya, Shelly Errington, David Marr, Ruth McVey, Anthony Reid, and Dennis Shoesmith. Jim Richardson and John Schumacher, S.J., sent me extensive typewritten critiques that pointed out basic errors and forced me to clarify my views. Bienvenido Lumbera and Isagani Medina generously shared their knowledge of Tagalog literature and helped me translate some difficult *Dalit* passages. Many other colleagues and graduate students, particularly those who participated in my History 207 seminars at the University of the Philippines, gave me much-needed moral support and the opportunity to articulate my thoughts. To all I owe a lifelong debt.

Support for the research and writing of this book was made possible through generous grants from the Cornell Philippines Project, Cornell Southeast Asia Program, and London-Cornell Project. A fellowship in the Department of Pacific and Southeast Asian History, Australian National University, provided me with additional research funds and ideal conditions for the completion of a book manuscript. Part of a Ford Foundation Southeast Asia grant enabled me to travel to Ann Arbor to examine the University of Michigan's Philippine collections.

To the following individuals, as well, I acknowledge a debt of gratitude: Carolina Afan, Rizalina Concepcion and Serafin Quiason for bringing to my attention important materials in the National Archives and the National Library; Doreen Fernandez for the loan of her photo-file on the Lapiang Malaya; Nicanor Tiongson for graciously inviting me to Malolos to observe the Holy Week rituals; the staffs of the various libraries and archives listed in the bibliography for their courtesy and help; and, finally, Esther M. Pacheco and her staff at the Ateneo de Manila University Press for patiently reminding me about deadlines, seeing through the transformation of my manuscript into a book, and completely retypesetting the manuscript for the book's third printing. Needless to say, none of the persons I have mentioned above are responsible for any errors of fact and interpretation in this book.

Valentin de los Santos, Lapiang Malaya *supremo* above a representation of *liwanag* (photo by Romeo Vitug)

CHAPTER 1

Toward a History from Below

One Sunday morning in May 1967, residents of Manila awoke to find a strange uprising in their midst. A little past midnight, street fighting had erupted along a section of Taft Avenue between the constabulary and hundreds of followers of a religiopolitical society calling itself *Lapiang Malaya*, the Freedom Party.[1] Armed only with sacred bolos, *anting-anting* (amulets) and bullet-defying uniforms, the *kapatid* (brothers) enthusiastically met the challenge of automatic weapons fire from government troopers, yielding only when scores of their comrades lay dead on the street. When the smoke from the encounter had cleared, only a few, if any, of the country's politicians and avid newspaper readers really understood what had happened. Who or what would shoulder the blame: depressed rural conditions, trigger-happy police, religious fanaticism, or, as intelligence reports claimed, Communists? After some weeks of public uproar, the incident quickly faded in people's memories. Except for those who had joined or sympathized with the uprising, the whole event was a momentary disruption of the familiar and explicable pattern of the nation's history.

The leader, or *supremo*, of the Lapiang Malaya was a charismatic Bicolano named Valentin de los Santos. Eighty-six years old at the time of the uprising, he had been involved with the militant sect since the late 1940s, building it up to a membership of around forty thousand drawn from the Southern Luzon peasantry. De los Santos's goals were very basic: true justice, true equality, and true freedom for the country. But it was his style of portraying and attaining

1. My brief account of the Lapiang Malaya is drawn largely from David Sturtevant, "Rizalistas—Contemporary Revitalization Movements in the Philippines," *Agrarian Unrest in the Philippines* (Athens, Ohio: Ohio University Center for International Studies, 1969). A more recent scholarly work is Elizabeth Pastores's "Religious Leadership in the Lapiang Malaya: A Historical Note," in *Filipino Religious Psychology,* ed. Leonardo Mercado, S.V.D. (Tacloban: Divine Word University, 1977).

these goals that made him appear a hero to some and a madman to others. He was, for example, a medium regularly communicating with *Bathala* (supreme god) and past Filipino patriots, above all Rizal. He linked the attainment of freedom with the Second Coming prophesied in the New Testament. And he subscribed to ancient beliefs in the magical potency of sacred weapons, inscribed objects (anting-anting) and formulaic prayers. Thus, when he declared himself a presidential candidate in the 1957 and subsequent elections, his challenge was regarded with amusement by regular politicians. His demand, in early May 1967, for the resignation of President Marcos was his final act of defiance against the political establishment which he believed at least since 1966 to be currying too much favor with alien powers.[2] The supremo's demand was summarily dismissed, contributing to the mounting tension that exploded in the infamous "Black Sunday" massacre. In the aftermath, the supremo was, according to an anonymous sect leader,

> taken to the Mental Hospital and pronounced insane. He was put in a cell together with a hopelessly violent case. Soon he was mauled and beaten while sleeping. He lost consciousness and was taken to an isolation ward. . . . After more than a week, he died without regaining consciousness. . . . The verdict of the attending physician was that he died of pneumonia.[3]

The Lapiang Malaya affair is not an isolated event in Philippine history. It is not an aberration in an otherwise comprehensible past. We should be able to find meaning in it, not resorting to convenient explanations like "fanaticism," "nativism," and "millenarianism," which only alienate us further from the kapatid who lived through it. But what we modern Filipinos need first of all is a set of conceptual tools, a grammar, that would help us understand the world of the kapatid, which is part of our world. Twentieth-century economic and technological developments have produced the modern Filipino culture to which we belong, but as Marx himself often pointed out, cultural transformation proceeds in an uneven, sporadic manner so that in a given historical situation we find cultural modes that reflect previous stages of development. In the interest of social reform we can either further accelerate the demise of "backward" ways of thinking (reflected in the Lapiang Malaya) in order to pave way for the new, or we can graft modern ideas onto traditional modes of thought. Whatever our strategy may be, it is necessary that we first understand how the traditional mind operates, particularly in relation to questions of change. This book aims to help bring about this understanding.

---

2. During the 1966 summit conference on the Vietnam War, approximately a thousand bolo-armed Lapiang Malaya members assembled in Manila to disrupt the conference proceedings. They were dispersed by the police without incident (Sturtevant, *Agrarian Unrest,* p. 21). The antiforeign sentiments of the group are fully described in Pastores's essay (op. cit.).

3. Sturtevant, *Agrarian Unrest,* p. 22.

The "Revolt of the Masses"

Anyone familiar with Philippine history will recognize the Lapiang Malaya's continuity with the Katipunan secret society of 1896. The triangular symbols, the colorful uniforms, the title "supremo" and even the very idea of a radical brotherhood stemmed from the Katipunan experience. In fact, our difficulty in understanding the Lapiang Malaya can be stretched backward in time: do we really understand what the Katipunan uprising was all about? There is no doubt that the post-1872 period up to and including the revolutions of 1896 and 1898 have been overstudied. But the overall framework of interpretation has remained rather constant. Just as pre-1872 accounts tend to focus upon the struggle of the native clergy for equal status with the friars, post-1872 studies usually deal with the activities of the native and mestizo elite that was to lead the nationalist struggle. This strongly evolutionary framework places a premium on the ideas and activities of the Filipino priests and intellectuals who gave form to the aspirations of the masses.

Briefly, the main historical themes are as follows. Economic changes in the nineteenth century, such as the opening of the islands to foreign trade and capital investment, led to the rise of a prosperous class of mestizos and native elites, or *principales.* For the first time, families could afford to send their sons to universities in Manila and Europe. Influenced by Western liberal ideas, educated Filipinos called *ilustrados,* or "the enlightened," were determined to have the radical changes in the mother country applied to the colony itself. In other words, they wanted to be treated equal to the Spaniards, the main obstacles to this end being the powerful religious orders that dominated colonial life. In spite of the ultimately narrow class interests behind their agitation, the ilustrados managed to stir up a nationalist sentiment among the masses by focusing upon friar abuse that was universally felt in varying degrees. And so, even as the reformist or assimilationist movement faltered and died in the early 1890s, the upsurge of nationalism was such that a separatist movement—the Katipunan—was able to take root among the masses. The Katipunan's uprising in 1896 triggered the revolution. But by 1897 the original secret society was superseded by a revolutionary government with republican aspirations. The culmination of such developments was the republic of 1898, however shortlived it was owing to its weak ilustrado leadership and the success of American military and political campaigns to destroy it.[4]

---

4. The literature on this period is fairly abundant. For example, see Onofre D. Corpuz, *The Philippines* (Englewood Cliffs, New Jersey: Prentice Hall, 1965); John Schumacher, S.J., *The Propaganda Movement,* 1880–1895 (Manila: Solidaridad, 1972); Cesar A. Majul, *The Political and Constitutional Ideas of the Philippine Revolution* (Quezon City: University of the Philippines, 1957); and the standard university textbook, *History of the Filipino People* (Quezon City, University of the Philippines, 1956) by Teodoro Agoncillo and Oscar Alfonso, and revised in 1977 by Agoncillo and Milagros Guerrero.

To return to my original question: have we fully understood the Katipunan within the framework summarized above? I first began to reflect upon this question after rereading Teodoro Agoncillo's *The Revolt of the Masses,* a classic work which not only brought Andres Bonifacio the recognition due him (which had been suppressed during American rule), but also gave succeeding generations of scholars plenty to think about.[5] The title of the book indicates Agoncillo's purpose—to rectify the tendency of historians before him to regard the revolution as the handiwork of upper-class, Hispanized natives.[6] He stresses instead that the Katipunan movement was initiated by petty clerks, laborers, and artisans in Manila, and that it was only later that educated and propertied Filipinos were, with some reluctance, drawn into the struggle.

Although I found the story of the Katipunan and its supremo, Bonifacio, vividly reconstructed by Agoncillo, I remained intrigued by the relationship of the title of the book to its body. The physical involvement of the masses in the revolution is pretty clear, but how did they actually perceive, in terms of their own experience, the ideas of nationalism and revolution brought from the West by the ilustrados? Agoncillo assumes that to all those who engaged in revolution, the meaning of independence was the same: separation from Spain and the building of a sovereign Filipino nation. We can rest assured that this was the revolutionary elite's meaning, which could very well be identical with that of revolutionary elites in Latin America and elsewhere. But the meaning of the revolution to the masses—the largely rural and uneducated Filipinos who constituted the revolution's mass base—remains problematic for us. We cannot assume that their views and aspirations were formless, inchoate, and meaningless apart from their articulation in ilustrado thought.

The dimensions of the problem become apparent in the treatment of the Katipunan's split into *Magdiwang* and *Magdalo* factions—an internal crisis that was resolved only upon Bonifacio's death. The latter's execution, ordered by the revolutionary government of Emilio Aguinaldo, seems to be rationalized by Agoncillo and other scholars as the predictable outcome of a power struggle between equally patriotic individuals for control of the revolution's leadership.[7] For the sake of unity, perhaps the tragic death of Bonifacio could be justified. Moreover, following an evolutionary perspective on nationalism, the dismantling of Bonifacio's brainchild—the Katipunan secret society—was

5. This was a prize-winning entry in the Bonifacio biography contest of 1948, but was published only in 1956 because of its then-controversial interpretation of the revolution.

6. See, for example, Gregorio Zaide, *Philippine Political and Cultural History,* rev. ed. (Manila: Philippine Education, 1957).

7. In narrating the power struggle, Agoncillo is sympathetic to the plight of Bonifacio but accepts Aguinaldo's rationalization of it. Carlos Quirino, however, has gone to the extent of being hostile to Bonifacio (see his introduction to *The Trial of Andres Bonifacio* [Manila: Ateneo de Manila, 1963]). The recent work by Jesuits Pedro de Achútegui and Miguel A. Bernad, *Aguinaldo and the Revolution of 1896: A Documentary History* (Quezon City: Ateneo de Manila, 1972) is useful for its documents but does not cast new light on the "power struggle."

perhaps necessary in order to preserve the viability of a revolutionary government that aspired to create a republic, certainly a more advanced political entity that articulated the aspirations of a wider community. In the history of the revolution, the Republic of 1898 overshadows everything; it is the central event to which everything else is pinned. Meanwhile, we are left wondering about Bonifacio—his passionate commitment, the vibrant language that inspired thousands to rise, the Katipunan's "strange" initiation rites, and the emblems and symbols that often took on a magical significance to the masses. If we, for the moment, lay aside questions of ultimate patriotism and political sophistication, and simply let Bonifacio and the Katipunan speak to us, perhaps a few controversies may be laid to rest.

Eventually, the problem we face is how to categorize the activities of post-1902 katipunans, religiopolitical societies and other peasant-based groups that waved the banner of independence and plagued the new colonial order up to the 1930s. The bulk of the principales who supported and led the revolution had accepted a revised program for the attainment of independence. Ilustrado politicians like Manuel Quezon, Sergio Osmeña, and Manuel Roxas now proclaimed themselves at the helm of the revolution, pragmatically setting the groundwork for independence as promised by the Americans. How then are the "troublemakers" to be viewed? Were Macario Sakay and his katipunan romantic idealists who failed to adjust to the "realities" of post-1902 colonial politics, just as Bonifacio had stubbornly failed to adjust to the widening scope of the revolution in 1897? Were the various religious leaders—messiahs, popes, supremos, and kings—who with their peasant followers formed their own communities, harrassed landowners and confronted the armed might of the constabulary, simply "religious fanatics" or "frustrated peasants" blindly and irrationally reacting to oppressive conditions? Were nationalist Filipino leaders justified in helping the colonialists suppress these "disturbances"? Even well-meaning historians tend to answer these questions affirmatively. Others regard these movements as curious, interesting but nevertheless minor sidelights compared to the politics of the metropolis. Still others sympathize to a great extent with their anticolonial and anti-elite aspects but fail to understand them in their own light. "Blind reaction" theories prevail; intentions and hopes are left unexamined. This leads to the foregone conclusion that early popular movements were largely failures, and continued to be so until they turned more "rational" and "secular."

"No uprising fails. Each one is a step in the right direction." These were the most memorable statements of Salud Algabre, a female organizer in the Sakdal peasant uprising of 1935, to her interviewer in 1968.[8] Her words may seem perfectly clear to us. The first thing that comes to mind is the notion that each movement learns from the experience, particularly the mistakes, of its predecessors. Though an uprising may be unsuccessful, it paves the way for future

8. David Sturtevant, "No Uprising Fails," *Solidarity* 1 (1966): 11–12.

victory But I think that Algabre's meaning runs deeper than this, and it is precisely the aim of this book to probe into this meaning. In this respect, my efforts follow upon the recent work of Algabre's interviewer himself, David Sturtevant, who attempted to view popular uprisings in their own terms and thus further clarified the meaning of the term "revolt of the masses."

When Sturtevant's dissertation appeared in 1959, no one had paid much attention to pre-1896 revolts, except insofar as they were anticolonial, "protonationalist," or paved the way for 1896.[9] Not until over a decade after 1959 would scholars follow upon Sturtevant's suggestion that, because of rural economic conditions and the persistence of traditional cultural forms, perhaps the peasantry viewed the nineteenth-century situation differently from that of their relatively more sophisticated and urbanized compatriots. The latter, toward the end of the century, noted a widespread provincial ferment, diagnosed it as popular antipathy toward Spain, and assumed that the rural masses would provide near unanimous support to essentially Western revolutionary aspirations. But what actually occurred during the tumultous era of the revolution, Sturtevant writes, was the appearance of a large number of popular movements in Luzon, some led by local "messiahs" and others by "bandit" chiefs, who embodied rural aspirations such as freedom from taxes, reform of the tenancy system, and the restoration of village harmony and communalism. A few of these movements even turned against the Malolos republican government when ilustrado and cacique elements wrested control of it in late 1898. As far as Sturtevant is concerned, the conflicts between "ilustrados and Katipuneros, Catholics and Aglipayans, *Manileños* and *provincianos,* landlords and tenants, regionalists and nationalists; pro- and anti-Americans" as they "contended for control of the truncated revolution" had little or no bearing on the "subplot of provincial protest."[10]

In an analytical sense, Sturtevant points toward a clarification of the "revolt of the masses" thesis by showing how variations in Philippine social structure gave rise to a peasant tradition of unrest, which is called the "Little Tradition," distinct from the elite-led movements for independence which belong to the "Great Tradition."[11] The rural masses had something of their own to say and Sturtevant decries the fact that the Filipino elite either refused to listen to or muffled these voices from below in order to preserve the image of national

9. David Sturtevant, "Philippine Social Structure and Its Relation to Agrarian Unrest" (Ph.D. dissertation, Stanford University, 1969). This dissertation has been extensively revised and published as *Popular Uprisings in the Philippines* (Ithaca: Cornell University, 1976). In discussing Sturtevant's ideas, I have relied on his dissertation and articles, the only works of his available when I started writing this book in 1973. Upon reading *Popular Uprisings,* however, I find that his analytical framework has remained unchanged.

10. Sturtevant, *Agrarian Unrest,* p. 1.

11. The terminology, originally coined by Robert Redfield, was applied to Southeast Asian history in the late Harry Benda's "Peasant Movements in Southeast Asia," *Asian Studies* 3 (1965) 420-34.

unity against colonial rule. It would have been a logical step for Sturtevant to apply his classification to the events of 1896-1897 and define the "Little Tradition" aspects of the Katipunan (which, after all, had a wide rural base). However, he avoids any discussion of the revolution itself largely because he accepts the Filipino elite's definitions of nationalism, independence, and revolution. By not looking for alternative, valid meanings of these terms within the "Little Tradition," he is led to conclude that the peasant-based, religious-oriented challenges to the republic were antinationalist, irrational, and doomed to fail.[12] Because of his inability to decode the language and gestures of peasant rebels, Sturtevant could at best interpret them in the light of psychological stress-strain theories. He says, for example, that they were "blind" responses to social breakdown. In contrast, he ascribes "rational" and "realistic" goals to elite—led movements. In his effort to classify each peasant movement according to its proportionate ingredients of the religious or secular, rational or irrational, progressive or retrogressive, nationalist or anarchist, he explains away whatever creative impulse lies in them rather than properly bring these to light.

The "revolt of the masses" thesis continues to fascinate scholars. Recently, Renato Constantino, in *The Philippines: A Past Revisited,* interpreted the Bonifacio-Aguinaldo conflict as a cooptation of the Katipunan mass movement by the Caviteño elite whose narrow class interests made them vacillate and compromise with the enemy.[13] Bonifacio, of lower middle-class origins and with a smattering of education, had been able to articulate the aspirations of the masses for primitive democracy and freedom from alien rule. Previous revolts had been "instinctual reactions to the social order," spontaneous but lacking ideology, fragmented because only the economic developments of the nineteenth century would provide the material basis for a truly national uprising. It was the Katipunan that forged the centuries-long tradition of unrest with the liberal ideas that the ilustrados had introduced. But because Bonifacio "had the instincts of the masses" whose desires were inchoate, his own declarations were "primitive," inchoate, and needed ilustrado articulation. Constantino, in effect, puts Bonifacio and the Katipunan at the head of "Little Tradition" politics.

The general contours of Sturtevant's study appear in the later chapters of Constantino's book on the mystical, millenial revolts that subsequently turned

---

12. David Steinberg seems to follow Sturtevant in asserting that the Katipunan was an urban phenomenon, with a leadership from the "minute, lower-middle class of white collar employees and from a few ilustrado intellectuals," and that peasant, on the other hand, "were far more involved in general in the religious dimensions of the struggle" ("An Ambiguous Legacy: Years at War in the Philippines," *Pacific Affairs* 45 [1972]: 72).

13. Renato Constantino, *The Philippines: A Past Revisited* (Quezon City: Tala Publishing, 1975). Since I got a copy of Constantino's work only in 1976, I was not able to use it in writing this book. Thus, the reader may find that some of my interpretations of, say, Bonifacio and Sakay are identical with Constantino's.

into more secular, class-conscious movements in the late 1930s.[14] But an important difference exists: whereas Sturtevant practically ignores the patriotic or nationalist dimension of postrevolution mystical movements, Constantino views these movements as "genuine vehicles for the expression of the people's dream of national liberation and economic amelioration."[15] Despite the absence of ilustrado leadership, the masses during the American colonial period kept alive the spirit of 1896 in their own primitive and fragmented style.

In a way, Constantino provides a touchstone for the present work. He presents a systematic and clear analysis of popular movements before, during, and after the revolution. The present volume deals with practically the same events during 1840-1910 but tries to look at them from within, that is, from the perspective of the masses themselves insofar as the data allow it. How, for example, did the masses actually perceive their condition; how did they put their feelings and aspirations into words? How precisely did Bonifacio and the Katipunan effect a connection between tradition and national revolution? How could the post-1902 mystical and millenial movements have taken the form they did and still be extremely radical? Instead of using preconceived or reified categories of nationalism and revolution as the matrix through which events are viewed, I have tried to bring to light the masses' own categories of meaning that shaped their perceptions of events and their participation in them. As Sturtevant tried to show, the conditions of rural life greatly influenced the masses' style of action. But the relationship was not deterministic, nor was their culture (i.e., the "superstructure") without some autonomy relative to their material life.[16] In early revolts, as we shall see, certain types of behavior often regarded as fanatical, irrational, or even "feudal" can be interpreted as peasant attempts to restructure the world in terms of ideal social forms and modes of behavior.

Understanding Philippine Society

The issues that this book is concerned with go beyond the subject of the masses and their participation in the revolution. All around us we hear of the

---

14. The immediate model for this interpretation of popular movements is Eric Hobsbawm's *Primitive Rebels: Studies in Archaic Forms of Social Movement in the 19th and 20th Centuries* (New York: Norton, 1963).

15. Constantino, *Past Revisited,* p. 389. (My italics.)

16. It is well known that Marx, in the preface to the *Critique of Political Economy* of 1859, totally eliminates the force of the "superstructure" (i.e., politics, law, religion, philosophy, and art) in history. But in his politicohistorical writings like *The Civil War in France* and especially *The 18th Brumaire of Louis Bonaparte,* Marx respects the autonomy and complexity of politics, the reciprocal interaction of various levels of society. The relative autonomy of the superstructure is recognized in Engel's letter to Joseph Bloch, where the former states that only "ultimately" or "in the last instance" did the economy determine the superstructure (Lewis Feuer, ed., *Marx and Engels: Basic Writings on Politics and Philosophy* [New York: Doubleday Anchor, 1959], pp. 397-98).

need to define the Filipino personality, style of politics, and social system. Yet the masses are hardly encouraged to participate in this effort. They make their statements in idealized portraits of rural life or, to take the other extreme, social realist representations of clenchfisted toiling peasants. Either way it is the elite, particularly the middle class, that puts its imprint on everything—from culture to national development and revolution. The standard interpretation of the revolution against Spain as the working out of ideas and goals stemming from the ilustrados is symptomatic of the widespread acceptance among scholars that the educated elite functions to articulate Filipino values and aspirations.

The model of Philippine society as patron-client oriented, wherein the patrons or elites are the source not only of money and favors but of "culture" as well, exemplifies the dominant view in current scholarship. The masses of poor and uneducated tao are indeed linked, through various forms of debt relationship and social conditioning to the rural elite, who in turn are indebted to patrons in the urban centers. In actual fact, the shape of present Philippine society is triangular, with a wealthy and educated fraction of the population at the apex. But problems arise when "normal" society is defined in terms of such a triangular structure with built-in mechanisms of self-preservation. When behavioral scientists today speak of social values like *utang na loob* (lifelong debt to another for some favor bestowed), *hiya* (shame), SIR (smooth interpersonal relations) and *pakikisama* (mutual cooperation), they give the impression that these values make Philippine society naturally tend toward stasis and equilibrium.[17] Since debtors are obliged to repay their benefactors, vertical loyalties to landlords and local politicians override horizontal relationships. The society is reduced to sets of rules and patterns of behavior that leave no room for "atypical" challenges to the social order. Conflicts and strains are smoothed out, defused with a minimum of disruption, instead of being resolved. Social change, when it unavoidably occurs, is attributed less to some inner dynamism of Philippine society than to external stresses and ideological influences.

If we accept most current definitions of the Filipino, we come up with something like the image of the smiling, peace-loving, religious, deferential, hard-working, family-bound and hospitable native. The masses, in particular, are regarded as passive acceptors of change on which the modern mass media can effectively train its guns. "Politics" for them is but a game they can allegedly do without or at least simply pay lip service to in lieu of direct participation.

---

17. See, for example, *Four Readings on Philippine Values* (4th ed. enl., IPC Papers No. 2) ed. Frank Lynch and Alfonso de Guzman II (Quezon City: Institute of Philippine Culture, Ateneo de Manila University, 1973). In the writings of Carl Landé, Mary Hollnsteiner, Charles Kaut and Jean Grossholtz, it is assumed that lowland Philippine society naturally tends toward equilibrium. The forging of reciprocal ties among individuals is viewed in terms of economic exchange, which is partly correct but cannot account for the solidarity found among peasant rebels or the "utopian" form of the communities they seek to create.

There is a lot of validity in this image. Social mechanisms do tend to preserve the existing socio-economic structure. The struggle for survival often relegates politics to the sidelines, particularly when the masses perceive that politics has generated into nothing more than *pulitika*—the bargaining and jockeying for power among politicos. There is a lot of truth in Remigio Agpalo's conclusion that "the *tao*, thinking first and foremost of the survival of himself and his family, is little interested in high-sounding policies, ideologies, or principles of good government and administration. What interests him is which party, group or person will give him a job."[18] However, we should guard against reducing Philippine society to this image. We should take into account the innumerable instances in the past when popular movements threatened to upset or overturn the prevailing social structure. Social scientists unable to view society in other than equilibrium terms are bound to conclude that these movements are aberrations or the handiwork of crazed minds, alienated individuals, or external agitators. On the other hand, many scholars sympathetic to these movements tend to fit them into a tight, evolutionary framework that leads to a disparagement altogether of cultural values and traditions as just a lot of baggage from our feudal and colonial past. The present study points out precisely the possibility that folk religious traditions and such cultural values as utang na loób and hiya, which usually promote passivity and reconciliation rather than conflict, have latent meanings that can be revolutionary. This possibility emerges only by regarding popular movements not as aberrations, but occasions in which hidden or unarticulated features of society reveal themselves to the contemporary inquirer.

To write history "from below" requires the proper use of documents and other sources "from below." Anyone who plows through the range of materials available, say, in Tagalog, soon realizes why a history from the viewpoint of the masses has been long in coming. Although most of the sources used in this work—poems, songs, scattered autobiographies, confessions, prayers and folk sayings—have been published or were known to previous scholars, they were utilized only insofar as they lent themselves to the culling of facts or the reconstruction of events. For these purposes, Tagalog sources have proven to be of limited value. That is why, in studies of popular movements, Spanish and English-language sources constitute the bulk of the documentation. No doubt the data in these sources are generally reliable and enable the narrative to be told. But since a language carries with it the history of its speakers and expresses a unique way of relating to the world, the exclusive use of, say, ilustrado Spanish documents in writing about the revolution, is bound to result in an ilustrado bias on issues and events which offer multiple perspectives. If we are to arrive at the Tagalog masses' perceptions of events, we have to utilize their documents in ways that extend beyond the search for "cold facts."

18. Remigio Agpalo, *Pandanggo-Sa-Ilaw: The Politics of Occidental Mindoro* (Ohio: Ohio University Center for International Studies, 1969), p. 4.

One characteristic of such Tagalog sources as narrative poems and songs is their apparent disregard for accurate description of past events. But factual errors, especially when a pattern in their appearance is discerned, can be a blessing in disguise. I can do no better than quote the pioneering social historian Marc Bloch on this matter:

> Nearly always, the nature of the error is determined in advance. More particularly, it does not spread, it does not take on life, unless it harmonizes with the prejudices of public opinion. It then becomes as a mirror in which the collective consciousness surveys its own features. [19]

When errors proliferate in a patterned manner, when rumors spread "like wildfire," when sources are biased in a consistent way, we are in fact offered the opportunity to study the workings of the popular mind. This is applicable not only to "folk" sources like riddles and epics but to works whose authors are known. The latter are usually analyzed as products or expressions of individual creative minds, despite the fact that poetry or history can only be written within the context of a system of conventions which delimit the text. As long as a writer intends to communicate, he has to imagine the reactions of his readers who have assimilated the system of conventions used. Knowing something of this underlying system enables us to transcend questions of authorship, which is problematic in many Tagalog sources. Once we have gained some idea of the structure of the popular mind, data from conventional sources like official reports and outsider accounts can be fruitfully used. For example, we can get at the full significance of the observation that Katipuneros wept after their initiation, only after we have analyzed and understood the complex of meanings behind acts of compassion, weeping, and empathy, which are abundantly illustrated in literature. In other words, "weeping" acquires meaning only if it is integrated into a system of unconscious thought.

The *Pasyon* and the Masses

One of the principal ideas developed in this study is that the masses' experience of Holy Week fundamentally shaped the style of peasant brotherhoods and uprisings during the Spanish and early American colonial periods. Instead of glorifying the ancient rituals of the *babaylanes* (native priests) as evocative of the true native spirit, the fact has to be accepted that the majority of the lowland Filipinos were converted to Spanish Catholicism. But like other regions of Southeast Asia which "domesticated" Hindu, Buddhist, Confucian, and Islamic influences, the Philippines, despite the fact that Catholicism was more often than not imposed on it by Spanish missionaries, creatively evolved

---

19. Marc Bloch, *The Historian's Craft* (New York: Vintage Books, 1953), p. 106.

its own brand of folk Christianity from which was drawn much of the language of anticolonialism in the late nineteenth century. The various rituals of Holy Week, particularly the reading and dramatization of the story of Jesus Christ, had in fact two quite contradictory functions in society. First, as Nicanor Tiongson has argued in his book on the passion play, or *sinakulo*, they were used by the Spanish colonizers to inculcate among the *Indios* loyalty to Spain and Church; moreover, they encouraged resignation to things as they were and instilled preoccupation with morality and the afterlife rather than with conditions in this world.[20] The second function, which probably was not intended by the missionaries, was to provide lowland Philippine society with a language for articulating its own values, ideals, and even hopes of liberation. After the destruction or decline of native epic traditions in the sixteenth and seventeenth centuries, Filipinos nevertheless continued to maintain a coherent image of the world and their place in it through their familiarity with the *pasyon*, an epic that appears to be alien in content, but upon closer examination in a historical context, reveals the vitality of the Filipino mind.

The *Casaysayan nang Pasiong Mahal ni Jesucristong Panginoon Natin* (Account of the Sacred Passion of our Lord Jesus Christ), first published in 1814, was the most common text used in nineteenth-century *pabasa*, or pasyon readings.[21] It is actually the second and the least-polished of three Church-approved pasyons that have seen print, but in this book I quote exclusively from it because of its popularity among rural folk, who refer to it as the *Pasyon Pilapil*. This popular name for the *Casaysayan* of 1814 originates from a traditional belief that it was written by a native priest named Mariano Pilapil, but recent scholarship has established that Pilapil merely edited the 1814 text, the author of which remains unknown.[22] The *Casaysayan* is also known as the *Pasyon Henesis* because, unlike the first pasyon composed by Gaspar Aquino de Belen in the eighteenth century, it begins with an account of the creation of the world and concludes with a glimpse of the Last Judgment based on the Apocalypse of St. John.

Bienvenido Lumbera has pointed out that the *Pasyon Pilapil* is, to a large extent, based upon De Belen's earlier pasyon. In commenting upon the latter, Lumbera stresses that it can in no way be viewed as a mere translation or rehashing of Spanish lives of Christ that its author seems to have been familiar with. A principal from the Tagalog province of Batangas, De Belen knew his audience well and was adept at handling the language in order to communicate Christian doctrines in a meaningful way:

---

20. Nicanor Tiongson, *Kasaysayan at Estetika ng Sinakulo at Ibang Dulang Panrelihiyon sa Malolos* (Quezon City: Ateneo de Manila University Press, 1975), p. 195.

21. In this study, I used a personal copy of the 1925 edition which does not, upon superficial comparison at least, differ from earlier editions. In quoting passages, reference is given to the page and stanza number in the 1925 edition.

22. See Bienvenido Lumbera, "Consolidation of Tradition in Nineteenth Century Tagalog Poetry," *Philippine Studies* 17 (1969): 389-440.

> Christ, Mary, Judas, Peter, Pilate and other figures from the New Testament are portrayed by the poet as though he were the first man to tell their story. Without falsifying the portraits in the Bible, Aquino de Belen, whether by temperament or art, avoids the stereotype characterizations created by pietistic tradition, and sees the characters as though they were his own countrymen.[23]

The *Pasyon Pilapil* has many characteristics of its predecessor. And yet it is different. Says Lumbera, "much of its verse is deplorably bad. Its author has no sense of rime or ryhthm, a lack made more obvious in the passages stolen from Aquino de Belen."[24] The educated, urbane De Belen would have been shocked and horrified to see this "bastardization" of his work.

The *Pasyon Pilapil* was, in fact, soundly criticized in the late nineteenth century by Aniceto de la Merced, a native priest, in a pamphlet titled *Manga Puna* (Critique). "This account," writes De la Merced, "will open your eyes to the errors, unnoticed but rampant in that book called *Pasiong Mahal,* which is really the work of an ignoramus."[25] The major criticisms of the *Pasyon Pilapil* are its incoherence, faulty scholarship, repetitiveness, and clumsy, inaccurate use of language. In 1906, De la Merced published his own version of the pasyon titled *El Libro de la Vida,* which Lumbera describes as "a *pasion* that is correct in every way . . . meticulous in its use of documentary evidence . . . 'safe' in its presentation and interpretation of biblical details." But despite all this and its "neat and polished" versification, Lumbera finds it the least interesting of the three pasyons.[26] It certainly did not threaten the popularity of the *Pasyon Pilapil.*

In contrast to the two "literary" pasyons of known authorship, the *Pasyon Pilapil* is a highly imperfect composition, one that probably does not deserve much attention from a literary or theological standpoint. It stands out mainly as—to paraphrase Marc Bloch—a mirror of the collective consciousness. In the late eighteenth and early nineteenth century, the text of Aquino de Belen's pasyon, in the course of being continually memorized, copied, and disseminated by professional readers and passion play (sinakulo) actors, experienced various subtle changes. This was aided by the practice, alluded to by Father Pilapil, of privately circulating manuscript versions of the pasyon which often contained doctrinal errors.[27] Whoever published the 1814 text saw the need for a properly edited pasyon incorporating changes introduced into De Belen's work as the latter came in contact and interacted with several generations of performers, copyists, and audiences. For example, the extraor-

---

23. Bienvenido Lumbera, "Assimilation and Synthesis (1700–1800): Tagalog Poetry in the Eighteenth Century," *Philippine Studies* 16 (1968): 639.

24. Lumbera, "Consolidation of Tradition," p. 390.

25. Ibid., p. 395.

26. Ibid.

27. See Fr. Pilapil's brief introductory note, dated 20 April 1884, in *Casaysayan nang Pasiong Mahal in Jesucristong Panginoon Natin* [Pasyon Pilapil] (Manila: J. Martinez, 1925), p.2.

dinary development of scenes in which Mother Mary plays a dominant role has to be attributed to the society's preoccupation with the bonds between mother and child. Authorship is irrelevant in the case of the *Pasyon Pilapil* because it bears the stamp of popular consciousness. The text itself, approved by the authorities and printed in presses owned by the religious orders, may not seem to contain striking heresies or innovations. A purely textual analysis can reveal only a faint reflection of how the various pasyons shaped, and in turn were shaped by, society. Nevertheless, it is beyond doubt that a text like the *Pasyon Pilapil* was, for all purposes, the social epic of the nineteenth-century Tagalogs and probably other lowland groups as well. This point will be clarified in later chapters as we look into the underlying perceptual frameworks of nineteenth-century popular movements.

Even if we, for the moment, limit our attention to the *Pasyon Pilapil,* as a text, its bearing on popular movements and social unrest can already be seen. For one thing, the inclusion of episodes relating to the Creation of the World, the Fall of Man, and the last Judgment makes the *Pasyon Pilapil* an image of universal history, the beginning and end of time, rather than a simple gospel story. In its narration of Christ's suffering, death, and resurrection, and of the Day of Judgment it provides powerful images of transition from one state or era to another, e.g., darkness to light, despair to hope, misery to salvation, death to life, ignorance to knowledge, dishonor to purity, and so forth. During the Spanish and American colonial eras, these images nurtured an undercurrent of millenial beliefs which, in times of economic and political crisis, enabled the peasantry to take action under the leadership of individuals or groups promising deliverance from oppression. One of these groups, as we shall see, heralded the country's passage from the dark, miserable, dishonorable age of Spanish rule to a glowing era of freedom *(kalayaan).*

The pasyon text also contains specific themes which, far from encouraging docility and acceptance of the status quo, actually probe the limits of prevailing social values and relationships. Take the extensive treatment of Jesus Christ's preparation to depart from home. This is a classic exposition—found in common soap operas and novels—of the role of utang na loób in defining an adult's response to his mother's care in the past. For all the comfort and love *(layaw)* that she gave her son, Mary asks, why must she lose him? Jesus, despite his attachment to his mother, can only reply that he has a higher mission to fulfill—to suffer and die in order to save mankind:

Ngayon po ay naganap na	The longed-for hour
ang arao ng aquing pita	when I shall save mankind
nang pagsacop co sa sala,	has now arrived,
Ina, i, ito ang mula na	Mother, from this day on
nang di nating pagquiquita.	each other we shall not see.
(78:7)	

There comes a time in a man's life when he has to heed a call "from above."

In the pasyon it is God's wish that is carried out; but what was to prevent the Indio from actualizing this "myth" by joining a rebel leader who was often a religious figure himself? To pave the way for this experience, the pasyon posits the possibility of separation from one's family under certain conditions. In a society that regards the family as its basic unit even in the economic and political spheres, this certainly goes "against the grain."

An even more significant idea found in the pasyon is that social status based on wealth and education has no real value. Traditional Tagalog society has, of course, been stratified according to wealth and education. The principalia class needed wealth to attract and maintain followers, using debt relationships to this end; education perpetuated this class and enabled a select few from below to enter it. The pasyon, again, contradicts this model by stressing the damage caused by "over-education" and wealth on the individual *loób* (inner self), which is where the true worth of a person lies. It is all right to be *maginoó* (the Tagalog equivalent of *datu*) as long as the external signs of power are matched by an equally beautiful *loób*.[28] In actual fact, the *loób* and *labas* (exterior) of the social elite in the pasyon tend to be out of fit, as the following metaphor signifies:

hinog, mabuti sa tingin	ripe, nice to look at
hilao cung pagmalasmasin	raw when closely examined
nacahihirin cung canin	chokes you when you eat it.
(156:9)	

From the Spanish perspective, what could be a more effective tool than the pasyon to discourage Indios from enriching and educating themselves to the point where they might constitute a threat to colonial rule. But from the perspective of the mass audience, the identification of the wealthy, educated pharisees, maginoó and *pinunong bayan* (local leaders) with Christ's tormentors could not fail to have radical implications in actual life. Take the following pasyon stanzas in which the priests and gentry demand that Pilate sentence Jesus to death:

At caming nagcacapisan	And we gathered here
dito sa iyong harapan	before your excellency
guinoo,t, pinunong bayan,	are aristocrats and town chiefs
di mo pa paniualaan	so you have no reason to doubt
sa mga sumbong ng tanan.	all our accusations.
Caming naghahabla rito	We plaintiffs here
di sinungaling na tauo	are truthful people
mayayama,t, maguinoo	gentlemen of rank and wealth

28. Colin, *Labor Evangelica,* 1663, in BRPI 40, p. 86. In Juan de Noceda and Pedro de Sanlucar's *Vocabulario de la Lengua Tagala* (Manila, 1860) *maginoo* is translated as "gentleman of rank."

houag nang panimdimin mo	so away with your misgivings
hatulan mo nang totoo.	hand down the verdict.
(114:6-7)	

Such terms as *maginoó, pinunong bayan, mayayaman* (wealthy) and even *di sinungaling* (honest) are used in an unflaterring context. In a society without freedom of speech and legitimate channels of protest, the pasyon made available a language for venting ill feelings against oppressive friars, principales, and agents of the state. This point will be clarified in later chapters of this book.

The most provocative aspect of the pasyon text is the way it speaks about the appearance of a "subversive" figure, Jesus Christ, who attracts mainly the lowly, common people *(taong bayan)*, draws them away from their families and their relations of subservience to the *maginoó,* and forms a brotherhood *(catipunan)* that will proclaim a new era of mankind. The friars must have been bothered occasionally by the political implications of the lowly Christ-figure, but the story could not be altered. The following passages illustrate how the masses could identify with Christ—poor, unlettered, and of humble origins:

Tanto rin naming lahat na	We all know, too
bayang tinubuan niya	the town he hails from
ito ay taga Galilea,	he is from Galilee,
tauong duc-ha at hamac na	a man poor and lowly
naquiquisunong talaga.	who shelters in others' roofs.
Ano pa at ang magulang	Furthermore, his father
isang Anloague lamang	is just a simple carpenter
ualang puri,t, ualang yaman,	devoid of fame and wealth
mahirap ang pamumuhay	living in poverty
ualang aring iningatan	without property of his own.
Ualang iba cundi ito	His behavior and character
asal niya,t, pagcatauo	are just as we described
nguni,t, cun itatanong mo,	but, you ask, can he claim
na cun may pagcaguinoo?	to be a gentleman of rank?
ay ualang-ualang totoo.	No, absolutely not.
(116: 4-6)	

The way that Christ's following multiplies presents quite a contrast to the traditional patterns of Philippine politics. This leader does not offer weapons, money, and security in exchange for loyalty. In fact, his followers must leave all these behind as the apostle Matthew did to his tax office and cash collections (48: 2). The kind of commitment to the cause that this leader evokes transcends personal considerations to the extent that his followers are willing to sacrifice their lives. The much-beloved story of Longinus, the soldier who pierced the side of Jesus, illustrates this. Having witnessed (and been transformed by) the blinding light of the resurrected Christ, Longinus informs the local authorities who, fearing the consequences, entice the other witnesses not to spread the news around:

Cami anilang napipisan dito,i, pauang punong bayan aming pangacong matibay, guinto,t, pilac cayamanan oficio at catungculan.	They said, we gathered here are all town chiefs we guarantee our promises of gold, silver, wealth jobs and high positions.
Tantong ibibigay namin ano man inyong hingin ito lamang ay ilihim houag nang sabi sabihin sa tauong sino ma,t, alin. (178: 11-12)	Rest assured that we will grant anything you ask just keep this matter secret don't spread the news to any person whatsoever.

As might be expected, particularly in a Philippine setting, the soldiers succumb to the bribes. Longinus, however, continues to announce the resurrection of Christ all over town until he is captured. Before he is stabbed to death, he confesses that in the past he was blind, but recent events enlightened *(lumiuanag)* him, showed him the right path *(daang catuiran)*, so that he is willing to die as his way of participating in Christ's passion.

According to Tiongson, Christ and the faithful in the sinakulo exhibit stylized forms of behavior. They are always timid *(kimi)*, modest *(mabini)*, gentle, sad, and lowly of behavior. What better image than that of a Christ who wouldn't disturb a fly *(di-makabugaw-langaw)*, to keep the Indios in a subservient, colonial state.[29] But can we be sure that the meaning of this image to us today was the same to Tagalog peasants in the nineteenth century? Longinus may look sad and act lowly in the sinakulo but his story, known to the audience, is one of defiance toward the authorities out of commitment to an ideal. Jesus Christ in the pasyon text appears as a rather harmless leader of humble origins but he manages to attract a huge following mainly from the "poor and ignorant" class. His twelve lieutenants are said to be neither principales nor ilustrados, nor the leader's relatives. They are simply

ducha at hamac na tauo ualang halaga sa mundo manga mangmang na tauo ualang dunong cahit ano. (49: 7)	poor and lowly people without worth on earth ignorant people without any education.

29. Tiongson, *Sinakulo*, pp. 194–95.

Yet, the pasyon account continues, these lowly men are charged by Christ with a mission and given special powers to carry it out:

Ito ang siyang hinirang ni Jesus na Poong mahal magpapatanyag nang aral gagaua nang cababalaghan dito sa Sangsinucuban. (49: 8)	These were the ones selected by Jesus the beloved master to popularize his teachings to perform astonishing feats here in the universe.

The pasyon abounds with passages like the above, suggesting the potential power of the *pobres y ignorantes,* the "poor and ignorant," to use the common ilustrado term for the masses. Whether the pasyon encouraged *subservience* or defiance, resignation or hope, will always be open to argument. The fact is that its meanings were not fixed, but rather depended on social context. Thus a historical approach is necessary.

A problem in dealing with early peasant movements in the Philippines is figuring out the extent to which they were religious, social, or political. Reflecting upon the pasyon text alone, I cannot see how the above categories can be strictly separated. It is true that many parts of the text, particularly the *aral* (lessons), exhort the audience to cleanse their souls in anticipation of a heavenly reward; it is equally true that the pasyon as a whole is about salvation. But the most dramatic and memorable parts of the pasyon are those whose meanings overflow into the sociopolitical situation of the audience. As the Jewish leaders complain to Pilate, Christ's teachings not only diverge from Moses' but also threaten the colonial state and its Jewish supporters:

Ang isa pang catacsilan nitong tauong tampalasan sinasapacat ang tanan, na houag mouis cay Cezar !malaquing calaluan!	Another treacherous act of this troublemaker is his plot with the people, not to pay taxes to Caesar, such great arrogance!
Cami,i, mayayamang lahat sumusunod tumutupad sa hari namin mataas, saca bucod iyang tungac magtatacsil na mangus.	We are all men of wealth who obediently follow our exalted king, in contrast to that blockhead who talks like a traitor.
Siya rao ay haring tambing sa boong bayang Israel ano pa,t, hinihilahil nitong lilo,t, sinungaling manga tauo,t, hinahaling.	He says he is presently king of all Israel this traitor and liar even puts the people in turmoil and turns them into fanatics.
Isa pang cabulaanan na sinasabi sa tanan	Here is another wild lie that he tells everyone—

di umano ay siya rao	out of nowhere he claims
Mesias na hinihintay	to be the awaited Messiah,
!laquing casinungalingan!	what a preposterous lie!
(115: 14-16, 116: 1)	

In the above passages, the gentry (i.e., the *mayayaman*) perceive Jesus Christ to be the leader of a popular movement not only against the Roman empire which exacts tribute from the Jews, but also against the traditional Jewish leadership. The "people" are flocking to a new king, a liberator (i.e., *Mesias na hinihintay)* who will usher in a new order. Could it be purely coincidental that the "religious" movements discussed in this book were led by "kings" and "liberators," that they turned against landlords and principales as well as the colonial regimes? I am not suggesting that the masses drew a one-to-one correspondence between pasyon images and their oppressed condition, although this may in some instances have been the case. What can be safely concluded is that because of their familiarity with such images, the peasant masses were culturally prepared to enact analogous scenarios in real life in response to economic pressure and the appearance of charismatic leaders.

Before the abolition of friar censorship by the republican and American colonial governments, the pasyon was one of the few literary works available to the rural population, and therefore could not fail to shape the folk mind. Its impact derived from the fact that, in the course of time, it coopted most of the functions of traditional social epics. Fray Diego de Bobadilla's seventeenth-century account tells us what these functions were:

> All the religion of those Indians is founded on tradition . . . . That tradition is preserved by the songs that they learn by heart in their childhood, by hearing them sung in their sailing, in their work, in their amusements, and in their festivals, and, better, yet, when they bewail their dead. In those barbarous songs, they recount the fabulous genealogies and deeds of their gods, of whom they have one who is chief and head of all the others. The Tagals call that god *Bathala mei Capal,* which signifies "God the Creator." . . . They are not far from our belief on the point of the creation of the world. They believe in a first man, the flood, and paradise, and the punishment of the future life.[30]

Compare the above with the following observations made in the early twentieth century. According to one account, during Holy Week "the old people forbid their children to sing or read a book other than the [pasyon] awit."[31] Another says that "everyone is obliged to read Jesus book [sic] about his life. People sing every phrase about his life. You can hardly find a boy or

30. "Relation of the Philippine Islands," n.d., BRPI 29, pp. 282-83.

31. Amanda Morente, "Social Customs of the People of Pinamalayan" (1916), BCTE, vol. 1, no. 2.

girl, man or woman, who does not know how to sing those phrases from Jesus' book."[32] In some towns, the pasyon was sung for twenty-four hours over a deceased person's body.[33] In other places, it functioned in courtship rituals. During Lent, says a 1917 source,

> sometimes a group of young men come in the evening to a young lady's house to sing the Pasion below her window. The young lady of the house is supposed to answer and sing some stanzas of the Pasion also. Often the young men are invited to come up and sing in the house. Gradually people gather in and around the house to listen to the singing.[34]

In fact, in his mideighteenth-century *Historia,* Fray Juan Delgado, while acknowledging that the Indios, "are very fond of singing the passion or history of the death of Jesus Christ, which is written in Tagalog verse," states sarcastically that the nightly ritual chanting of the pasyon, "has been converted into a carnival amusement, or to speak more plainly, into a pretext for the most scandalous vices."[35] This friar account, while biased and exaggerated, does remind us of Bobadilla's earlier comment that the Indios sang their epics even "in their amusements."

The widespread use of the pasyon not only during Holy Week but also on other important times of the year insured that even the illiterate tao was familiar with the general contours of the text. The common pabasa, or reading session, called for people to assemble in a house, where a little altar was set up around which two or three individuals sang alternate stanzas. If the gathering was considerably large, the owner of the house provided a temporary tent outside which could accommodate practically the whole barrio population. The pasyon singers, who knew the complete text by memory, were divided into an even number of pairs, half in the house and the rest in the tent, and the singing would alternate back and forth between them. Styles of singing varied, as they still do today. Although the Spanish melodic influence is dominant, one particular style called *tagulaylay,* in which a complete stanza is chanted in one breath with fancy curls and trills, harks back to pre-Spanish modes of singing.

Another way in which the pasyon text reached out to a wider audience was through the sinakulo. During the Spanish period, the play was performed near the church or *convento,* under the watchful eye of the friar. A stage was erected and a cast of characters, dressed to represent pasyon figures, acted out the various episodes, reciting or singing their lines from memory. Somewhat

---

32. Maximo Penson, "Superstitious Beliefs in Our Town (San Miguel,Bulacan)" (1917), BCTE, vol. 3, no. 147.

33. Serviliano Mascardo, "Ceremonies for Dying and Dead Persons in Lopez (Tayabas)" (1916), BCTE, vol. 1, no. 12.

34. Tarcila Malabanan, "Social Functions among the Peasants of Lipa, Batangas" (1917), BCTE vol. 2, no. 59.

35. In BRPI, vol. 40, p. 231 (n. 192).

complementing the sinakulo was the *estacion,* a Good Friday reenactment of the *via dolorosa* of Christ. Through the town streets and the surrounding fields, a penitent carried a heavy cross, periodically jeered and tortured by others dressed in Jewish or Roman garb. There were other public rituals that taught or reminded the people of the basic themes of the pasyon: the *huling hapunan* (Mass of the Last Supper), the *salubong* (meeting) of Christ and the Virgin Mary, the sermons of the parish priest, and the many processions. Having described the various statues of Christ, Mary and the saints borne in procession, a student in 1916 concluded that "they are generally dressed in such a way as to suggest what they represent. The whole scene means much to the people especially to ignorant ones who need to have knowledge of religion not only by words and principles but by demonstration."[36]

The point of all the rituals—it would take a separate volume to describe them all—was not merely to entertain or dazzle the masses. Undoubtedly there were lively moments, particularly in the sinakulo, with its many episodes sprinkled with folk humor. But even these can be interpreted in the general context of narrowing the gap between "biblical time" and human or "everyday time." In traditional Tagalog society, at least, Holy Week was that time of the year when the spiritual and material planes of existence coincided; when, to put it in another way, the people themselves participated in Christ's passion. Take the following account of how Lent was observed in Bulacan in 1917:

> People care little about eating any kind of meat, because the priest told them not to eat. . . . So they eat only fruits and all vegetable food. The priest orders them to do this so that their love for Christ may not be false. They say that if you eat the meat you are exactly [sic] eating the dead body of Christ. If you are cutting wood for fuel, you are cutting the head of Jesus, and if you are riding on a vehicle your vehicle travels along the body of Christ, etc. Hence every movement you make is always referred to Christ.[37]

"On Good Fridays," observed another student of 1916, "the people do not take a bath for they believe that the water contains Jesus' blood."[38] We can draw up a long list of the rules and obligations observed by most members of the community during Holy Week: when to cease work or the kinds of manual work allowed, what social activities to engage in, what to wear, what to eat, even when to bathe. Even if one did not go to the extent of becoming a

36. Asuncion Arriola, "How 'Holy Week' is Celebrated in Gasan, Marinduque" (1916), BCTE, vol. 1, no. 6. See Tiongson's description (*Sinakulo,* pp. 172–73) of Holy Week rituals around the 1920s, the "golden age" of the sinakulo and related dramas.

37. Penson, "Superstitious Beliefs."

38. Morente, "Social Customs."

flagellant or being crucified, his personal behavior during Holy Week was geared toward a wider social drama.[39]

The pasyon, then, was not simply sung, heard, or celebrated by the masses in the nineteenth century. It was lived, both individually and socially, during Holy Week and oftentimes beyond it. Furthermore, its meaning went beyond the doctrine of Christ's redemption of man by his passion, death, and resurrection. For traditional Tagalog society, Holy Week was an annual occasion for its own renewal, a time for ridding the loób of impurities (shed like the blood and sweat of flagellants), for dying to the old self and being reborn anew, and, through its many social events, for renewing or restoring ties between members of the community. Even the world of nature was affected: it was believed that at the point of Christ's death the elements signified their participation in the pasyon through the sudden covering of the sun by passing clouds, the falling of droplets of rain, or even thunder and lightning.

Power and Anting-Anting

Holy Week was also the time when anting-anting were obtained or tested for their efficacy. In view of the fact that these amulets or special powers played a significant role in the thinking and motivation of peasant rebels, bandits, soldiers and even generals of the revolutionary army, more than a passing mention must be made of them.

One method—which has many variations—of obtaining anting-anting was to exhume the body of an unchristened child, or an aborted fetus, placing this inside a bamboo tube pierced at the bottom. The liquid that slowly oozed out was collected in a bottle and saved for Holy Week, during which time it was sipped by an aspirant until Good Friday. Initiation rites were held on Holy Saturday or Easter Sunday to test the anting-anting powers of the individual.[40] A different way of obtaining anting-anting, this time in the form of an object, was to go to the cemetery on midnight of Holy Wednesday or Thursday and place bowls of food, a glass of wine and two lighted candles on a tomb. Before the candles burned out, the food and drink would have been consumed by

39. It is perhaps useful to draw a parallel here with the conception of reality in late antiquity and the Christian Middle Ages as described by Erich Auerbach: "In this conception, an occurrence on earth signifies not only itself but at the same time another, which it predicts or confirms, without prejudice to the power of its concrete reality here and now. The connection between occurrences is not regarded as primarily a chronological or causal development but as a oneness within the divine plane, of which all occurrences are parts and reflections" *(Mimesis: The Representation of Reality in Western Literature* [Princeton, New Jersey: Princeton University, 1953], p. 555).

40. Teodoro Kalaw, *Cinco Reglas de Nuestra Moral Antigua: Una Interpretación* (Manila: Bureau of Printing, 1935), pp. 7–8; Severo Magpantay, "Kabal" (1915), BCTE, vol. 1, no. 57; Mariano Gonzales, "Stories About Anting-Anting" (1915), BCTE, vol. 4, no. 183.

spirits who would leave a white stone in one of the empty vessels. A struggle for possession of this anting-anting would then ensue between the aspirant and earth-spirit called *lamang lupa.*[41] Only extraordinarily brave or daring men used this method; these were the ones, it is said, who usually became rebel or bandit chiefs. The more common, and less risky, way of obtaining anting-anting was simly to get hold of objects used in or associated with Holy Week rituals. The immense Lenten candle called *cirio pascual*, the candles used in the ceremony of total darkness (particularly the last one to be extinguished), the monstrance, the communion table, and even the bell that rang at 3:00 p.m. on Good Friday, were broken into fragments to serve as anting-anting. In some towns, pieces of paper inscribed with magical incantations were immersed in holy water on Easter Sunday and thereby became anting-anting.[42] We can add many more details, which are mentioned casually in sources of a "folkloric" nature, such as the following from Paete, Laguna:

> Our great revolutionists and rebels used various forms of anting-anting. The one possessed by Asedillo, Ronquillo and even our common "beteranos" were in the form of medallions made of copper or bronze, wherein images of the Sacred Family were engraved together with Latin scriptures . . . The only time these "anting-anting" medals were acquired was during the ceremony of the church on Good Friday.[43]

Despite the frequent mention of anting-anting in documents and in interviews of Katipunan veterans—who are sometimes referred to as "men of anting-anting"—the subject has not been given the scholarly attention it deserves.[44] The problem, perhaps, originates from the refusal of the "modern, rational and scientific" mind to study, much less accept the reality of, other conceptual systems. This results in a severe limitation on what can be studied about the past since much of it is simply incomprehensible to the present; the temptation to adopt reductionist approaches is irresistible. In the case of anting-anting and early popular movements, we have to suspend temporarily our common-sense notions of what power is all about in order to understand such phenomena.

---

41. Gonzales, "Anting-Anting"; Benito Reyes, "Lenten Fiestas in Manila and Neighboring Towns" (1937) BCTE, vol. 4, no. 183.

42. Robert Woods, "Origin of the Colorum," *Philippine Magazine* 17 (January 1930): 513; Fermin Dichoso, "Some Superstitious Beliefs and Practices in Laguna, Philippines" *Anthropos* 62 (1967): 64; and Dominador Fernandez, "Superstitious Beliefs of the People of Lilio" (1918), BCTE, vol. 2, no. 81.

43. Historical Data Papers (on Paete, Laguna Province, PNL).

44. Hermogenes Caluag, "Some Tagalog Beliefs and Maxims" (1915) BCTE, vol. 1, no. 156. Anyone examining the Beyer Papers and the Historical Data Papers—both largely based on folk interviews—will notice how stories of revolutionary *beteranos* inevitably bring up the subject of their anting-anting.

According to Benedict Anderson, Western political thought treats power as an abstraction, a way of describing relationships between individuals and groups. Through analyses of relationships and patterns of behavior, it has come to be generally accepted that the sources of power are such things as wealth, social status, formal office, organization, weapons, manpower, and so forth. In traditional Javanese culture, however, power is "not a theoretical postulate but an existential reality." Anderson describes it as "that intangible, mysterious, and divine energy which animates the universe . . . [and] is manifested in every aspect of the natural world, in stones, trees, clouds, and fire." The Javanese idea of power derives basically from the animistic conception of a "formless, constantly creative energy" permeating the universe, a conception which amalgamated with Brahmanic, Buddhist, and Islamic elements to produce a uniquely Javanese theory of politics. Particularly significant for our study of Philippine movements is the Javanese mode of accumulating power, which involves such practices as extreme asceticism, meditation, sexual abstinence, ritual purification, and various types of sacrifices in order to "focus" or "concentrate" in oneself some of the energy suffusing the universe. The idea of purity is connected not necessarily with moral questions, but with the idea of concentration of power versus its diffusion. The hermit who deprives himself of earthly comforts paradoxically accumulates power, while an individual who engages in wordly pleasures loses that steadfastness and "tense singleness of purpose" which keep one's power from dissipating.[45]

According to a contemporary Indonesian intellectual, "a central concept in the Javanese traditional view of life is the direct relationship between the state of a person's inner being and his capacity to control the environment."[46] It is because the state of a leader's inner being is manifested through certain signs that people flock to him. Among these signs is the *tedja* (radiance) which, says Anderson, "was thought to emanate softly from the face or person of the man of power."[47] Another sign, particularly in the case of rulers, is sexual fertility. It is also expected that a man of power surround himself with objects or persons held to have unusual power. A ruler's palace, for example,

45. Benedict R. O'G. Anderson, "The Idea of Power in Javanese Culture," in *Culture and Politics in Indonesia,* ed. Claire Holt, Benedict R. O'G. Anderson, and James Siegel, (Ithaca, N.Y.: Cornell University, 1972), pp. 1–70.

46. Soedjatmoko, "Indonesia: Problems and Opportunities," quoted in Anderson, "Idea of Power," p. 13.

47. Anderson, "Idea of Power," pp. 16–17. Anderson also speaks about the *wahju* (divine radiance), which was seen in different shapes and forms but more often as a star or ball of light streaking through the sky. A sign of a leader's power, the wahju's movement "typically marked the fall of one dynasty and the transfer of the light-source to another." I am reminded of my interviews with Jose Baricanosa, the late president of the Watawat ng Lahi (Flag of the Race) sect based in Calamba and his adjutants, during which it was said that Baricanosa's choice as successor to the previous leader was confirmed when a ball of bright light landed near him during a ritual.

> would be filled not only with the traditional array of pusaka (heirlooms), such as krisses, spears, sacred musical instruments, carriages, and the like, but also various types of extraordinary human beings, such as albinos, clowns, dwarves, and fortune-tellers.[48]

The point is that the proximity of these objects and persons enabled the ruler to absorb some of their power. Their loss was regarded as a disaster. It meant the loss of some of the ruler's power and signalled the impending collapse of the dynasty. Military defeats and the diminution of the ruler's wealth and personal following were regarded as mere manifestations of the deteriorating state of the ruler's inner being.

One of the principal notions that will be developed in later chapters of this book is that of the loób, or inner being. We will see how loób is intimately connected with ideas of leadership and power, nationalism and revolution. It is worth bearing in mind that the Tagalog case is in many respects not unique. For the Javanese, too, the state of the inner being is traditionally perceived as the determinant of overt political phenomena. There is a continuity between a leader or group's success and its inner concentration of power. Seen in this light, the traditional Filipino attachment to anting-anting makes sense. These are not merely objects that magically protect their wearers. They point to a complex system of beliefs and practices that underlie much of the behavior of peasant rebels and to some extent their leaders. For the power that is concentrated in an amulet to be absorbed by its wearer, the latter's loób must be properly cultivated through ascetic practices, prayer, controlled bodily movements and other forms of self-discipline.[49] For an amulet to take effect, the loób of its possessor must have undergone a renewal and purification. These ideas are common to Javanese and Tagalogs. But historical circumstances have given a unique shape to Filipino beliefs and practices. This is where Holy Week and the pasyon enter the picture.

In his little volume on anting-anting, Retana speculates that during the period of Spanish conquest, the Indios, who had "half a Christian conscience and half pre-Spanish," wanted to get the best of both worlds. So they came up with the first *libritos*—prayers to San Agustin, San Pablo and others—which actually were anting-anting. At least, says Retana, the natives had something

---

48. Ibid., p. 12.

49. In his list of restrictions or practices to be observed before an anting-anting takes effect, Magpantay ("Kabal") includes the following: "He must not taste vinegar nor eat any kind of sour or salty food; he must not be a coward; he must face if possible any danger . . . he must not feel proud that he has this cabalistic quality; he must not tell a lie; he must not make use of his human affection and worldly desire for at least one year . . . [he must] pray every evening before retiring usually the Our Father, at least three times." For a description of the elaborate rituals associated with anting-anting in battle, see Katherine Mayo, *The Isles of Fear: Truth About the Philippines* (New York: Harcourt, Brace & Co., 1925), pp. 192–93.

"useful" without having to pray to their *anitos* and other idols.[50] During the later centuries of Spanish rule a further reshaping of indigenous notions of power appears to have taken place. At first glance, the pasyon seems to be about the salvation of men's souls. The poor, meek, and humble of heart will attain a place in heaven. But in the story itself, the state of people's loób has an immediate effect in this world. Judas is treacherous because his loób is "disoriented" and "hard as rock"; in the end, he hangs himself. On the other hand, those whose loob are pure, serene, and controlled have "special powers" granted to them by Christ. They can control the elements, cure the sick, speak in different tongues, interpret signs, and foretell the future. These are precisely some of the powers one hopes to obtain through anting-anting. Is it any wonder, then, that anting-anting were obtained, tested or "recharged" during Holy Week? Surely the friars did not intend the pasyon themes of self-purification and renewal to amplify indigenous notions of concentrating the "creative energy" of the universe in one's loob. But in the end, the colonized had their way.

As previously mentioned, once we know how the masses perceived reality in the nineteenth century, documentary sources can be more fruitfully utilized. For example, in February 1897, a news correspondent noted that all those in Aguinaldo's army wore "scapularies and crucifixes around their collars . . . and also a band of red cotton cloth having another anting-anting secured inside." But most curious of all was that

> among other followers he had two youths appropriately dressed as pages who accompany him everywhere and who seemed to be considered as persons of no little importance by the others. One of the youths in particular has attracted attention which is explained by others of his followers in this way. This interesting youth possesses the supernatural qualities of anting-anting.[51]

It is now obvious that, by keeping a boy of unusual anting-anting by his side, Aguinaldo hoped to absorb some of his power. And if Aguinaldo did not believe in anting-anting (an unlikely fact), he had to conform to what his peasant soldiers believed a man of power should be and have. To the "intelligent officials," says Miranda, an anting-anting was "a simple stimulant to infuse valor and maintain that serenity and cold-bloodedness which all the armies of the world need."[52]

Ricarte, in his memoirs, tells us the story of how Eusebio Di-Mabunggo, head of the Filipino defenders of Cacaron de Sili, distributed among his men

50. Wenceslao Retana, *Supersticiones de los Indios Filipinos: Un Libro de Aniterias* (Madrid, 1894), p. xliii.

51. Manuscript copy of the article in the *New York Herald* (in PIR-SD 780-A [reel 44]). PNL.

52. Claudio Miranda, *Costumbres Populares* (Manila: Imprenta "Cultura Filipina," 1911), p. 64.

pieces of round paper with a cross written in the middle and surrounded by Latin words. As he uttered a magical formula, his men swallowed the pieces of paper, believing that this would keep them from harm. By doing this, they absorbed the power concentrated in the hostlike pieces of paper associated with the death and resurrection of Christ. No less important was the fact the Eusebio uttered a magical formula to "activate" the anting-anting. Also, "he told his men that whoever was reached by his gaze *(tanaw)* at the moment of battle, and was hurled his mysterious blessing (*basbas*), would be free from any danger and hardship in life."[53]

Obviously, Eusebio Di-Mabunggo had such a great concentration of power in him that it affected others through his penetrating gaze. This particular episode in Philippine revolutionary history tells us that the Filipino people, led by charismatic leaders, fought doggedly against the Spaniards. But more than that, it points to the conceptual world underlying the struggle of the masses. To the nineteenth-century peasant, Eusebio's gaze was perfectly intelligible and rather commonplace. After all, the heads of statues and images of Christ and the saints were believed to emit a certain glow, particularly from their wide, staring eyes. What is more, extraordinary individuals like possessors of anting-anting and popular leaders were noted for the radiance about their faces, their ability to cast "compassionate glances" on their followers. But let us move a step further. In documents and emblems, the Katipuṇan Society is imaged as a brilliant entity suffusing with light a country darkened by its colonial past. Is this somehow related to what has been said about individual pasyon and individual salvation, to ideas of brotherhood and national liberation? The answer hopefully will be found in the ideas and activities of popular movements from the Cofradía de San Jose to the Santa Iglesia, which this book describes and elucidates.

---

53. Artemio Ricarte, *Himagsikan nang manga Pilipino laban sa manga Kastila* (Yokohama, 1927), p. 109; Miranda (*Costumbres*, p. 61) has a similar description of a whole company of soldiers, prior to battle, eating "hosts or wafers on which were written prayers in crude Latin."

Altar illustration in the church of the Tres Personas Solo Dios on Mount Banahaw, which carries on the tradition of Hermano Pule's Cofradía de San Jose

CHAPTER 2

Light and Brotherhood

In October 1841, Spanish government forces battled for ten days an outlawed religious confraternity encamped on the slopes of Mount San Cristobal, in the Tagalog province of Tayabas.[1] The story of this revolt is familiar to students of Philippine history. In standard classroom texts, the revolt is regarded as a precursor to the nationalist movement at the turn of the nineteenth century. More recently, it has been treated as one of the string of millenarian revolts, rumblings of the "Little Tradition," that have punctuated the Philippine rural scene up to the present.[2] David Sweet, in the best account of the revolt so far published, looks at the event as the response of the peasantry to "chronic experience of humiliation and of discouragement from the practice of traditional customs, combined with exasperation at having to pay heavy taxes and labor dues to a government which made itself felt principally by imposing economic restrictions."[3] A peasant movement arose when a leader appeared who effectively articulated these problems and proposed a way out of them. This leader was Apolinario de la Cruz, known to his followers as Hermano Pule who, continues Sweet, "was able to attract and mobilize supporters because he preached a convincing message of redemption to the Tagalog peasantry."[4]

Sweet states that the religious character of the movement was "a strength rather than a weakness. It was its very other–worldliness which gave it

---

1. Tayabas has been renamed Quezon province.

2. David Sturtevant, "Philippine Social Structure and Its Relation To Agrarian Unrest" (Ph.D. dissertation, Stanford University, 1958), p. 121.

3. David Sweet, "The Proto-Political Peasant Movement in the Spanish Philippines: The Cofradía de San Jose and the Tayabas Rebellion of 1841," *Asian Studies* 8 (April 1970): 114.

4. Ibid.

organizational and revolutionary potential."[5] He does not, however, dwell upon the nature of this religious character, being content with the view that some sort of syncretism of pre-Spanish and Christian beliefs was the basis of the brotherhood's ritual and ideology. The aim of this chapter is precisely to demonstrate how the revolt's religious character was a "strength rather than a weakness." It is not enough to say, as previous writers have, that the revolt was the outcome of conflicts between social groups or a peasant reaction to the frustrations of life. All peasant-based revolts are of such a nature to some extent. Our concern is how Apolinario de la Cruz and his fellow cofrades perceived the meaning of their actions and the revolt itself.

In the previous chapter, we saw how the religious life of the peasantry, dominated as it was by the themes of the pasyon, offered to them an image of reality that was potentially disruptive to settled forms of existence. While religion as impressed by the friars upon the people encouraged resignation to "things as they are" as being part of God's design, there was also the possibility that individuals might respond to certain themes, paticularly those connected with Christ's passion, death and resurrection, that have "subversive" implications. After all, biblical history proceeds in terms of cataclysmic events. Beneath the flux of everyday life operates a divine plan that is known to the faithful only through certain signs, or *tanda*. The divine plan can also be known by reflecting upon certain mysteries or metaphors, called *talinhaga,* with which the pasyon abounds.

Reflecting upon talinhaga, a prime activity of Hermano Pule's confraternity, was not simply a process of thinking. As the leader implies in his letters, it was part of a lifestyle of prayer and devotion, involving the total orientation of one's being toward an order of reality in which the disruption of one's "normal" role in society, including death itself, was a distinct possibility. The events that culminated in the bloody revolt of 1841 was not simply a blind reaction to oppressive forces in colonial society; it was a conscious act of realizing certain possibilities of existence that the members were made conscious of through reflection upon certain mysteries and signs. Furthermore, since what we are talking about is part of the world view of a class of people with a more or less common religious experience, the connection between the events of 1840-1841 and later upheavals in the Tagalog region can be posited. Sweet has pointed out correctly the danger of making a causal connection between this revolt and the Cavite Mutiny of 1872, the Katipunan Revolt of 1896, and the Colorum revolts of the early twentieth century.[6] But certain common features

---

5. Ibid., p. 115.

6. Ibid., pp. 112-13. Sweet, however, goes to the opposite extreme of attributing "specific ideologies and purposes" to each Colorum outbreak. R.G. Woods, in his "The Strange Story of the Colorum Sect" (*Asia* 32 [1932]: 450-53), detects some continuity which is rejected, for lack of documentation, by Sweet.

of these upheavals, or the way these events were perceived, indicate that connections do exist. These lie perhaps, not in a certain chain of events, but in the common features through time of a consciousness that constantly seeks to define the world in its own terms.

Apolinario de la Cruz was born around 1814 of relatively well-to-do peasant parents in the town of Lucban, Tayabas province. Having received primary religious instruction, he decided, at the age of fifteen, to enter the monastic life for which purpose he came to Manila in 1830. Being an *Indio,* however, frustrated his plans of entering the religious orders. Eventually he took a job as lay brother, or *donado,* at the San Juan de Dios Hospital, a charitable institution. Sinibaldo de Mas, who claims to have known Apolinario when he was confined for a time at the hospital, describes him as a "quiet, sober, unobtrusive young man, exhibiting nothing of the hero or the adventurer."[7] At this time, Apolinario was also a member of the Cofradía de San Juan de Dios, a brotherhood open to Indios and affiliated with the hospital. He seems to have been attracted to mystical theology, picking up scraps of knowledge either by reading or listening to sermons in church. Eventually he became an accomplished lay preacher with an ability to move the hearts of the faithful that caused concern among some Spaniards who also witnessed the ease with which he solicited monetary contributions from his audiences.[8]

In 1832, Apolinario helped organize a group of nineteen provincemates, who had settled in the poor suburbs of Manila, into a confraternity, the Hermandad de la Archi-Cofradía del Glorioso Señor San Jose y de la Virgen del Rosario (Brotherhood of the Great Sodality of the Glorious Lord Saint Joseph and of the Virgin of the Rosary). There was nothing unusual then about this association. Like many others of the same type scattered throughout the islands, the Cofradía de San Jose was an offshoot of a medieval Spanish institution "whose religious function was the practice of piety and the performance of works of charity." Phelan notes that the Jesuits had introduced sodalities in the Philippines as instruments to consolidate Christianization. He describes the duties of members as the performance of two acts of charity:

> The first was to visit the sick and the dying to urge them to receive the sacraments and to persuade the infidels to request baptism. The purpose of these visits was to discourage the ill from appealing to clandestine pagan priests for consolation. The other act of charity was for members to attend funerals. The presence of sodality members, it was hoped, might discourage ritual drinking, a custom which the clergy was anxious to suppress.[9]

---

7. The bulk of my narrative treatment of the Cofradía is based on Sweet's article, "Proto-Political Peasant Movement." Sweet's source is Sir John Bowring, *The Philippine Islands* (London, 1859), p. 70.

8. Sweet, pp. 100-1; also in more detail, *Promovedores, origen y progreso de la Cofradía,* March 1842 (manuscript, unpaged, PNA).

9. John Leddy Phelan, *The Hispanization of the Philippines* (Madison: University of Wisconsin Press, 1959), p. 74.

Lucban, Apolinario's hometown, had several of these sodalities. A nineteenth-century Spanish traveler, Juan Alvarez Guerra, notes that "few towns in the world have as many cofradías, hermandades and religious archicofradías." These groups constantly filled the town church with men and women preparing for the various fiestas and celebrations. Guerra was particularly attracted to a cofradía called the Guardia de Honor de Maria, a women's association "which entertains no distinction of class or age." Its members were distinguished by a silver medal hanging on a blue band or belt. The basis for its organization was the perpetual veneration of the Virgin, for which the *hermana mayor* (elder sister) assigned three sisters at a time praying in shifts throughout the day and night.[10] The Cofradía de San Jose founded by Apolinario de la Cruz was therefore an ordinary phenomenon in those days. It was a small organization, probably overshadowed by well-established cofradías composed of wealthier Lucban residents. The archbishop of Manila, in fact, did not deem it necessary to grant it formal recognition as a confraternity because it had but a modest number of original founding members. Thus, from its founding in 1832 to around 1840 it existed unnoticed by the authorities.

Sometime in 1839 or 1840 the Cofradía, for reasons unknown to us, seems to have undergone a rapid expansion. The original nineteen members were now called *fondadores* (founders). They dispatched representatives to towns in the provinces of Tayabas, Laguna, and Batangas. As soon as these representatives were able to enroll a dozen people in the brotherhood, they became known as *cabecilla* (headman) and had one vote each in the supreme council. Members were required to pay a *réal* per month to cover the cost of their meetings and monthly Masses. The High Mass performed on the nineteenth of each month was the high point of their ritual activity, after which they would hold a "reunion" in the house of a cabecilla, recite the Rosary, listen to letters from Apolinario, and then partake of a communal meal. Eventually these activities aroused the suspicion of the curate of Lucban, Fr. Manuel Sancho. He accused the Cofradía of engaging in heretical activities and on 19 October 1840, led a raid on one of its reunions.

Real trouble with the government came when Apolinario tried to gain official recognition for the Cofradía in order to avoid unnecessary conflict with local authorities. Various applications sent to both ecclesiastical and civil authorities in 1840 were either turned down or laid aside. But when Governor-General Oraa eventually reviewed the petition in mid-1841, he was struck by a clause which excluded Spaniards and mestizos from joining the organization without Apolinario's personal permission . Upon Oraa's recommendation, the hospital dismissed Apolinario, who promptly went into hiding in Manila in order to avoid arrest. Meanwhile, in Lucban and Majayjay, civil and ecclesiastical authorities joined forces in mounting a witch-hunt of Cofradía

10. Juan Alvarez Guerra, *De Manila á Tayabas*, 2nd ed. (Madrid, 1887), pp. 63-64.

leaders and members. Fleeing the towns, the cofrades congregated on the slopes of Mount San Cristobal led by Apolinario, whom they now hailed as "king." In October 1841, government forces attacked and overran the Cofradía encampment at Aritao, killing hundreds of Apolinario's followers. Their leader was captured and executed soon after.

Cofradía Rituals and Prayers

What the Spaniards found most striking about the rebels was the state of excitement or frenzy in which they fought and their almost "irrational" disregard for personal safety as they confronted a vastly superior government force. This "irrational" quality has often been ascribed to other peasant-backed revolts in the archipelago as well.[11] Katipuneros, Colorums, and Sakdalistas are described as having fought with a seeming disregard for death, thus resulting in appalling casualties on their side. The psychological explanation, which also finds its way into analyses of the Muslim *juramentado* phenomenon, not only fails to account for the elaborate ritual that accompanies such acts but also reduces the people involved to the status of "passive reactors," a convenient way of ignoring their creative historical role. This impasse will be avoided only when these ostensibly "irrational" acts are placed in the context of a coherent world view. Fortunately, it is possible to reconstruct an "inner history" of the Cofradía from pieces of devotional literature and Apolinario's correspondence in Tagalog that have been preserved in the Philippine National Archives.

How would an ordinary Tayabas peasant have perceived his act of joining the Cofradía? As soon as he made his intentions known to a cabecilla, he was made to undergo some simple rituals. First, he and other neophytes were brought by a hermano mayor, or "elder brother," to the town church to attend a *Misa de Gracia* (Thanksgiving Mass). According to Dolendo, who seems to have interviewed ex-cofrades in his native Tayabas province, the neophytes prostrated themselves on the dusty pavement of the church, "asking for divine light, supernatural grace in order that at that precise moment they may be strengthened in their new state of being."[12] They whispered "ancient prayers." It was not an occasion for fanfare; no choir singing was heard. There was "nothing but total, sepulchral silence, and hardly is heard the monotonous murmurs of their prayers, which reach up toward the infinite."[13] The neo-

---

11. Sturtevant adduces psychological explanations. In this article "Guardia de Honor—Revitalization within the Revolution" (in *Agrarian Unrest in the Philippines* [Athens, Ohio: Ohio University Center for International Studies, 1969], p. 4), he follows Wallace in using such phrases as "hallucinatory states," "otherwordly convulsion," "mounting irrationality," "social seizure," and "aberration" in relation to peasant revolts of the "millenarian" type.

12. Teodorico Dolendo, "Los Sucesos del Mag-Puli," RENFIL 2 (21 August 1911): 223.

13. Ibid.

phytes also went to confession to purify themselves of the sins of the past, and were awarded a plenary indulgence.[14]

The key element in the simple ritual was the recitation by memory of certain prayers. These were repeated a certain number of times and in a given order, Apolinario himself insisting upon memorization and proper form.[15] The most frequent prayer, judging from Apolinario's letters, was the Holy Rosary, which was recited in full (i.e., the fifteen mysteries). No less important, and perhaps more so in terms of our analysis, are a prayer and a hymn (dalit) which appear among the documents captured during the various raids on Cofradía reunions. The prayer referred to is the *Sulat na paquiqui-alipin sa mahal na Poong San Josef* (Declaration of submission to the beloved Lord St. Joseph). The fact that it was printed in great numbers is an almost certain indication of ecclesiastical approval. But this does not prevent us from viewing it in terms of the Cofradía, for whom the document served as a proof of membership when signed by the individual.[16]

The declaration begins this way:

> O Casantosantosang Josef, Ama, at Panginoon co: Acong si . . . . . ay nag papatirapa sa iyong manga paa, alipin ni Jesus Sacramento, at nang Casantosantosang Virgen Maria.
>
> O Most Holy Joseph, Father and Lord, I [signature] prostrate myself before your feet, a servant of Jesus of the Sacrament and of the Most Holy Virgin Mary.

Clearly, the enslavement or submission is not to St. Joseph alone but to the Holy Family, which in the pasyon and other religious manuals of the time, is set forth as the model of unity and solidarity. St. Joseph holds a special place in Cofradía prayers simply because he is their patron and special intermediary. The lines that follow make this dedication to the Holy Family more pronounced:

> Homahain aco at napa aalipin sa iyo, at nang caiyo
> bagang tatlong manga Panginoon cong si Jesus, Maria, y
> Josef, ay sumaaquing puso.
>
> I come before you, humbly submitting myself,
> so that you three Lords of mine—
> Jesus, Mary and Joseph—may be in my heart.

---

14. Apolinario de la Cruz (AC) to Octabio San Jorge (OSJ), Manila, 18 May 1840 (PNA).

15. Ibid.

16. Several copies, some containing signatures, were found among the papers in the Apolinario de la Cruz bundle, PNA. A copy was also found among "religious documents" captured from the Santa Iglesia (PIR, Box I-25, PNA), a proindependence "millenarian" movement of the early twentieth century (see chapter 6).

As a sign of submission, the cofrade promises to "pay taxes" to St. Joseph (a reference to the Cofradía's monthly dues) and to pray, daily, seven Our Fathers, Hail Marys and Gloria Patris:

> Pacundangan sa iyong pitong saquit, at ligaya na quinamtan mo, noong casama mo ang iyong yniybig na Esposa.
>
> In honor of the seven trials and the happiness that you [i.e., St. Joseph] experienced when you were united with your beloved wife.

The word *pacundangan,* here too freely translated as "in honor of," connotes the intention to participate in the object or experience referred to. For example, it is used in the pasyon to mean participation in Christ's experience:

Lagnat liping pagcagutom	Fever, dizziness, headache, hunger
casalatan nang panahon	scarcities that plague the times
patiisin natin yaon	should all be endured now
pacundangan na sa Pasion	in honor of the Passion
ni Jesus na ating Poon.	of Jesus our Lord.

In the Declaration, St. Joseph's experience is twofold: unity and happiness with Mary, and the endurance of his seven trials. Because he successfully underwent the trials out of love for Mary and Jesus, he was rewarded in heaven. That is why, explains the Declaration, St. Joseph has become a source of light *(liwanag)* to others.

The cofrade's declaration of submission initiates a life of constant pacundangan, or attunement, to the "way" of suffering-toward-happiness revealed by St. Joseph. To guide him through this experience, he asks St. Joseph to shower him with light emanating from his eyes:

> Silayan mo aco ng manga mata na iyong aua, at tangapin mo aco, at ypaquibilang sa iyong manga mapapalad na alipin.
>
> Gaze at me with your compassionate eyes, and receive me, count me as one of your fortunate servants.

The cofrade's experience is made comprehensible because it is illumined from without; it partakes, the Declaration further states, of the "boundless joy" of St. Joseph. The cofrade accepts a life of trials with the hope that he will receive happiness of soul, "and the peace of a good conscience, a good (or beautiful, *maganda*) life, and a fortunate death." With St. Joseph's help, the Declaration concludes, the compassion and care of the Holy Family will be showered upon the cofrade, so that he will have enthusiasm (*sigla*) and joy, his sins will be forgiven, and he will ultimately see the Holy Family and be with them. This hope of intimate togetherness with the Holy Family ends the prayer.

It was most likely in the spirit of the above prayer that the Cofradía sought to inculcate a deep sense of egalitarianism and fraternal love among its members. Common submission to the Holy Family was the condition that bound them together as brothers and sisters. During their monthly reunions, after the reading of Apolinario's letters and the recitation of prayers, the cofrades would sit together at a cena fraternal, a fraternal supper, without distinctionas to ageor sex."There reigned an atmosphere of intimate cordiality and happiness; contentment seized their hearts. They considered themselves siblings *(kapatid)* and for this reason served each other."[17]

At this time, too, the neophyte was required to recite the mysteries of the Holy Rosary. These encapsulate the basic themes of the pasyon, from the Angel Gabriel's annunciation to Mary, to Christ's resurrection. What other significance could this have had but to remind the cofrade of the true path of life which is revealed to the multitude during Holy Week when the pasyon is sung or reenacted?

The third Cofradía prayer or hymn we shall examine is the *Dalit sa caluwalhatiansa langit na cararatnan ng mga banal* (Hymn to the peace in heaven that will be attained by the faithful), a poem of forty-two stanzas found among the Cofradía papers in the form of a little handwritten prayerbook. Essentially, the *Dalit* describes a vision of the state of perfection that reigned in Eden and that will be recovered in heaven. It appears to have been one of the pieces of mystical literature that Apolinario de la Cruz picked up while in Manila. It was first published in 1645, along with a translation of a Jesuit retreat manual, by an Augustinian friar, Pedro de Herrera, one of the earliest missionary poets in the Tagalog language.[18] The original poem of forty-seven stanzas was trimmed to forty-two stanzas probably by Apolinario himself, who may have found the last five stanzas too didactic and out of keeping with the powerful vision in the main body.[19] That Apolinario appropriated the poem for the Cofradía's use is indicated by a note at the end of the manuscript version that states: "This is what will be seen by those who ascend beginning 19 February 1840." The *Dalit* is thus associated with the period in which the Cofradía was undergoing rapid expansion; one wonders if it was one of the reasons for the Cofradía's attractiveness.

The *Dalit* begins with the statement that its contents are to be understood as a special vision of the future:

Arao nacapitapita	That day most eagerly awaited
lalong caligaligaya	becomes even more joyful
cun an macaguiguinhaua	should the source of fulfillment
matingnan ng ating mata.	be seen with our eyes.

---

17. Dolendo, "Los Sucesos," p. 222.

18. The manual bore the title *"Meditaciones, cun manga mahal na pagninilaynilay na sadia sa Santong Pag-eexercicios"* (Meditations, when one ponders holiness during holy retreats).

19. The complete text of the *Dalit* appears in appendix 1. Stanza numbers are given after direct quotations from the *Dalit*.

The contents, therefore, if properly understood, will ease the cofrade's present trials. For such knowledge gives him an external standpoint from which to view his earthly existence. Heaven is a state of perfection:

Ang magaling at ang totoo na sundin sundin ng tauo ang yamang dimacabuyo sa langit matotoo. (25)	All goodness and truth that men strive toward but never quite attain [on earth] will be fulfilled in heaven.

The *Dalit* describes this condition of perfection as an image of possibilities of being, a horizon in view of which the members of the Cofradía could direct their daily activities. It would be difficult, if not possible, to understand many of Apolinario's statements and various accounts of the Cofradía's activities if we failed to grasp the image of the future that colored and shaped them.

The *Dalit* is easily dominated by the image of liwanag. This can be explained by the fact that the idiom of darkness and light can be used to describe the world as well as the individual self. Liwanag is the horizon of being in terms of which eveything can be explained; there is presence or absence, degrees of intensity, purity, permanence and concentration, of liwanag. In the *Dalit*, heaven is the state of pure and permanent liwanag. It contrasts with the union of men on earth which, Apolinario says, is also a state of liwanag but a fragile one, since its liwanag is impermanent.[20] Perhaps that is why Apolinario states elsewhere that liwanag's source is beyond the world, and that union is liwanag because it receives its energy from this ultimate source, heaven.[21] Extraordinary men, like Apolinario himself, could be regarded as sources of light, though in general the ordinary cofrade was more a recipient rather than a source of light. In heaven, according to the *Dalit*, every person will be a source of light. No one will cower before God, but rather will

Titingnang pagcaraniuan siyang mata't titigan ualang humpay ualang hoyang (22)	Look at the eye himself as an everyday sight, will stare at it intensely, and without end.

The radiance of men in heaven cannot be looked at by earthly beings because it is blinding:

Ang sa arao na liuanag at ang sa bouang banaag culang liuanag, at hamac con sa canila'y harap. (26)	The light of the sun and the rays of the moon will be poor and dim beside them.

20. AC to the Cofradía, Manila, 1 September 1840 (PNA).
21. AC to the Cofradía, Manila, November 1840 (PNA).

The reason, according to the *Dalit*, that heaven is pure liwanag is because its inhabitants live in a condition of perfect unity. This contrasts with the impermanence of unity among men on earth and the consequent threat of darkness, or *dilim*. There are many ways in which the idea of perfect unity is presented in the hymn. Unity, in one sense, is exemplified by the dissolution of individual differences in appearance. That is why, in heaven, all bodies will be "under one roof" *(isa ring pisan)* and will uniformly take on the appearance of Christ:

Baguntauo ma't dalaga	Young men and women
manga tauo mang naona	and their predecessors
magulang caya't bata pa	parents and even children
mag cacasing parapara. (14)	all will look alike.

And the scars that reveal one's personal history—wounds, blindness, lameness, etc.—will not be present in the bodies of the heavenly (29-30). In a way, however, this absence of outward blemishes is only a reflection of the purity of loób that has been cultivated while on earth:

Dilima cocotya cotya	There will be no mockery
hobo mang sa hihilata	though one be naked and on his back
con ualaman sala't sama	if he has no sin or evildoing
ualan sucat ycahiya. (28)	there is no shame.

In other words, appearance is irrelevant if the soul is clean; one can stand naked before others and not be mocked because in essence (loób) they are the same.

Perfect unity means that the social positions that differentiate men on earth will be dissolved:

Ang mahal ma't ang mababa	High-born or low,
ang mayaman ma't ang ducha	rich or poor,
mag sising musing mucha	all will look alike
ang Dios din ang may panata.	this is God's vow.

Furthermore, the elements that threaten the fragile bonds defining human associations will be eradicated. Envy, arrogance, anger, and selfishness will no longer exist; only love will remain to bind men to each other:

Ualan capanaghilian	There is no envy
ualaman capalaloan	there is no arrogance
ang silang lahat na'y banal	they are all devout
nag ca ca ybig ybigan.	they all love one another.
(18)	

Perfect unity also means the dissolution of kinship ties on earth. This is implied in the following stanza:

<table>
<tr><td>Cun ang Ama mo't ang Yna
sa infierno'y maquita
di mabauasang ligaya
asal dima ngongolila.
(33)</td><td>If your father and mother
in hell you see
still undiminished joy you'll have
you won't behave like an orphan.</td></tr>
</table>

The community in heaven is, in fact, a new family of which God is the father. There one finds the perfection of the concept of suprakinship unity which the Cofradía sought to realize on earth. Kinship ties were, in fact, often obstacles to the smooth operation of the brotherhood. Conflicts between children and parents, and between husband and wife, often erupted in connection with membership in or withdrawal from the Cofradía. Related to this matter is the idea that human vacillation, perhaps the greatest threat to the Cofradía, no longer exists in heaven. Apolinario constantly encouraged the cofrades to have control of their loób, to guard against the temptation to submit to family pressures, and finally to remain steadfast in the face of hardships being experienced by the brotherhood. Many cofrades failed to attain such control of self, and left the brotherhood. In heaven however,

<table>
<tr><td>Ualan sala salauahan
budhi ualang calabcaban
di macapag bagong lagay
mag pa sa cailan mang arao.
(327)</td><td>There is no ficklemindedness
consciences are not tormented
there is no changing of states
forever and ever.</td></tr>
</table>

The intimate association with Joseph, Mary, and all other saintly beings that is hoped for in the concluding lines of the Declaration of Submission is attained in heaven. Love bridges the gap between all beings, whether they be saints or ordinary devotees. Even

<table>
<tr><td>Ang Dios namang maycapal
pinagcacaybiganan
ang silang lahat ay banal
nag cacaybig ybigan. (19)</td><td>God the Supreme Creator
is treated as a loved one [or friend]
they are all devout
they all love one another.</td></tr>
</table>

Furthermore,

<table>
<tr><td>Ang cacasa casamahin
Angeles nama niningning
sila'y cacapanayamin
at cacao caosapin.</td><td>Their companions will be
the brilliant angels
with whom there will be
dialogue and plain talk.</td></tr>
<tr><td>Marteres cacabatiin
Virgenes cacatotohin</td><td>Martyrs will be acquaintances
virgins will be friends</td></tr>
</table>

Confesores cacasihin	confessors will be loved
pauang nag aaloningning	all of them resplendent.
(39-40)	

This last line "all of them resplendent" exemplifies in one more way the juxtaposition of ideas of love and liwanag. The image of heaven in the *Dalit* depicts the fulfillment of the Cofradía's aspiration toward oneness with the other and its search for liwanag.

Membership in the Cofradía brings to the individual special knowledge, a concommitant of being in the liwanag that suffuses the community. Among men or earth, however, knowledge (*dunong*) and a "good mind" (*magandang isip, mabuting isip*) are usually found among leaders and only to a lesser extent among the common brethren. In heaven, everyone receives the ultimate form of knowledge. Seeing God face to face implies not only being together in liwanag but also simultaneously receiving knowledge of all things:

Maguin pantas at paham	Whether sage and highly educated
diman nagaral napagal	or ignorant
ysip nila'y susubuan	their minds will be fed
ng mataas na aral. (38)	with the highest knowledge.

Thus,

Ang ysip nila'y matalim	Everyone's mind will be sharp,
ang ala ala'y gayondin.	and so will be their memory.
Talos mangamaroronong	Even the tiniest infant
manga mumuntiang sanggol.	will be like a sage.
(35-36)	

The *Dalit* does not say what will be known. We can only assume that the mind, being in pure liwanag, sees things as they really are. An example of what this means is found in the pasyon: on Mount Tabor the blinding light radiated by Christ brings about a transformation in the apostles, who are able to see Jesus as he really is. Adam had this property before he sinned; thereafter, he had to shield his eyes from God's blinding light. In heaven, one recovers this ability to stare directly at the liwanag radiated by God.

One last point about the *Dalit* concerns its relationship to amulets, or *anting-anting*, which Spanish authorities accused Apolinario of distributing, in the form of little scapulars hung about the neck, to the cofrades. Some of the characteristics of being in heaven the *Dalit* describes are precisely those claimed by persons who possess anting-anting. Stanzas 5 to 7, for example, describe the ability of heavenly persons to move with agility and speed, like birds in flight, "faster than the wink of an eye." Stanza 4 is about the ability to proceed with one's actions without hindrance or danger. The whole subject of liwanag is related to anting-anting in that the more efficacious of the latter are said to radiate light; and certain persons with powerful anting-anting also radiate light. One gets the strong impression that the little prayerbook which contains the *Dalit* was regarded by the cofrades as a powerful object, perhaps an anting-anting. From descriptions of anting-anting gathered from various sources, it may be concluded that its efficacy depends upon the proper execution of certain rituals and the following of strict rules. That is why, when tragedy strikes, the anting-anting is not blamed inadvertently; this object really is a sign that points to a different order of reality to which the wearer attunes his existence. Rebirth is its fundamental theme; one in possession of anting-anting often fights to the end because he anticipates suffering and death.[22] In 1840, a critical year, the prayerbook would have been the cofrade's anting-anting. Images of heaven are meaningless unless the individual accepts the idea of dying to the world in order to attain the perfect state.

A thin line separates anting-anting and the prayers of the Cofradía; all are intimately connected with action. Time and time again, Apolinario exhorted the cofrades to pray; in critical times, prayer was the only recourse to give strength and direction to the individual. It must be emphasized that prayer was not a form of escaping from present reality, but of enabling the loób to enter it with serenity. In a letter written during the interrogation of members by the governor, Apolinario reminds the brethren that prayers to God should be "true" prayers and not the outpouring of fears.[23] "True prayer"" lies in the relationship between prayer and control of self, the total orientation of one's loób in a certain direction. With "true prayer" as in certain forms of anting-anting, the individual can face death calmly because his existence is "situated" in a frame of reference that makes death the door to perfection.

Apolinario's Teachings

Apolinario de la Cruz's letters to the Cofradía were addressed either directly to the brethren or to the hermano mayor, Octabio San Jorge. They were read to the assembled cofrades as part of the activities of their monthly reunions. Apolinario instructed Octabio on the mode in which his letters were to be read, in order that everyone would be entirely informed of their contents.[24] The Spanish authorities were particularly disturbed by the "spirit of sedition" that they allegedly found in letters confiscated during a raid on 19 October 1840.[25]

22. Cf. "Anting-anting," RENFIL 3 (1913): 1369; "Amuletos guerreros de la pasada Revolucion," RENFIL 1 (7 October 1910): 17; cf. also the series "El Anting-anting," by Paco Venegas, starting in RENFIL 2 (21 September 1911): 370; Kalaw, *Cinco Reglas de Nuestra Moral Antigua*, pp. 7-8; Retana, *Supersticiones de los Indios Filipinos* (Madrid, 1894).

23. AC to OSJ, Manila, 4 January 1841 (PNA).

24. *Promovedores, origen y progreso* (PNA.)

25. Ibid.

The only message of a "seditious" (because of its racial connotations) nature that can be found in the letters is the stipulation that mestizos were not to be allowed into the brotherhood without Apolinario's consent.

According to Dolendo, the cofrades relied heavily on Apolinario's letters in organizing their activities.[26] The reference here, it seems, is to the myriad of details in the letters concerning preparations for coming reunions, the collection of dues, dispatching of messengers, and the like. Dolendo further says that the cofrades listened "with reverence and also some curiosity to Hermano Pule's letters, from which the multitude gained profound insight."[27] Does Dolendo mean that the cofrades became conscious of certain ideas that were new and, therefore, subversive to Spanish eyes? Or were these ideas already there, implicit in the society's values and religious experience, merely given form by a creative and articulate leader?

The ideas in the letters are expressed through images. Phenomena occurring in the Cofradía, or in the world for that matter, are not allowed to remain situated in the context of everyday life but are charged with meaning through juxtaposition with transcendental ideas. Thus, when Apolinario wants to refer to the fact that a few cofrades have changed their minds and are leaving the brotherhood, he says that thin, high clouds are covering the rays of the sun.[28] The opposition of darkness and light seems to be the most frequent and powerful image utilized in the letters. When he wants to encourage his brothers to behave in a certain way, or when he wants to express his relationship with them, Apolinario invokes images from the pasyon and other familiar texts. At times, the continuous stream of images that he brings up to emphasize a point leads to a blurring of distinctions between the "everyday world" and the "pasyon world." The letters had a compelling hold over their audience precisely because of their form. The cofrades were not merely told what to think; rather, the images used by Apolinario enabled the cofrades to organize their experience. In sum, the leader's advice, encouragement, scoldings, and interpretations of events raised everyday life to a level that was both transcendental and coherent—transcendental in the sense that the present was viewed in relation to the time of the pasyon (e.g., the Day of Judgment being the focus of present action); coherent in the sense that everything—conflict, suffering, and death included—had meaning.

The most vexing problem that Apolinario addresses himself to in the letters is the wavering of loób. The test of a cofrade's commitment to the brotherhood and to the Holy Family was his ability to withstand persecution by outsiders and to resist the temptation to live an easier life by withdrawing. Apolinario became particularly concerned about the problem after September 1840. That

---

26. Dolendo, "Los sucesos," p. 222.

27. Ibid.

28. AC to the Cofradía, Manila, November 1840 (PNA).

month Manuel Sancho, the curate of Lucban, refused to perform the monthly Mass financed by the group after discovering the potentially "subversive" organization flourishing in his parish. On the night of 19 October, Father Sancho set out with the *gobernadorcillo* and several principales to raid a reunion of the Cofradía. This resulted in the arrest of 243 people and the confiscation of the cash box, the correspondence of Apolinario and two large portraits of the leader done in the style of popular images of saints.[29] About a month after this incident, Apolinario wrote specifically to advise his brothers not to let their loób retreat (*urong*) in those trying times. Apparently, a few had already turned their backs on the Cofradía, for Apolinario was firm in stating that these people were no longer to be regarded as *casama* (companions, comrades). What was happening to the cofrades

> ay para lamang ysang panganoring tomaquip sa cicat ng arao, anopa at sa aua ng Dios ay magliliuanag din tayo at ang anomang carouaguinan ay tiisin at nasa panahon, sapagcat Dios ang may bigai at cia rin naman ang bibihis sa atin.

> is merely as if thin high clouds were covering the rays of sun, but through God's mercy there will be liwanag in us, and any oppression should be endured as it is part of the times, for God has willed it and He, too, will bathe us in glory.

He reminded the cofrades of the Masses they should attend during the following month; that they should not neglect these, in spite of dangers and threats by the curate, because eventually they would profit from their sad plight (*"macababaui rin tayo sa cahapisan"*). Apolinario concluded by exhorting the cofrades to carry on with their activities, particularly the raising of funds to pay for further Masses and reunions. They should "let their hearts go forward" (*solong naman ang loób*).[30]

Early in 1841, the situation of the Cofradía turned from bad to worse when the provincial governor, Ortega, acceded to Father Sancho's insistent requests for civil intervention by ordering the gobernadorcillo of Lucban to cooperate in stamping out the Cofradía. This may have been the background to Apolinario's letter of 4 January advising Hermano Mayor Octabio San Jorge of disruption he expected on the Cofradía's forthcoming "day of unity." In such an event, the cofrades should not be "perplexed" (*icabacla*). If they are called upon by the governor to render testimony, they must tell him about the hardships inflicted upon the Cofradía; they must not be afraid to state that they have been truly maltreated. The important thing, according to Apolinario, is to face the suffering squarely, not to turn their backs on it. In their prayers to

---

29. Sweet, "Proto-Political Movement," p. 105. A description of the portraits is given in a letter of Fr. Manuel Sancho to Fr. Antonio Matheos, Lucban 19 October 1840 (PNA).

30. AC to the Cofradía, Manila, November 1840 (PNA).

God, they should "revel in the dignity of being human beings" (*lumagay sa casiyahang pag catauo*) rather than pour out to Him their fears and uncertainties.[31]

On 10 February 1841, Apolinario, in a similar but more strongly worded letter, urged the members of the Cofradía to be resolute (*pacatitibayin ang loób*) in calling out to God the Father, the beloved Virgin, and Saint Joseph. Echoing the "Declaration of Enslavement," he reminds the cofrades that suffering is necessary and that it will bear fruit in eternal peace. But there are some whose "loób waver in their commitment to our union" (*loób na nag uurong sulong ng paquequesama sa ating Kaisahan*). These individuals ought to think, because "perhaps darkness is beginning to overcome them" (*baca nadidiliman lamang*) or perhaps because they have "become forgetful in these times" (*nacalilimot sa panahong ito*). They should remember what their fate will be when the *oras na tadhana* (the fated hour) arrives. Indeed, continues Apolinario, a few have already betrayed the cause, but the fondadores cannot be blamed for this, for they are

> nag papamata lamang cung sanang sa isang bulag at saca ng mga mulat cayo ay hindi ipatuloy ang caliuanagang banta, ay dapat yatang consumihan ng D. ang isang ganganoon at uica ng mga Campon ng D. ay dapat ihalimbaua ang ganoon sa Babuy na punong dumi na bauat taong macaquita ay nadirimarim.[32]

> merely the eyes that enable the blind to see, and when you have become aware yet do not continue to follow the path of liwanag, it is fitting that God let you waste away, for in the words of God's disciples these ought to be likened to pigs so filthy that when seen by anyone brings great disgust.

Vacillation of loób was not a phenomenon among the ordinary cofrades alone. The hermano mayor himself, Octabio San Jorge, seemed to have been troubled at one point. Not only did he suffer some conflict with his parents, but he also was subjected to unusually intense interrogation by the governor.[33] These may have been some of the "punishments" Apolinario refers to in an undated letter to him, in which he tells his trusted casama Octabio not to seem as if darkness were falling upon him (*nahihilom*) and not to do things "that do not stem from the loób." Think about better things to do in these times, Apolinario continues, and bear in mind that

> ang anomang nasapit at nagdaan ay caloob ng langit, ang mga parusang binata mo yaon naman ay hindi parusa condi lalong malaquing gracia sa ycaliliuanag nitong Cofradía yayamang napag aninao muna ang limang Mistiriong toua.[34]

---

31. AC to OSJ, Manila, 4 January 1841 (PNA).
32. AC to OSJ, Manila, 1 February 1841 (PNA).
33. AC to OSJ, Manila, 25 April 1841; AC to OSJ, Antipolo, Rizal, undated (PNA).
34. AC to OSJ, Antipolo, Rizal, undated (PNA).

> whatever has passed is bestowed by Heaven, that the punishments you endured are not really punishments but rather an outpouring of grace that brings liwanag to the Cofradía inasmuch as they have been made to perceive the five joyful mysteries.

This letter differs from the previous ones examined in that it is addressed specifically to the hermano mayor. Apolinario reminds Octabio that, as one of the leaders of the confraternity, he should have exemplary control of himself or "a genuinely transformed loób" (*tunay na napag cumberting loób*). Only then can he serve as a beacon (ilao), which means, among other things, caring wholeheartedly for the parishioners under his wing and not giving them "a posture of being upset about things that get them nowhere" (*postura sa mga pagca aburidong ualang casasapitan.*)[35] The connection between ideas of liwanag and self-control is evident here: Liwanag is radiated by the union of men, by heavenly beings, and by extraordinary human beings who possess powerful anting-anting. But, as in the case of Octabio, a leader has liwanag to the extent that he has a "genuinely transformed loób"; his "charisma" rests not necessarily upon wealth, status or education but upon a "beautiful" loob that attracts others. According to Apolinario, "upright leadership is properly bringing to awareness those of restless loób who are being swayed by temptations rising from the earth" (*ang tapat ding pag amo sa canila ang catampatang pagpapa ala ala sa mga balinong loób na napadadala lamang sa tucsong singau̧ ng Lupa*). Having the right qualities, Octabio San Jorge can thus be regarded by Apolinario as his *camay sa canilang boong cadahunan* (right hand in the community).[36]

How do men control or steady the wavering of their loób? On one occasion, Apolinario urged the cofrades "not to change what is in the loób" in the face of prolonged suffering: *Pilitin ninyong tabanan*, "force yourselves to remain steady," he said. *Taban*, here, literally means "to grasp in order to maintain equilibrium, so as not to fall." This is the correct attitude to take, and will be a sign to God and St. Joseph who will not abandon them.[37] In other writings of Apolinario, it is evident that the visible sign of the extent of self-equilibrium among the cofrades is the degree of liwanag that suffuses the community. But still, what does the cofrade do to maintain this state? The answer is found in what Apolinario means by having a good mind (*mabuting isip*). In a passage cited earlier, he implies that "thinking" is a state of being aware of the

---

35. *Ilao* (lamp, beacon) and *liwanag* (light) can both be translated as "light." Liwanag, however, implies more of a condition of light; "brightness" and "illumination" are other possible translations. *Ilaw* refers to pinpoint sources of light, such as a candle or a light bulb.

36. AC to OSJ, Antipolo, Rizal, undated (PNA).

37. AC to the Cofradía (PNA). This letter is unfinished and unsigned. Place of writing is not indicated.

panahon, the age or times in which events are situated.[38] Their efforts, their tribulations, have meaning in a wider context which should be reflected upon. In another letter, Apolinario specifically encourages reflection upon his teachings so that "with the mercy of St. Joseph, those who are falling into darkness may learn to have constant clarity of mind" (*con aua ni S. Josef ay ypaquiquilala sa nadidilimang sinabina ang ysang mabuting palagi ang isip*).[39] Briefly stated, the doctrine he stresses is that they ought to be in a position wherein "the loób expects the experience of bitterness before attaining the happiness sought" (*hinihingi ng ating loób na ipagcaloob ang capaitan bago ang ligaya'y paratingin sa humihinging camocha nanga natin*). But if one who asks for life tires of lowly suffering and oppression (*carouaguinan*), he will not reach his goal. This person "will not be within the fence" (*uala naman sa bacod ng ysang nagbacod*), a reference to the parable of the lost sheep. Obviously perturbed by the incidence of vacillation and weakness of loób among the cofrades, Apolinario cries out: "If that is the cooperation we have in this good union, then it is worthless" (*Cung ganoon ang paquiquisama sa mabuting caisahan ay ualang cabuluhan*). In the end these erring individuals, these cofrades who do not "think," are compared to bad seeds that sprout only to be devoured by beasts.[40]

A good or clear mind, then, sees the connection between suffering and the attainment of a "good union of men." The significance of Apolinario's reminder that, after all, Octabio's endurance of his trials made the brethren perceive the five joyful mysteries and brought liwanag to the Cofradía, is that the brethren were made to understand, by his example, the need for keeping their loób whole in the face of hardship, for the sake of the confraternity's wholeness.

"Seeing," being in liwanag, demanded constant prayer. By declaring his enslavement to the Holy Family, by constantly reciting the mysteries of the Rosary or singing the *Dalit* to Heaven, the cofrade was able to discipline himself, maintain himself in a condition of awareness. In this way, every threatening event, rather than cause doubts and fears, was situated in a meaningful context. As a sign that liwanag permeated their prayer sessions, the cofrades carried lighted candles. In fact, among Apolinario's orders was that the candle before St. Joseph's image should not be extinguished until after the completion of prayers.[41]

The case of Octabio mentioned earlier reveals that the leaders of the Cofradía were extraordinary individuals because they had exemplary control

38. AC to OSJ, Manila, 1 February 1841 (PNA).
39. Ibid.
40. Ibid.
41. AC to OSJ, Manila, 12 May 1840 (PNA).

of their loób; consequently they could be, like Octabio, lamps that guided others who faltered or, as Apolinario said of the fondadores, eyes that gave sight to the blind. In Octabio all the requirements of a good leader were fulfilled. He had suffered persecution both from his family and from the authorities as a result of his activities with the Cofradía. After some apparent wavering at the beginning, he managed to stand firm, and this experience was put at the service of others. A particularly clear statement of Octabio's function is found in a letter from Apolinario during the height of persecution by the authorities. Octabio is urged to intensify his caring for the brethren, "so they won't be scattered about" (*manabog*):

> Ang namamali ay aralan, at yturo sa capatagan, at huag paraig sa mga tocso.[42]
>
> Teach those who are in error, and show them the straight path, so that they will not be overcome by temptation.

Octabio's ability to lead was acknowledged by the Spanish authoritites in a report of March 1842, pointing out that he had certain qualitites "not common among Indios, and he could establish among them a regimen of order where previously there was a tangled confusion."[43] This image of confusion turning into order is consistent with the image of Octabio as the lamp that revealed to men the straight path. Without the light of the lamp, men would lose their way, wandering in all directions.

The image of the lamp or beacon that guides men through the thorny path of life is a familiar one in Tagalog literature. In the poems they wrote as introductions to published religious texts such as manuals and lives of saints, early Tagalog poets referred to these writings as beacons at sea, guiding those ships set out to find God.[44] For example, one of the earliest Tagalog poems, composed in 1605, has precisely this theme:

May bagyo ma,t, may rilim ang ola,y, titiguisin, aco,y, magpipilit din aquing paglalacbayin tuluyan cong hanapin Dios na ama namin . . .	Though it is stormy and dark I'll strain my tearful plaints and struggle on— I'll set out on a voyage and persist in my search for God our father . . .
Cun dati mang nabulag aco,y, pasasalamat	Though blinded in the past, I'll give thanks

---

42. AC to OSJ, Manila, 23 February 1841 (PNA).
43. Promovedores, origen y progreso (PNA).
44. See Bienvenido Lumbera, "Tradition and Influence in the Development of Tagalog Poetry (1570-1898)" (Ph.D. dissertation, Indiana University, 1967, chapter 2).

na ito ang liuanag	for this light
Dios ang nagpahayag	which God let shine
sa Padreng nagsiualat	upon the priest who has
nitong mabuting sulat	made known
	this noble book.
Naguiua ma,t, nabagbag	Though tossed and dashed
daloyong matataas,	by huge waves
acoy magsusumicad	I'll trash my legs
babagohin ang lacas:	and renew my strength—
dito rin hahaguilap	in this [book] will I grasp
timbulang icaligtas.[45]	for the buoy that saves.

No doubt the Spanish friars found the image of a ship at sea a powerful vehicle to convey Christian ideas to the predominantly riverine and sea-faring inhabitants of the lowlands. In the pasyon, we find this well-known—to Filipinos at least—reference to the Virgin Mary, Star of the Sea:

Yaong Mariang pamagat	This woman named Mary
bituing sacdal nang dilag	a star unequalled in brightness
ay siyang nagliliuanag,	is the source of light
sa tanang nagsisilayag,	to all who set sail
sa calautan nang dagat. (12:9)	far out at sea.

The image of a ship crossing stormy seas, guided by light, perfectly fits conceptions of passage from one state of life to another, a transition that, for example, each cofrade had to make from the very moment he signified his intention to become a member. Not surprisingly, then, do we find Apolinario using this very image in an undated letter that must have been written sometime in mid-1841 when, dismissed from the hospital, he was hiding out in Manila prior to his return to Tayabas. Most of the contents of the letter are illegible, and there are passages which hint at the difficult situation of the writer, such as his wearing "tattered clothes." One passage, however, stands out clearly: *Cayo ay nanga uacauac at cami natiualag sa laot ng dagat* (You are abandoned to the mercy of the elements [as in a shipwreck] and we were separated in the middle of the sea).[46] We clearly find here an image of the Cofradía as a ship, a body moving as one toward some destination. At this particular point, however, a shipwreck has occurred. *Nanga uacauac* also means "isolated"; the cofrades seem to have lost their point of reference and are groping in a state of semidarkness. This is a result of separation from their leader, who is a guiding lamp, or, as he says in other letters, their steersman

45. From "May bagyo ma't may rilim." (Though it is stormy and dark) by an anonymous poet, Manila, 1605. Text and translation are from Lumbera, ibid., appendix, p. 1 A.

46. AC to the Cofradía, Manila, undated (PNA).

(*may manebo*).[47] Perhaps it is more accurate to say that they are separated from Apolinario's teachings, for at the end of the above letter he says that it deeply saddens him to recall the teachings which the cofrades seem to have forgotten.

A Tagalog Christ

Apolinario's relationship to the Cofradía can be gleaned from occasional passages in his letters. There are, in general, two seemingly contradictory images of himself. On one hand, as in the passage below, he appears as a poor and lowly person:

> Canilang alalahanin acoy isang Pobre, naualang pinagcuconan ng yaman, at laque sa cahirapan ang aquing pulangan.[48]
>
> Let them bear in mind that I am a pauper, without personal source of wealth, and that my following [or army] was raised in poverty.

On the other hand, Apolinario never leaves a doubt that he was a source of authority, knowledge, and compassion. He gives the impression at times that the cofrades were dependent upon him for support as children are to their mothers. Once, when the authorities banned their reunions, he scolded the cofrades:

> Cayo rin ang may cagagauan, caya tayo nag caganito ay mga ualang pag ysep at ala ala, sa gagaling galing ay nag pa casera cayo sa mga pagsonod ng mga caotosan sa atin, aba sino yniong tatauaging Panginoon ngayon, sino ang tatacbohan ngayon ninyo, sa aquin ay ualanang maydadaing sa aquin ngayon aco ay ualang calacasan na parang date.[49]
>
> It's all your doing, that's why we have become like this. You did not think nor care. You have destroyed us all by your failure to follow my orders correctly. So now whom shall you call 'master'; whom shall you turn to? You can no longer turn to me for help for I have lost my former strength.

At one point, he warned those who had brought ill will to the Cofradía: "Even if I am young, I still have the power to punish" (*Cahit acoy bata ay mayroon din namang ycapag paparusa*).[50]

---

47. AC to the Cofradía, Manila, 1 September 1840 (PNA); AC to OSJ, Manila, 1 February 1840 (PNA).

48. Ibid. The letter is signed "The Pauper Apolinario de la Cruz."

49. AC to the Cofradía, Manila, 1 October 1840 (PNA). Although signed by Apolinario de la Cruz, the script of this letter differs somewhat from the rest.

50. AC to the Cofradía, Manila, 1 September 1840 (PNA). A Spanish source *(Promovedores, origen y progreso)* claims that Apolinario inflicted corporal punishment upon erring cofrades, but this is not corroborated elsewhere.

The only way this apparent contradiction can be explained is by seeing the above images in conjunction with the model of Christ in the pasyon. In Christ we are acquainted with an individual who combines in his person the seemingly contradictory aspects of divinity and humanity, humility and overwhelming strength. He is simultaneously lord and servant, victim and victor. He is described as "unlettered," and yet exceeds all others in knowledge. He is poor, and yet dispenser of all wealth. He washes and kisses the feet of his disciples, and angrily drives away the merchants at the temple. His final victory is attained only through the lonely ascent of Calvary, and death.

At several points in Philippine history, there have appeared extraordinary individuals who were perceived by the masses as embodiments of the Christ model. An example is Jose Rizal, one of the few popular martyrs who belonged to the *ilustrado* class. It was his death and not his life (except for some enigmatic statements in his writings) that served as a sign to the people.[51] Apolinario de la Cruz is another Christ-like figure in Philippine history, apparently remembered not for his particularly unique individual attributes but as a powerful sign of Christ's presence among men. Folk memories of his personality have been shaped in terms of the pasyon image of Christ. The following account of his life at the San Juan de Dios Hospital was published in 1915 by Gabriel Beato Francisco, an educated Tagalog writer who, apparently, relied heavily upon popular accounts existing among elderly people in his native Tayabas province:

> When he became a brother in the orphanage of San Juan de Dios, Apolinario took it upon himself to carry an alms box as he went from house to house in the Manila area. In doing the rounds of begging, he never took off the black cloak draped about his body as a sign of piety and dedication to the Lord, and he never let go of the alms box until it was filled and too heavy for his hands to hold. Apolinario remained this way in appearance, and the head of the orphanage was not aware of his inner feelings.
>
> In the early days of his service, he used to return to the orphanage every afternoon with the box of pickings from the nearby towns. Later, he received permission to take to the provinces the box filled with pachouli and balsam scent, which was placed before [religious?] portraits to be kissed by those who had pious intentions. Day by day, Apolinario journeyed farther and farther away from

51. This is evident in Tagalog poems honoring Rizal in which parallels are often drawn between Rizal and Christ, particularly concerning the mode of Rizal's death in Bagumbayan, the "Calvary" of the country (Cf. "Bagumbayan," RENFIL 4, 2 [14 July 1913]:189). Of all of his works, the poem "Mi Ultimo Adios" (My Last Farewell), first translated into Tagalog by Diego Mojica and Andres Bonifacio, is most popular among the masses. Rizalista sects have interpreted certain passages as prophetic of his second coming (see Iglesia Watawat ng Lahi, *Bagong Liwanag* [Calamba, 1970]).

> Manila. In spite of his exhaustion, Apolinario reflected that "if San Juan de Dios is poor, even more abject is the situation of the country."
>
> Driven by these thoughts he reached, in his journeys, the towns bordering the lake of Bae, and from there headed for his hometown in Tayabas. He made himself even more lowly (*nagpakababa*). He attended Mass everyday and he not only went around bearing a pious mien but also invited the common people to form a brotherhood.[52]

This account contains many details which are charged with meaning. Apolinario's descent to extreme "lowliness" parallels Christ's experience on earth. Francisco's informants, probably left with only bits and pieces of "facts" about the man, put them together in a collectively meaningful portrait modelled upon Christ whom they knew from the pasyon:

Asal ay caaua-aua	His manner was pitiful
bago,i, Dios na daquila	though he was God
tiquis nagpacababa	he deliberately humbled himself
nang may cunang halimbaua	as a model
ang tauong hamac sa lupa.	for lowly man on earth.
(86:13)	

The act of journeying around the countryside, culminating in the formation of a group of men presumably attracted to Apolinario's way of life, is reminiscent of Christ's wanderings in search of disciples. The gesture of carrying a heavy alms box, to the point of exhaustion, invokes the image of Christ bearing his Cross. The black cloak (*sapot*) he wore as a sign of piety is itself a sign to Tagalogs of the individual's readiness to face death.[53]

It is not enough to say that, in folk memories, Apolinario de la Cruz's life was interpreted in pasyon terms. In his time, as today, Lucban and its neighboring towns were known for the intensity of their religious festivals. We can be sure that their inhabitants were familiar with the life of Christ, even to the extent of singing pasyon passages at work; the intensity of their faith affected their daily lives. This the Cofradía thrived on. We can understand the phenomenon better through the notion of *damay*, which sums up the individual's relationship to the pasyon. *Damay*, which today usually means sympathy and/or condolence for another's misfortune, has a much older meaning of "participation in another's work."[54] The whole point of the singing of the pasyon is the

---

52. Gabriel Beato Francisco, *Kasaysayan ni Apolinario de la Cruz na may pamagat na Hermano Pule* (n.p., 1915), pp. 31-32.

53. Cf. Teodoro Kalaw, *Cinco Reglas*, pp. 6-7, for a description of the black-coated *tirong*, or man of adventure.

54. Juan P. de Noceda and P. Pedro de Sancular, *Vocabulario de la Lengua Tagala* (Manila: 860), p. 103.

evocation of damay with Christ; the text itself is filled with examples that suggest this mode of behavior: expressions of sorrow and compassion, tearful weeping, individuals helping Jesus carry his Cross, changing their state of loób to lead a pure life and follow Christ's example. The various details of Apolinario de la Cruz's life should be regarded as his expressions of damay with Christ.

In one of his letters, Apolinario speaks about having done some form of begging prior to the founding of the Cofradía. Referring, for example, to the amount of 5,000 pesos in the organization's coffers, he says that he devoted eight years of "toil and exhaustion, day and night" (*pagod at puyat, arao gabi*) toward building up this fund without which the Masses and rituals of the Cofradía cannot be held.[55] This is just one of the ways, he adds, through which he has expressed his "care" for the Cofradía. He uses the phrase *ysang nagpagat* (one who has pursued) in reference to himself, an obvious parallel to the image of the Good Shepherd tending the flock night and day.[56]

In other letters, this image of the humble leader of men is extended to include the fondadores as a group. In February 1841, Apolinario wrote that the fondadores are the *maralita*, the lowly people, who attract others to their way of life. To the cofrades the fondadores offer love and compassionate care, day and night.[57] There is no indication here of the role of status, gained through wealth and higher education, in defining relations between leaders and followers. Rather, the powerful image of Christ in the pasyon has served to overturn a "traditional" situation in which the *principalia* is the only group of people "deserving" respect and deference. To the cofrades, at least, an individual who was *maralita* could be a leader because he was a sign that Christ was once again among men.

Apolinario's letters are replete with other images that point to his Christ-like relationship to the Cofradía. Added to the image of the Good Shepherd is the image of the Gardener caring for plants that are about to blossom. In late 1840, Apolinario, advising the Cofradía to desist from holding reunions in order to allow the tense situation to subside, remarked: "and we shall be separated, so what shall be done since I, the gardener, can no longer water you?" (*at naghihiualay na tayo, ay anong gagauin acoy ang nag halamang di macapagdilig sa inyo?*)[58] In this connection, Apolinario speaks about the "bad seeds" *(masama na binhi)* that sprout into weeds, referring to certain indi-

55. Referring to the task of collecting dues, Apolinario warns Octabio that "this matter brings about a bad union." Furthermore, there were a few individuals who apparently joined the Cofradía in order to inquire about the 5,000 pesos in its fund. Apolinario was aware of the temptation caused by such a huge sum, and how a few greedy individuals might "wish to give a bad example to our unions" (AC to OSJ, Manila, 1 September 1840 [PNA]).

56. Ibid.

57. AC to OSJ, Manila, 1 February, 1841 (PNA).

58. AC to Cofradía, October 1840 (PNA).

viduals who join the Cofradía with bad intentions.[59] But even if seeds do sprout into leafy plants, they are unfulfilled beings until they blossom and bear fruit. This common folk saying is best summed up in the following passage from the pasyon:

Sapagca,t, ang tauo pala	This is because man
ay catampatan mamunga	has the potential to bear fruit
nang manga gauang maganda	in good works
at cung dili,i, mapapara	and if this isn't so
sa sinumpa ngang higuerra.	he is like the cursed fig tree.
(72:2)	

Apolinario's tending the garden—the Cofradía—is a labor of love aimed at helping men realize the full potential of their beings. It is in terms of the image of the gardener sprinkling the water of life that Apolinario says he showers upon Octabio the sacred blessing of his care and compassion, which is plentiful in his inborn love for the whole community:

> Sabogan cana uari ng mahal na gracia at Santong Vendicion ng Calinga co at auang laganap sa aquing catutubong pag-ibig sa boong comonidad.[60]

The fondadores were, in a sense, a mirror of certain possibilities of existence to which the ordinary individual could respond. Their leadership implied leading others to view their own lives from an external standpoint and from then on to decide whether they should make that "leap of faith" in commitment to the brotherhood. The "function," then, of leadership in the Cofradía was analogous to the singing of the pasyon narrative: to evoke damay and the development of potentialities of loób.

In a letter of March 1841, Apolinario emphatically states that the fondadores have never "squeezed anybody's neck" (*pinisa sa liig*) or threatened anyone with a dagger to join their union; it was all done out of "willingness" (*bolontad*) of loób and nothing was accomplished with the whip. That is why, he concludes in the letter, the only action that can be taken against those who definitely intend to back out is to strike their names off the list.[61] In another passage quoted previously, he reminds the cofrades that the fondadores enable the blind to see, but when they have become conscious and yet do not follow the path of light, it is but fitting that God will let them waste away.[62] Here we get the sense that the individual is fully aware of his actions; the decision is his whether or not to undertake that passage from one state to the other that is illumined by light. Indirectly, Apolinario expresses the same idea

59. AC to OSJ, Manila, 1 February 1841 (PNA).
60. AC to OSJ, Antipolo, Rizal, n.d. (PNA).
61. AC to OSJ, Manila, 15 March 1841 (PNA).
62. AC to OSJ, Manila, 10 February 1841 (PNA).

in telling the cofrades, on 1 February 1841, to reflect upon the Father's revelation to the Son when the latter was in the garden sweating blood.[63] This revelation is clearly stated in the pasyon:

Sa pagca Pastor cang tunay nitong mundong cabilugan ang ovejang sino pa man, cundi masoc sa bacuran hindi nga masasacupan. (94:11)	In your role as pastor in this global world any sheep, no matter who, that fails to enter the fence will not be saved.

Implied here is that the sheep have the freedom to choose whether or not to enter the fence. This is the composite image of Apolinario, the Good Shepherd of the Cofradía, pursuing the disoriented sheep, beckoning them to a union which ultimately they can reject.

In a letter of July 1840, Apolinario consoles his brothers:

> Huoag ang aalala ala ay ang na caraan na para ng pagdaranan pa yamang cayoi ypinag papabor ng cahinusayang Gaua na sucat ycapag alab ng Sintang tunay cay S. Josef at sa Amang Dios naysa tatlo sapag catauo niya.[64]
>
> Don't let your minds dwell on the past as if that has to be lived again, for I have favored you with good works which have fed the flame of true love for St. Joseph and God who has three Persons.

Two facets of the meaning of personal response are revealed in this statement. First, there is a break with the past, "which does not have to be lived again" because the act of commitment to the Cofradía is a total passage from one state of being to another. Second, response is indicated by a "flame of true love," synonymous with "awakening" or "becoming conscious," as the sentence following the above passage implies:

> Munti bagang diquit con an mga batang masusunod sa atin ay agad maguising nitong ating capisanan at siyang pagcalachang asal, at ano pa tayo ay manga matay man ay may masasabing ating pamana sa canila.[65]
>
> It's as if there is a small but radiant glow (diquit) should our children be immediately awakened by our brotherhood and grow up in the best of behavior, so that even if we shall die we can say that we have left them an inheritance.

In this passage we again encounter the problem of where the glow, a form of liwanag, is really located. A close reading seems to indicate that it is the

63. AC to OSJ, Manila, 1 February 1841 (PNA).
64. AC to Cofradía, 5 July 1840 (PNA).
65. Ibid.

union of men itself; Apolinario, in fact, often tells his cofrades that they are joined together in light, *nag oonion ng caliuanagan.* And since *diquit* also means "kindling" or something used to start a flame, Apolinario seems to be expressing a *talinhaga,* a metaphor about the Cofradía's expansion and permanence. The glow is increasing in intensity or spreading over a wider circle. Earlier in the same letter, in fact, Apolinario warns against refusing membership to anyone, except mestizos *(dogong mistesa),* who need his personal permission. So many have already joined that three towns are fully organized and the respective branches of the Cofradía can now operate autonomously.

If the idiom of *liwanag* is applicable to both the individual and the group, Apolinario uses still another metaphor with two levels of significance, as in the following invocation in connection with a membership drive:

> Aquing ytinatauag sa mahal na patron ng A. Cofradía na mag cabohos ang mga loob ng tauo, con baga sa cahoy o sa halaman ay mamolaclac ng sagana at toloy magbunga nang madlang caaliuan.[66]
>
> I call upon the help of the beloved patron of the Cofradía to make the loób of men overflow, just as a tree or plant might fully bloom and eventually bear the fruit of happiness for all.

This image has been dealt with previously in connection with the individual's (then compared to a tree) realization of his full potential.[67] But in this particular passage, the tree seems to stand for the Cofradía itself. As he states elsewhere, the brethren are the leaves *(boong cadahunan).* This alternation of reference to the individual and the whole is possible because the whole is an organic entity, moving as one. Apolinario himself puts it nicely in the same letter: "To be joined together we must follow like one body" (*Nang tayo ay mag caoompoc ay mag sunuran parang ysang catau-an*).[68] Each member sustains the brotherhood by an outpouring of his own loób.

Apolinario was particularly insistent upon the responsibility of local heads (cabecillas), in particular, to proselytize others: "Those who refuse to seek other people should not hope for my victory" (*ang ayao homanap nang tauo ay houag nang omasa ng aquing Victoria*) was his warning to some of the local leaders who apparently had doubts and fears regarding certain persons who wished to join the Cofradía.[69] Their actions seemed half-hearted to Apolinario, who believed that proselytizing was not a matter to be treated lightly, being a task that deserved the total devotion of body and soul.[70]

---

66. "Listahan," by AC, Manila, 5 July 1840 (accompanies a letter to the Cofradía bearing the same date; PNA).
67. See above, p. 67.
68. "Listahan," op.cit.
69. Ibid.
70. AC to the Cofradía, Manila, 5 July 1840 (PNA).

This importance given to the active seeking out of new members can only be understood fully through the notion of *lakaran* (lit., "journey of foot"), a word used as a proper noun by Apolinario because of its institutional, if not symbolic, aspect. It refers to the long treks that assigned members of the Cofradía undertook to spread the word to other localities. The scope of a lakaran can be inferred from a list, drawn up by Apolinario, of towns that three female cofrades were to pass through. This particular lakaran embraced four provinces of southern Luzon. Also listed down were the names of four men who were to accompany alternately the women in "those dangerous places not fit for women to pass through alone."[71] In another letter, Apolinario explains to Octabio that several men now in Octabio's custody were forced to refrain from sea travel because of depredations by "Moros and Englishmen who take captives in the sea." Because of these dangers, they are to journey on foot instead.[72] Evidently, the lakaran was a very dangerous undertaking, not to mention the physical exhaustion involved. Can we not say, then, that the importance Apolinario gives to proselytization is related to the experience of hardship that the lakaran involves? The "straight path" implies the experiencing of trials and suffering with serenity that comes from control of the self. Furthermore, Apolinario could inspire others to undertake the lakaran because he himself had, in his earlier days, wandered about the southern provinces, begging and preaching.

What we have said about the term *lakaran* will appear again and again in our discussion of other social movements. Even prior to the appearance of these movements, the term would have been familiar to the ordinary Filipino. A pilgrimage, a mission, an ascent—all these were perceived in terms of Christ's example in the pasyon: a lakaran from place to place to spread the word, a lakaran that knows no turning back and ends in Calvary. The swiftness and vigor of the Cofradía's expansion is difficult to explain unless lakaran is viewed as part of the individual cofrade's life of damay with Christ. In this way, liwanag gradually spread its rays over the landscape of southern Luzon. Spanish officials were understandably alarmed when it dawned on them that the Cofradía phenomenon was beginning to involve not only the province of Tayabas but also Laguna, Cavite, Batangas, and Camarines.

The Aritao Commune

When in late 1840 an order of excommunication against the Cofradía failed dismally to stop its growth and the continued collection of monthly dues from thousands of people, the curate of Lucban joined forces with the gobernador-

71. "Listahan," op.cit.
72. AC to OSJ, Manila, 25 April 1841 (PNA).

cillo and the provincial governor in attempting to intimidate the members. These difficulties forced the Cofradía, in early 1841, to transfer its center to Majayjay, Octabio San Jorge's hometown in nearby Laguna province. Monthly reunions were continued there. It was during this period that Apolinario's letters concerning the need for steadfastness of loób were written. Finally, sometime in August or September 1841, as a result of pressure from the friars and growing suspicion in Manila that the Cofradía was anti-Spanish, the central government ordered the organization suppressed and its leaders arrested. A reunion was raided on the evening of 19 September, resulting in the capture of several leaders, Octabio included, and incriminating correspondence from Apolinario. One of the letters revealed Apolinario's hiding place in Manila, and the government moved to have him arrested.[73]

Most of the leaders of the Cofradía escaped arrest, however, because the governor of Tayabas decided to return to Manila. The task of rounding up the leaders was left to the gobernadorcillo of Tayabas, whose wife was a member of the Cofradía. Having been allowed to escape from the towns, the leaders, now armed and considered outlaws, established contact with Apolinario, who had likewise escaped arrest in Manila, in the town of Bay. From there, they marched together around the western slopes of Mount San Cristobal, reaching the barrio of Isabang, which they decided to make their strongfold. A call was made to cofrades in all regions to assemble at Isabang for a novena—nine days of prayer and purification. According to the curate of Lucban, the Cofradía was successful in "communicating this fact with incredible speed, and with the prestige of the founder drawing a large number of people of all sexes, ages, and conditions, converting that solitary place within a few hours into a large and bustling encampment."[74] Responding to the call in the first couple of days were about three thousand people, including about two thousand armed with lances and a few rifles. Within a week, the number seems to have doubled.[75] One estimate gives the total figure as eight to nine thousand, including women and children.[76] The Cofradía in Isabang continued as it had begun in the towns, "with the difference that from that time it formed a group or society apart, the members considered themselves proscribed." They lived an "orderly and regular life. Each worked for his maintenance without abandoning his religious ideals and duties."[77]

---

73. For a more detailed account, cf. Sweet, "Proto-Political Peasant Movement," pp. 105-6.

74. From Sancho's report, in Sweet, "Proto-Political Peasant Movement," p. 107.

75. These are the figures given by Juan Manuel de la Matta in the official report of the rebellion (cf. Sweet, "Proto-Political Peasant Movement," p.107).

76. Fr. Antonio Matheos, curate of Tayabas, to Governor-General, Tayabas, 24 October 1841 (PNA).

77. Robert G. Woods, "Origin of the Colorum," *Philippine Magazine* 16 (7 December 1929): 428–29. Woods says he relied upon certain Tagalog manuscripts for his information about the Cofradía.

Apolinario's alleged objective was to occupy the nearby town of Tayabas and hold the novena in the parish church. Having opened negotiations with the gobernadorcillo and the acting governor, Apolinario might have achieved his goal peacefully had it not been for the vigorous opposition of the principales, who were afraid of looting, and the parish priest, who correctly anticipated that the central government would take military action. The gobernardorcillo managed to delay the Cofradía's attack until the town's defenses could be set up.

When Governor Ortega returned to Tayabas from Manila on 22 October, he hastily formed a contingent of ill-prepared constables, headmen, and *polo* laborers.[78] He offered amnesty to Apolinario, who promptly rejected it. On 23 October, a force of 300 led by Ortega attacked the Cofradía camp, but had to make a terrified retreat before a much larger force of cofrades, who were in a state of battle excitement. The governor, abandoned by his own men in the field, was captured and killed. Refused a Christian burial by the cofrades, his body was left in the care of a party of pagan Aetas who had come down from the Sierra Madre to join the rebels.[79] The killing of a Spanish governor was looked upon by the Cofradía as a "transcendental occurrence," further increasing their determination.[80]

The Cofradía next transferred its stronghold to a higher and more strategic location—Aritao—an open field between two rivers, protected in the rear by the slopes of Mount San Cristobal. A double palisade was built in which the cannon captured from Ortega's party was installed. Occupying the center of the camp was "a large palm-thatched chapel of bamboo, the inside walls of which were hung with colorful tapestries and religious paintings, where Manong Pule presided over the 'mysterious prayer sessions and ceremonies' of the *novenario.*"[81]

It is during this period of armed revolt that a different picture of Apolinario emerges. According to Spanish sources, the leader spent his time secluded in a small house beside the chapel, surrounded by trusted men prepared to die for his protection and devout women who attended to his every need.[82] The cofrades were allowed to see him only at certain times of the day and with great ceremony. He was now called by his followers "king of the Tagalogs."

---

78. *Polo* was forced labor performed by every male in the community, except chieftains and their eldest sons, a certain number of days each year.

79. Sweet, "Proto-Political Peasant Movement," p. 108. This interesting alliance between the Cofradía and a pagan mountain people is discussed in Sweet, p. 110.

80. Salvador de Roda, senior administrator of the government monopoly trade, to superiors (Tayabas, 23 October 1841; PNA). Roda accompanied a contingent of 300 men in the fighting.

81. Sweet, "Proto-Political Movement," p. 109.

82. There were rumors that Apolinario was "surrounded by beautiful, young single women who came in rotation to satisfy his needs and pleasures" (Leandro Tormo Sanz, *Lucban [A Town the Franciscans Built]* trans. from Spanish by Antonio Serrano [Manila: Historical Conservation Society, Vol. 20, 1971], p. 100; see also Sweet, "Proto-Political Peasant Movement," p. 109).

During this time, too, the leader made many predictions and promised which are absent from his letters. The cofrades were made to believe that, at the time of battle, invisible soldiers would be summoned and the angels would swing the tide of battle in the Cofradía's favor. Also, as soon as the battle started a big lake would open up and swallow the advancing enemy troops.[83] Another belief was that the cofrades would fight "without fear and contrary to the respect which these natives have for the Spaniards." They believed that their hearts would be as firm as the mysterious sword with which Apolinario baptized them, and they would be invulnerable to Spanish bullets. Finally, during the battle two voices would emanate from Tayabas and be answered by two rumbles from Mount Amolog. The mountain would open and the *Yglesia* (lit., "Church") would appear, uniting all the brethren. Manila would be inundated; the waters from the sea would drown all who were not cofrades, the latter being aided by a great armada.[84]

Previous scholars and writers who have examined the Cofradía have had to rely almost exclusively upon Spanish sources. Spanish accounts, however, date from 1840 and concentrate heavily on the armed revolt of October 1841. The reports show a fascination with the "superstitious beliefs" of the cofrades and the figure of Apolinario as king. Following the official line that the revolt was purely politically motivated, Spanish reports tend to picture the leader as a demagogue and manipulator of gullible minds. A modern Spanish historian admits that, among the Spanish observers of the time, "there was a tendency to conceal the facts and to emphasize the worst, presenting Apolinario as a monster of vice."[85]

In the context of the conceptual framework that we have attempted to elucidate, what can be said about the "Aritao phenomenon"? Although the "superstitious" beliefs reported by Spanish accounts were extracted through interrogation and are, therefore, probably inaccurate or incomplete, they nevertheless can be placed in an intelligible context.

Active membership in the Cofradía was a way in which peasants in the region could make ideal social forms and moral values, as imaged in religious rituals such as the pasyon, a permanent condition of their existence. In the *Dalit* to heaven discussed earlier, they got a glimpse of the perfect state of being, a condition which the Augustinian author of the *Dalit* would have reserved for the afterlife, but which Apolinario de la Cruz promised as a possibility for the cofrades in this world as well. What are our efforts for, he said, if not "to sustain our souls and bodies?" *(sa cabuhayan ng calolouat catau-an)*.[86] The very existence of the Cofradía was the realization of a mode

---

83. Sanz, *Lucban*, p. 99.
84. Promovedores, origen y progreso (PNA).
85. Sanz, Lucban, p. 100.
86. AC to the Cofradía, Manila, 5 July 1840 (PNA).

of existence as long as, through various forms of meditation and work, the members' loób were attuned to it. Returning to the "Aritao phenomenon," then, it is logical for the cofrades to have perceived their expulsion from the towns as a further "dying" to a past characterized by hierarchical social patterns and relationships. As long as they continued to live in the towns, the "old" would threaten the "new." On the slopes of Mount San Cristobal were families uprooted from the often closely knit kinship systems of the towns, men and women separated from their spouses, children or parents, and brought together in a new society.[87] Being a "community apart" heightened the bonds of solidarity among the brothers and sisters of the Cofradía, bringing them a step closer to the ideal of perfect unity.

The question of why the cofrades responded en masse to the leader's call for a reunion at Isabang must be posed. One way of approaching this is to regard the "fantastic" prophecies of Apolinario as divine signs, for biblical history to which Apolinario was attuned, is cataclysmic: Beneath the flux of causal events operates a divine plan that, hidden to human eyes, structures history according to a series of abrupt events leading to the final day of judgment. These "abrupt events" can be anticipated by the faithful through certain signs. Apolinario was probably pointing to these when he advised the cofrades always to be aware of the "meaning of these times."[88] Victory is "just behind the curtain of this age" *(nasasa cabila nang tabing lamang sa Panahong yto.)* Before the curtain is finally drawn, all must trust *(panalig)* in God, the Virgin, and the Cofradía's patron, St. Joseph.[89] During the actual revolt, Apolinario could be more specific in his interpretation of the signs of the times—thus his prophecy of a great flood and the appearance of the Yglesia from the depths of the mountain. These are, of course, signs of the Apocalypse.

Merely pointing this out, however, does not answer the question of why the cofrades fought to the end. Discounting the "irrationality" explanation, we note, in the pasyon, the repeated warning that the perception of signs of change should lead to a change in loób, so that the individual is attuned to, and participates in, the unfolding event. This is suggested, in the Cofradía's case, by the rebels' belief that, during the battle, they would fight without fear and with hearts of steel, and that they would be invulnerable to Spanish bullets. This is precisely the kind of behavior expected of one who has anting-anting. He can fight well because his acts are situated in a frame of reference in which the attainment of difficult tasks rests upon a pure and serene loób. Divine aid

87. Examples of the break-up of families are given by Sweet, "Proto-Political Peasant Movement," p. 107. He points out that many of the faithful at Isabang were women, "the most 'fanatical' of Apolinario's followers, of whom it was said later that they had been given the task of crucifying all the Spaniards who fell into their hands when the rebellion was victorious" (ibid.).

88. AC to OSJ, Manila, 10 February 1841 (PNA).

89. AC to OSJ, Manila, 2 March 1841 (PNA).

is not forthcoming if the loób wavers; salvation is not in sight if one is not prepared to leave the world behind. According to a Spanish observer, the cofrades "were prepared to die for [Apolinario] and for the sustention of his brotherhood."[90] Almost a century later, men would look back at these events as the "Golgotha" of Hermano Pule.[91]

It is not clear whether Apolinario in fact designated himself "king of the Tagalogs," for he vehemently denied this in a statement made after his capture. This title, he insisted, was used in jest by his lieutenant, Apolonio Purgatorio.[92] Spanish reports, however, are unanimous in claiming that the cofrades used the title in referring to their leader, at least during the armed revolt. While it is doubtful that Apolinario arrogated to himself the title "king," it is perfectly understandable for the cofrades to have spontaneously perceived him as a kingly figure.[93] If Apolinario, in his letters, could effectively invoke images of the Gardener and the Good Shepherd—i.e., the Tagalog Christ—surely the idea that Apolinario was *their* Christ the King would have suggested itself to his followers. To the authorities, however, a Tagalog king could be regarded as a political threat to Spanish rule. Although there is no evidence that Apolinario ever incited the cofrades to revolt against Spain, the Cofradía had to be suppressed because of the social implications of its "heretical" practices, particularly the way it upset the traditional relationship between the parish priest and his Indio congregation—that of a superior to an inferior. According to Robert Woods, who claims to have used old Tagalog papers in his 1929 research,

> Many persons asserted that there was no resistance on the part of those of the Brotherhood. Those defenseless persons, following the principals of a sect whose aim was ennobling, were put to the sword without mercy, for the sole crime of having disobeyed the vicar, and if anyone did resist, it was in self-defense at the moment of danger.[94]

The commune at Aritao was, within a short time, surrounded by troops from Manila and peasant volunteers from the surrounding provinces. A second amnesty offer was promptly spurned by Apolinario. The cofrades, say the Spanish sources, were in a high state of excitement, spoiling for a fight. On 31 October, an advance party of government troops was attacked by the cofrades, waving a red flag, fighting "with more vigor and enthusiasm than

---

90. Salvador de Roda to superiors, Tayabas, 23 October 1841, (PNA).

91. *Dahong Pang-alaala sa Bayan Tayabas* (Quezon province, 1928), p. 7.

92. *Promovedores, origen y progreso* (PNA). The author of this report concludes that Apolinario was motivated by ambition.

93. According to E. Arsenio Manuel, the title Apolinario himself assumed was "supreme pontiff" but his followers crowned him king (*Dictionary of Philippine Biography*, vol. 2 [Quezon City: Filipiniana Research Society, 1970], p. 159).

94. Robert Woods, "Origin of the Colorum," *Philippine Magazine* 16 (December 1929): 429.

military know-how and prudence."[95] Sinibaldo de Mas comments that the cofrades "came for the battle dancing," implying controlled and ritualistic movements.[96] In a short while, however, the military superiority of the government force pushed the rebels back behind their palisades. Fortunately at this moment their Aeta allies released a shower of spears and arrows, which delayed the Spanish advance.

Eventually, the palisades were breached. Government soldiers and peasant volunteers poured into the encampment, followed by Spanish cavalry. The cofrades defended their position house by house. Those guarding Apolinario's headquarters died to a man while their leader managed to escape into the forest. After some four hours of battle, it was all over. Three to five hundred rebels lay dead.[97] Some five hundred cofrades, including about three hundred women, were taken prisoner. The rest managed to flee to the dense forests of Mount Banahaw, where they were not pursued. On the government side, there were only eleven wounded.[98]

Apolinario was captured the day after the battle as he tried to seek refuge among ex-cofrades in Sariaya. After a summary trial he was shot, his body cut up into pieces, his head put in a cage and displayed atop a pole stuck along the roadside leading to Majayjay. Among the witnesses at the execution was Father Sancho, the curate primarily responsible for the suppression of the Cofradía in Lucban, who reported that Apolinario de la Cruz "died serenely and showed unusual greatness of spirit."[99] On the same day, two hundred of the prisoners, comprising most of the males, were executed. Questioned, before their death, about their purpose in rebelling, their answer was: "To pray."[100]

Apolinario de la Cruz, and probably his followers as well, died with serenity and "greatness of spirit" because death was the fulfillment of their hopes, the final passage to a condition of pure liwanag where they would be face to face with God and other beings in paradise. Death at the hands of the "establishment" was, after all, an event familiar to them through the story of Christ; it would have been but one more act of damay for them to die for their cause. Apolinario taught the cofrades to accept suffering, even death, for the sake of their union. Perhaps he was right; perhaps those hundreds of deaths contributed to the survival of an ideal. For the inhabitants of the region continued

---

95. Sweet, "Proto-Political Movement," p. 10, quoting Fr. Sancho's account.

96. In Sanz, *Lucban*, p. 99. This is most likely accurate, for when the Colorum joined the Katipunan revolt in 1896 they walked to battle as in a church procession, dressed in white garb (Artemio Ricarte, *Memoirs* [Manila: National Heroes Commission, 1963], p. 84).

97. The number killed in battle varies widely. Sinibaldo de Mas puts it at 240 (*Lucban*, p. 99); Woods ("Colorum," p. 429), puts it at 800, according to his information; Barrows (in Manuel, *Dictionary*, vol. 2, p. 159) puts it at "about a thousand."

98. Sanz, *Lucban*, p. 100.

99. Ibid.

100. Ibid.

to remember Apolinario de la Cruz, believing that he was alive in the land of paradise and would return someday to help his people.[101] But even more than the memory of a specific man and a specific movement, it was the vitality of the pasyon tradition that made it possible for ordinary folk to recognize the appearance of other Christ-like figures, each bringing the same message of hope that Apolinario brought. In this way did he live on in those that came after him.

The New Jerusalem

According to Spanish records of 1870, Apolinario de la Cruz, together with his disciple Apolonio Purgatorio (who was killed in 1841) and the Virgin Mary, appeared to several persons and revealed to them the path that must be taken toward the attainment of liwanag: the Cofradía must be rebuilt and people taught the proper modes of prayer and devotion. Spanish authorities were once more alarmed upon learning that reunions were being held regularly, one of such reunions in fact taking place in the house of Apolonio Purgatorio's widow. The new cofradía, they discovered, was called "Cofradía of St. Joseph, St. Apolinario and St. Apolonio." As the magistrate Salvador Elio put it, "this is to say that they sanctify . . . the event [of 1841] and those two criminals are recognized as martyrs."[102]

At the time (1870) Spanish authorities discovered the revived Cofradía, its leader was Januario Labios, who was linked in a way to the old Cofradía by virtue of the fact that his father-in-law, Andres Labios, was considered by the inhabitants of the locality to have been involved in the 1841 revolt. The old man Andres used to walk about the barrios in the vicinity of the mountain, telling the inhabitants of his communications with the Virgin and Apolinario and how they had taught him prayers and rituals which gave him powers of invisibility and invulnerability to certain types of physical harm. As a result of his teachings, his son-in-law Januario "underwent a transformation" and himself took to wandering in the mountain and the surrounding barrios, praying and proselytizing.[103] He "seduced the imagination of the inhabitants" by telling them of his talks with Apolinario, Apolonio and the Virgin, of how they had revealed to him the form of the Cofradía to be revived and the new religious practices to be instituted. In return for the perseverance of the

101. Alfred Marche, *Luzon and Palawan*, trans. by C. O. Ojeda and J. Castro (Manila: Filipiniana Book Guild, 1970), p. 82. Marche was a French explorer who visited the Philippines in the 1880s. His travels took him to the sites where Apolinario passed through.

102. *Ynforme del Sr. Magistrado D. Salvador Elio*, Manila, 27 July 1870 (PNA); Interrogration and statements of Fr. Francisco Rosas, parish priest of Tayabas, 16 June 1870, (PNA). Information about the resurgence of the Cofradía in 1870 comes from documents in the Apolinario de la Cruz bundle in the Philippine National Archives.

103. Emilio Martin, alcalde mayor of Tayabas, to the Governor-General, *Sobre reorganización de la Cofradía de San Jose*, Tayabas, 19 June 1870 (PNA).

cofrades, they would be granted "eternal felicity for their souls in the afterlife, and in this life the abolition of tribute and above all, independence."[104]

The writer of the above report, Alcalde Mayor Emilio Martin, says that *independencia* was the ultimate goal of Labios's Cofradía. If this information is accurate and not merely a product of Spanish paranoia about the event, the use of the term independencia may reflect changes taking place in Manila.[105] After the successful revolution of 1868 in Spain and the establishment there of a liberal government, a new governor-general, Carlos Maria de la Torre, was sent to the Philippines in 1869 to introduce liberal reforms. De la Torre's liberal ideology as well as behavior was appreciated by the native elite. During his short-lived administration (1869-71), he encouraged freedom of speech, abolished censorship of the press, and in general stimulated the reformist spirit among various segments of the educated elite. It is possible that news, however distorted, of these "sensational" events in the capital managed to filter out to the rural areas. Could this have been regarded as one of the signs of impending cataclysmic change, that thus led Labios to promise independencia? As we shall see, during and after the revolution at the turn of the century, similar leaders appropriated the word independence (*kalayaan*), giving it meanings often unintended by the elite who introduced the term.

Alarmed civil and ecclesiastical authorities in Tayabas certainly suspected a link between Manila liberal politics and the reorganization of the Cofradía, for its "subversive" nature was evident in the members' refusal to pay tribute or perform the annual personal service. But the authorities found it hard to believe that a simple peasant like Januario Labios could be behind the whole affair. They also could not imagine that a man of no education was able to devise the unusual prayers and rituals of the Cofradía. In the interrogation of some captured members, an attempt was made to secure statements to the effect that Januario received inspiration, counsel or orders from other persons presumably higher up in the social scale. But in each case, the respondents "failed to understand the limits of the question," implying that the idea that wealthy or educated people inspired the movement was incomprehensible.[106]

Among the documents captured during a raid on Mount Banahaw were several notebooks of Tagalog writings about the life of Christ and some

---

104. Martin to the Governor-General, Tayabas, 19 June 1870 (PNA).

105. According to the French consul in Manila, the word "independence" was uttered as a "rallying cry" in the Philippines at the uprising of the Tagalog soldiers of the Tayabas regiment in Manila in response to the Hermano Pule affair (Horacio de la Costa, *Readings in Philippine History*, [Manila: Bookmark, 1965], p. 215).

106. *Declaración de Gregorio Enrique*, 18 June 1870; *Declaración de Tiburcio de Rojas*, 18 June 1870; *Declaración de Crispina Romero*, 18 June 1870; all before the alcalde mayor, Tayabas (PNA). The same inability to produce the wanted statements because of the failure to understand the question is evident in the interrogation reports of other Cofradía members.

medicinal prescriptions and prayers. The writings about Christ were probably copied out from a published pasyon, and attests to the importance of the singing of the pasyon in the rituals of the pilgrims and cofrades.[107] Some of the other prayers, however, were utterly incomprehensible to the authorities who examined them. Although containing some Latin and Spanish words, they were "in reality . . . neither Latin nor Castellan and they are scraps of prayers from some breviary or missal, badly copied."[108] This led some Spanish investigators to the theory that Labios, who recited these prayers, was a madman. But interrogation of Cofradía members always led to the latter's insistence that their leader was not mad. One of them, Gregorio Enriquez, stated emphatically: "He was not mad; in fact his mind functioned in a totally regular and determined manner."[109]

In order to explain the above details, we must regard Januario Labios as a prophet, and therefore a link between two dimensions of time. His ability to communicate with the Virgin and Apolinario would have been interpreted by those who learned about it as a sign of the "divine" and the "everyday" intersecting. The only response they knew was to listen and participate in the event that was to unfold. Elio described it this way:

> Januario says he is in direct communication with God and the Saints and this supernatural assertion is enough for the Yndios to believe in him. No extraordinary event, after the apparition, serves to corroborate his assertion, but this is not important for the Yndios who submit to his orders and over whom he exercised a despotic rule.[110]

In this context, we can understand why some of the prayers recited by Januario were incomprehensible. Their content alone was unimportant; their incomprehensibility indicated the inability of the rational faculty of mind to know the workings of divine time. More important was the mode in which the prayer was recited and the consequent effect on the listener. In order to clarify this, let us quote what a pilgrim says about the "incomprehensibility" of prayers (the writer describes the effect upon the pilgrims of Maestro Mintoy's recitation of a prayer):

> Sabihin pa baga ang tuwa't ligaya
> ng lahat ng taong nasagot sa kanya,
> dahil sa mabuting tumuod ng letra
> ang pagsasalita'y na sa punto'y coma.

---

107. This is mentioned by Artemio Ricarte, *Memoirs*, p. 82.
108. *Ynforme del Sr. Magistrado D. Salvador Elio*, Manila, 27 July 1870 (PNA).
109. *Declaración de Gregorio Enriquez*, Tayabas, 18 June 1870 (PNA).
110. *Ynforme,* (PNA).

> Would you believe the delight and joy
> of all the people who responded,
> as he pronounced the letters so well
> speaking with perfect rhythm.

At gayon din naman itong dinarasal
ay matutuwa ka't parang tinutunghan,
sa galaw ng dila maliliwanagan
ang puso ng taong nasa sa kadiliman

> The same was true of the prayers
> how delightful they were as if,
> by his tongue's movement came liwanag
> to the heart of a man in darkness.

Lalo't ang marami latin na salita
kung aking pakinggan ay aywan kung tama,
sapagka't hindi ko napag-uunawa
ang gayong termino latin ma't kastila.[111]

> Especially since the many Latin words
> could not be verified when heard,
> because I am unable to comprehend
> such Latin or Spanish terms.

To this pilgrim, as well as to the cofrades of 1870, it was the sound of the teacher's voice reciting the prayers that brought joy and liwanag. The experience of listening was one of the feeling, not of deciphering or understanding. What, to others, might have seemed like noise was, to the pilgrims, similar to music in a key that their religious experience enabled them to respond to.

Labios, through his powerful speeches, enabled his listeners to organize their everyday experience in terms of a divine plan. No longer would the hopes and fears of his peasant followers remain incoherent; change could be looked forward to. There would be a great storm and deluge. Homes and buildings would be destroyed; rivers and streams would overflow their banks. In order to prevent the inundation of their fields and the destruction of their homes, they must deepen the beds of streams and fortify their houses with two posts, in the form of a cross, embracing the extreme southern points of the sides of the house. But more important was that the cofrades must pray. They must make

---

111. Simeon Aranas, *Kaligaligayang Bundok ng Banahaw*, vol. 2 (Manila: P. Sayo, 1927), pp. 17–18. Aranas talks about his experience of the pilgrimage to Mount Banahaw sometime during the Spanish colonial period.

the pilgrimage to the mountain and there undergo "penitence," which would mark their initial separation from or dying to the world that will be destroyed when the cataclysm finally occurs. And they must form the brotherhood that would herald the kind of relations between man and man that the society of the future would bring. This, plus freedom from taxes and forced labor, was what "independencia," or whatever the original Tagalog word was, signified.[112]

In response to Januario Labios's call, people from Tayabas, Batangas, and Laguna came to undertake the pilgrimage through the mountain. As one of the cofrades himself noted, it was extremely difficult, especially for young women and the elderly, to approach the mountain retreat. Leeches abound in the forests. And yet people continued to arrive.[113] The parish priest and civil authorities panicked upon realizing that the teachings of Labios, without being related directly to the spread of liberal ideas in the metropolis at that time, were leading the *pobres y ignorantes* to defy the status quo. Contrary to the image of the passive and acquiescent Indio peasant, the members of the Cofradía refused to pay taxes and fulfill the annual personal service. They also disavowed any connections with the priests of the Catholic Church, for their church, they claimed, was in the mountain.[114] That is why an armed force was sent to disperse the community. Many were arrested; Labios's fate, however, could not be ascertained. The invading party also cut down sacred trees and attempted to destroy the sacred rock which formed part of the cult.[115]

The provincial governor's account of the punitive expedition to the mountain in 1870, gives us the first description of a cult on the slopes of Mount Banahaw and its sister slope, Mount San Cristobal. There were baths where the pilgrims were baptized. Farther up the slopes were seven trees successively marked "first heaven" to "seventh heaven." There was also a huge rock called *Iglesia Mayor* by pilgrims, with a flat top upon which lighted candles were left to burn. Marriage ceremonies were also conducted beside this rock. In conclusion, the governor says: "Those which the inhabitants call temples, hermitages, and holy places, are represented only by rocks, trees, and streams."[116]

---

112. *Declaración de Feliciano Yobion y Caballero*, Tayabas, 16 June 1870; statements of Fr. Francisco Rosas, parish priest of Tayabas, 16 June 1870, and of Martin to the Governor-General, Tayabas, 19 June 1870 (PNA).

113. *Declaración de Feliciano*, 16 June 1870 (PNA); Emilio Martin, who led an expedition to the mountain, says that the lower slopes can be inhabited for two weeks at most, but "the places which the ignorant mind of certain people of this province considers sacred, and which are located in the interior of almost impenetrable forests, cannot be inhabited for three days by even the strongest native without his succumbing, [being] filled with insects and always without sunlight" (Martin to Governor-General, Tayabas, 2 July 1870 [PNA]).

114. Martin to the Governor-General, Tayabas, 19 June 1870 (PNA).

115. Ibid., 2 July 1870 (PNA).

116. Ibid.

Writing in 1887, the French explorer Marche gives a fuller description of the cult. He points out that, to the inhabitants of the region, the holy land is Mount Banahaw. One finds there such spots as the river Jordan, Purgatory and Calvary, all regarded as having been sanctified by Apolinario de la Cruz himself:

> The spots that he had sanctified are always, although secretly, very much frequented. One brings sick people there, in order to take a bath in the water of Jordan or at the miraculous springs, which heal all those who have faith.[117]

The Purgatory, an immense cave in the mount of Calvary, "served for a long time as refuge to the prophet and his disciples. . . . All of these places are the object of veneration by the natives who still secretly gather there."[118] Marche also mentions that a recent gathering of the pilgrims had been raided by the *guardia civil* at the request of the parish priest of Dolores, the town where the pilgrimage usually starts.

By the time the revolution against Spain began in 1896, the cult was an established center for the Lenten pilgrimage, attracting not only Tagalogs but people from all over the archipelago.[119] An organized priesthood of men and women existed. Branches of the society or brotherhood flourished in other areas, headed by pastors trained at the mountain.[120]

Why were people attracted to make the pilgrimage? Let us quote a few stanzas from a pilgrim's *awit.* At the beginning, the pilgrim describes the town of Dolores, the starting point of the pilgrimage, and how people from faraway towns journeyed there.

Sa panahong yaon ay kasalukuyan
bayan ng Dolores sa kapayapaan,
nasasa ligaya tungkol namamayan
parang paraiso nitong taong buhay.

In those days the town of Dolores
was in a state of peace,
the inhabitants were happy
it was like paradise to the living.

Ang lugar na ito ay parang bagong langit
at kabalitaan bayan ng Dolores,

---

117. Marche, *Luzon and Palawan*, p. 82.

118. Ibid.

119. In 1912, the population of Dolores, staging area of the pilgrimage, was 5,000, of which only around 500 were members of the Colorum society. However, "tens of thousands" of members from "other towns and distant provinces" flocked annually to the site (Severino Gala, *Dasala't Dalit ng Kolorum* [Maynila, 1912], pp. viii-ix).

120. Ricarte, *Memoirs*, pp. 82-83.

kinawiwiliha't ang iba'y naalis
sa sariling baya't doon dumarating.

> The place was like a new heaven
> news of Dolores spread far and wide,
> so fascinating it was that some left
> their hometowns to go there.

Halos balang oras gabi linalamay
ng lahat ng tao bata't matanda man,
purong umaalis sa kasarilinan
at doon sila nagsisipamayan.

> For days and nights everyone
> young and old journeyed there,
> they all left their own homes
> and settled down in Dolores.

Dahil sa malaki akay ng ligaya
tanang kahirapa'y winalang halaga,
ipinagbibili ang munting nakaya
sa kasarilina't doon dinadala.[121]

> Because of the joy that led them on
> they paid no attention to hardships,
> they sold their meager properties
> and brought the rest there.

Dolores and the surrounding countryside are described in detail, with a constant repetition of the theme that the beautiful place is like paradise. The people who inhabit it, namely, the members of the brotherhood, are described as pure of heart. The author mentions, in particular, certain elders whose names are Maestro (Teacher) Casinto, Tandang (Elder) Albino, Antoling and Sabelo:

Ito'y puro-purong may honor na tangan
puso'y malilinis at may kapurihan,
ang una'y sa Dios may pagsintang tunay
tapat ang pag-ibig di nadurungisan.

> They all hold a position of honor
> their hearts are pure and upright,
> for one thing they love God truly
> a love that is sincere and pure.

Bukod pa sa rito'y ang iba't iba pa
na natahang tao bata't matanda na,
purong malilinis lalo ang dalaga
na naghahalaman ng buong ligaya.[122]

---

121. Aranas, *Kaligaligayang Bundok,* p. 6.
122. Ibid.

The other residents too
young and old alike,
are pure of heart like the maidens
who tend the gardens with joy.

The beauty of the natural surroundings is thus matched by the purity and love in the hearts, or loób, of the people.

Dolores, then, is an image of paradise which beckoned pilgrims from all over the archipelago who understood its meaning because of their common religious experience. They understood that Dolores was only a sampling of the liwanag and fulfillment that awaited them at the end of their pilgrimage, which was none other than the lakaran practised by the Cofradía of 1841. According to a 1915 account of customs in Lipa, Batangas, pilgrims used to go either on foot or in carts, never in a carromata for "such a mode of travel is very different from Christ's journey to Calvary and 'Do as Christ did on earth' is always a pilgrim's motto."[123] The pilgrim's awit chronicles the week-long experience on Mount Banahaw involving much climbing, crawling through narrow caves, and intense prayer in the heat of the sun. If Dolores was a beckoning paradise, it certainly was no picnic or recreation spot; pilgrims went there to experience hardship and exhaustion so that paradise could be experienced in the loób:

Ang nasa loob ko'y itong kahirapan
ay ang hahalili itong katuwaan,
kaya ko sinapit ang ganitong bagay
nang makilala ko ang kaliwanagan.

I kept to heart that this hardship
would be followed by great joy,
for I underwent this experience
in order to be in liwanag.[124]

The climax of the pilgrimage was the ascent to Calvary, a hill "in a spot similar to the poetic descriptions in the Pasion Mahal, or rather something resembling the blurred and imperfect woodcuts in the book."[125] The ascent, was bloody and difficult, but without it the pilgrimage had no meaning:

Ang tarik ng bundok ay sakdal ng taas
ang tinutuntunga'y ang batong matalas,

---

123. Julian Lopez, "Social Customs and Beliefs in Lipa, Batangas," Manila (1915), BCTE, vol. 1, no. 64.

124. Aranas, *Kaligaligayang Bundok*, p. 32.

125. Woods, "Origin II," *Philippine Magazine* 26 (January 1930): 515.

at may isang batong pasan sa balikat
na may labin-isang kilo ang katumbas.

> The mountain was extremely steep
> we clambered over sharp stones,
> each carrying on his shoulder
> an eleven-kilo rock.

Matalas na bato pula kung pagmasdan
nagsugat ang aking buong talampakan,
tiniis ko kahit ako'y mahirapan
marating ko lamang ang kaitaasan.

> The sharp stones appeared red
> cut and bloody were the soles of my feet,
> I endured all this hardship
> just to reach the summit.

Sa inutay-utay ng aming paglakad
buong katawan ko sa pawis ay tigmak,
nagtitiis ako kahit anong hirap
makadamay lamang sa kay Kristong hirap.

> As we made our way slowly
> my body was drenched in sweat,
> I was enduring all kinds of hardship
> in *damay* with the hardship of Christ.

Mag-aalas siete nang kami magmula
sa puno ng bundok na dakong mababa,
nang a las doce na katawa'y nanghina
dalawang paa ko'y umuurong yata.

> We started at seven in the morning
> from the lower base of the mountain
> when it was noon my body weakened
> my legs seemed to falter.

Sa malaking hirap ako'y nag-uutay
pasan ko ang bato na may kabigatan,
dalawa kong paa'y di na maihakbang
na nagkakahalo ang gutom at uhaw.

> In such great hardship I went slowly
> bearing the heavy rock on my shoulder,
> my feet could hardly move ahead
> hunger and thirst compounded the pain.

Bukod pa sa rito'y ang mga babai
may dala rin naman paris ng lalaki,
kaya kahi't anong hirap ang mangyari
sa mga kasama'y di makapagsabi.

Moreover, our women companions
also carried rocks, like the men,
thus no matter how trying it was
we could not complain to our companions.

Mag-aala una nang kami umabot
sa kataluktukan ng Kalbariong bundok,
sa kalagitnaa'y may malaking Krus
ang bunton ng bato ay talu-taludtod.

It was almost one o'clock
when we reached the peak of Calvary,
upon which stood a large Cross
with piles of rocks at its foot.

Dala naming bato pasan sa balikat
sa puno ng Krus duon inilapag,
ang aming maestro pagdaka'y nangusap
sa amin at ito ang ipinahayag.

The rocks we bore on our shoulders
we dropped by the foot of the Cross,
and then our teacher spoke
and this is what he said:

Mga kapatid ko ang puso'y linisin
tayong kalahatan purong magsikain,
at kung makasundo bago manalangin
sa Dios na Amang Panginoon natin.

My brothers let us cleanse our hearts
in purity let us share our meal,
and when we have come together
we shall pray to God the Father our Lord.

Nang nahahanda na ang pagkaing mahal
ang aming maestro'y pumuno sa dasal,
at nang matapos na'y nangagsabay-sabay
sumubo ng kanin kaming kalahatan.

When the holy food was ready
our teacher led the prayer,
and when it was over we all
together partook of the rice.

Matapos kumain ay magpasalamat
kami sa Lumikha ng sangmaliwanag,
bago isinunod ang pamamahayag
sa lahat ng mga kapatid na liyag.

Having eaten we all gave thanks
to the Creator of the universe,

then the teacher resumed his sermon
to all of the beloved *kapatid*.

Isilid sa inyong puso't alaala
na kaya narito'y hindi sa ligaya,
kun di sa pagdamay kay Hesus na Ama
sa pagsakop nito sa sanglibutan sala.

Implant in your hearts and memories
that we are not here for happiness,
but in *damay* with Jesus the Father
in his redemption of sinful mankind.

Pagka' t ang ligaya sa mundong ibabaw
katulad ng bulang nasa karagatan,
na di nalalao't munting oras lamang
di paris ng tuwa sa langit na bayan.[126]

Because happiness in this world
is like foam on the ocean,
that exists only briefly
compared to the joy in the land of heaven.

Then the pilgrims all prayed the rosary and the "seven supplications" kneeling in the heat of the sun, arms outstretched before the Cross. Because of their common experience of damay with Christ's pasyon, now they were truly brothers.

---

126. Aranas, *Kaligaligayang Bundok*, p. 32.

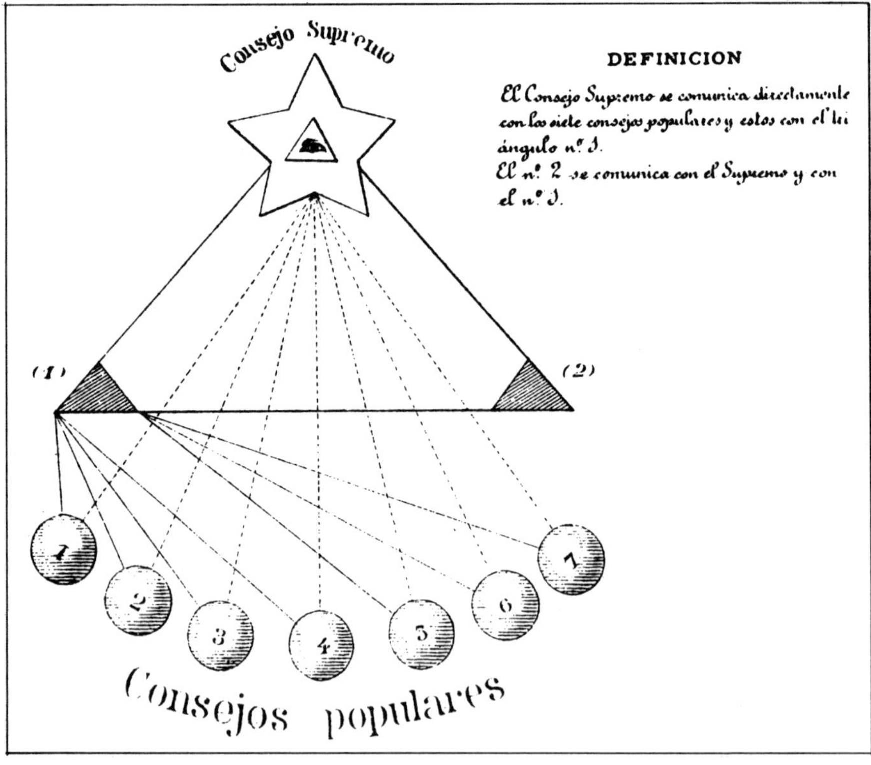

The triangular basis of the 1896 Katipunan's organization, the lines representing the flow of authority and communications from the *supremo*, or "eye," to the popular councils below (based on statements of Katipuneros; from Jose del Castillo, *El Katipunan* [Madrid, Imprenta del Asilo de Huerfanos, 1897], facing p. 108)

CHAPTER 3

Tradition and Revolt: The Katipunan

The armed uprising against Spain in 1896 was initiated by a secret society called *Kataastaasan Kagalanggalang Katipunan ng mga Anak ng Bayan* (The Highest and Most Honorable Society of the Sons of the Country). The flame of rebellion that began in the outskirts of Manila spread quickly throughout the countryside of central and southern Luzon, as Katipunan chapters and other groups concertedly turned against the symbols and representatives of Spanish rule. It was during this time that the Cofradía based at Mount San Cristobal underwent a tremendous expansion. It attracted many, predominantly peasants, who had fled to the mountains and forests of southern Luzon in order to escape the bloody reprisals being inflicted by the Spanish army upon the populace at large. The Colorum Society, as the brotherhood came to be called, soon became involved in the revolution largely through the efforts of a pastor *(pator)* named Sebastian Caneo, a native of Taal, Batangas, who later settled in San Pablo, Laguna.[1] He was primarily responsible for interpreting separation from Spain as a sign that the world was about to undergo a substantive change, for which his brotherhood must prepare through prayer and participation in the struggle.

---

1. The word "colorum" seems to have been derived from the phrase "per omnia saecula saeculorum," with which the Cofradía ended its prayers. "Colorum" also means, in contemporary Philippine usage, any unlicensed property or business. This reflects to a certain extent today's popular image of these religious groups (See Milagros Guerrero, "The Colorum Uprisings: 1924–1931," *Asian Studies* 5 [April 1967]: 65).

According to Santiago Alvarez, a prominent Katipunan leader who provides us with the bulk of information about the Colorum participation in the revolt, the prominence of Caneo resulted from a miracle that occurred in the hills of eastern Cavite.[2] It was then a time of drought when, all of a sudden, a spring of water began to flow from a crack on a dry mountain top. Caneo first saw it as he was walking, and out of surprise or fear fell on his knees and prayed. The people who happened to be nearby all knelt with awe at the miracle. Soon the word spread around that Caneo was a prophet whose devoutness and concern for his fellowmen in thirst caused God to respond with the miracle. From that time on people began to gather about Caneo, not only because of the sign but also because of his "gentle and good manners." He instructed them on the ways of leading a pure and devout life, and informed them of the cult center at Banahaw where the sage prophet, Agripino Lontok, lived as a hermit.

Caneo perceived that the Katipunan revolt against Spain was a sign of an approaching cataclysm that would bring about the fulfillment of the faithful's hopes. But the brotherhood was not going to stand aside while the divine plan for the world unfolded itself. Man had to participate in the process. For Caneo this meant that the *kapatid* (brothers) must strengthen themselves through prayer and join the revolt against Spain. Thus, he called upon his assistants, Juan Magdalo and Eligio Dius-Diusan, to gather as many of the brethren as possible in preparation for the struggle for *kalayaan* (liberty). He told them that according to the *Santong Boces* (Holy Voice), with whom he communicated in the caves of Banahaw, the Spaniards would be forced to surrender without a fight by means of the following strategem: They would all march to the Spanish garrison at Tayabas, the provincial capital, each of them bearing a piece of rope, about a yard long, tied around their waists. As they approached the *cuartel* of the *guardia civil,* they would throw these pieces of rope at the Spaniards, who would be miraculously tied up. Their real weapon would be intense prayer. Caneo announced his plan to the sage, Agripino Lontok, who gave his blessing to Caneo saying that, indeed, everything should be done for the defense of the country's kalayaan, and that through prayer their victory would be assured by God.

Caneo's assistant, Juan Magdalo, wrote to all the pastors in the vicinity, asking them to gather all the brethren, men and women alike, at the foot of Banahaw. Before about five thousand people who were immediately assembled, Juan Magdalo announced that they had been commanded by the Santong Boces to fight for their country's kalayaan and that their strongest weapon would be prayer. He then outlined their battle plan, particularly the

2. Santiago Alvarez, "Ang Katipunan at Paghihimagsik" (typescript), 25 July 1927 (PNL). Artemio Ricarte, a former colleague of Alvarez in the Magdiwang wing of the Katipunan, also wrote about the Colorum in his *Memoirs* (Manila: National Heroes Commission, 1963), pp. 82-84.

manner in which the ropes were to be thrown.[3] Obviously it was to be a ritualistic movement, involving great bodily control.[4]

At the dawn of 24 June 1897, a huge procession of men, women and children, all praying in unison and carrying lighted candles, entered the town of Tayabas. The older pilgrims wore long white robes, similar to the attire of Christ's apostles. In the middle of the procession was a *caro* (a platform upon which a saint's statue is borne during processions) on which stood Juan Magdalo dressed in the attire of John the Baptist. As they neared the soldiers' quarters, the guardia civil opened fire upon seeing the devotees reach for the ropes around their waists. At the first volley, scores of men and women of all ages fell dead or wounded. The devotees broke from their ranks and fled in the direction their leader, Juan Magdalo, was running.

When Sebastian Caneo brought up the subject of the massacre before the Santong Boces on the mountain, the reply was: "They did not have enough faith *(kulang ng pagsampalataya)* and during the time of battle those who died or sustained wounds had failed to utter my name." When Caneo repeated these words to the kapatid, they regained their serenity. Alvarez notes that "this explanation was sufficient, and all were happy with the continuation of their devotions (*sampalataya*), without even feeling sadness and loss at the death of their brothers, spouses, children or parents." They brought candles which they arranged along the banks of a deep stream, on the slopes of the mountain, believing that the souls of the departed pass through there on their way to heaven.[5]

The entry into Tayabas appears to have been the only occasion in which the Colorum fought as a group during the war against Spain. Nevertheless, as Alvarez and Artemio Ricarte point out, the brotherhood was always ready to aid Katipunan fighters who came for help and protection. The cult center at Mount San Cristobal had been transformed into a patriotic shrine by mid-1897, at the latest. Patriotic martyrs like Fr. Jose Burgos and Jose Rizal were said to be living there, apparently to render prophetic advice to pilgrims.[6]

Agoncillo views the Colòrum fiasco of 1897 as no more than "an interesting sidelight" to the real struggle going on elsewhere. He concludes that "this painful experience taught the Colorum a lesson: henceforth, they were not to

---

3. Alvarez, "Ang Katipunan," pp. 378–79.

4. See also chapter 2, p. 62, which describes the Cofradía of 1841 as going to battle "dancing." Such control of external movement reflects the firm control of loób that has been attained through prayer. This is consistent with the notion, expressed in various parts of this study, that no discontinuity exists between external appearance and internal states of being.

5. Alvarez, "Ang Katipunan," p. 380-81.

6. Telesforo Canseco, "Historia de la Insurrección Filipino en Cavite" (1897), Archivo de la Provincia del Santísimo Rosario, p. 98 (page reference is to the typescript in the Ateneo de Manila's Rizal Library).

concern themselves with the revolution but instead contribute in kind to the rebels as their patriotic duty."[7] Sturtevant surprisingly ignores this event altogether, perhaps because it blurs the distinction he makes between the revolution (a "Great Tradition" phenomenon) and messianic movements (a "Little Tradition" phenomenon).[8] Actually, the incident of 1897 is a manifestation of how the revolution, in its Katipunan phase, was perceived from below. Santiago Alvarez, in his account, hardly regards the Colorum as a curiosity. In fact, he notes that, with the exception of the brotherhood's unique rituals and devotions, it was "just like the Katipunan of the Sons of the People at the time brotherly love had not been dissolved."[9] This is a key statement, which not only connects the Cofradía and the Katipunan but almost makes a distinction between two phases of the revolution characterized by the presence and absence of brotherly love. By seeing the Katipunan as only one of many types of brotherhoods that Filipinos from all walks of life were attracted to join, and by asking ourselves what part these brotherhoods played in the interpretation of everyday experience, we may begin to assess the real impact of the revolution upon the masses.

Unfortunately, rather than attempt to describe the revolutionary experience, scholars have chosen to focus on the evolution of the struggle from its Katipunan, or secret society, stage to various stages of revolutionary government culminating, in 1898, in a constitutional republic. By positing, at the outset, that the Filipino people had a common goal—independence—scholars have simplified the problems of the revolution, reducing them to personality difference, regional differences, military weakness, corruption and the like. The execution of the Katipunan's founder, Andres Bonifacio by Emilio Aguinaldo and other prominent Cavite leaders, for instance, is "explained away" by the argument that, although both Bonifacio and Aguinaldo sought the same goal—independence—one or the other had to be cast aside for the sake of revolutionary unity. Bonifacio's execution is taken as a sign that the "secret society" phase of the revolution had given way to a more progressive "national" movement led by a more capable military leader, Aguinaldo. But is it true that progress had taken place simply because of the use of more sophisticated political language and forms by a few men in power? Have we bothered to investigate what those who joined the Katipunan or even the Cofradía de San Jose and the Colorum, were trying to voice out regarding the shape of the society they wanted to create? Perhaps there is more in Bonifacio than the rabble-rouser and frustrated leader.

---

7. Teodoro A. Agoncillo, *The Revolt of the Masses* (Quezon City: University of the Philippines, 1956), pp. 194–96.

8. David Sturtevant, "Guardia de Honor: Revitalization Within the Revolution," *Asian Studies* 4 (1966): 342.

9. Alvarez, "Ang Katipunan", p. 376.

A serious obstacle to a contemporary understanding of the Katipunan is the established view that the rise of nationalism culminating in the revolution of 1896-1900 was purely a consequence of heightened Westernization in the nineteenth century. The general argument is that the rise of liberalism in Spain and the opening up of key Philippine cities to world trade encouraged the formation of a well-to-do native and mestizo class that could afford to send its son to Europe, Hongkong, Singapore, and Japan to study. It was only during their stay abroad that these young, educated Filipinos, called "ilustrados," realized what freedom meant. To quote a respected scholar, "they learned languages, read history, discussed politics and joined the lodges of freemasonry. Most important of all was their discovery that they, as Filipinos, were not inferior to other peoples, certainly not to Spaniards."[10] This heightened consciousness led to the dissolution of the "aura of authority and the halo of grace" that had bound Filipinos to the colonial order. Realizing such injustices done to them, as forced labor, taxes, and inequality before the law, the ilustrados began to wage a propaganda campaign aimed to make Filipinos and Spaniards equal within the existing colonial framework; they wanted reforms, not independence. In spite of their limited aims, however, the ilustrados are credited with having first conceived of a Filipino national community.

Thus, the fact that a self-educated, lower-middle-class clerk named Andres Bonifacio founded the Katipunan in 1892, is excessively attributed to the influence of ilustrados like Del Pilar and Rizal. Furthermore, Bonifacio's movement is placed in an evolutionary framework: since the ilustrado efforts at reform were constantly frustrated, the time had come for a complete break with Spain by means of armed revolution. It is emphasized that Bonifacio, though not an ilustrado, was nevertheless well-read on Rizal's works, and on such topics as the French revolution and the lives of United States presidents. These things considered, however, no one has seriously asked why the revolutionary impulse had to start "from below." Nor have the Tagalog writings of Katipunan leaders and other documents of the period been viewed beyond their obviously patriotic content, as the articulation of folk perceptions of change. The acceptance of the independence ideal by the masses has been interpreted in terms of the vertical patron-client ties that link the lower and upper classes of society. Thus, a discontinuity exists, in our present understanding of the revolution, between "folk traditions" and the liberal ideas of the nineteenth century that are said to have triggered aspirations for change.[11] In

10. Onofre D. Corpuz, *The Philippines* (Englewood Cliffs, N.J.: Prentice-Hall, 1965), p. 61. The most comprehensive work on the ilustrados in Europe is John N. Schumacher, S.J., *The Propaganda Movement: 1880–1895* (Manila: Solidaridad, 1972).

11. That the events of the revolution have not been interpreted in terms of traditional ideas can perhaps be traced to the social and cultural background of Filipino scholars. Bred in the intellectual milieu of Philippine universities, they have unconsciously inherited the nationalist and revolution-

fact, very rarely are folk traditions referred to except as political, manipulative devices to gain mass support for the movement. Some even see the concept of a secret society and the "bizarre" initiation rites of the Katipunan as totally Masonic in origin. Little has been done to alter or amplify the observations of a Spaniard in 1897 that the masses responded to the revolutionary call with intense resolve because of their volatile character, their "propensity toward the portentous," their "blind obedience" to their patrons, their "stoicism in the manner of the fakirs," and their susceptibility to the rule of their superstitious imagination.[12] In other words, the majority of those who fought in the revolution are regarded as essentially passive beings suddenly mobilized into action by "blind obedience" to patrons or supernatural forces.

That the "poor and ignorant" masses who swelled the ranks of the Katipunan had certain ideas about the world and their places in it, ideas quite different from those of the "better classes" of society, is hinted at by Isabelo de los Reyes in statements based on interviews of hundreds of Katipuneros in 1898. "It would seem," he says, "that the Katipunan was an association to be feared, because it was composed of common ignorant people, yet although the plebeian thinks little, for this little he will die before giving it up." Later on, De los Reyes says the same thing more emphatically:

> I have said, and I will repeat a thousand times, that the Katipunan was a plebeian society; that is certain. But never have I wished to say that it was insignificant; on the contrary, the people speak little and perhaps think little, and I wish to say, perhaps without the artificial complication of a cultivated intelligence, but the little they think is intense, forms their second nature, and that which they believe is their faith, is fanaticism in them and works miracles, moves mountains, creates new worlds and other prodigies.[13]

Unfortunately, De los Reyes does not elaborate upon what the intensely held ideas of the masses were. But he does assert outright that "the limit of the aspirations of the Katipunan was a communistic republic," and that the masses had great faith in the Katipunan's triumph which would bring about a "community of property," a "brilliant future . . . in an atmosphere of liberty and

---

ary language of the ilustrados who not only dominated the post-Bonifacio stages of the revolution but left behind the bulk of written documents upon which histories have been based. The perspective, therefore, has been that of the educated nationalist glancing with puzzled or condescending approval at the "poor and ignorant" who prayed and waved amulets as much as they fought.

12. Juan Caro y Mora, *La Situación del País*,, 2d edition (Manila, 1897), pp. 13, 59.

13. Isabelo de los Reyes, "The Katipunan: Origins and Development," July 1898, in John R.M. Taylor, *The Philippine Insurrection Against the United States,* vol. 1, pp. 209–10. The same appears as *Report on the Philippine Revolution of 1896—1897* (Madrid, 1898), originally in Spanish in BIA 2291–96.

general happiness, based on honourable work for all."[14] These are socialist ideas, to be sure and it might be argued that De los Reyes's radical sympathies, which he himself admits to, colored his interpretation of the Katipunan. But he insists that his conclusions are based on what "the thousand and one" Katipuneros confided to him. In the absence of De los Reyes's original interviews, is there a way of reconstructing the masses' perceptions of the Katipunan and their role in it?

If we cease, for the moment, to regard the Katipunan as a radically unique phenomenon or as the mere creation of individuals like Bonifacio and Jacinto, then we can begin to examine its roots in Philippine society and culture. We can begin to discover continuities in the form and language of movements before and after it. One perceptive Spanish observer of the Katipunan seemed to find little difference in the behavior of leaders and followers of past and present revolts:

> If you put Diego Silang in Andres Bonifacio's place, Juan de la Cruz Palaris in Emilio Aguinaldo's place, Juan Marayac in Mariano Llanera's place, you would find in them the same personalities, the same obscure caciques of old, using the same methods to attract and sustain a following. Apolinario enrolled them in the cofradia of St. Joseph; the present chiefs enroll the people in the Katipunan brotherhood. Diego Silang called himself a petty chief *(cabo)* of Jesus Nazareno; Emilio Aguinaldo appropriated the title of special agent of God for the liberty of his brothers.[15]

There was also a difference, of course. We have to examine carefully the sense in which these movements are all the same or continuous, and where the Katipunan strikes a new chord. There had been katipunans, or associations, prior to the Katipunan, and many continued to flourish independently during the revolution. There were friar-sponsored groups like the Catipunan nang Sagrada Familia (Catipunan of the Holy Family), the Guardia de Honor de Maria (Guards of Honor of Mary), and the Catipunan nang Laguing Pag-eestación (Catipunan Devoted to the Stations of the Cross), not to mention the countless sodalities in the towns. Others were purely native and antiestablishment, like the Gabinista, the Colorum and *remontado* hill communities.[16] In order to mobilize large numbers of Filipinos, the revolutionary Katipunan had to speak the common language of katipunans, tap the undercurrent of popular

---

14. Ibid.

15. Caro y Mora, *La Situación,* p. 13. Silang and Palaris were eighteenth-century rebels in the Ilocos and Pangasinan regions. Llanera was a Katipunan leader from Nueva Ecija province.

16. The Guardia de Honor, Gabinista and *remontado* groups are examined in later chapters. See R.P. Gregorio Azagra, *Maicling Casaysayan nang Catipunan nang laguing Pageestación* (Manila, 1894), for an interesting use of *pasyon* language to define a conservative, religious Katipunan.

expectations and hopes, and channel the people's energies toward achieving independence from Spain.

Katipunan Manifestos

One way to understand the swift spread of the Katipunan society in 1896 is to examine the contents of the one and only issue of its organ, *Kalayaan*, that was disseminated among the populace of central and southern Luzon. Only about one thousand copies were printed, but these were passed from hand to hand. Pio Valenzuela, one of the organizers of the Katipunan, says that around the end of March 1896, when copies of *Kalayaan* had been distributed over a fairly wide area, "hundreds of people nightly joined the Katipunan in the municipalities of San Juan del Monte, San Felipe Neri, Pasig, Pateros, Marikina, Caloocan, Malabon, and other places." Bonifacio himself was surprised at the rapid growth of the society. From the time he had founded it in 1892 to the appearance of *Kalayaan* in January 1896, it had only some three hundred members. But from the middle of March to the outbreak of hostilities against Spain in August 1896, its membership rose sharply to 30,000. Valenzuela attributes the sharp rise in membership to "the effect of the periodical on the people."[17]

The most important item in the *Kalayaan* issue is Bonifacio's manifesto, "Ang Dapat Mabatid ng mga Tagalog" (What the Tagalogs Should Know).[18] Its importance stems from the fact that it places the struggle for independence in a framework of meaning which is "traditional." In the first three paragraphs, Bonifacio interprets the past, beginning with an account of the "Fall" of the Tagalog race:

> Ytong katagalugan na pinamamahalaan ng unang panahon ng ating tunay na mga kababayan niyaong hindi pa tumutungtong sa mga lupaing ito ang mga kastila ay nabubuhay sa lubos na kasaganaan, at kaguinhawahan. Kasundo niya ang mga kapit bayan at lalung lalo na ang mga taga Japon sila'y kabilihan at kapalitan ng mga kalakal malabis ang pag yabong ng lahat ng pinagkakakitaan, kaya't dahil dito'y mayaman ang kaasalan ng lahat, bata't matanda at sampung mga babae ay marunong sumulat ng talagang pagsulat nating mga tagalog. Dumating ang mga kastila at dumulog na nakipagkaibigan. Sa mabuti nilang hikayat na di umano, tayo'y aakain sa lalung kagalingan at lalung imumulat ang

---

17. "The Memoirs of Pio Valenzuela" (original in Tagalog), in *Minutes of the Katipunan* (Manila: National Heroes Commission, 1964), p. 107; Agoncillo, *Revolt*, p. 96.

18. In Teodoro Agoncillo, ed. *The Writings and Trial of Andres Bonifacio* (Manila: Bonifacio Centennial Commission, 1963), pp. 68–69. I have made a new translation, not because Agoncillo's is inadequate but because certain nuances of Tagalog terms relevant to this study are not brought out in his translation.

ating kaisipan, ang nasabing nagsisipamahala ay ng yaring nalamuyot sa tamis ng kanilang dila sa paghibo. Gayon man sila'y ipinailalim sa talagang kaugalian ng mga tagalog na sinaksihan at pinapagtibay ng kanilang pinagkayarian sa pamamaguitan ng isang panunumpa na kumuha ng kaunting dugo sa kanikanilang mga ugat, at yao'y inihalu't ininom nila kapua tanda ng tunay at lubos na pagtatapat na di mag tataksil sa pinagkayarian. Ytoy siang tinatawag na "Pacto de Sangre" ng haring Sikatuna at ni Legaspi na pinaka katawan ng hari ng España.

In the early days, before the Spaniards set foot on our soil which was governed by our compatriots, Katagalugan enjoyed a life of great abundance *(kasaganaan)* and prosperity *(kaginhawaan)*. She maintained good relations with her neighbors, especially with Japan, and maintained trade relationships with them all. That is why there was wealth and good behavior in everyone; young and old, women included, could read and write using their own alphabet. Then the Spaniards came and appeared to offer to guide us toward increased betterment and awakening of our minds; our leaders became seduced by the sweetness of such enticing words. The Spaniards, however, were required to comply with the existing customs of the Tagalogs, and to bind their agreements by means of an oath, which consisted of taking blood from each other's veins, mixing and drinking it as a sign of genuine and wholehearted sincerity in pledging not to be traitorous to their agreement. This was called the "Blood Compact" of King Sikatuna and Legaspi, the representative of the King of Spain.

Rizal, in his annotations to Morga's *Sucesos de las Islas Filipinas* (1609), had pointed out that an indigenous civilization flourished in the archipelago before the arrival of the Spaniards, and it has rightly been assumed by historians of the revolution that Bonifacio's manifesto was inspired by the writings of ilustrados like Rizal. What we are calling attention to is not the historical content of Bonifacio's work but its form and language. Whether Bonifacio was a Mason or a Catholic is irrelevant here; to communicate what he regarded as a matter of sublime importance to each Filipino, he used the form that traditionally conveyed such matters—the pasyon form.

To begin with, Bonifacio uses the words *kasaganaan* (root word: *sagana)* and *kaginhawaan* (root word: *ginhawa*), to describe the pre-Spanish situation. These are common attributes of paradise. The word *ginhawa* connotes, besides "prosperity," a general ease of life, relief from pain, sickness or difficulties. Furthermore, the Tagalogs, he writes, could read and write, and thus had knowledge, just as Adam and Eve could name all the plants and animals in paradise. The mention of good relations and trade with the neighbors of Katagalugan further defines the condition of wholeness of the pre-Spanish past.

Then the Spaniards arrived, offering increased prosperity and knowledge if the Tagalogs would ally with them. Any reader of the manifesto would immediately think in terms of the pasyon story, particularly when Bonifacio says that the leaders of Katagalugan "became seduced by the sweetness of such enticing words." For in the pasyon the delightful existence of Adam and

Eve begins to fall apart precisely when Eve, because of her "weak mind," succumbs to the words of the serpent. The serpent's words, however, are not a true reflection of his loób, which is "always in confusion and turmoil" because of envy (8:3). The serpent's description matches that of the Spanish friars in Katipunan documents. The Tagalogs accepted the offer of union, of "genuine and wholehearted sincerity" symbolized by the blood compact between Sikatuna and Legaspi. Only later did they realize that the outward appearance of the Spaniards did not match their true intention. The mutual, or dyadic, relationship that had been established was false. Bonifacio dwells on its implications:

> Buhat ng ito'y mangyari ay bumibilang na ngayon sa tatlong daang taon mahiguit na ang lahi ni Legaspi ay ating binubuhay sa lubos na kasaganaan, ating pinagtatamasa at binubusog, kahit abutin natin ang kasalatan at kadayukdukan; iguinugugol natin ang yaman dugo at sampu ng tunay na mga kababayan na aayaw pumayag na sa kanilay pasakop, at gayon din naman nakipagbaka tayo sa mga Ynsik at taga Holanda ng nagbalang umagaw sa kanila nitong katagalugan.
>
> Ngayon sa lahat ng ito'y ano ang sa mga guinhawa nating paggugugol nakikitang kaguinhawahang ibinigay sa ating Bayan? Ano ang nakikita nating pagtupad sa kanilang kapangakuan na siang naging dahil ng ating pag gugugol! Wala kung di pawang kataksilan ang ganti sa ating mga pagpapala at mga pagtupad sa kanilang ipinangakung tayo'y lalung guiguisingin sa kagalingan ay bagkus tayong ibinulag, inihawa tayo sa kanilang hamak na asal, pinilit na sinira ang mahal at magandang ugali ng ating Bayan; Yminulat tayo sa isang maling pagsampalataya at isinadlak sa lubak ng kasamaan ang kapurihan ng ating Bayan; at kung tayo'y mangahas humingi ng kahit gabahid na lingap, ang naguiguing kasagutan ay ang tayo'y itapon at ilayo sa piling ng ating minamahal na anak, asawa at matandang magulang. Ang bawat isang himutok na pumulas sa ating dibdib ay itinuturing na isang malaking pagkakasala at karakarakang nilalapatan ng sa hayop na kabangisan.
>
> Since then, for three hundred years, we have been giving a most prosperous life to the race of Legaspi; we have let them enjoy abundance and fatten themselves, even if we ourselves were deprived and hungry. We have wasted our wealth and blood in defending them even against our own countrymen who refused to submit to their rule; and we have fought the Chinese and Hollanders who tried to take Katagalugan from them.
>
> Now, after all this, what prosperity *[ginhawa]* have they given to our land? Do we see them fulfilling their side of the contract which we ourselves fulfilled with sacrifices? We see nothing but treachery as a reward for our favors; as their fulfillment of the promise to awaken us to a better life, they have only blinded us more, contaminating us with their lowly behavior, forcibly destroying the good customs of our land. They have awakened us to false beliefs, and have cast into a mire the honor *[puri]* of our land. And if we beg for scraps of compassion, their reply is banishment and separation from our beloved children, spouses, and

parents. Every sigh we utter is branded by them a great sin and punished with inhuman cruelty.

In the first place, the Tagalogs are said to have fulfilled their obligations to the Spaniards. But the Spaniards, declares Bonifacio, have refused to honor the pact; they have incurred a heavy debt *(utang)* to the Filipinos which they "pay" in the form of treachery *(kataksilan).* In a society whose smooth functioning hinges a lot upon honor and reciprocity, such treachery on Spain's part is disruptive; the world of the Tagalogs is disjointed and confused. The "fall" of the Tagalogs is expressed in terms of increasing blindness or absence of *liwanag*. This condition precisely has enabled the people to accept for so long an inauthentic relationship that has reduced them to "lowly behavior" and dishonor. They have failed to respond to a sign of *lingap* (compassionate care), even when the Tagalogs in their suffering beg for it. Because there is no love, compassion and honor, the conditions are present for the breaking of the relationship.

The next paragraph begins with a continued description of the effects of Spain's inability to have compassion and her increasing cruelty to the Tagalogs. There is much weeping and wailing in the land from orphans, widows, and parents bereft of their children: "Now we are drowning in the flood of tears from mothers whose children's lives have ended, and orphans crying for their parents." Bonifacio's description of the pain and hardships of the people is reminiscent of the lengthy pasyon passages describing not only the suffering Christ but also of those like his mother, Mary, who participated in Christ's experience. The description of hardship and weeping in the pasyon is meant to evoke, from the reader or listener, compassion and *damay*, signs of response and a change in the *loób.* In similar fashion, Bonifacio dwells on the language of suffering and oppression and then, having "softened" the *loób* of his audience, shifts in midparagraph to a discussion of the changes that must take place:

> Ano ang nararapat nating gawin? Ang araw ng katuiran na sumisikat sa Silanganan, ay malinaw na itinuturo sa ating mga matang malaong nabulagan ang landas na dapat nating tunguhin, ang liwanag niya'y tanaw sa ating mga mata, ang kukong nag akma ng kamatayang alay sa atin ng mga ganid na asal. Ytinuturo ng katuiran, na wala tayong iba pang maantay kundi lalut lalung kahirapan, lalut lalung kataksilan, lalut lalung kaalipustaan at lalut lalung kaapihan. Ytinuturo ng katuiran, na huag nating sayangin ang panahon sa pagasa sa ipinangakong kaguinhawahan na hindi darating at hindi mangyayari. Ytinuturo ng katuiran ang tayo'y umasa sa ating sarili at huag antain sa iba ang ating kabuhayan. Ytinuturo ng katuiran ang tayo'y mag kaisang loob magka isang isip at akala at ng tayo'y magkalakas na maihanap ang naghaharing kasamaan sa ating Bayan.
>
> What should be done, then? The sun of reason that shines in the East clearly shows, to our eyes long blind, the way *[landas]* that must be taken; its liwanag

> enables us to see the claws of those of inhuman character who brought us death. Reason *[katwiran]* shows that we cannot expect anything but more and more hardships, more and more treachery, more and more contempt, more and more enslavement. Reason tells us not to waste our time waiting for the promised *ginhawa* that will never arrive. Reason tells us that we must rely upon ourselves alone and never entrust our right to life to anybody. Reason tells us to be one in loób, one in thought, so that we may have the strength in finding that evil reigning in our land.

The word "reason" does not quite bring out the root meaning of *katwiran,* which is "straightness." This connotation is important because in the context of blindness or darkness what is lost is the ability to keep to the "straight path." Katwiran is also associated with the liwanag of the sun which shows the "way" (*landas*). The direction from which liwanag comes—the East—is associated with the life-giving powers of the rising sun, with rebirth, and also is the destination of the "way of the cross." The "sun of reason," then, is a beacon that enables the Tagalogs to "see," but does not by itself restore wholeness; it merely points to the path toward death that must be taken. It is characteristic of both Katipunan and Colorum appeals that the mere awaiting of ginhawa is discouraged, that man must participate by "taking the straight path." Specifically, the Tagalogs must not "entrust their right to life to anybody" but instead be one in heart and thought, meaning that "wholeness" can no longer be defined in terms of a pact between the Tagalogs and "Mother Spain" who shows no love. The Tagalogs must die to this relationship and be "reborn" in a new condition of wholeness—i.e., katipunan or kalayaan.

In a footnote to his classic study of the Katipunan, Agoncillo discusses the confusion in scholarly circles over the meaning of the letter *K* in a Katipunan (Magdalo faction) flag of 1896. The letter *K,* in old Tagalog script, occupied the center of a sun with an indefinite (later reduced to eight) number of white rays. Did the *K* signify "Kalayaan" as General Ricarte contends, or "Katipunan," according to General Aguinaldo? Accepting the latter's view, Agoncillo demonstrates that the *K* must have stood for "Katipunan," the organization's name, although he admits that by 1897 it may have changed its significance to "Kalayaan," "probably because the din of battle and the intense nationalistic feeling forced into the consciousness of the revolutionists the aptness of the letter *K* to symbolize their ideal—Liberty."[19] The apparently unsettled issue perfectly illustrates the multiplicity of meanings that signs like the letter *K* in the center of a radiant sun had to Katipuneros, particularly rank-and-file members, who interpreted them in terms of their experience. What, indeed, is the difference between "katipunan" and "kalayaan," between "brotherhood" and

---

19. Agoncillo, *Revolt,* p. 326.

"liberty"? The root word *laya* does not appear in Noceda and Sanlucar's eighteenth-century Tagalog dictionary; there is only *layao*, defined as "bodily pleasure," "satisfaction of necessities," and "giving to another what he wants." Recently, Jose Villa Panganiban has tried to make a clear distinction between *layà* (freedom) and *layâ* or *layaw* (much pampered, willful, self-abandoned). He says, "Distinguish, between *layà* and *layâ*. Consequently, between *kalayaan:* freedom, independence, liberty and *kalayaán*: self-abandonment, libertinage. However, those untrained in language make no such distinctions."[20] Panganiban's last comment is of utmost importance. It suggests that a term like *kalayaan* has several layers of meaning. What the experience of the people contributed to its meaning is no less important than the definition that nationalist leaders assigned to it.

The meaning of "wholeness" or "becoming one" implied by the term *katipunan* is also contained in *kalayaan*. Prior to the rise of the separatist movement, *kalayaan* did not mean "freedom" or "independence." In translating into Tagalog the ideas of "liberty, fraternity, equality" learned from the West, propagandists like Bonifacio, Jacinto, and perhaps Marcelo H. del Pilar built upon the word *layaw* or *laya,* which means "satisfaction of one's needs," "pampering treatment by parents" or "freedom from strict parental control." Thus, *kalayaan,* as a political term, is inseparable from its connotations of parent-child relationship, reflecting social values like the tendency of mothers in the lowland Philippines to pamper their children and develop strong emotional ties with them. Childhood is fondly remembered as a kind of "lost Eden," a time of *kaginhawaan* (contentment) and *kasaganaan* (prosperity), unless one was brought up in abject poverty or by an uncaring *(pabaya)* stepmother. In "kalayaan," revolutionists found an ideal term for independence that combined separation from a colonial ruler (i.e., a mother who showed cruelty instead of love) and the "coming together" of people in the Katipunan. Katipunan is kalayaan in that it is a recovery of the country's pre-Spanish condition of wholeness, bliss and contentment, a condition that is experienced as layaw by the individual, who is thus able to leap from the "familial" to the "national."[21] As a revolutionary document puts it, the

---

20. Juan de Noceda and Pedro de Sanlucar, *Vocabulario de la Lengua Tagala* (Manila, 1754), p. 177; Jose Panganiban, *Diksyunario-Tesauro Pilipino-Ingles* (Quezon City: Manlapaz, 1972), p. 623.

21. A comparison between *kalayaan* and the Tausug *karayawan* is instructive. Literally, *karayawan* means "goodness." It also implies a state of pleasure and happiness in the afterlife. Anthropologist Thomas Kiefer's informants described it as "analogous to a state of perpetual orgasm." Since the religious merit of a killer is transferred to his victim, most Tausug fighters believe that if they die in battle they will be automatically "inside of karayawan" (*The Tausug: Violence and Law in a Philippine Muslim Society* [New York: Holt, Rinehart, and Winston, 1972] p. 128-29). It seems to me that in the Tagalog context, dying for kalayaan could mean automatically entering a state of bliss in heaven, particularly if the struggle is interpreted as a pasyon.

"Katipunan of Man" is none other than the extension of the experience of unity between mother and child.[22]

In the final paragraph of the manifesto, Bonifacio speaks of the "light of truth" *(liwanag ng katotohanan)* that will rise, revealing to all men that the Tagalogs—here defined as all Filipinos—have feeling *(pagdaramdam)*, honor or purity of loób *(puri)*, hiya and, finally, damay. This liwanag, then, reveals an image of the possibilities of existence that will be realized in the redemptive process, an image of a condition that was lost when the Tagalogs succumbed to the sweet words of Spain. It shows the "holy and sacred teaching" that will "tear through the curtain that blinds our thinking." This liwanag, concluded Bonifacio, is the Katipunan.

The second major item in the first issue of *Kalayaan* is a manifesto by Emilio Jacinto, a man of some education who was called the "eye" of the Katipunan.[23] In this manifesto, kalayaan is personified and appears to a youth (Katagalugan) who is in darkness.

In the introductory lines, the interplay of images of darkness and light establishes the profound nature of the manifesto: "It was a dark night. Not a star shone in the dark sky of this horrible night." Head bowed, face resting on the palms of his hands, a youth contemplates his miserable state. Beside him is an oil lamp, the room's only source of illumination, which will remain flickering for the duration of the narrative, signifying an interval of awareness or revelation that interrupts the enveloping gloom.

The youth is about to surrender to anger and frustration when someone taps him on the shoulder. He hears a "sad and sweet-sounding voice" that asks: "Why do you weep? What pain or affliction rends your heart and tarnishes your youth and strength?" The youth looks up and sees, in the dim light, a shadow surrounded by a halo of white vapor. "Oh merciful shadow," he replies, "my grief has no cure, no consolation. What I have to say is of no importance to you. But why have you come to interrupt my weeping?" The shadow replies that she always appears whenever ignorance and stupidity cause the hardships and sufferings of men and nations. She will always appear until men are released

---

22. "Ang Katipunan ng Tao" (manuscript; Box 9, PIR-PNL). The author is most probably Apolinario Mabini.

23. In Wenceslao Retana, *Archivo del Bibliófilo Filipino*, vol. 3 (Madrid, 1895-1905), pp. 52-64. The original has not been found, and Agoncillo himself had to rely on the Spanish translation in Retana and on a translation, presumably by Epifanio de los Santos, in *The Philippine Review* (July 1918). This manifesto is not found in the published collection of Jacinto's writings, *Buhay at mga Sinulat ni Emilio Jacinto* (Manila: Jose P. Santos, 1935), edited by Jose P. Santos. In other words, it appears that an extant copy of the influential first (and only distributed) issue of *Kalayaan* has not been found. Even the translation by De los Santos, Agoncillo concludes, is from the Spanish version in Retana. I have made a new translation based on this Spanish text.

from blindness and can think clearly, until men realize that, without her, "true and perfect happiness" can never be extended over the face of the earth. Still the youth cannot recognize the visitor, who claims in astonishment:

> Does this mean that you don't recognize me anymore? But I am not surprised, for it has been more than three hundred years since I visited your land. It is the will of your people to adore false gods of religion and men, your fellow-creatures, that is why my memory has been erased from your minds.
>
> Do you want to know who I am? Then listen: I am the origin of all things great, most beautiful and praiseworthy, precious and dignified, that is possible for humanity. Due to me heads of kings fall; thrones are demolished or transferred, crowns of gold destroyed; due to me the flame of the 'Holy Inquisition' in which the friars tortured thousands upon thousands of men, was extinguished. For my cause men unite, each one forgetting his selfish interests, seeing nothing but the good of all; because of me slaves are rescued and lifted up from the mire of degradation and shame, the pride and malice of their cruel masters broken . . . . My name is Kalayaan.

Having recognized Kalayaan, the youth proceeds to tell her about the mockeries and sufferings inflicted upon his people, in the hope that she will pity and give them protective care. The grievances take the form of contradictions between the Christian teachings and the actual practices of the Spanish friars:

> "We," they say, "are hungry," and they who teach us to feed the hungry reply: "Eat the refuse and the crumbs of our savory fare and our sumptuous board."
>
> My brothers say: "We are thirsty," and they who teach us to give drink to the thirsty, reply: "Drink your tears and sweat, because we will see to it that there shall be enough of both."
>
> My brothers clamor: "We are without clothes; we are completely naked," and they who command us to dress the naked reply: "We shall, right now, wrap your bodies in chains, one above the other . . ."
>
> My brothers say: "A little love, a little clemency and compassion," and the superiors and chiefs who govern us judicially and spiritually reply: "These men are filibusters, enemies of God and Mother Spain; exile them!"

The youth asks Kalayaan if the grievances are sufficient cause for despair and tears. In a somewhat sarcastic vein she replies that tears are only for those without life and blood in their veins to avenge the wrongs inflicted upon the people. "To weep in one's house, in the silence and darkness of night, is inconceivable; it is all the more improper for a youth . . . it is not proper." The youth, however, cannot conceive of any other recourse: "From the time we were in our mother's womb we have learned to suffer and endure all kinds of affliction, contempt, and rebuff. What more can you ask us to do but weep?" He cannot understand Kalayaan's advice that men cast away their "bad inclinations." With the youth eventually speechless, Kalayaan proceeds to explain:

> Listen. In the early days, when the good customs of your ancestors were not sunk in cowardice and isolation or imprisonment, the Tagalog or native people lived in the shade of my protection, and in my bosom she was happy and breathed the air that gave her life and strength. Her knowledge was increased by my light and she was respected by her neighbors. But one day, which must be execrated and accursed, Slavery arrived saying that she was Virtue and Justice, and promised Glory to all who would believe in her.
>
> Notwithstanding the fact that she came disguised with a mask of loveliness and goodness, and was smooth and affectionate in her behavior, I recognized her. I knew that the happiness of the country was over, that she had pierced your unhappy people . . . and your brothers believed in her and almost adored her . . . and forgot me, even abhorred me and were irritated by my presence . . . . But now your sighs have reached me, filled me with sadness, which is why I have come. And now I must leave.

The youth begs Kalayaan to stay, to have pity and once more take the Tagalogs into her fold. She replies that indeed her heart feels the suffering of the Tagalogs, and that it is precisely her calling to come to the aid of the afflicted. "But no man is worthy of my protection and care who is not fond of me, does not love me and is not able to die for me. You can announce this to your compatriots." Suddenly, the flame of the oil lamp flickers and dies.

Some of the nuances of the Tagalog language such are found in Bonifacio's manifesto are missing in Jacinto's manifesto, which is available only in Spanish translation. Nevertheless, the translation seems to be faithful enough to the original, for we find in it certain images that point to a "traditional" frame of meaning in talking about revolution and independence. The flickering oil lamp illuminating the room is reminiscent of the solitary candle during Easter Vigil rituals and the candles the cofrades lighted during prayer to signify the presence of liwanag. For the episode is a moment of liwanag in which a connection is made between human and pasyon time in the person of Kalayaan. She comes in the form of an apparition with a "sad, sweet-sounding voice," which reminds us of Apolinario's appearance in 1870 and the Santong Boces that bade Caneo to join the revolt against Spain.

The youth had known Kalayaan before, in a time that corresponds to Bonifacio's pre-Spanish past. His failure to recognize her now reflects his blindness. Kalayaan has to explain what she is and in doing so reveals herself in terms of possibilites for man: elimination of despotism and cruelty, unity and love among men, liberation of slaves, and punishment of oppressors. In other words, she is the condition in which society is turned on its head.

Knowing who Kalayaan is gives the youth hope that she will show pity on his people. He proceeds to enumerate their grievances—not only the friars' cruelty but also the discontinuity between their words and their intentions. They had come preaching fine Christian precepts only to seduce the natives; their eventual cruelty to the natives who ask for compassion is only a reflection of the lack of fit between external appearance and interior state. The pasyon repeatedly warns against being seduced by "appealing exteriors" which are all *daya,* or trickery. The enslaved condition of the youth and his people is a result of weakness in loób, and a way out of this condition is pointed to by the pasyon. The youth, however, cannot see this "way" because of his blindness; all he does is weep and despair in spite of Kalayaan's advice that the Tagalogs shed their "bad inclinations." Kalayaan has to explain further, and at this point the manifestos of Jacinto and Bonifacio converge.

The youth can comprehend the future only when Kalayaan explains his past and present in terms of the pasyon. Thus, she elaborates upon her previous assertion that the Tagalogs had known her, that under her "protective care" they had experienced happiness, prosperity, and knowledge—a condition akin to layaw. Then Slavery came and, like the serpent in paradise, offered ultimate glory to the Tagalogs, who were seduced by Slavery's appearance of beauty, goodness, and "smoothness." They "forgot" or no longer recognized Kalayaan in a classic case of failure to show utang na loób, a familiar situation exemplified by Judas's turning away from his maestro who loved him, and failing to "reflect upon" the motherly care that Mary had shown him:

Di mo na guinunam gunam	And you [Judas] did not reflect upon
ang madlang pagpapalayao	the *layaw* showered upon you
sa iyo nang Virgeng mahal	by the Holy Virgin,
ano mang canin sa bahay	whenever there was food in the house
ala-ala cang matibay.	she never failed to remember you.
(90:5)	

Having realized the worthlessness of the pieces of silver, Judas was cast in despair which he never overcame. For the youth, however, there is hope: first, in recognizing Kalayaan and the layaw she showered upon his ancestors; then in heeding her call for the oppressed to love her and be willing to die for her. The "future" Kalayaan points to is the people's experiencing of the pasyon, a dying to a state of darkness. The next morning, a "smoldering project" is seen in the youth's eyes. Liwanag is in him because he is now conscious of the "way" that must be traversed.

Initiation Rites

When a person signified his intention to join the Katipunan, he was sponsored by a member who brought him, blindfolded, to a secret place where initiation rites were performed. The underlying meaning of these rites has never been adequately examined. Outwardly, they appear to be Masonic. But if they were truly so, could unlettered peasants have embraced the Katipunan as truly their own? Our key to understanding the rites is De los Reyes's statement that "at first, [Katipunan leaders] adopted the Masonic formulas, but later simplified them to suit the cultural level of the members, who belonged to the workmen and peasant classes."[24]

When the blindfold was removed inside the ritual chamber, the first thing that met the neophyte's eye was an oil lamp on a table before him. A woman who joined the society described the experience of being blinded by this light: "I was in a tiny room lit only by a single *tinghoy* lamp that was flickering like a person out of breath. The light was blinding to my eyes."[25] As the neophyte became accustomed to the dimly lit surroundings, he discerned tablets on the walls with the following warnings:

> If you have strength and valor, you may proceed.
> If only curiosity has brought you here—go away!
> If you do not know how to control you passions—go away. Never will the gates of the venerable and respected Society of the Sons of the Country open for you.[26]

In some cases, the same warnings were voiced by an officer called *mabalasik,* a sort of "terrible brother" who guarded the entrance to the gates of the society. The initial experience of blinding light, or liwanag, was accompanied by a firm resolve in the loób of the individual. He would not move a step closer toward the light if he did not have strength, valor, and at least the firm intention to control his "passions."

The neophyte was next required to answer the following questions in a printed questionnaire: (1) What was the condition of the country in early times? (2) What is her condition today? (3) What will be her condition in the future? The replies to the questionnaire were taught to the neophyte by his sponsor, and were similar to what Bonifacio said in his manifesto: before the Spaniards came, the country enjoyed perfect harmony, wealth, and intercourse with other nations of Asia. Then the friars came and taught the external forms of Catholicism and its shallow trappings, blinding the natives to the true nature of religion through spectacular and costly festivals. What must be done was to recover the country's condition of kalayaan, freedom and independence, by means of faith, valor, and perseverance.[27]

This stage of the ritual was meant not merely to make the neophyte aware of certain facts about his country and its future but to place them in a meaningful context. It is significant that the dark initiation hall was illuminated

---

24. De los Reyes, "The Katipunan," p. 202.

25. "Mga dahon ng kasaysayan (Sa kalupi ng isang babaing naanib sa Katipunan)," RENFIL 2 (7 October 1911): 455.

26. Agoncillo, *Revolt,* p. 48; Gregorio Zaide, *History of the Katipunan* (Manila: Loyal Press 1939), p. 6.

27. Zaide, *History,* pp. 6-7; Agoncillo, *Revolt,* pp. 48-49.

by a single "blinding" oil lamp, with all its connotations. The Katipunan initiate would, in fact, have found many aspects of the ritual familiar. His experience of religious rituals would have facilitated his understanding of Philippine history as a "fall" that would be followed by redemption. In a variation of the initiation ritual used by a katipunan of 1900, the message is clear to every Indio: joining the society entails one's "last agony" and death, an experience analogous to Christ's redemptive act:

> (Leader): Who is this who has never been initiated who wants to take part in the works of the temple?
>
> (answer): One who wants light and who wants to be a Son of the People.
>
> (Leader): Profane man, think well whether you are able to fulfill all of these obligations. If at this very hour the society demands your life and your body, are you able to give them? The sound of the bells which you have just heard, what does it mean?
>
> It means that you are quitting your former life as the man in his last agony is quitting his, and your anguish is the sign of your separation from your past life, at the same time it is the sign of your entrance into the society where you will see the true light.[28]

In the world of the Colorum pilgrim, paradise is at the end of a long and torturous search which takes place during Holy Week. Paradise is the equivalent of liwanag which, to quote the author of the pilgrim's *awit*, is the aftermath of the experience of hardship.[29] These notions are also found in the literature of the Katipunan revolt against Spain. The revolutionary experience is conceived of as a search for kalayaan, a term which, in Katipunan literature, is often juxtaposed with liwanag and paradise.[30] In the portion of the initiation ritual quoted above, the neophyte arrives at the gates of the society in search of liwanag and brotherhood, and then he is told that he must die to his past life in order to enter the society where he will see the true liwanag.

These themes are brought out even more vividly in an unpublished manuscript detailing a Katipunan form of initiation.[31] The title of the document,

---

28. Katipunan oath and form of initiation, English translation in PIR-SD55 and Taylor. *Philippine Insurrection,* vol. 1, p. 219. I have not found the original Tagalog document.

29. Simeon Aranas, *Kaligaligayang Bundok ng Banahaw* (*awit*), vol. 1 (Manila: P. Sayo, 1927), p. 32.

30. Cf. "Ang Liuanag sa Katipunan" by Soliman, in "Documentos de la Revolución Filipina" (1952), PNA. This document, which is undated, states basically that the Katipunan is a "great light," which means "the true recognition of the unparalleled power of the Lord God" which also revealed the cruel exploitation by the Spaniards and the fact that the Filipinos owe no *utang na loób* (debt of gratitude) to Spain in spite of what the friars have always insisted.

31. PIR-SD 514-10. Another copy of the manuscript is found in a bundle of papers on the *sandatahan* formed by Ricarte in Manila in 1899, and also called "Banal na Kalayaan" apparently based in San Francisco de Malabon, Cavite (PIR, reel 160, frame 271ff.)

Pagbubukas ng Karurukan (lit., "Opening of the Pinnacle"), refers to the gates of the society at the summit of what is presumably a symbolic mountain. The neophytes are said to pass from *kapanatagan* (level surface) to *karurukan* (tip of an elevation); the image of Mount Calvary is clearly alluded to. At the beginning of the ritual, the mabalasik, or "terrible brother," interrogates the neophytes in the following manner:

> Ikao ay sino? At ano ang dito ay iyong hinahanap? Nababatid mo baga kapagkarakang dito ay matatagpuan mo ang iyong hinahanap? At sino ang may sabe sa iyo? At sino ang nagbunsod sa iyo at nagkaroon ka ng ganitong hangad?
>
> Di mo baga nababatid na kapagkarakang ikao ay masanib sa katipunan ito ikao ay mabibingit sa katakotakot na kapahamakan gaya ng matapon sa iba't iba o malalayong lupa o ang maualay kaya sa piling ng iyong pinakaguiguilio na magulang, asaua, anak at kapatid ay hindi ka natatakot? Paris ng mapiit sa malungkot na bilangoan o ang maakiat sa kakilakilabot na bibitayan at patain ng kadustadusta? Di ka nalalaguim na dumaluhong sa gayon karami at ualang pag itan kamatayan?. . . . Ikao ay magtapat.

> Who are you? And what are you searching for here? Have you learned that you will find here what you are searching for? And who told you this? And who revealed this to you so that you came to have this purpose?
>
> Do you not know that once you have joined this katipunan you will be at the threshold of the most frightful dangers, such as being thrown into various faraway places or being separated from your most beloved parents, spouses, children, and relatives? Are you not now afraid? Do you not fear being imprisoned in a lonely cell or ascending the scaffold to meet the ignominious death? Do you not dread rushing to the attack in the face of certain death?. . . . Tell us the truth.

The first paragraph implies that the neophytes have learned about kalayaan and have come to find it. The image beckons them to the society, just as the vision of an earthly paradise beckons pilgrims to Banahaw. But once at the threshold, they have to affirm their wish or willingness to die to past relationships, to their previous attachments to home and family. This process of separation is linked to the actual struggle: they will face imprisonment and execution, will fight with courage even "in the face of certain death" because from the moment they affirm their willingness to join the society they have accepted death in order to seek kalayaan. After they have answered all the above questions in the affirmative, the mabalasik says: "If that is so and you still insist upon joining this katipunan follow me." The neophytes are taken to the door of the next chamber, the *karurukan*, or pinnacle. Responding to the mabalasik's knock, the *pangulo* (leader) instructs Brother *Taliba* (Sentinel) to interrogate the stranger who knocks at the gate. "Where have you come from?" he asks, to which the fiscal representing the neophytes replies:

> Buhat sa lusak ng pagkaalipin inagao sa kuko ng bulag kapagkatapos ay naglagos sa balabalaking kapansanan at kapahamakan ngayo'y naririto't tumatauag sa mahal mo pong pintuan at hinahanap ang kalayaan.
>
> We have come from the mire of slavery, saved from the claws of blindness; we have repeatedly passed through various obstacles and dangers and now are here calling before your holy gate in search of kalayaan.

The phrase "holy gate" *(mahal na pinto)* in this and other initiation documents is another indication of the connection between Katipunan and pasyon idioms. In the latter, the word "gate" first appears in the episode where Adam and Eve are driven out through the "gate of paradise" which is then shut close and guarded by an angel. The passage through the gate marks, for Adam and Eve, the beginning of a life of "exhaustion, hunger and fear, incomparable hardship":

Ano pa,t, hindi maisip pangamba at madlang saquit narating nila,t, nasapit nang pumanao at umalis doon sa lupang mariquit.	And we cannot imagine the fear and manifold pain thrust upon them when they departed from the radiant land.
At cung canilang maquita doon at maala-ala, ang una nilang guinhaua hapis lumbay sabihin pa ng canilang caloloua. (10:15-16)	And when they look back and remember their former *ginhawa* such sorrow and loneliness afflicts their soul.

The gate of paradise marks the boundary between suffering and a life of ginhawa, between darkness and liwanag. Elsewhere in the pasyon and related texts, the "holy gate" is alluded to as the barrier to man's complete fulfillment until opened by the completion of Christ's passion and death. In explaining why the door, or gate, of the synagogue was closed when Christ entered Jerusalem, the pasyon reveals a *talinhaga:*

Sapagca,t, si Cristong Ama at dili pa nagdurusa nang mahal na Pasion niya, ay totoong nasasara ang pintong mahal na Gloria.	Since Christ our Father had not yet suffered his holy passion so the holy gate of glory was truly shut.
Tutumbuquin capagcouan niyong Cruz niyang tangan at ang pinto nang Simbahan	This will be struck squarely by the cross he will bear and the gate of the synagogue

ay agad namang bubucsan	will at once open;
ito,i, siyang cahulugan.	this is what it means.
Ay cun, ito,i, maganap na	When this is done
at sa Cruz maiparipa;	and when he is crucified
pagcamatay nga sa dusa,	and has died in suffering
siya namang pagcabuca	at that moment will open
niyong pintuan sa Gloria.	the gate of glory.
(71:1–3)	

In 1840, Apolinario de la Cruz referred to "the holy gate of the nineteenth day" *(mahal na pinto ng Arao Diesynuebe)*—the day of the Cofradía's Mass—as a stage they have reached on the way to the "holy land of peace" *(mahal na Bayan ng caloualhatian)*.[32] Not surprisingly, the Colorum also appropriated the notion of a "holy gate" in their rituals. The narrow cave entrances and other passages through which the pilgrims passed, often with great physical effort, were called *pinto*. Special prayers were said at these entrances to avoid, so the belief went, being crushed by the pillars of the gates. According to one account, "far from the chapel of Amang Dios is a gate where the keeper loudly asks for the name of the pilgrim and all other necessary information. Then giving him a supply of wax candles he is allowed to begin his subterranean trip." For the Colorum pilgrims, the gates were visible markers of the experienced stages of hardship and concomitant purification and control of loób, culminating in the ascent of Calvary.[33]

The term "holy gate," then, has various layers of significance. Katipunan leaders merely added another layer, a "nationalist" one, by incorporating it in the "opening of the pinnacle." Having knocked on the "holy gate in search of kalayaan," the neophytes are told by the leader that they must "prepare the loób for every test of hardship that will be inflicted." Then the neophytes are subjected to certain trials of ordeal, such as jumping into a well or crawling through a narrow tunnel. The parallel with the trials that a pilgrim undergoes in Banahaw is unmistakable. Moreover, the meaning of the experience is similar. As the initiates emerge from their ordeal, the mabalasik presents them to the leader, who replies: "In that case, brother mabalasik, you have not noticed any drawing back of their loób." Here we are reminded of Apolinario de la Cruz, who once said that Octabio had a "truly converted loób" because he had experienced many trials. The gate of the society is opened; the new Katipuneros have died to their former state of blindness and disorientation. Only then are they allowed to sign the oath of membership with their own blood.

---

32. Apolinario de la Cruz to the Cofradía, Manila 6 July 1840 (PNA).

33. Aquilino Atienza, "The Kolorum" (1915) BCTE, vol. 1, no. 39; Severo Magpantay, "The Kolorum and the Spiritismo" (1916) BCTE, vol. 1, no. 41; Aranas, *Kaligaligayang Bundok*, p. 44 and passim.

At the end of the ceremonies, the leader gives a sermon beginning with the following appeal:

> Yniirog kong piling mga kababayan, kahahagan mo ako, nasaan baga ang taglay mong lakas na na sisimpan, malaon ng arao at ipinagkakait sa akin. Ydulot mo nga at damayan akong na sa malabis na pagcaapi at hirap na di maaguanta. Agauin niño ako sa kuko ng lilo. Ako baga ay nalimutan mo na? . . . (titiguil ng kaonte) . . .
>
> Ako ang matandang kalayaan na na bibilibiran ang katauan ng katakot na tanikalang bakal at napipilan ng hibong maraya at ng matapos ay pinagbabantaan patain. Ako ang guinhaua ng unang panahon na naualay sa lahing tagalog at nag dudulot ng sarisaring guinhaua sa puso, hañguin mo ako upang tayo ay magsasama sa lubos na kapayapaan, huag kang mang hinayang sa kaonting dugong pupuhunanin at magaganti ko rin na ualang takal sa biyaya. Yayamang sumapit na ang panahon dapat ipaghiganti ng napakaayop nating bayan sa mga kuhilang kastila ang dugong hihibok hibok sa pamamahala ng abang frayle.

> My beloved compatriots, have compassion for me. Where is the strength you possess that has been saved up through all these years and kept from me? Offer it to me, and have damay for me in my state of unbearable oppression and hardship. Save me from the claws of traitors. Have you already forgotten me? (pause)
>
> I am old Kalayaan whose body is wrapped in frightful chains of metal, subjected to deceitful temptations and threatened with death. I am the ginhawa of former times that gives many kinds of ginhawa to the heart. Rescue me so that we can be together in ultimate peace. Do not feel regret at the blood you shall shed as *puhunan* (investment) for you shall be rewarded a thousandfold with grace. For the time has come for our most humiliated country to seek revenge from the Spanish betrayers for the blood that has flowed during friar rule.

Most notable about the sermon is the fact that the leader is only a vehicle through whom personified Kalayaan speaks. This phenomenon manifests an old Tagalog view (which the friars attempted to suppress) that disembodied spirits may enter the "personalities" of certain mediums and speak through them.[34] Even though it is not specifically stated in the sources, it may be said that Apolinario de la Cruz was not dead in 1870 but lived in the person of Januario Labios. In later periods, as we shall see, Jose Rizal and Felipe Salvador spoke to the people through leaders that came after them. In much the same way did "old Kalayaan," or Mother Country, embodying the ginhawa of former times, enter the "persons" of Katipunan leaders and speak through them. Notable also is an instruction scribbled in the manuscript of the initiation ritual, about the mode of presenting Kalayaan's appeal. The tone of the exhortation should be one of plaintive evocation. The leader should speak with the gentle,

---

34. Cf. Marcelino Foronda, *Cults Honoring Rizal* (Manila: R.P. Garcia, 1961), passim.

supplicating language of a woman in chains who seeks compassion from her sons. In other words, the message must be experienced as well as understood. In the previous chapter, we hinted that Januario Labio's apparently meaningless Latin prayers should be examined in terms of their sound effect rather than their literal translation. Likewise, Katipunan appeals cannot be understood apart from their sounds and mode of presentation. We can liken the leader's speech to poetry or music, its "effect" analogous to a *kundiman's* (love song). Here is a description of what happens when a *kundiman* is sung:

> One of them will sing a song, a pure Tagalog song which is usually very sentimental, so sentimental that if one should listen to it carefully watching the tenor of words and the way the voice is conducted to express the real meaning of the verses, he cannot but be conquered by a feeling of pity even so far as to shed tears.[35]

Compassion or pity for Mother Country is precisely what the Katipunan applicants experienced during their initiation. To put it another way, they had damay with her sufferings. This explains why, at the end of the ceremonies, the Katipunan brothers had tears in their eyes.[36]

Tears and plaintive supplications are only signs of damay. In essence, damay involves a complete change in loób. In the pasyon context, it means a decision to avoid wrongdoing, to follow instead Christ's example. In the Katipunan, having damay implies a commitment to struggle for kalayaan. Toward the end of the sermon, the leader tells his brothers to have humility, to give their lives so that the country may be saved, to think about old Kalayaan as they go off to battle. He talks of the struggle as traversing the "way," in the process of which there is unity, love and purity of self:

> Talastasin naman niño pili kong kababayan na ang nilalandas ng Katipunan ito ay isang daan pagkakaisa, pagtitinginan at pagdadamayan na di magmamalio magpahangan libing. At sa katipunan ito talastasin niño na iniuauaksi ang masasamang asal, masasamang loob at lalu pa at higuit ang kapalaluan palibhasa ay ang tinutungo ay ang isang uagas at dalisay na kalinisan magpahangan kailan. Kababaan loob at pamumuhunanan ng ingat na buhay at madlang kaya upang ipagtanggol ang bandila ng tumatangis nating Religion at sariling bayan.
>
> Bear in mind, my chosen compatriots, that the way travelled by this Katipunan is the way of unity, mutual caring and mutual damay that will not perish even unto death. And bear in mind that in this Katipunan, bad behavior and bad loób and pride in particular, are renounced, for the object of our journey is the purest and most immaculate existence that can ever be attained. Be humble of loób and

35. Juan Pagaspas, "Native Amusements in the Province of Batangas" (1916) BCTE, vol. 2, no. 166.

36. Agoncillo, *Revolt*, p. 50.

sacrifice your lives and all your resources in order to defend the banner of our tearfully lamenting religion and native land.

Return of King Bernardo Carpio

The significance of many little details which has escaped previous scholars can be seen in the light of what has been said so far. For example, in April 1895, about a year before the start of the revolution, Andres Bonifacio and eight leading members of the Katipunan went on a week-long excursion in the mountains of San Mateo, southeast of Manila. Previous scholars have not seen anything more in this event than a search for a safe haven in the mountains to retreat to in the event of difficulties in the struggle; indeed, that is the reason one of the survivors gave Agoncillo in an interview in 1949. Could it be merely coincidental, though, that the group chose the Holy Week of April, from Holy Tuesday to Holy Saturday, to make the climb? Led by an old man named Tandang Pelis, they reached their destination—the caves in Mount Tapusi—on Good Friday. In the "cave of Bernardo Carpio," Bonifacio wrote with a piece of charcoal, "Long live Philippine Independence!" and each Katipunero signed his name with trembling hands and tears in his eyes.[37]

The ascent of Mount Tapusi, more than being a search for a safe haven, was a gesture of deepest significance to the Katipunan and to the inhabitants of the region. For the peasants believed that the legendary Tagalog folk hero—Bernardo Carpio—was imprisoned in the caves of the mountain, awaiting the day when he would break loose and return to free the people. Let us examine the implications of the Katipunan's choice of the "cave of Bernardo Carpio" as its place of refuge.

Bernardo Carpio was one of the favorite characters in awits and komedyas of the nineteenth century.[38] Although his story originates from the *Mocedades* of Spanish writer Lope de Vega, the Tagalog version, set in the traditional "dodecasyllabic quatrain" form, departs from the Spanish original in several ways. In the main, the story is familiar. Bernardo Carpio is the bastard son of a courtier and the sister of the king of Spain. The king, learning about the illicit

---

37. Santos, *Buhay at mga Sinulat,* p. 16; Kasandugo (pseud.), *Ang Katipunan at si Gat Andres Bonifacio* (manuscript, n.d., p. 82, PNL); also Agoncillo, *Revolt,* p. 70. Agoncillo's informant was Guillermo Masangkay, who was with the group that made the "pilgrimage."

38. *Historia Famosa ni Bernardo Carpio* (Manila: J. Martinez, 1919), originally published in 1860. For a full analysis of this awit and its relationship to nationalist writings, see Reynaldo Ileto, "Tagalog Poetry and Perceptions of the Past in the War against Spain," in *Perceptions of the Past in Southeast Asia,* ed. Anthony Reid and David Marr (Singapore: Heinemann, 1979). For publication details on this and other awits, see Damiana Eugenio, "*Awit* and *Korido:* A Study of Fifty Philippine Metrical Romances in Relation to Their Sources and Analogues" (Ph. D. dissertation, University of California at Los Angeles, 1965).

romance, banishes the courtier and detains his sister in a monastery. The boy grows up to be a great general, a staunch defender of the Spanish crown, only to find out that his true parents are unknown. So he makes it a vow to search for his parents. In the course of his adventures, a letter drops from heaven telling him where his father has been imprisoned. Unfortunately, his father dies in his arms. This does not prevent Bernardo from legitimizing his tie to his parents. He brings his father, covered with a cloth on the pretext that he must not be exposed to cold air, to the king's palace, where the wedding with the king's sister takes place. Only when father, mother, and son are formally reunited does Bernardo pretend to discover that his father is dead.

The awit does not end here, as it does in the Spanish originals. Bernardo, having declined the Spanish throne, continues his travels in search of idolaters to destroy. He arrives before a churchlike structure with two lion statues by the entrance. Because the gate is shut, he kneels outside and prays. A bolt of lightning strikes and destroys one of the lions. Angered by the lightning's challenge, Bernardo hurls the other lion away and vows to search for the lightning and destroy it. Not far away, he sees two mountains hitting each other at regular intervals. Then a handsome youth—an angel—appears in dazzling brightness and tells Bernardo that the lightning has entered the mountain. God commands that Bernardo shall not see, much less capture it. When the angel himself takes the path of the lightning, Bernardo stubbornly follows, the twin peaks closing in on him.

Bernardo does not die, however. Some report seeing him in a dream, asleep, his body stretched out on a slab of stone. A man enters the cave where Bernardo lies and converses with the imprisoned hero, who says: "I am Bernardo Carpio who has lain here for a long time. If you want to acquire my strength, give me your hand, let's be friends." Seeing the many skeletons lying around the marble bed, the stranger offers instead a piece of bone, which crumbles to pieces when Bernardo holds it. Then Bernardo tells him

> You are lucky. Because you are intelligent, I am your friend on whom you can depend. Take the little cross near my head as a gift from me. When you are in danger, just say devoutly 'Christum' and the danger will be averted by the power of the Son of God. I am being punished here by God for my sins, but God is good and I am still alive. I am hoping that the time will come when I can arise from my imprisonment. So go, and tell the people about my condition, so that they will be reminded that Jesus after he was interred rose again. In the same manner, I that am now confined in my stone bed inside a cave will, in time, be able to return to the land. For Almighty God has his reasons; He singles out one man as saviour of the oppressed. So tell the oppressed people that their Bernardo will soon rise and save them.[39]

39. Eugenio, "Philippine Metrical Romances," pp. 136–37. This account of the stranger's visit to the cave does not appear in the 1919 edition I used. Eugenio bases her account on a much later (1949) edition. Commentators like Rizal *(El Filibusterismo,* trans. Leon Ma. Guerrero [New York Norton, 1968], p. 35), Teodoro Kalaw (*Cinco Reglas de Nuestra Moral Antigua* [Manila: Bureau c

The Tagalog version of the story thus ends in a manner curiously reminiscent of Colorum rituals. Bernardo Carpio follows the lightning, a form of liwanag, to the gates of paradise, the pillars of which consist of twin peaks hitting each other. Because his loób has not been fully cleansed, he is barred from entering paradise. When he follows the angel, nevertheless, he is cast in a limbo, a state of sleep. He is alive, a potential of power, and only the completion of a redemptive event will bring about his freedom. Only then will he, together with the oppressed people who participate in the liberation process, see paradise.

Rizal was very much aware of the folk belief in a "king of the Indios" imprisoned in the San Mateo cave who would one day return to free the people. "For no apparent reason," comments Rizal, "the natives called him King Bernardo, confusing him perhaps with Bernardo del Carpio." A disgruntled rig driver in *El Filibusterismo* is made to mutter with a suppressed sigh: "When he [Bernardo Carpio] gets his right foot free, I shall give him my horse, put myself under his orders, and die for him. He will free us from the constabulary."[40] In the decade or so prior to the rise of the Katipunan, the Bernardo Carpio story appears to have been appropriated by the peasants as one way of imaging their hopes for a better life, free from oppression and foreign rule. And while Rizal was content to note down this fact, Andres Bonifacio built upon it in mobilizing the Indios against Spain.

Of all the Tagalog plays with which Bonifacio, as an actor, was deeply familiar, the Bernardo Carpio play was his favorite. In his copy of the awit, he even went to the extent of changing Spanish names of places, events and mountains to Tagalog ones.[41] What, one wonders, struck Bonifacio about this awit? The answer is clear if we see Bernardo Carpio, no longer as a Spanish hero, but a Filipino whose life constitutes a talinhaga. Here is a boy whose energy cannot be utilized properly and meaningfully because his parents' identities are unknown to him. Only when he has repudiated his deceitful stepfather and his patron the king is he able to set out in search of his imprisoned parents. When, like a flash of liwanag, his parents' names are revealed to him by heaven, Bernardo becomes ever more aware of his mission in life. Among other things, he undertakes the supremely political act of intimidating the French court into dissolving Spain's vassal status to her.

Bonifacio and other Filipino nationalists of some education appear to have found in the Bernardo Carpio story a popular perception of events on which

---

Printing, 1947], p. 18, and Claudio Miranda (*Costumbres Populares* [Manila: Imprenta "Cultura Filipina," 1911], p. 62) verify the existence of this belief in the late nineteenth century, in spite of our uncertainty as to whether or not it appeared in the published awit.

40. Trans. Leon Ma. Guerrero (London: Longmans, 1961), p. 35. The book was originally published in 1891.

41. Agoncillo, *Revolt*, p. 67.

to hinge their separatist ideas. The Filipino people would, like Bernardo, discover their identity only by repudiating their false parents—Spain and the friars. Bonifacio eloquently expresses this in the following stanzas from the poem *Katapusang Hibik* (Final Lament):

Sumisikat na Ina sa sinisilangan
ang araw ng poot ng katagalugan.
tatlong daang taong aming iningatan
sa dagat ng dusa ng karalitaan.

Mother at the horizon, has risen
the sun of Tagalog fury;
three centuries we kept it
in the sea of woes wrought by poverty.

Walang isinuhay kaming iyong anak
sa bagyong masasal ng dalita't hirap,
iisa ang puso nitong Pilipinas
at ikaw ay di na Ina naming lahat.[42]

Your children's hut had nothing to hold it up
during the terrible storm of pains and troubles,
all in Filipinas are one of heart—
no longer a mother you are to us.

Like Bernardo's outburst of strength, the people's emergence from a condition of ignorance and suffering is accompanied by a release of their energy, or "fury," in a fruitful manner. And finally, the Filipino people themselves would conclude the Bernardo Carpio story by participating in the culmination of his pasyon—his emergence from the depths of his mountain grave. Miranda notes that, north of Manila, "the masses were awaiting the liberation of Bernardo Carpio, a character in a Tagalog legend, from the two enormous cliffs of Biak-na-Bato so that he may exterminate the *cazadores* who defended the Spanish outposts. They say *paa na lamang ang kulang* [only a foot remains pinned]."[43] Meanwhile, continues Miranda, the masses, armed only with bladed weapons, were fighting ferociously to the end.

For Bonifacio and his men who trekked to Mount Tapusi during the Holy Week of 1895, the search for Bernardo Carpio's cave had two levels of meaning. On one hand, it was purely military, a search for a haven. On the other, it was a gesture of identifying with the folk hero entombed in the mountain. No wonder many came to the cave to be initiated into the

42. From "Katapusang Hibik ng Pilipinas" in Agoncillo, *Writings and Trial*, pp. 75–77; and Bienvenido Lumbera, "Tradition and Influences in the Development of Tagalog Poetry (1570–1898)" (Ph. D. dissertation, Indiana University, 1967), appendix, pp. 46–47.

43. Miranda, *Costumbres*, p. 62.

Katipunan. We can also understand why Bonifacio's hand trembled with fierce emotion as he wrote on the walls of the cave: "Long live Philippine Independence!"[44] This slogan must be interpreted in its entire form—*Panahon na! Mabuhay ang Kalayaan!*—which was the battlecry of the Katipunan.[45] Its common translation as "The time has come! Long live Liberty!" does not quite capture its meaning. *Panahon na!* (It is time!) implies, not only that the revolution has begun, but that a totally new era (panahon) is about to succeed the old which has irreversibly winded down. And *Mabuhay* should be translated literally as "May it live" or "May it come to life." "Long live" or "Cheers" fails to capture the meaning of the struggle as the experience of hardship in order to redeem or give life to a "dead" or "slumbering" condition called kalayaan.

Bonifacio's appropriation of the Bernardo Carpio story served the same purpose as the pasyon layer of Katipunan appeals discussed earlier. They both enabled the masses to grasp the meaning of nationalism and separatism through the mediation of familiar awit and pasyon language. Bonifacio's poem *Katapusang Hibik* (Final Lament), which we earlier linked to the theme of Bernardo Carpio's liberation through repudiation of his false parents, also recalls the pasyon in its use of the image of the "rising sun of Tagalog fury." In the resurrection scene there is the following striking passage:

Mamimitac at sisilang	The dawn was breaking
ang arao sa Silanganan	the sun rising in the East
nang lumabas sa baunan,	when from the grave emerged,
yaong sumacop sa tanan	the redeemer of all mankind
siya na ngang pagcabuhay	he had truly come alive.
(177: 12)	

Compare this with the language of the Katipunan in which the dawn, rising sun, lamp flame and other images of liwanag are associated with the awakening or "coming alive" of kalayaan, Mother Country, the youth, Bernardo Carpio, and even the martyrs Rizal, Gomez, Burgos and Zamora. Obviously, without the masses' experience of the pasyon, the revolution against Spain would have taken a much different form.

Lakaran of the Sons

Often ignored documents like poems, songs and even dreams are rich in allusions to the revolution's framework of meaning. The following poem is attributed to Procopio Bonifacio, brother of Andres:

---

44. According to Zaide, it was Aurelio Tolentino who scribbled "Viva la Independencia Filipina" on the wall (*The Philippine Revolution* [Manila: Modern Book Co., rev. ed., 1968], p. 98).

45. Teodoro Agoncillo and Milagros Guerrero, *History of the Filipino People*, 5th ed. (Quezon City: R.P. Garcia, 1977), p. 200.

Oh inang Espanya, humihinging tawad
kaming Pilipino na iyong inanak
panahon na dumating na magkatiwatiwalag
sa di mo pagtupad, masamang paglingap.

O Mother Spain, we Filipinos
your children, ask forgiveness
the time has come for us to separate
because of your neglect,
your lack of motherly care.

Paalam na aking Espanyang pinopoon,
kaming Pilipino humihiwalay na ngayon
ang bandera namin dulo ng ta [sic]
ipakikilala sa lahat ng nacion.

Farewell, revered Spain
we Filipinos are now leaving you
our flag waving on a . . .
will be displayed before all nations.

Lakad, aba tayo, titigisa ang hirap
tunguhin ang bundok at kaluwanagan ng gubat
gamitin ang gulok at sampu ng sibat
ipagtanggol ngayon Inang Pilipinas.

Let us, lowly men, walk on, each
to experience hardship
head for the hills and forests
use our knives and spears
let us now defend Mother Filipinas.

Paalam na ako, bayang tinubuan
bayang masagana sa init ng araw.
Oh maligayang araw na nakasisilaw
kaloob ng Diyos at Poong Maykapal.[46]

Farewell, land of my birth
land of plenty in the warmth of the sun.
Oh joyful, blinding sun
a gift of God the Lord Creator.

What is striking about the first stanza of the poem is that the Filipinos are seeking Mother Spain's *forgiveness* for their act of separating from her. Why this sentimental moment, if Spain had oppressed the Philippines for so long? The poem can be understood only if the revolution itself is viewed not merely as the overthrowing of a foreign power but as a transition between two worlds. As mentioned earlier, wholeness is in Philippine society commonly spoken of

46. Jose P. Santos, *Si Andres Bonifacio at ang Himagsikan,* 2d printing (n.p., 1935), p. 18.

in terms of the bond between mother and child. Together they form a self-contained universe bound by ties of love and utang na loób. A tearful crisis usually occurs when the grown-up son or daughter has to leave home. The preoccupation with the mother-child separation theme has left a strong imprint on Tagalog literature. In the pasyon's development through the centuries, for instance, the dialogues between Christ and the Virgin Mary grew all out of proportion, making the pasyon just as much an epic of Mother Mary's loss.[47] In effect, the everyday theme of separation was raised to a higher level of meaning.

In Bonifacio's poem, the Filipinos are about to embark upon the struggle, which is imaged as everyman's *lakaran*. Just as the start of Christ's passion is marked by his emotional and painful separation from Mary, so does the struggle of the Filipinos, following the contours of tradition, begin with separation from Mother Spain. In the pasyon text, lengthy dialogues between Jesus and Mary, and between Mary and God the Father, bring to light the irreversibility and "fatedness" of the event. The Day of Redemption has come, Jesus tells his mother, and so we must separate (78:7). In the poem there is a striking parallel in the declaration: "The time has come for us to separate." Bonifacio goes on to exhort his compatriots: "Let us, lowly men, walk on, each to experience hardship / head for the hills and forests." The struggle is imaged as an arduous journey on foot, a lakaran, toward the "hills and forests" where for centuries Indios "fleeing from the bells" found refuge. Bonifacio sees the struggle as a lakaran-unto-death—hence his farewell to the land—but with death comes more liwanag over the land. Kalayaan is imaged as the blinding light of the sun, just as, in the pasyon, the outcome of the lakaran-unto-death is a radiant "victory." Rising from his grave, Christ is described as:

lubos ang pagcaliuanag	completely engulfed in liwanag
nitong nanalong nang gubat	was he who had gone to the hills
na icalauang Personas. (177:13)	this victorious second Person.

In the poems of the Bonifacio brothers, a dominant theme is the changing of mothers—from Spain to Inang Bayan (Mother Country). Now it is not only the separation from Mother Spain that the pasyon tradition rendered intelligible to the masses. The very notion of Mother Country rode on popular images of the Virgin Mary, who appears in the pasyon as the ideal Filipino mother, behaving in the traditional fashion as the son persists in his untraditional mission.

There is a story told by Aurelio Tolentino that one night, as Andres Bonifacio, Emilio Jacinto, himself and others were asleep in Tandang Sora's house in Balintawak, one of them dreamt of a beautiful woman leading by the

---

47. Cf. Bienvenido Lumbera, "Consolidation of Tradition in Nineteenth-Century Tagalog Poetry," *Philippine Studies* 17 (July 1969): 391–93.

hand a handsome child. The woman looked exactly like the Virgin Mary in church statues, except that she wore a native costume, the *balintawak*. The child was dressed in peasant garb, armed with a glittering bolo, and shouting "kalayaan!" The woman approached the dreamer to warn him about something. Roused from his sleep, he narrated his dream to his companions, who all concluded that the Virgin was warning them against proceeding to Manila that morning. They all decided to tarry a while longer in Balintawak. Later, the news arrived that the Katipunan-infiltrated printing shop of the *Diario de Manila* had been raided by the guardia civil. Without the Virgin's warning, alleged Tolentino, Bonifacio would have been captured along with the others and executed, and the revolution delayed indefinitely.

The story may be entirely apochryphal, but it was deemed fit to be published in the newspaper *La Vanguardia*—the successor to *El Renacimiento*—sometime before Tolentino's death in 1915. The point is, such a story was entirely credible to Tolentino's audience. Why was the Virgin in native costume; why was she leading a Katipunero by the hand? Was she Mother Country herself? For the popular mind there was no clear distinction, no crisis of meaning as one image flowed into the other. One of the reasons why, as we shall see, religiopolitical groups and the Philippine Independent Church swelled with peasant members during the days of the republic and the succeeding years was because "nationalist" and "religious" idioms merged in them. Bishop Gregorio Aglipay, for example, continued to instill among his adherents the teachings of Mabini, Rizal and Bonifacio. But at the same time, without hesitation, he could proclaim: *Ang Virgen sa Balintawak ay ang Inang Bayan* (The Virgin at Balintawak is the Mother Country).[48]

A fine example of how meaningful images of the revolution are combined in a popular song is the following kundiman:

> Sa dalampasigan ng dagat Maynila,
> Luneta ang tawag ng mga kastila
> ay doon binaril ang kaawaawa
> pobreng Pilipino, martir nitong Lupa.
>
> > On the shores of Manila bay
> > called by the Spaniards "Luneta"
> > there was shot the pitiful
> > humble Filipino, martyr of this land.
>
> Naramay sa dusa ang ating tanggulan
> panganay na Burgos at bunsong si Rizal
> sa inggit at takot ng prayleng sukaban
> pinatay at sukat, walang kasalanan.

---

48. Gregorio Aglipay, *Pagsisiyam sa Virgen sa Balintawak: Ang Virgen sa Balintawak ay ang Inang Bayan,* Tagalog trans. Juan Evangelista (Manila: Isabelo de los Reyes, 1925). The *La Vanguardia* article by Tolentino is partly reproduced on the back of this *novenario*.

Our defenders fell into grief
the eldest Burgos, the youngest Rizal
sons without stain of guilt
were treacherously killed by the envious, fearful friars.

Hindi na inisip ang kanilang buhay
kung ito'y matapos tapos din ang layaw,
paris na nga ngayon, ang kinasapitan
kaming Pilipino'y kusang humiwalay.

They did not think of their lives
when life is ended, so is *layaw,*
just as it is now, it all ended up
in we Filipinos willingly separating.

Oh mga kalahi! Lakad, pagpilitang
tunguhin ang bundok, kalawakang parang,
gamitin ang gulok at sibat sa kamay,
ating ipagtanggol lupang tinubuan.

Oh compatriots! Walk on, strive
to reach the mountain and the forest
use the bolos and spears in your hands,
let us defend the land of our birth.

Huwag manganib, Inang Pilipinas
sa kahit ano mang itakda ng palad,
di kami tutugot hanggang di matupad
itong kalayaang ating hinahanap.[49]

Fear not, Mother Filipinas
whatever fate has in store for us,
we will not cease to struggle until
the kalayaan we search for is found.

The first thing to be noted about this kundiman is that its composer is unkown, and that several versions of it exist. The longest, though incomplete, version published by Ronquillo in 1910 lacks a title; two others are titled *Ang mga Martir* (The Martyrs) and *Ang Dalampasigan* (The Seashore), respectively.[50] Ronquillo comments that "the author of the poem evidently had a very confused mind, expressed himself unintelligibly, and knew nothing about the life of Burgos." Such information points, if not to the folk origins, at least to the

49. From Carlos Ronquillo, "Mga Kantahing Bayan," RENFIL 1 (28 August 1910): 23.

50. Ibid.; Consejo Cauayani, "Some Popular Songs of the Spanish Period and their Possible Use in the Music Program of our Schools" (M.A. thesis, University of the Philippines, 1954), pp. 110–11; Felipe de Leon, "Poetry, Music, and Social Consciousness," *Philippine Studies* 17 (1969): 278

folk appropriation of the song. Although the poetry is "crude" from the literary critic's view, it nevertheless reveals popular perceptions of events, more than sophisticated or urbane Tagalog poetry does.

There is a preoccupation with the martyrdoms of the ilustrados Burgos and Rizal who, because of their mode of death, belong to the family of folk heroes. They are *pobre* (poor) not necessarily because of their economic status but because of their identification with the paradigm of the poor and suffering Christ. The friars, of course, are described just like the pharisees—guardians of the official religion who are motivated by "envy and fear" to condemn innocent men to death. In the third stanza, the martyrdoms of Burgos and Rizal and their consequent loss of layaw are juxtaposed with the separation of the Filipinos from Spain—as if each patriot who participates in the struggle reenacts the experience of the martyrs. In the fourth stanza, we have again the image of the lakaran. With Mother Country hovering in the background, her sons pursue the struggle, not ceasing until kalayaan is found.

As long as the struggle is perceived as a sacred mission—a people's pasyon—the path toward kalayaan is narrow and straight, and there is no turning back until the end is reached. In view of this, it no longer appears irrational that Katipunan units mostly armed only with bladed weapons and sticks fought the Spaniards with determination. A Spanish observer notes that the Katipuneros seemed to be "hallucinated unto death." When, for example, the Spanish army recaptured a Katipunan town, "the masses were made to believe that they had to return and retake it," so that the river was reddened with the blood of the slain, both Filipino and Spanish. And having been "defeated a hundred and one times and driven to the mountains," the "fanaticized" masses were made to believe in the aid of a foreign power or a supernatural being.[51] Isabelo de los Reyes notes that the natives of Pandakan were not frightened when some of their men were executed by the Spaniards:

> The peasants, far from being intimidated by these tests, wept with enthusiasm and emotion at having in this immortal association a glimpse into the brilliant future of the Philippines, and they wept with emotion at finding that their country thought them worthy of saving it from its then sad situation.[52]

The tears of the "country people" were not the result of what is usually termed "sentimentality." They reveal to us that the people had damay and compassion and thus took the path in search of kalayaan.

Was kalayaan ever attained during the Katipunan revolution? In a description of the liberated town of San Francisco de Malabon, Cavite, Santiago

---

51. Caro y Mora, *La Situación,* p. 14.
52. De los Reyes, "The Katipunan," p. 209.

Alvarez seems to capture the experience of kalayaan during the latter days of September 1896:

> The people were truly happy, free to enjoy life in all sorts of ways. Food was plentiful; all things were cheap; there were no perversities, no robberies, no thefts, no pickpockets. Everyone had love for his fellow men, and in every place the Katipunan's teaching of brotherly love held sway. Frightful threats of death, like the whistling cannonballs, were viewed calmly as everyone simply ducked to avoid them. And with hope in the grace of God, the children, elders, women and men had no fear of death . . . no news of the enemy's advance was ever cause for fear. . . . The cannon bursts were no longer feared and even came to be regarded as fireworks in a celebration. . . . The women's stores were open all day and night; singing, dancing, feasting beneath the trees, gambling and cockfighting everywhere, served to make them forget the impending sacrifice of their lives and blood. But at the first sign of fighting, all the men and women would straighten up and grab their weapons of war.[53]

Other sources confirm that the first few months of the revolution were remembered particularly during the difficult years of the war against the United States as some kind of a "Lost Eden."[54] The experience of release from Spanish rule was indeed exhilarating. Food was cheap and plentiful. And there was an attempt, at least, to practice the Katipunan ideals of love, brotherhood and good moral conduct. But this was a fleeting experience. Not only would the Spanish armies return in force, but in the liberated areas, principalia rivalry and vacillation would harm the revolution from within. When Andres Bonifacio arrived in late 1896 to unite the warring Magdalo and Magdiwang factions of the Katipunan in Cavite, little did he realize that he would die at the hands of *pinunong bayan*.

Ironically, Bonifacio's downfall can be traced to his preoccupation with "sacred ideals" and moral transformation. He was led to this not so much by his personality and Masonic background as his familiarity with popular perceptions of change. Folk poetry and drama undoubtedly provided him with basic insights into the "folk mind." Between him and Apolinario de la Cruz in fact exists a strong affinity. Their sermons and exhortations, rooted in the people's language and experience, drew similar responses and gave rise to similar problems. In Bonifacio's case, the concept of national unity as each citizen's rebirth in a society of liwanag was found by others to be unworkable

53. Alvarez, *Ang Katipunan,* pp. 78-80. San Francisco de Malabon was the capital of the Magdiwang wing of the Katipunan which invited Bonifacio, who was then in Morong, to become their leader in late December 1896.

54. The writings of Diego Mojica and Eulogio Tandiama about the war against Spain are examined in the next chapter. In the PIR can be found many letters to President Aguinaldo from participants in the "first revolution" who looked back with longing to the early months of victory.

in a time of massive recruitment of revolutionists. For example, Roman Basa was expelled or withdrew from the Katipunan because he wanted to do away with "the tedious process of initiation, which Bonifacio never wanted to give up."[55] In fact, Emilio Aguinaldo and others practically abandoned the initiation rituals while retaining Katipunan rhetoric to incite the people to revolt.[56]

In Cavite, Bonifacio got embroiled in the question of kingship which scholars briefly mention but understandably avoid discussion of. Santiago Alvarez, an eyewitness, says that, as the welcome parade in honor of Bonifacio wound its way from Noveleta to San Francisco de Malabon, some people in the crowd shouted "Mabuhay ang Hari!" (Long live the King!), to which Bonifacio replied "Mabuhay ang Inang Bayan!" (Long live Mother Country!)[57] Aguinaldo, in his memoirs, adds that the cabinet of the Magdiwang government conferred upon Bonifacio the highest title they could give: *Haring Bayan* (sovereign). He describes what happened as Bonifacio and the Magdiwang leaders visited the towns under their jurisdiction:

> They gave speeches and lessons about love of country and said other inspiring words concerning our kalayaan. How overjoyed the people *(taong bayan)* were, so filled with pomp and solemnity was their reception that it seemed as if a real king had arrived.[58]

Scholars have paid scant attention to Aguinaldo's insistence that conflict between the two wings of the Katipunan was inevitable because the Magdiwang faction was Maka-Hari (monarchist), while the Magdalo faction was Republikano.[59] Our sympathies in this modern age tend to lie with Aguinaldo.[60] But if we put ourselves in the context of his time, we can understand why some people greeted Bonifacio as the Filipino king. Some fifty-five years prior to that incident, Apolinario de la Cruz, whether he, liked it or not, was crowned "king of the Tagalogs" by his peasant followers. For did not the masses, steeped in the world of awit and *korido*, await the coming of

---

55. E. Arsenio Manuel, *Dictionary of Philippine Biography,* vol. 1 (Quezon City: Filipiniana Research Society, 1955), p. 93.

56. Emilio Aguinaldo, *Mga Gunita ng Himagsikan* (Manila: n.p., 1964), p. 53 and passim.

57. Alvarez, *Ang Katipunan,* p. 116. Agoncillo translates the crowd's greetings as "Long live the ruler of the Philippines" (*Revolt,* p. 204).

58. *Mga Gunita,* pp. 140–41. In Laguna, too, several towns looked up to Bonifacio as "the Supremo, the King of the People" (Antonino Guevarra to Emilio Jacinto, 8 May 1897, in Epifanio de los Santos, *The Revolutionists: Aguinaldo, Bonifacio, Jacinto* [Manila: National Historical Commission], p. 133).

59. Ibid., p. 143.

60. For example, Carlos Quirino (*The Trial of Andres Bonifacio* [Manila: Ateneo de Manila, 1963], p. 8) states that "when acclaimed publicly upon his first arrival in San Francisco de Malabon that December, [Bonifacio] allowed them to hail him with the words 'Mabuhay ang hari ng bayan'"

Christ the King or Bernardo Carpio, the Tagalog king? Telesforo Canseco, an admittedly profriar witness, says that while people in his town lamented the execution of Spanish priests, many prayed for "the triumph of the insurrection" and, during Holy Week, the coadjutor led public prayers for "the triumph of the king of the Tagalogs." Was this king Bonifacio himself? Or was it Bernardo Carpio? For Bonifacio himself, as Carlos Ronquillo reports, told his followers that their legendary king Bernardo would descend from Mount Tapusi to aid the Katipunan rebels. Whatever the exact rumors were, the fact is that Bonifacio was so adept at tapping popular feelings to serve his revolutionary ends that he was unavoidably incorporated into the folk view of events.[61] He and some Magdiwang leaders, notably the poet Diego Mojica, appear to have encouraged such beliefs in the hope of consolidating their government's hold over the people.[62]

Bonifacio eventually drew the ire of the leading citizens, not the people of Cavite as some would have us believe. They called him an ignoramus, an outsider from Tondo, a poor military strategist, a Mason, a monarchist, a *tulisan* (bandit) even. But beneath these accusations, most of which are valid, lies the simple fact that Bonifacio's Katipunan, if allowed to progress, would have threatened existing boundaries and hierarchies in the province. A comparison of Bonifacio's case with that of other leaders of popular brotherhoods and secret societies like Apolinario de la Cruz, Sebastian Caneo, and Felipe Salvador, reveals similar reactions on the part of the *maginoó* or *pinunong bayan* toward upstarts with a powerful message to the masses. In

---

(Long live the king of the people!). Later, Quirino asserts that "to the rank and file of the insurgents, who were confirmed believers in a republican form of government, the words 'king' and 'viceroy' suggested an odious connection with the colonial power oppressing their country." The evidence I have collected does not support this view of the "rank and file."

61. Canseco, "Historia de la Insurrección," p. 98; Kalaw, *Cinco Reglas,* p. 18; Carlos Ronquillo, "Ilang talata tungkol sa Paghihimagsik ng 1896–97" (Ms., Hongkong, 1898, in The University of the Philippines Main Library).

62. John N. Schumacher, "The Religious Character of the Revolution in Cavite, 1896–1897," *Philippine Studies* 24 (1976): 399-416. Schumacher stresses the difference between the religious masses of Cavite and the "fundamentally anticlerical and antireligious color" of the Katipunan, mainly due to Bonifacio's influence. This distinction appears forced and ultimately irrelevant. Bonifacio's condemnation of the clergy was based on the latter's failure to live up to its religious ideals. His much-publicized torture and execution of some Spanish friars was undertaken not on religious grounds but on the conviction that they were involved in political acts against Filipino nationalists. Bonifacio's attitude toward the friars was perhaps imprudent as it gave Aguinaldo and others an opportunity to feed the rumor mills. Schumacher painstakingly proves what would have been obvious to Bonifacio: that the masses were steeped in the traditions of Catholicism. Bonifacio's close friendship with the staunchly religious poet and revolutionary, Diego Mojica, suggests that they strove to harness these traditions rather than, as Schumacher implies, destroy them. Schumacher, however, rightly concludes that research on the revolution "which ignores the Catholic character of nineteenth-century Filipino society" (p. 416) can never adequately explain the response of the masses.

keeping with this pattern, it is significant that Bonifacio's counter-accusations harp on the sad state of his rivals' loób. In a letter to Emilio Jacinto, he describes the Magdalo leaders as "envious" *(mainggitin)*. "The selfishness *(pagkagahaman)* of Magdalo," he says, "is truly nauseating *(nakasusuklam)* and even led to many reverses." In two other letters, he reiterates the connection he perceives between state of loób and military defeats. On 24 April 1897, he tells Jacinto that the enemy took three or four towns without a fight and that other towns will be similarly captured if *kasakiman* (greed) and *pag-iimbot* (selfishness) continue to reign; this, he concludes, is "the sole cause of the misfortune *(kasawian)* of these pueblos." In another letter, Bonifacio attributes frequent enemy attacks on certain towns to "infighting and lack of unity among the leaders who continue to have hardness of loób *(matitigas ang kaloóban)* while ordinary people suffer."[63] These charges all reveal Bonifacio's preoccupation with inner transformation as a condition for revolution.

In the preface to his essay *Liwanag at Dilim,* Emilio Jacinto describes Bonifacio as "bearing on his shoulder all the burdens on the face of the earth" *(pumapasan ng madlang kabigatan sa balat ng lupa)*.[64] No other image would have brought home to his audience the nature of Bonifacio's commitment to the struggle. After all, Jacinto states later on, kalayaan is a *panatang lakaran*—a goal that one devotes his life to pursue—which involves hardship and the shedding of blood.[65] Bonifacio, at the age of thirty-three, did give his life in the struggle for kalayaan. But almost in anticipation of the future struggle, his executioners were his own compatriots. One early morning in April 1897, he and his companions were attacked by a detachment of Aguinaldo's army. Understandably, the Katipunan supremo was stunned by the sight of kapatid killing fellow kapatid. Himself wounded in the neck, he was carried to Naik, the capital, where began a mock trial that ended five days later in Maragondon. There the Bonifacio brothers, Andres and Procopio, were pronounced guilty of plotting to assassinate President Aguinaldo and overthrow the revolutionary government. On 10 May 1897, the two were brought to the hills of Maragondon and shot; because of the lack of reliable witnesses, the precise details of their deaths may never be known.

With Bonifacio's execution came the final dissolution of the Katipunan secret society in favor of a truly "national" revolution. This is the standard interpretation, at least. From an organizational point of view, undoubtedly Aguinaldo was now able to form a government with a broader principalia base, culminating in the birth of the Filipino nation. But, as we shall see in later

63. In Agoncillo, *Writings and Trial,* pp. 82–86, 88, 91. English translations on pp. 13–17, 19, 21–22.

64. In Santos, *Buhay at mga Sinulat,* p. 26.

65. Ibid., p. 35.

chapters, the Katipunan survived in various forms, often taking stands opposed to those of the revolutionary center. This phenomenon can be understood if we view Bonifacio's Katipunan as the embodiment of a revolutionary style, a sort of language which enabled the ordinary Indio to relate his personal experience with the "national." Granted that the Katipunan of Bonifacio was not the totality of the revolution, its appeals for a national rebirth, the redemption of Mother Country and the struggle for kalayaan became part of every revolutionary leader's vocabulary in arousing the people. The language born in the early stages of the struggle far outlived the personalities who created it.

Revolutionary seals, 1898–1900

CHAPTER 4

The Republic and the Spirit of 1896

The proclamation of Philippine independence in 1898 climaxed the popular struggle against Spain waged by the revolutionary army and the revived Katipunan. Ironically, however, independence brought less than fulfillment to the actual participants in the war. It signified a final break with the Katipunan definition of *Inang Bayan*, Mother Country, as a brotherhood of her sons who have experienced the passage from darkness to light by participating in her redemption. The *ilustrados* who quickly took over the affairs of the new nation succeeded in institutionalizing their definition, borrowed from the West, of "sovereign nation" as a bounded territory encompassing all of its inhabitants who pledge loyalty to the government and constitution. As interpreted by the *principales* and ilustrados who flocked to the capital at Malolos, separation from Mother Spain had brought forth a new entity—*Inang Filipinas* (Mother Philippines)—and it was the task of the "better classes" to solidify "national unity" so that the Philippines could take her proper place in the international community.

On President Emilio Aguinaldo fell the unenviable task of preserving the Filipino elite's conservative definition of the state while, as a commander-in-chief of the army, channeling the people's energies toward the war with the United States. Perhaps no other individual could have played that role. Aguinaldo was a veteran of the early national struggles. His successful military exploits, attributed no doubt by many to his powerful *anting-anting,* conferred an aura of power about him. He was considered by his followers "as possessed of magic powers; he could foresee the future; he was invulnerable; he had a magic sword by waving which he could turn bullets in their flight."[1]

---

1. John R.M. Taylor, *The Philippine Insurrection against the United States*, vol. 2 (Pasay City: Eugenio Lopez Foundation, 1971), pp. 121, 175.

In the eyes of many, he was no different from Apolinario de la Cruz, who liked to appear before his followers brandishing a luminous, magical saber.[2] Furthermore, Aguinaldo was an effective orator, familiar with the traditional idiom of struggle. "His words," says Taylor, "produced an effect upon his hearers which men who have to read them in translation will not understand. There is a strong love for music and poetry among the Filipinos and Aguinaldo's florid speeches moved them strongly."[3] Whatever he had to say in public had to reconcile the views and interests of all classes of society, no matter how grave the inherent contradictions were.

The republic's ideas of nationalism and revolution can be gleaned from the following excerpt of a speech by Aguinaldo before local principales who were to form "revolutionary municipal councils":

> Pacatantoin nating lahat na Filipinos na tayo'y anac na parapara nang isang Ina; nang inang Filipinas: palibhasa'y pagcamulat natin ay inanducha na tayo sa caniyang candungan, pinasamyo ng bango nang caniyang hangin, liniuanagan nang caniyang arao at binuhay na parapara sa bunga nang caniyang lupa. Caya ang lahat na naturales, lahat nang mestizong castila para nang mestizong Sangley sa Pilipinas ay pauang isang anac ni bathala dito, isang larauan niya at isang capatid co. At ano ang gagauin nating mga capatid nang mabiguiang lugod ang mairuguin nating Inang Bayan, cundi ang magcaisang loób sa caniyang icabubuti.
>
> Sa pagcaca isang loob ang lahat nang provincia nitong Pilipinas, cahit ano mang lalayo ay maglalapit at maboboo sa isang nais—ang nais ng pagcasarinlan at ualang pagcasalilungan![4]

> Let all of us Filipinos understand that we are all children of a single Mother, of Mother Filipinas: since from the time we left her womb she has sheltered us under her care, let us breathe her fragrance, brought us the light of her sun and nourished us with the fruits of her soil. For this reason all her native inhabitants, all the Spanish mestizos as well as the Chinese mestizos in the Philippines are like a single child of God here, and in each one I see God's image and a brother of mine. And what better offering can all of us brothers give to make our loving Motherland happy, than to be one in *loób* for her sake?
>
> In the effort of becoming one in *loób* of all the provinces of the Philippines, even those that are distant will be brought closer in a union of views and aspirations—namely, independence and freedom from foreign domination!

Reference in the speech to the protection and light of Mother Filipinas reflects consciousness of the new entity born out of the separation of Spain and

---

2. Robert G. Woods, "Origin of the Colorum," *Philippine Magazine* 16 (December 1929): 429

3. Taylor, *Philippine Insurrection*, p. 175.

4. "Talumpati na isinalaysay nang Presidente M. Emilio Aguinaldo at Famy sa Cavite Viejo n 3 ng Agosto ng 1898" (PIR-SD 457.3). Also printed in Spanish.

Filipinas. It is also an image that invokes the spirit of the 1896 revolution. But the idea of unity that follows is ultimately based not on the *experience* of unity but on the fact that each inhabitant of the nation is an image of God. That is why many of the ilustrados, wealthy principales, and *mestizos* who had generally been unsympathetic or hostile to the 1896 struggle could, because of education, wealth and social status, be placed on an equal (or even higher) plane with veterans of the Katipunan.[5] Either missing or entirely subdued in this and other speeches and manifestos emanating from the government is the Katipunan idea that unity is accomplished through the transformation and "direction" of each Filipino's loób or, to put it differently, in the individual experience of the struggle. The absence of the notion of participation in the redemption of Mother Filipinas reflects the ilustrado and upper *principalia* composition of the Malolos government and congress. Cabinet President Apolinario Mabini, born of very poor parents, was one of the few exceptions. This may well explain the harrassment he was subjected to in Malolos in 1899, and his later condemnation of Aguinaldo's manner of governing. For Mabini was not convinced that the nation could come into being by definiton and the mere possession of all the external trappings. In the introduction to his "Decalogue," he echoes Bonifacio's earlier complaint that self-interest, jealousy, and favoritism among self-proclaimed revolutionaries were destructive of the common good. "A veritable blood-letting is necessary," writes Mabini, "in order to shed so much vitiated and corrupt blood, inoculated in your veins by your stepmother in order to bind you to eternal thankfulness. Therein lies the internal revolution which I proposed."[6]

Aguinaldo's speech to the principales defines "nationalism" as "a union of views and aspirations" centered on independence, or "freedom from foreign domination." Because the ilustrados reserved for themselves the right to define Filipino "aspirations" and had, in fact, defined independence as political autonomy or self-government by Filipinos, radical interpretations of independence from elements of the "poor and ignorant class" (to paraphrase the ilustrados) were branded as "antirevolutionary" by the leaders of the republic. The internal problems that Malolos had to contend with were largely caused by the ramification of the independence ideal among the populace. The revolutionary message of the 1896 Katipunan—that independence (*kalayaan*) would bring about a condition of brotherhood, equality, contentment (*kaginhawaan*) and material abundance (*kasaganaan*)—had been communicated so effectively to the people, that by the time separation from Spain was fully

5. See Aguinaldo's apologetic proclamation, "To the Katipunan," Cavite, 15 July 1898 (Taylor, *Philippine Insurrection*, vol. 3, p. 162). Aguinaldo tells the Katipunan not to "grow disheartened" when it sees that the office is bestowed "upon those who have not been our companions" since, after all, the whole country is the Katipunan.

6. "Decalogue," May 1898 (Taylor, *Philippine Insurrection*, vol. 3, p. 48).

attained in 1898, broad economic and social changes were expected by many rank-and-file Katipuneros and peasant fighters.

The language of revolutionary literature and slogans urging the people to fight could often be interpreted in broader terms than originally intended. Take the following *catotohanan* (truth) that appeared in the newspaper *Ang Kaibigan nang Bayan* (The Friend of the People) on 2 February 1899:

> Ang bunga nang pagbabaca ay itong sumusunod:
> Nababauasan ang capalaluan nang marurunong.
> Nababauasan ang calupitan nang malacas.
> Dumudunong ang mangmang.
> At nadadagdagan ang diquit nang mundo,
> palibhasa'y nabubucsan ang isip nang caramihan.[7]
>
> The fruits of stuggle are the following:
> The educated become less arrogant.
> The powerful become less cruel.
> The ignorant gain knowledge.
> And the world grows more radiant and beautiful,
> as the minds of the masses are opened.

Social levelling is implied in the above "truth." How could readers of the newspaper not expect it after struggling so hard? In the following song of earlier vintage, social inversion is the fruit of victory:

Ang kastila kung lumaban ayao sila ng tagaan ang gusto nila ang barilan mi trinchera pang kanlungan.	When the Spaniards fought they avoided hand to hand combat preferring the security of trenches from which to fire their guns.
Wala na! Tapus na ang Maynila; sumuko ng lahat pati kura; ang konvento nila at hacienda ibinigay sa aming lahat na.	It is all over! Manila is taken; friars and all have surrendered; their conventos and estates have all been given to us.
Ang kura sa Bulakan nananalakay sa parang sapagkat siya'y pinagutusan ni Don Salgario del Pilar.	The parish priest of Bulacan was furiously tilling the fields having been ordered to do so by Don Salgario del Pilar.

7. PIR, Box 7, PNL.

Sa Bulakan, ang kastila	In Bulacan, the Spaniards
doon silang lahat mistulang alila:	all were practically servants:
taga pamili sa tiangi ng isda	going to market to buy fish
at taga gawa ng lahat ng bagay.[8]	doing practically all the chores.

"It is all over!" proclaims the song, and then follow the economic and social consequences of the event: redistribution of friar property, and erstwhile colonial rulers becoming tillers and household servants. The revolutionary elite was anxious to leave it at that, to limit the meaning of the song to the defeat and humiliation of Spain. But the hopeful among the oppressed and those who fought doggedly to achieve this victory expected more sweeping changes. To them the above song expressed the beginning rather than the end.

Challenges to Malolos

Toward the end of 1898, the Malolos-based government began to receive alarming reports from provincial officials in both central and southern Luzon concerning the spread of "anti-revolutionary" movements. These peasant bands ignored directives from government officials, even going to the extent of threatening the lives and properties of the wealthy. The complex background of such discontent has been described in an incisive study by Milagros Guerrero.[9] She points to the ilustrados' resistance to "internal revolution," the localism and abusiveness of many municipal officials, and the exigencies of the guerrilla resistance. For one thing, the imposition of the *cedula personal* and other forms of revenue and labor service simply recalled the "dark age" of Spanish rule. Furthermore, the control of local government by the principales gave them an opportunity to assert ownership of vast tracts of land, some of which were claimed by less sophisticated and powerless tillers. The realities of national independence were far from the expectations, nurtured during the war, not only of a release from the burdens of Spanish rule but of a society "turned upside down." Even from the earliest days of victory, Mabini was aware of the contradictions that would plague the republic:

> While forming part of the Malolos Government, the complaint was made to the writer by certain alarmed individuals that this talk of liberties had caused to

8. Honesto Mariano, "Popular Songs of the Revolution," (Manila, 1915) BCTE, vol. 4, no. 198.

9. Milagros Guerrero, "Luzon at War: Contradictions in Philippine Society, 1898–1902" (Ph. D. dissertation, University of Michigan, 1977). Guerrero gives a thorough account of socio-economic developments which I have only lightly touched upon.

> germinate in the minds of the masses certain socialistic or communistic ideas which forbode no good for the future of certain properties of doubtful origin.[10]

As it was perceived that the acts of the revolutionary center contradicted its language of struggle and redemption, many religiopolitical brotherhoods turned away from it. Their ranks swelled in the latter part of 1898 as disappointed peasants and other aggrieved parties sought alternative vehicles for the pursuit of their ideals.

One of the more "spectacular" cases of disorder that Malolos had to contend with was the so-called Pensacola affair in Zambales, northwest of Manila. The brothers Teodoro and Doroteo Pensacola were veterans of the war against Spain, having been responsible for liberating a town or two from Spanish rule. But when the towns of the province were reorganized according to the government decree of 18 June 1898, the Pensacola brothers encouraged the populace to disobey the local principales who controlled the municipal governments, and to refrain from paying the "personal contributions" required by the government. They began to form parties in the towns to oppose all orders from Malolos and were even successful in inducing some detachments of the revolutionary army to abandon their posts and form a rebel group. The Pensacola brothers harrassed "various wealthy and educated persons" of Botolan, Zambales, with the aim of forcing them to leave the town,

> their object being to secure their real property and distribute it among their followers, as according to their doctrine it was already time for the rich to be poor and for the poor to become rich, endeavoring to make the people believe that the ignorant should direct the towns and the intelligent be subordinated to them; with these extravagant theories, they have succeeded in deceiving the masses and securing their adhesion.[11]

This report, coming from a government administrator, does not quite give us the outlook of the Pensacola brothers themselves. But it is clear how the outcome of the war against Spain was easily perceived by the masses of Zambales as an inversion of traditional relationships in society.

In the previous chapter, we pointed out the ideological kinship of the Katipunan and the Colorum of southern Luzon, and how in 1897 Sebastian Caneo led the latter against the Spaniards. But as the leadership of the revolution came to rest increasingly in ilustrado hands, resulting in government

---

10. *El Comercio*, 1 February 1900, p. 7 (BIA 2291–96, USNA). See also Cesar A. Majul, *Mabini and the Philippine Revolution* (Manila: National Commission, 1964), p. 37 and passim.

11. Wenceslao Viniegra to Aguinaldo, Iba, Zambales, 13 November 1898 (Taylor, *Philippine Insurrection*, vol. 3, p. 401). For a more detailed account, see Guerrero, "Luzon at War," pp. 170-175.

neglect of local problems, a change occurred in the Colorum's posture vis à vis the revolutionary center. In late 1898, Caneo's group, now calling itself the "Katipunan ni San Cristobal," was ordered suppressed by the Malolos government for having aims that were "almost diametrically antirevolutionary."[12] Branches of this katipunan were discovered in the provinces of Morong, Batangas, Laguna, and Tayabas. In the latter three provinces, the *Magbubundoc* (lit., "uncouth mountain dwellers"), as the Colorums were also called, had a following of over thirty thousand by September 1898. Manuel Arguelles, the provincial governor of Tayabas, in an urgent report to Aguinaldo bewailed that the "heretic" and "absurd" ideas of the Katipunan ni San Cristobal were encouraging the *gente proletaria* to abandon their fields, to the detriment of the landlords. Many servants were leaving the homes of their masters. In general, they were "a constant threat to public order" but it was fruitless, and dangerous, to pursue them because they were "prepared to die in defense of their cause."[13]

The ilustrado Arguelles also noted that this katipunan's leader, Sebastian Caneo, was a man of no education at all and "a great impostor." And yet by wandering around, preaching his message, he was able to undermine the traditional dominance of the principales and ilustrados. Arguelles himself offered an explanation for this: "Since the country today is passing through a critical period, it seems that the spread of this society is swift . . . and geometrically proportional."[14] What Arguelles meant was that the spread of the Katipunan ni San Cristobal directly followed upon the overall state of dislocation in the country in the wake of the war against Spain. This war was tantamount to a cataclysm leading to a total reordering of the universe. The Colorums were mobilized by Caneo to support it wholeheartedly, inspired by the promise of a perfect society in which the faithful of the earth would be united in a community of brotherhood and equality. The style of Bonifacio's Katipunan, its use of traditional imagery and its ethos of brotherhood, encouraged this fusion of popular "religious" aspirations and new, patriotic goals. Caneo's use of the Katipunan name in late 1898, at a time when the original secret society was proscribed by the government, suggests that the Katipunan ethos lived on and gave form to hopes that the revolution would still run its course.

Similar movements sprouted at about the same time all over Luzon. A little-known group calling itself "Cruz na Bituin" (Cross of Stars) and the Santa Iglesia, which will be described in a later chapter, flourished in the provinces of Pampanga, Bulacan, and Tarlac. Pangasinan and the southern Ilocano

---

12. Jose Elises to Aguinaldo, Antipolo, 3 November 1898 (Taylor, *Philippine Insurrection*, vol. 3, pp. 395–96).

13. Manuel Arguelles to Aguinaldo, Bacoor, 10 September 1898 (PIR-SD 242).

14. Ibid.

provinces saw the rapid growth of the Guardia de Honor.[15] Flooded with reports of "disturbances" in the countryside, President Aguinaldo, in February 1899, appealed to "those various katipunans" to unite with the country as a whole. Announcing that the Americans had come to succeed the Spaniards, that they intended to make the Filipinos worship the friars again, and that they would hand back to the latter the properties that belonged rightfully to the people, Aguinaldo assured the nation that the congress, government and army were one in loób with the people in the struggle. However, many brothers who, confused by certain teachings, refused to abolish their katipunans:

> Dito sa Mundo'i hindi natin maiaalis ang manga kahirapan, at yaon ay taga nang laman nitong lupang atin kinatahanan—datapua't kung sino man ang may agravio o kahirapan tinataglay, huag sanang bigla biglang hihualay sa Katipunan natin manga Filipinos, at gagaua nang ibang partido, dahil sa yo'i makasisira totoo sa atin linalakad na independencia.[16]
>
> In this world, there will always be hardship, and that is inflicted by the conditions of the land we live in—however, if anyone bears grievances or hardship, let him not suddenly turn away from the katipunan of us Filipinos and form another party, for that damages our budding independence.

What frustrated Aguinaldo was the difficulty of reconciling the interests of the peasantry and the nation, as he and other leaders saw it:

> Yuan na nang lahat ang mga partidos at iba pang nakakagulo sa ating pagkakaisa, at tayong lahat ay mag-isa na lamang nang pangalan—Filipinos—señal baga na isa lamang tayong nacion, isa lamang tayong loób, at isa lamang tayong Katipunan.[17]
>
> Let us leave behind all these parties and other things that cripple our unity, and let us all be one in name—Filipinos—a sign that we are one nation, one loób, one katipunan.

Aguinaldo gave the parties concerned ten days to present themselves and air their grievances. Otherwise, those caught would be imprisoned for two years or, particularly for members of the Santa Iglesia, Guardia de Honor, and Cruz na Bituin, death would be meted out.[18]

Another phenomenon that disturbed the Malolos government was the increasing frequency of labor strikes directed mainly at foreign-owned compa-

---

15. See Guerrero, "Luzon at War," for an exhaustive treatment of the Guardia de Honor.

16. "Manga Kapatid na Filipinos," Malolos, February 1899 (Draft in Aguinaldo's handwriting, PIR-SD 490.3).

17. Ibid.

18. Ibid.

nies based in American-occupied Manila. Again, this was unheard of in pre-Katipunan days and must be attributed to the desire of workers to realize certain possibilities which had opened up to them with independence. In late 1898, some laborers in Manila instigated a strike against a Chinese-owned tobacco factory. Then followed a strike of domestic servants and local artisans of Manila. Teamsters, tram and railway operators, shopkeepers and employees of private firms followed suit.[19] The strikes aimed at lowering or eliminating taxes as well as securing wage increases. They had, however, clearly also a political dimension. Among the most enthusiastic participants were members of the Katipunan being revived by Gen. Teodoro Sandiko in the occupied district. According to Taylor, the upper classes of Manila were already tacitly, if not openly, supporting the Americans at this time. Thus, Sandiko could only appeal to the "poor and ignorant." Many of those who rallied to the revived Katipunan or *sandatahan* (army) were Katipuneros of 1896–97, imprisoned by the Spaniards but released by the Americans who found the Manila jails overflowing with political prisoners. Assuring the Americans that he was merely forming athletic clubs, Sandiko disguised his organizational activities until the general strike occurred. When interviewed about it, he called the strike a good thing because "it tends to better the situation of the laborers—that is, the poor class."[20]

These events, however, perturbed the Malolos government. The revolutionary provincial governor of Manila, Ambrosio Flores, in a proclamation, exhorted the inhabitants of Manila to follow their habitual occupations, to disregard the nationality of their employers, and to seek redress for grievances through "legal and prudent methods." Continuing, he said:

> In no case should you resort to violence or cause disorders which only serve to belie your naturally pacific, docile and honorable character. . . . Furthermore, can you not understand . . . that at this time when the future of our country is being decided, when the whole civilized world has its eyes fixed upon us to see if we possess the requisite ability and culture for self-government and if we sufficiently guarantee order to protect foreign interests in our country; can you not see, I repeat, that at this precise moment the disturbances you cause by these strikes, your reasons not being known to the outside world, may give rise to false impressions concerning the depth of our national character?[21]

What we should especially note is the preoccupation with the outward form of the republic in order to merit recognition by the "whole civilized world." This

---

19. Ambrosio Flores, provincial governor, "To the Inhabitants of the Province of Manila," San Juan del Monte, 4 October 1898 (Taylor, *Philippine Insurrection*, vol. 3, p. 378).

20. Sandiko to Aguinaldo, October 1898 (PIR-SD 458.7, in Taylor, *Philippine Insurrection*, vol. 2, pp. 140–45).

21. Flores, "To the Inhabitants," p. 378.

is a particularly ilustrado conception which rests upon a disjunction between internal states and outward forms. To ilustrados like Flores, unity seems to rest not upon the release of energy and potential through mass mobilization but in the preservation of order—"to protect foreign interests"—within the republic, which in turn is based upon mass acquiescence to the vertical relationships of pre-Katipunan days. In order to sustain this argument, Flores takes refuge in a definition of the Filipino character as "naturally pacific, docile and honorable," and ultimately blames the strikes on "foreign influences" and on enemies trying to "disparage the virile and powerful Philippine race."[22] For decades, Spanish friars and officials had said the same thing of the "docile" natives who gave trouble. But the natives may have found this understandable, if not predictable. In their beloved *pasyon*, did not the pharisees accuse the "foreigner" *(iba ang tinubuan)* Jesus of bringing disorder to once-peaceful Judea (118:7)?

Aguinaldo himself echoes Flores in a proclamation issued in the midst of a railroad strike in Pangasinan in September 1898. The laborers did not report for duty in order to pressure the foreign-owned company to increase wages. Aguinaldo's attitude toward them is clear even from the first sentence of the proclamation in which he says he finds it worthwhile to address the strikers because the workers, having a "submissive disposition," will listen to him. Later he insists that the idea to strike cannot have come from the natives themselves and must have been "advised by our enemy in order that the foreigners may have occasion to criticize us." But Aguinaldo also points out that the strikers' attitude "shows our union which is the fountain and strength of our present struggle against the Spaniards." Somehow this hesitance to either condemn or praise reflects Aguinaldo's intermediate position between masses and ilustrados, and partly explains why he could hold the republic together for a time in spite of its leaders' essentially conservative outlook. Eventually, Aguinaldo tells the strikers that their action is mistaken, and explains why:

> Our union does not lie in what you have done—refusing to go to work with the railroad company. There should be a union in hailing the sacred liberty of our native land and in defending the same from being again taken from us by the Spaniards or by any other foreign nation. Our union should not consist in small things, as what you have done, i.e., refusing to go to work, which discredits you and all of us in the eyes of other nations who are now observing us.[23]

22. Ibid., p. 379.

23. "Proclamation" (printed in Tagalog), Malolos, 23 September 1898 (Taylor, *Philippine Insurrection*, vol. 3, p. 360).

Again we find a preoccupation with the external appearance of [illegible], which leads Aguinaldo to define "union," first in terms of comn[illegible] cence to an abstract notion of "sacred liberty of our native land, [illegible] in terms of the Filipino nation's identity vis à vis foreign nations. The st[illegible] concrete experience of unity is dismissed as irrelevant.

The ilustrados, confronted by the awesome specter of American armed might, soon proved themselves incapable of maintaining their commitment even to republican independence when American overtures for collaboration were made. By 1899, serious splits had developed in the government between pro- and anticapitulationist factions. Somehow, the superficial and indecisive leadership, combined with personal rivalries for power, was reflected in increasing disunity among factions of the army and flagging morale on the part of the common soldiers. The "mood" of the time is expressed in a poem about a common soldier's sorrow at leaving home ("which is like the fondest paradise") in response to orders to march to the frontlines:

> Sa saliuang palad ano'i ng dumating
> sa lilim ng touang nilalasap namin
> arao ng juivis ng aming tangapin
> ang otos na halos sa buhay quiquitil.
>
> > When the stroke of misfortune arrived
> > we were secretly enjoying our happy life
> > it was Thursday when we received
> > the orders that almost choked us.
>
> Na ang pagcasabi otos na mahigpit
> nayong Sanjamayor ay lisaning pilit
> huag maliliban at agad omalis
> itong aquing otos ay ganaping pilit.
>
> > The strict orders said:
> > you must leave barrio Sanjamayor
> > do not delay, march immediately
> > force yourselves to obey this order.
>
> Nang aming matantot cusang maalaman
> nayong Sanjamayor cusang malilisan
> nagulo ang isip puso't alinlangan
> sa biglang paglasap ng capighatian. (3-5)[24]
>
> > As soon as we fully understood
> > that we had to leave Sanjamayor
> > our minds were in turmoil, our hearts in doubt
> > at this sudden taste of anguish.

---

24. "Awit," by a certain "Gaspar" (manuscript, PIR-SD, Box I-19, PNL). Sanjamayor is a barrio of San Francisco de Malabon, Cavite, one of the strongholds of the revolution of 1896.

Reluctantly, the author and his friends carry out the orders. Throughout the forty-eight stanzas of the poem, there is no reference to the standard Katipunan themes of "love," "brotherhood," or "defense of Mother Country." Instead we find a personal account of loneliness, of hardships caused by the harsh environment and American "guerillas," of boredom and the desire to return to the heavenly barrio. In stanza 17, there is even mention of some companions who, unable to endure it all, have gone home. The author understands that suffering is a progressive dying to the world, death being the avenue for reward (in heaven?), but he is not sure of his commitment to the hardship of the struggle. His cynicism and vacillation betray the absence of a social meaning for the event in which he participates:

Ang iba pang dusa'y dicona sabihin
at ualarin yatang titingin sa amin
sa aua ng Langit ito'i natiis din
cahit anong hirap ay nabata namin.

> The other sorrows I won't bother to mention
> for no one is likely to render a compassionate glance
> we endured it all through heaven's mercy
> patiently suffered through all hardships.

Ang buhay nga namin sa mundo'i ualana
catimbang ng hirap dinadaladala
ngonit ang panahon capagdumating na
ang bihis sa dusa ay ating lahat na.

> Our life in this world fades away
> in proportion to the hardship we bear
> but when the fateful day arrives
> the reward for suffering will be ours.

Marahil pay cami ang siang mainis
yoracan ng paa ang pagmamasaquit
at aapuhapin guinhauang sumapit
at sa lalong longcut cami'y ibubulid.

> But perhaps we might become disgusted
> trample underfoot, with disdain, our sacrifices
> and blindly grope for a life of comfort
> and fall into even greater sorrow.

Recovering the Past

It is during the same period (ca. 1899) that we begin to find essays and poems that suggest a groping for the social meaning of the revolution. With the breakdown of spirit and morale during the latter part of the republican period, individuals concerned about the turn of events interpreted their past, present, and future in terms of the experience of 1896. The narration of the Katipunan revolt assumed the form of epics like the pasyon, restored a dimension of meaning to the troubled present and pointed to the "way" that ought to be taken.

In September 1899, a small and poorly printed tabloid entitled *Ang Bayang Kahapishapis* (The Deeply Grieving Country) appeared in the town of San Francisco de Malabon, where Bonifacio and the Magdiwang wing of the Katipunan had had their headquarters.[25] It was edited by Diego Mojica, a poet and former president of the Katipunan in San Francisco de Malabon. In the first issue, Mojica states that he has started the publication to announce humbly to his *kapatid* (brothers) certain matters and truths related to the "straight and holy path" (*Santong Matuid*), so that they will discover the "delightful things" that come with the right way of life prescribed in the Holy Scriptures (*santong casulatan*). When the lives of the kapatid are ordered and oriented in this manner, they will obtain freedom and peace; in their souls will shine "that pure beacon of light and brilliance" (*yaong dalisay na ilao ng puspos cariquitan at caliuanagan*) rivalling the stars in the sky.

Although Diego Mojica seems to have been a devout person, having written several pieces of religious poetry including the *Pasiong Bagong Katha* (New Pasyon Composition), his concern in the above passages was not merely for the devout and moral life in itself.[26] His newspaper was conceived with the growing sad state of the country in mind. In another article in the same issue, Mojica writes about the light (*ilaw*) of Mother Filipinas which is flickering under the onslaught of the Americans. But, he continues, heaven is bound to help the Filipinos, and he ends with the saying: "King Nabucadanosor likened himself to a beast, but humility and lowliness saved the good Moses" *(tumulad sa hayop ang Haring Nabucadanosor, ngunit ang capacumbabaan ang nagligtas sa mabait na Moses)*. Reflected in this saying is the connection between struggle and the state of one's loób. It is not implied that the individual must simply be passive and seek refuge from the turmoil of the world by turning inward. Nor does it mean that the masses must, in their lowliness, follow their leaders blindly. Heaven will help the Filipinos if they pattern their lives after the lowly but powerful and victorious Christ. Each inner transformation and perhaps death for the country will hasten the coming of kalayaan. The light of Mother Filipinas is flickering because men of the republic have turned away

25. This tabloid seems to have been connected with Sandiko's revival of the Katipunan. Only two issues (nos. 1 and 2) have been found and are in Box 7, PIR, PNL.

26. His religious poetry include the following titles: "Ang Anghel at ang Demonio sa Bawa't Isang Tao" RENFIL 1 (28 January 1911): 34; "Gelona Católica," RENFIL 1 (28 April 1911): 34; (7 May 1911): 33; and "Pasyong Bagong Katha," RENFIL 1 (21 March 1911): 33. These were all composed much earlier than their publication dates.

from the experience of the "straight and holy path;" the resulting state of their loób is manifested in external events.

The same ideas are developed in Mojica's view of the past. He devotes the whole front page of the newspaper's second issue to an article entitled "Ang Catapusang Arao ng Agosto 1896" (The Last Day of August 1896), which treats of the beginning of the war against Spain in Cavite, in which he participated. Mojica does not really relate what happened, or what he did; what he does is try to recapture the meaning of 1896. To perceive this meaning in his work is to regain a sense of the "straight and holy path":

> A las once ng umaga ng arao ng lunes catapusang arao ng Agosto ng 1896 ng simulan sa bayang S. Francisco Malabon ang cahambal hambal at caapi aping panghihimacsic o revolucion at somonod naman ang lahat ng bayang sacop ng Hocomang Cavite, inaring langit ng mga matatapang at bayaning loob ang calunos-lunos natangis ng bayan, luha, buntong hininga at camatayan, ipina-ngahas ang ilang baril na luma, sibat na bucaue at mga guloc sa Cuartel ng Guardia Civil at Hacienda ng mga Frayle napauang sagana sa mga sandata at iba pang cailangan ucol sa paquiquilamas, anopa't ang ngalit ng bayan ang lalong humigad na sagasain at pucsain ang mga caauay, ng mga arao at oras na yaon nahimlay sa libing ng limot ang caruagan at caalisagaan, bumubucal ang tapang sa libo libong puso, bait at cabayanihan, iisa ang loób at pagdaramdam palibhasa't isang lahi at mag cacayacap sa patong patong na dusa ng casahulan at caalipinan, hindi lumampas ang labing limang arao at tumahimic ang boong Hocomang Cavite nasupil ang mga cuartel at Hacienda pinangco ng caruagan ang mga caauay hinahong ipinagcaloob ang canilang mga sandata at iba pang mga casangcapan, marami ang napatay sa canila at nanga sugatan.
>
> It was eleven o'clock in the morning of Monday the last day of August 1896, when San Francisco de Malabon began the sad and oppressive war or revolution, and all the rest of the towns in the jurisdiction of Cavite followed suit; the most pathetic weeping, the tears, sighs and dying of the country were taken to heart by the brave and heroic of loób; several rusty muskets, spears, and bamboo sticks were dared pitted against the *cuartel* of the civil guard and the hacienda of the friars, which were well-armed and provisioned, in spite of which the fury of the country spread even more, overrunning and annihilating the enemy; during those days and those times, cowardice and indolence rested in the grave of the forgotten; in many thousands of hearts sprung forth bravery, goodness and heroism, loób and feelings were one, for they were one people, in each other's embrace they had suffered the grief of subjugation and enslavement; hardly five days had passed when the whole jurisdiction of Cavite quieted down, the cuartel and hacienda were overrun; the enemy, overcome by cowardice, peacefully surrendered their weapons and supplies, many among them were killed or wounded.

The whole event is told in a single sentence. Mojica did not see fit to break up the account into smaller segments because the lengthy sentence is itself an image of a complete process—the beginning, the spread, and end of a popular uprising. Rather than being pure narrative, the account tries to capture through language the experience of 1896. The event, he says at the outset, is "sad" and "oppressive." The original word for "sad" is *cahambalhambal*, which connotes a dismal or doleful atmosphere that "infects" people in it; it is often used to describe the mood in a funeral. The original Tagalog word translated as "oppressive" is *caaping-api*, which literally refers to a pitiful situation that evokes compassion. Both *cahambalhambal* and *caaping-api* denote the pasyon framework in which the event and its narration are situated.

Mojica states that the revolt took place when people "took to heart" the "pathetic weeping, tears, sighs and dying of the country." The word "pathetic" is, in the original Tagalog, *calunoslunos*, a word which evokes a sympathetic feeling of pity. Thus it not only "describes" the sad state of the country but, together with the words for "weeping, tears, sighs and dying," evokes the experience of pity in the reader. This is essential in view of Mojica's intention, in 1899, of reviving the spirit of 1896. The revolt of 1896 took place when men's loób carried *damay* and compassion.

Mojica uses the phrase *inaring langit*, which I have translated as "taken to heart," to describe the people's response to the country's suffering. But the literal translation of inaring langit is "to interpret as heaven-sent," and may also be translated as "to respond [to something] as a sign of heaven." The implication here is that the experience of pity for the suffering country also meant situating events in the context of divine time. This would explain the force that is suddenly released and which "overruns" and "annihilates" the enemy. The people can fight with "rusty muskets, spears and bamboo sticks" against a well-equipped enemy because they are acting out an event whose outcome is, in a way, part of a divine framework. The force or "fury" mentioned is, however, not heaven-sent but concomitant to men acting out the event. This involves a movement in the loób of each individual which releases the potentialities of "courage, goodness and heroism" while casting off "cowardice and indolence." In the common experience of suffering, compassion, struggle, and self-control is found the basis of unity, the "oneness of loób and feeling."

The whole first sentence is thus about the country's experience of her pasyon—a redemptive act, the completion of a divine plan, the painful death to a former state of being. That is another reason why the event is sad, even though the outcome, as we could expect, is rebirth, described in the next sentence of Mojica's account:

> Nabuhay ang panghihimacsic o revolucion ng taong 1872 na minulan sa loob ng Hocomang ding ito, nabuhay ang binhing pag cacaisa at masaquitan, nabuhay ang dati at mahitic na pagiirogan nabuhay at halos laganap na sa boong Catagalugan, parang mga buhay rin ang mga bayani at guinoong Burgos, Zamora, Gomez, Rizal, at iba pang may tapang at dalisay na pag daramdam, hinamac nila ang camatayan dahil sa pag ibig sa lupang tinubuan at sa di mabilang

> na cadugo na nabuburol sa buntong ng dusa at caruaguinan, ang canilang mga libingan iguinagalang at binubuisan ng *ay!* at luha hindi mapaparam sa ala-ala ng Catagalugan ang canilang pag panao sa mundo.
>
> The revolt of 1872 that was also started in this jurisdiction, came alive, the seed of unity and mutual concern came alive, that bountiful love of former days came alive and spread throughout Katagalugan; as if the heroes Burgos, Zamora, Gomez, Rizal and others with courage and pure feelings came alive; they had spurned death because of love for their native land and love for the countless brothers buried in the heap of suffering and oppression; their graves are revered and showered with sighs and tears, remembrances by their brothers of their departure from this world.

Then Mojica condemns Spain and the friars who caused the people's suffering and oppression:

> O hangal na Ina! Sino ca ngayon?. . . . Ay sa aba mo! Hulugan mo ang iyong mapait na dili at pag sisisi. Simula sa balintatao ng iyong calilohan ay gunitain mo ang cahina hinayang na Filipinas na iyong ipinaganyaya. Uala cang dapat pang higantihan cundi ang mga Frayleng lumapastangan sa iyong Gobierno at nangagpapangap na sila'i cahalili at catoto ni Jesus. Si Jesus baga'i may mga pabuisan . . . may bodega ng pilac, nagpapatay ng tauo, nag patapon, o destierro at iba pang parca pumangit na bagay? Uala si Jesus nito, cundi pauang santong capacumbabaan, sa crus na cahirapan sa lahat ng bagay ang naguing buhay, Cordero, at Hari sa pagibig at panghihinayang sa lahat ng quinapal, siya ang nag pacamatay, ng tayo'i mabuhay na lahat; datapua ang Frayle, ang ibig ay macuyom ang sang daigdigan, sila na ang mag Hari at macapangyarihan lahat, sila ang mabuhay at tayo ang mamatay.
>
> Oh stupid Mother! What have you become now!. . . . How destitute you are! Let fall your bitter reflections and regrets. Through the eyes of your treachery, gaze at Filipinas whose misfortune you, now regretfully, caused; you can only seek vengeance from the friars who blasphemed your government and pretended that they were the soldiers and successors of Jesus. Did Jesus undertake tax collections . . . did he have storehouses of silver, did he have people killed or exiled and do other ugly things? Jesus did none of these; he was but holy lowliness, he bore the cross of hardship that all things may come alive, he was the lamb, a king in love and compassion for all of creation. He caused himself to die, so that all of us may live; the friars, however, wanted the world in their fist, they wanted to be king and exercise power over all, they wanted to live and us to die.

Mojica's explicit reference to the figure of Christ as a model to be followed answers the question of how leading a life according to the "straight and holy path" will make the light of Filipinas shine brightly once more. Mojica emphasizes the need for humility, love, compassion, the willingness to die so that others may live, because the events in his time showed a departure from the "straight and holy path" that the Katipunan of 1896 had taken. Perhaps Mojica never forgave the Aguinaldo group for purging him from the revolutionary ranks, aside from executing his friend Andres Bonifacio.[27] Now he could justifiably hint that the ilustrados who, in the heyday of the republic, had indulged themselves in the glory and status of office were vacillating in their commitment to the revolution. The president of the Filipino republic himself, in violation of the model that Mojica suggests, seemed to relish the power and glory of high office. Such behavior was what undoubtedly led Mabini, while in exile in Guam, to make the following comments:

> Mr. Aguinaldo believed that one can serve his country with honor and glory only from high office, and this is an error which is very dangerous to the common welfare; it is the principal cause of the civil wars which impoverish and exhaust many states, and [it] contributed greatly to the failure of the Revolution. Only he is truly a patriot who, whatever his post, high or low, tries to do the greatest possible good to his countrymen. . . . True honor can be discerned in the simple manifestations of an upright and honest soul, not in brilliant pomp and ornament which scarcely serve to mask the deformities of the body.[28]

Ricarte, in the original Tagalog version of his memoirs, concurs with Mabini, adding that the latter's admonitions "are fully deserved by a man who willingly deviated from purity of heart and the clarity of *katwiran*."[29]

Aside from the contradiction between ideal and actual modes of leadership, Mojica's essay implies a contrast between the irresistible power released by the Katipunan uprising of 1896 and the flickering light of Mother Filipinas in 1899. Mojica's narration of the "last day of August 1896" was, in both form and content, an attempt to recapture the experience of 1896 that was moving beyond the grasp of the present. If to us the attempt is not fully successful, it is because of the inherent limitations of the narrative form. Traditional Tagalog poetry and music are more effective forms for recapturing the experience of compassion, unity, revolutionary energy, and loss. Fortunately, there are a few examples of these which we can fruitfully analyze.

Poetry and Revolution

During the Filipino-American war, *awit* (metrical romances) about the war with Spain appear to have been circulated in rough, pamphlet form. One such awit, most likely written by Eulogio Julian de Tandiama (whom we know next

---

27. Artemio Ricarte, *Memoirs* (Manila: National Historical Commission, 1963) p. 52.

28. *The Philippine Revolution*, trans. Leon Ma. Guerrero (Manila: National Historical Commis-ion, 1969), p. 67.

29. *Himagsikan nang manga Pilipino Laban sa Kastila* (Yokohoma, 1927), p. 82.

to nothing about), was the *Casunod nang Buhay ng Ating manga Capatid* (Sequel to the Life Story of our Brothers).[30] In terms of the events it narrates in 122 stanzas, it appears to say nothing new. It deals with the oppressive acts of the friars, the rise of the Katipunan, the unsuccessful attempts of the Spanish government to stamp out the revolution in 1896 and 1897, the truce of January 1898, and the final defeat of Spain in mid-1898.

An almost identical awit appears, in a highly abbreviated form, in the June 1911 issue of *Renacimiento Filipino*.[31] Entitled *Ang Paghihimagsik Laban sa España* (The War against Spain), it is only fifty-two stanzas in length. Moreover, its first twenty-two stanzas are an altogether different composition, although we shall show later that its equivalent in the longer version has the same meaning. This version was transcribed by Carlos Ronquillo, Aguinaldo's personal secretary during the revolution and an eminent Tagalog man of letters in this century.[32] His comments about the awit are particularly interesting. He makes no mention of the existence of a published version, which is curious, since he was an avid collector of Tagalog literary marks. He says that the awit was copied down from a beggar who used to sing it regularly. In fact, he calls it a "beggar song" because "it is also the beggars who possess it and never forget it."[33] Ronquillo's statement is borne out by the existence of still another transcription of the awit dated as late at 1921. Jose Estrella, then a young student at the University of the Philippines, copied down what he calls a *Kantahing Pulube* (Beggar Song) from a "wandering minstrel who obtained his living by singing songs." Estrella says this of the "minstrel": "the one who wrote this or composed the verses . . . is excusable due to the fact that he is an illiterate man, who was born blind, as he told me. He can make rhyme readily."[34] The Estrella version of the awit is even shorter—twenty-six in all—but it preserves the unifying theme of the original.

Ronquillo notes that, at least in the version he copied down, there are many mistakes of fact and omission. Many prominent revolutionaries, like Candido Tirona, Mariano Trias, Miguel Malvar and others are not mentioned; on the other hand, Antonio Montenegro, who never led soldiers in the war is glorified among the heroes. Furthermore, there is no mention, says Ronquillo, of the

---

30. Tandiama's name does not appear in the two copies I have examined, but similarity of style suggests that this awit is a sequel to his earlier work *Ang Cahabaghabag na Buhay na Napagsapit nang ating manga Capatid* (The Pitiful Life-story of our Brothers), n.d.

31. RENFIL 1 (7 June 1911): 34; concluded in 1 (14 June 1911): 33. The full text appears in appendix 2.

32. Teodoro Agoncillo, *Revolt of the Masses* (Quezon City: University of the Philippines, 1956), p. 58. Ronquillo began a series in *Renacimiento Filipino* called "Mga Kantahing Bayan." He also wrote a series of articles on the passing of certain traditional Tagalog beliefs and practices. Ronquillo's valuable contribution to Tagalog literature and ethnography is evident from paging through the issues of RENFIL.

33. RENFIL 1 (7 June 1911): 34.

34. Jose Estrella, "Old Tagalog Songs" (1921) BCTE, vol. 10, no. 352. Full text appears in appendix 3.

revolutionary government of Naik, the "departmental government" in central Luzon, the "republican government" at Biak-na-Bato and other developments all of which took place within the time span of the awit.[35] The ilustrado view that the revolution evolved from Katipunan or secret society stage to a republican stage is simply ignored by the awit and, implicitly, in folk memories of the revolution. There indeed was an evolution in political organization but, as we shall see, that was not what the revolution meant to the masses.

As far as the "unmentioned" leaders are concerned, we might note that some of them are mentioned in the longer awit version, but the latter contains even more insignificant names, e.g., Leon Juanching, Isidoro Carmona, Juan Gutierrez. The personalities of these leaders and men are in fact irrelevant to the theme of the awit. Estrella comments that "the facts of the story are somewhat obscure. But the way the story progresses is somewhat convincing."[36] Ronquillo himself admits that the awit is about the "spirit" of the war rather than about personalities and events per se:

> Masasabing boong diwa ng naging dahil ng Panghihimagsik ay naibadha riyan. Iyang ang katas. Iyan ang sigaw ng bayang noo'y napilitang manghimagsik at humanap sa sariling lakas ng lunas na kailangan sa malubhang sakit na idinaraing.[37]
>
> It can be said that the whole spirit of what brought about the war has been traced [in the awit]. That is the essence [sap, *katas*]. That is the cry of the country that was forced to wage war and to find in its own strength the cure that was needed for the grave illness that made her moan in pain.

Ronquillo could make the statement because he was a participant in the revolution. But why is it that by 1910 or earlier, only beggars and the like remembered and sang the awit? We shall note in future chapters that the Katipunan ethos was, in fact, kept alive in this century among the so-called poor and ignorant people. The awit itself, from internal evidence in the longer version, seems to have been composed during the latter days of the republic and is a statement about the increasing loss of "Katipunan experience" since the war against Spain. A similarity exists between the awit and the writings of Diego Mojica we have looked into. They both speak about the experience of revolution, the force or energy that comes from the union of men. The three versions we have of the awit emphasize this energy and its overpowering effect on the Spaniards. Ultimately, personalities and events are subordinated to the images of union and energy that constitutes the "essence" of the awit. It must be noted that the awit's content analyzed below is in the form of regulated verse

35. RENFIL 1 (14 June 1911): 33.
36. Estrella, "Old Tagalog Songs."
37. RENFIL 1 (14 June 1911): 33.

recited or sung.[38] What Mojica tried to communicate through the careful use of prose would have been rendered more effectively by the singer of the awit.

The awit begins with the image of a relentless storm:

Sa dahas ng unos na di magpatantan
na bumabagabag sa nangangalacal
siyang di itiguil sa puyat at pagal
ng manga bihasa sa pagpapatayan.

> So violent and unrelenting is the storm
> that disrupts the activities of traders
> and rages on through the tireless efforts
> of those who are hardened to slaughter.

The storm is said to disrupt the whole of Filipinas, "from the good clerics down to the people who are trampled upon."[39] Its relation to death is immediately established: the image of the ceaseless slaughter of men (*pagpapatayan*) is juxtaposed with that of a storm that destroys and uproots. The storm, which in other stanzas finds its equivalent in the word *gulo* (chaos, turmoil), begins at a certain point in the past and rages unceasing up to the time in which victory over Spain is complete. The storm is the temporal framework of the awit, the context in which events take place. The theme is stated repeatedly in the course of the poem, and is recognized by the stress patterns of the first two lines of the awit:

Sa dahás ng unós na dí magpátantán
na bumábagábag sa nangángalácal

The phenomenon of disruption is said to have originated with the friars. Unlike other types of revolutionary literature, however, this awit does not portray the friars as the archetype of evil. It averts the direct flow of moral outburst by inserting complimentary adjectives in what is otherwise an enumeration of their misdeeds. In the stanzas describing the activities of Father Gil (the discoverer of the Katipunan), he is said to be "all right" (*maigui*). It is out of his "goodness" (*cabutihan*) that many are shot or exiled. He is awarded "honors" for his services. He is "famous" (*bantog*); by his "beautiful handling of things" his name is acclaimed even in Spain. The awit, of course, does not approve of Gil's acts, one of which was to open a campaign of terror against

---

38. Unfortunately we do not know the tune to which it was sung. For some notes on the adaptation of revolutionary poetry to existing well-known melodies (particularly the *kundiman*, or love song), see Antonio Molina, *Ang Kundiman ng Himagsikan* (Papers of the Philippine Institute of National Language, vol. 4, no. 22 [February 1940]).

39. For full text of the awit, see appendix 4. References are made to stanza numbers.

suspected members of the Katipunan. But the use of poetic irony, verging on the humorous, limits condemnation. Even the Spanish government which Gil served is merely described as "mute" (*pipi*). The awit, as we shall see, is not a condemnation of Spain's brutal acts, nor is it supposed to portray the triumph of good over evil.

Friar Gil's discovery of the Katipunan is not mentioned explicitly. But he is said to participate in the creation of chaos (3). His role in the awit is to illustrate that a condition of chaos has set upon the land. "As if at a certain appointed hour" (7), the "good" friars everywhere begin to persecute the "wealthy and educated" citizens of the towns. The simultaneity of the friars' activities everywhere contributes to the impression that the event is almost fated rather than the result of an insidious plot.

The descriptions in stanzas 8-12 build up an image of a multitude of innocent individuals from disparate towns being compressed into a limited space, i.e., the "prison":

> Na cun caya lamang parang lumuluag
> sa siquip ang madla na nasasa-hirap,
> cun binabaril na o caya ipatpat
> sa mga destierro ang cahabaghabag . . .
>
> > Only did relief come
> > from this crowded state
> > when they were killed
> > or exiled, these pitiful men . . .
>
> Bagamat, sa carcel nama,i, naiiuan
> na di nararamay sa pinarusahan,
> di maglipad buan bubugso na naman
> macapal na tauong taga ibang bayan.
>
> > Though the prison had a few left
> > of those who escaped punishment
> > hardly a month passed when it again overflowed
> > with masses of people from other towns.
>
> Ano pa,t, ang lagay carcel nang Bilibid
> na gripong mistula ang nacacaparis,
> maguing arao gabi ang balang umiguib
> hindi nagcuculang ang nasabing tubig.
>
> > Bilibid prison in fact could be
> > likened to a faucet
> > which though used day and night
> > was never without water.

The description of the "pitiful" principales serves as the introduction to the rise of the Katipunan which, in a sense, is prefigured by the coming together of individuals in prison; the image of the ceaseless flow of water is analogous to the common flow of blood (i.e., the blood compact) that symbolizes Katipunan unity. But the experience of the principales is still different in that they are forcibly compressed into one.

The transition to the episode of the Katipunan's "coming to being" is made by reiterating the image of the storm:

Ang bilis nang dusa na di magpatantan
nang tanang pinunong na sa bayan-bayan
doon sa pahirap ay lalong naglatang
ang init nang loob nitong CATIPUNAN. (14)

> The grief of all the principals in the towns
> was sweeping and unrelenting,
> in this mounting hardship the heat of the Katipunan's loób
> intensified, burst into flames.

The first two lines of the stanza recall the main theme introduced in stanza 1 by the identity of stress patterns and the presence of the word *magpatantán*. *Dusa* (grief) does not seem to be merely a private emotion but moves in a "rushing manner" and so has the quality of an uprooting force, the equivalent of *unos* (storm) in stanza 1. It is then implied that this "rushing" grief led to the rise of the Katipunan, expressed in terms of the "bursting into flames" of the "heat" of the Katipunan's loób. But why should the Katipunan, composed largely of nonprincipalia elements be ignited by the experience of the principales? The answer lies in the image of "grief" and "hardship" of the principales, which is made an element of the overall chaos. Grief and hardship, irrespective of the personalities or class that experienced them, evoke and release in society such emotive forces as damay and compassion. In this context, we recall Mabini's comment that, in spite of the fact that the martyrs Burgos, Gomez, and Zamora "had striven for the right of a class and not of the people in general," their execution brought about "deep pity and pain for the victims. This pain wrought up a miracle; it caused the Filipinos to think for the first time of themselves."[40] In Mabini's view, the experience of damay in 1872 involved all classes of society and signified a budding national consciousness. In stanza 14 of the awit, damay is a social experience, a Katipunan experience. Since damay is a manifestation of a whole and controlled loób, the Katipunan's loób radiates heat and flame, just as Christ and other individuals of exemplary loób radiate *liwanag*.

The first "gathering of men" (*tipon*, root word of *Katipunan*) takes place at Balintawak. The awit does not say that Bonifacio organized this group. Many men simply "come together" and then follow their leader, the "intelligent"

40. *The Philippine Revolution*, pp. 27–28.

(*matalino*) Bonifacio. The second leader mentioned, Valentin de la Cruz, together with his many companions are the first to bring chaos (*gumulo*) to Santa Mesa. The key word here is *gumulo*, whose stem, *gulo*, is often used to refer to battles or to the general situation in which the Katipunan mobilizes. An alternative word used is *pagpapatayan* (killing of each other), which we shall translate as "holocaust." In stanza 54 the battlefield is called *campong patayan* (field of death).

We mentioned previously that the image of the uprooting storm (unos) provides the temporal framework of the awit. Chaos (gulo) and holocaust (pagpapatayan) are like the storm in being manifestations of a fundamental disruption in the order of things. In order to understand how an entity such as the Katipunan can be conceived of as arising out of a disruption in the world order, we have to refer to the pasyon's particular use of the "storm" and "chaos" images.

In the pasyon, the word *gulo* first appears in reference to the turmoil among most inhabitants of Jerusalem upon hearing various rumors concerning the Messiah's birth. Later on Herod, the pharisees, and "leading men of the towns" regard Christ's teaching as the cause of gulo among the common people. Anas, for example, confronts Jesus:

ano bagang manga saysay	what kinds of things
ang iyong iniaaral	do you preach to the people
nacagugulo sa bayan? (107:4)	that brings such *gulo* among them?

Or as Pilate says before sentencing Christ:

Anila ay itong tauo	They say this man
palamara't ualang toto	is a traitor without friends
sa hari pa'i maglililo,	disloyal even to the king,
boong baya'y ginugulo	putting the whole land in *gulo*
ang ugali'i binabago. (136:5)	changing attitudes and customs.

Christ's presence among men brings about gulo because it changes attitudes toward the self and society. It may even be said that traditional relationships in society are disrupted; for example, the pharisees accuse Christ of causing men to disobey their king, Herod. This gulo, however, is still only a prelude to the gulo that comes about as soon as Christ has died on the cross. Suddenly there are "unceasing earthquakes" and other manifestations of chaos:

Ito na,i, ang siyang mula	This was the beginning
niyong caguluhang paua	of all that *gulo*
ang panaho,i, nalumbay nga	the seasons grieved
pagcamatay na mistula	over the true death
ng Panginoong May-gaua . . .	of the Lord Creator . . .
Ang dilang bagay sa mundo	All things in the world
sampung apat na elemento	including the four elements

para parang nangagulo	seemed to be in *gulo*,
at nangag-ibang totoo	being truly altered
at sa lagay nila,t, estado.	from their normal states.
(167:2,4)	

The pasyon explains at length that the chaos in the elements of the universe is really a sign that the material world, apart from man, has sorrow and pity for the dead Creator. This juxtaposition of chaos and compassion gives us another insight into the awit's similar juxtaposition of damay, storm/chaos, and the rise of the Katipunan. On the matter of the storm imagery, clearly the pasyon line *lindol ay di magpatantán* (the unceasing earthquake) parallels the awit's recurrent motif *unos na di magpatantán* (the unceasing storm). This is found in another line of the pasyon, *quidlat ay di magpatantán* (the unceasing lightning), in relation to the Apocalypse. Moreover, the resurrected Christ himself tells his mother: "The storm (*unos*) of suffering and pain / has ceased and passed" (181:8).

The final appearance of the storm/chaos theme is in the treatment of the Apocalypse. Gulo is a sign of the second coming of Christ. As the pasyon describes it, the earth and even the heavens will turn into gulo. The sun will darken, the sky turn bloodred. Stars will flicker and fall to the ground. Wild animals will swarm into the towns. Huge tidal waves will inundate the land, and terrible sounds like that of armies clashing will be heard.

Magugulong di cauasa	Unbearable *gulo*
ang mga tauo sa lupa	shall people on earth suffer
ang lahat ay mamumutla	they shall turn pale
di mabibigcas ang dila	their tongues paralyzed
at mangauaualang diua.	their senses lost.
Di na mangagcacatoto	No longer friends
bata't matanda sa mundo	young and old shall be
ano pa nga't gulong-gulo	for *gulo* shall reign
at capoua rin Cristiano	and fellow Christians too
mangagbabacang totoo.	shall fight each other truly.
(207:10–11)	

Other aspects of the gulo will be the appearance of traitors and anti-Christs. Those who oppose the anti-Christs will suffer martyrdom. But this gulo is also a sign of the coming of the Kingdom. Forty days will pass in which men will be given a chance to change their loób and share in the coming victory. Storm and chaos thus provide the context in which men come together in Christ.

Our discussion of the layers of meaning in the word *gulo* illustrates the relationship between the awit and the Indio's experience, and helps explain why beggars and the like continued to remember it. For through it they could hold on to what Ronquillo calls the "essence" of the revolution, which is not the armed revolt or the military battles per se, but rather the condition of chaos and uprootedness in which men come together in the Katipunan. It is the force—i.e. the flame and heat—of this apocalyptic event that actually confronts the superior military strength of the Spaniards. Thus when General Blanco, having learned about the "swift spread" of the Katipunan, sends the *guardia civil* to the front, the result is disastrous; the flame spreads even faster when the "good Spaniards" attempt to extinguish it:

Uala ring nangyari tanang inacala
nitong manga punong mabuting castila,
hangang linalabas lalong lumalala
yaong Catipunan na lumilipana. (18)

> In vain their efforts were
> thought these good Spanish chiefs
> suppression only intensified
> the Catipunan's rapid spread.

Stanza 19 is about the rise of the Katipunan in Cavite province. At this point, the two versions of the awit become identical. The notable difference in the first 22 stanzas comprising the Ronquillo variation is that the stirrings of revolt are conceptualized in terms of the breaking of an *utang na loób* relationship between the Filipinos and Mother Spain.

The awit begins with an acknowledgment of a debt of "education" to Spain accompanied by profuse thanks. In return for what is regarded as Spain's love for her "youngest child," the Filipinos have "shed blood" to defend their mother against her enemies, particularly the Moros. But in time the Filipinos are treated like animals, especially at the instigation of the friars. This violates the Katipunan definition of human relationship. A Katipunan document states that love between mother and child is what distinguishes man from beast, "catipunan" being but an extension of this primordial love.[41] In treating the natives like animals, says the awit, Spain even negates the possibility of love's existence. In stanza 8–16, the atrocities of the friars are vividly listed, but this description is made meaningful only as it reflects the breaking down of the bond between mother and daughter because there is no love:

Ito baga ina ang iyong pagkasi
na kami'y lunurin sa luhang marami,
sa maraming hampas ng mga prayle?
Diwa'y binigyan ka ng kuwaltang marami! (6)

> Is this, Mother, your kind of love
> that you left us to drown in a flood of tears
> from the friars' many blows?
> Perhaps with lots of money you were bribed!

41. "Ang Catipunan ng Tao" (manuscript; PIR, Box 9 PNL).

Is there a connection between this image and the "chaos" in the written version of the awit? In a sense, the breaking of an utang na loób relationship between Mother Spain and daughter Filipinas is equivalent to uprootedness and chaos. The Ronquillo version, in fact, makes this more specific:

At sumikat na nga sa Kasilanganan
ang araw ng puut ng ating si Rizal,
tatlong daang taong laging iningatan
sa dagat ng dusa at karalitaan.

> And in the East rose
> the sun of our Rizal's anger
> for three hundred years submerged
> in the sea of sorrow and suffering.

Mula nang isuhay kaming iyong anak
sa bagyong masasal ng dalita't hirap,
iisa ang puso nitong Pilipinas
na ikaw ay di na ina naming lahat.

> Ever since your children held fast
> in the raging storm of suffering and hardship
> Pilipinas was one of heart
> in no longer calling you "mother."

We have here a close copy of the opening stanzas of Andres Bonifacio's poem *Katapusang Hibik ng Pilipinas* (The Final Lament of Pilipinas). That a wandering beggar used to chant it in the streets of Cavite testifies to Bonifacio's influence among the "folk." But we must also explain why these particular passages stuck in the folk memory, and how the beggar's version differs from Bonifacio's. If Agoncillo's transcription is accurate, the second stanza of Bonifacio's poem begins with the lines *walang isinuhay kaming iyong anak/ sa bagyong masasal ng dalita't hirap,* which Agoncillo translates as "We, your children, had nothing to shore up/ against the terrible storm of suffering."[42] In the beggar's version, clearly the "sun of Rizal's anger" shores up the children during the storm of suffering. The "storm" is a metaphor for the revolution against Spain, while the "sun of anger" recalls the image of flame and heat that accompanies the Katipunan's spread. These images are juxtaposed with the last two lines: the heart of Pilipinas becomes one as the bond between her and Mother Spain is broken. Taken as a whole, the stanza situates the breaking of the utang na loób relationship within the context of an "intense storm," a time of utter disorder, during which a simultaneous horizontal "ordering" or

---

42. Teodoro A. Agoncillo, *Writings and Trials of Andres Bonifacio* (Manila: Bonifacio Centennial Commission, 1963) pp. 9, 75.

"coming together" takes place in the Katipunan. This is the "essence" of the war as the beggar captured it.

The stanzas that follow, in both versions, deal with the spread of the Katipunan in Cavite. The event is presented in the image of spreading turmoil by virtue of the prosody of the verse. In the enumeration of place names in stanzas 19–20 and elsewhere, the lines become interrupted more frequently by commas and by the stringing together of place names. The following is an example:

> Hocomang Cavite nama,i, nagsiquilos
> Noveleta,t, Cauit, Bincaya,t, Imus,
> Pasay at Palanyag, Las Piñas umayos
> Zapote at Silang at taga Bacood.
>
> > The province of Cavite began to stir
> > Noveleta, Cauit, Binakayan, Imus,
> > Pasay and Palanyag, Las Piñas all got organized
> > those, too, from Zapote, Silang and Bacood.

Although the tempo of recitation never changes, the breaking up of the lines into elements that follow each other in quick succession does give the effect of speed.

The coming together of men which takes place in a condition of chaos is itself a process of ordering. In stanzas 19 to 21, the various places are said to have "put themselves in order" (*umayos*) as they joined the holocaust or as they "moved into action" (*cumilos*) in the gulo. There cannot be unity without disruption. Even the "naughty" (*maldiqueño*), a probable reference to bandits and vagabonds, are caught up in the movement which centers on Imus, where the "illustrious" (*bunying*) Aguinaldo resides.

Then comes an enumeration of outstanding leaders who have "emerged" from the gulo:

> Na sa gulong yaon lumitao ang ngalan
> bayaning Jimenez taga Bagong-Bayan,
> saca si Licerio na tauong Montalban
> may sari-sarili silang manga caual.
>
> > In that *gulo*, there emerged the names
> > of patriot Jimenez from Bagong-Bayan
> > and Licero native of Montalban
> > each with his own soldiers.
>
> Saca si Julian sa tapang ay bantog
> tauong Mariquina na magandang loób.
> at yaong sargento na taga Sampaloc
> may manga caual din silang bucod-bucod.

> Also Juan renowned for valor
> native of Mariquina with a beautiful loób,
> and that sergeant from Sampaloc
> they too had their own soldiers.

Lumitao ang Luis saca si Eusebio
Antoniong bayaning bunying Montenegro
na ang tatlong itong ngalang sinabi co
may sari-sarili na manga vasallo.

> There appeared Luis and Eusebio
> the illustrious patriot Antonio Montenegro
> these three names I have mentioned
> had their own vassals.

Na sa gulong ito siyang pagcatanghal
nang taga Malibay na Pio del Pilar,
ito,i, pinuno rin na maraming caual
na natatalaga sa cacastilaan. (23–26)

> In this *gulo* became famous
> that Pio del Pilar, native of Malibay
> he was also a leader with many soldiers
> all poised against the Spaniards.

Many prominent patriots are omitted from this list, while some like "Jimenez" and "Luis" cannot be identified and are probably local Katipunan chiefs. Ironically, Julian [de la Cruz] and Antonio Montenegro are placed practically side by side. De la Cruz was a brigadier general appointed by the Biak-na-bato government, while Montenegro never led men in battle and was, in fact, a prime suspect in the cold-blooded murder of De la Cruz in November 1897.[43] The personalities mentioned are not significant in themselves. They are emptied of meaning in the awit. Being an extension of the previous enumeration of place names constitutes their "value" in the work. Each patriot is identified with a particular locality and a particular cluster of followers—a conventional picture of political leadership in the Philippines. But strung together in the awit, in the thematic context of chaos and spreading conflagration, these particularities merge into a whole, the Katipunan. Thus, the very form and recitation of the awit conveys the meaning of unity.

Soon thereafter, the storm motif is reiterated, with gulo being substituted for unos:

43. Juan Aguilar to the Director of War, Sampaloc, 25 October 1898 (Taylor, *Philippine Insurrection*, vol. 1, pp. 407-8).

Na ang gulong yaon na lumalagablab
matay mang pugnawin di maampat-ampat. (29)

> The gulo that was raging like wild fire
> could not be controlled, despite all efforts.

Reiterating the theme at this point signals the beginning of the narrative of armed confrontations between Katipuneros and Spaniards (including their native allies). Events are clearly situated in a context of gulo, of a disruptive momentum seemingly fed by suprahuman forces. In stanza 30, General Blanco in panic sends a letter to the Queen of Spain announcing merely that "in the present gulo a multitude of people cannot get along well." Viewed from the Spanish side, the phenomenon is pure disruption, the breaking of "traditional" ties, a movement of the Tagalogs away from the previous center—Spain. From Blanco's standpoint, people can't seem to get along with each other. But from the Katipunan's standpoint, the people "have organized themselves" (*nagsiayos*). Blanco, the "renowned general," and the "honorable Queen" are not objects of hatred or disdain in the awit. Rather, they play necessary roles in the unfolding of the themes of chaos, separation, unity, and power.

The Queen of Spain responds by sending a contingent of around fifty thousand men to reinforce Blanco's troops:

Isinabog nitong bantog na general
sa madlang hucuma,t, manga bayan-bayan,
nang sa Catipunan sila,i matanauan
di na tiniguilan ang pagpapatayan.

> These men were set loose by the famed general
> throughout the provinces and towns,
> when they were sighted by the Catipunan
> a never-ending holocaust took place.

Maguing arao gabi,i, ualang bigong quilos
manga cazadores parang sinasalot,
lalo na,t, ang tauong manga taga Imus
castilang pinatay ay catacot-tacot. (31–32)

> Day or night, no action ever failed
> a plague seemed to strike the Spanish troops
> the people of Imus, in particular,
> killed an awesome number of Spaniards.

Instead of voicing out triumph, the awit, referring to the number of Spaniards slaughtered by the people of Imus, finds the effects of the Katipunan's power frightening. The image of the plague devastating the *cazadores* (lit., "hunters") corresponds to the destructive aspect of the flame raging beyond the control of the human will.

News of the massacre is communicated to Blanco as the fact that "the gulo cannot be set in order" (33). He responds to the situation by ordering his troops to initiate a seige of Imus, the capital. In addition, the Spanish naval squadron in Manila Bay bombards the town. During several months of continuous bombardment, however, the cannon shells and bullets aimed at Imus "only bury themselves in the sand" (35). There does not seem to be a human explanation for this; a mysterious force seems to have guided the missiles to their harmless graves. The Spaniards neither wish to take Imus by deceit (*dayaing macupcup*) nor overrun the town's fortifications and trenches, because they are afraid (*natatacot*). In stanza 70, a tiny band of thirty-eight Katipuneros causes a hundred well-armed troops to flee by simply lighting firecrackers. The cazadores have not noticed that the Katipunan band has only six rifles; it is the sound of the firecrackers that portends disaster.

One of the charges filed against Bonifacio during the 1897 power struggle in Cavite was that he "was bribed by the friars in order to establish a Katipunan and launch the Filipinos in a war without arms against the well-armed Spanish government."[44] The first part of this accusation is, of course, preposterous, but the second part would have been the conclusion of more "sophisticated" leaders weighing the outcome of the war primarily in terms of military strengths and weaknesses. In fact, it has often been said that Bonifacio paled before Aguinaldo in military matters and would have completely bungled the war had not the latter stepped in. Fair enough; yet, what was the background of Bonifacio's thinking, obsessed as he was by the Katipunan idea? The awit provides an insight into a mode of thought of the time by not portraying the war as a contest of armed might. The phenomenon is not comprehensible in terms of the norms of battle accepted in other countries:

Ano,t, itong guerra ay pinagtatachan
nang ingles at frances, japon at aleman,
sa cañon at mauser ang inilalaban
nitong Catipunan ay itac na pañgal.

> This war, in fact, was viewed with astonishment
> by the English and French, Japanese and Germans,
> against cannon and mauser rifles
> this Katipunan pitted nothing but dull blades.

Lahat nang pinuno nitong cazadores
sa labanang yao,i, nagsisipagngitngit,

44. Agoncillo, *Revolt of the Masses*, p. 238. The complaints received by Aguinaldo regarding Bonifacio's behavior, says Agoncillo (ibid.), "were probably not true but nonetheless believed in by the majority." It should be added that the rumor campaign waged by the anti-Bonifacio principales was responsible for this accusation.

dahilan sa capal armas nilang gamit
ang catagalugan ay hindi magahis.
(36–37)

All the Spanish leaders
were furious in that battle
for in spite of their innumerable firearms
the Tagalog they could not overpower.

Clearly, the Katipunan strength is not in armed might but in the invincible power generated by the people's unity, a power symbolized by the rays of the sun or a triangle in Katipunan flags and seals.

Realizing that armed might along will not cause the Katipunan to budge, the Spaniards resort to deceit (*daya*), the particulars of which are not stated. They cannot win this way, however, because Emilio [Aguinaldo] has *magandang isip*, a phrase which literally means "a good (or beautiful) mind." In stanza 15, Bonifacio is said to have "intelligence." In stanza 47, the qualities that render Katipunan leaders immune from deceptive plots are *tapang* (valor) and *dunong* (knowledge). At the outset, the awit's conception of true knowledge must be distinguished from the knowledge acquired through formal education, which is associated with being ilustrado. In the language of the Katipunan, a distinction is made between the perception of *ningning* or "glitering," empty externals, and true knowledge that sees the reality of things because liwanag permeates the mind.[45] In other words, true knowledge is associated with a state of being or loób permeated by liwanag. This concept is fundamental in the pasyon: the pharisees and *pinunong bayan* disdainfully refer to Christ and his disciples as poor, humble, and uneducated, but there is not doubt as to who have "good minds." In chapter 2, we pointed out that in Apolinario de la Cruz's definition, a "good mind" is that which sees the relationship between "suffering" and the attainment of a "good union of men." "Knowing" implies a loób that maintains its equilibrium in the face of threats or pressures to abandon its commitment to a cause. Apolinario de la Cruz thus provides the explanation for the awit's conjoining of "valor" and "knowledge" as qualities that frustrate the enemy's deceptive plots.

In stanza 42, the Spaniards are described as being in an "oppressive" situation. General Blanco's "deep sadness" renders him practically ill. We have come to a point in the awit where the "enemy" is portrayed in practically the same terms as the principales who suffered under the friars. Blanco's sorrow is intended to evoke compassion, pity for the innocent, although he is the commanding general of the Spanish forces. But in a sense he is innocent.

---

45. Emilio Jacinto, "Liwanag at Dilim," 1896, in J.P. Santos, *Buhay at mga Sinulat ni Emilio Jacinto* (Manila, 1935), pp. 26-46.

The force of the Katipunan belongs to an order against which armed opposition from a foreign enemy is powerless. The foreigners can be pitied because they are not, and have never been, a real threat.

The real threat comes from within:

Na cun caya lamang na auas-auasan
dahil sa ilongong dito,i, nagsidatal,
at ang macabeong tauong salangapang
nangacong matibay sa bunying general. (43)

> [Blanco's] sadness was alleviated
> only by the timely arrival of Ilonggos
> and Macabebes, roguish people
> who made a firm pledge to the illustrious general.

For the first time in the awit, an enemy of the Katipunan is morally condemned. The "roguish" traitors promise to overrun Imus and capture Aguinaldo alive. Blanco even orders an iron cage built. But the plot fails:

Hindi rin naganap binanta sa loób
nitong manlililo na may asal hayop,
ang pinagnasaa,i, niligtas nang Dios
at itong nagnasa buhay ang natapos. (46)

> The threats from the loób
> of these traitors, beastly characters
> were nevertheless frustrated,
> the intended victim was saved by God
> and the plotters' lives cut short.

The Macabebes cannot be placed on the same plane as the cazadores or even friars. Moral condemnation and death are their due. For if power comes from the coming together of men in the Katipunan, traitors weaken this power by subverting the whole. The Macabebes, and not the Ilonggos, are singled out because the Kapampangans in later stanzas are considered participants in the Katipunan phenomenon. The punishment of death accorded the traitors is even more significant when contrasted with the outcome of events in the preceding episode. There, "the Spanish leaders, soldiers and friar-curates are not killed, but taken captive" (41). This outcome, says the awit, is what makes the battle "astonishing" (*catacataca*). But why should traitors die, if Spanish lives can be spared? The answer lies in stanza 47:

Caya ang sinoma,i, di dapat mangahas
na sa catapangan at dunong na ingat,
mahaba,t, maicsi chapin ma,t, chinelas
ay may manga paang naguiguing casucat.

> That is why no one should dare wreak violence
> on those who have valor and knowledge;
> long or short, clogs or slippers
> each has a pair of feet that fits.

The last two lines of the stanza is a common folk saying that warns against envy. The acts of the Macabebes are motivated by envy; that of the cazadores by their loyalty to Spain. The moral condemnation of the Macabebes is reminiscent of the pasyon where envy, always associated with a distorted loób, is the reason given for the behavior of the serpent, Herod, the pharisees and Judas. Envy, which reflects the condition of the traitors' loób, is the very antithesis of damay and love. By undermining the very conditions of Katipunan, the traitors threaten to destroy the whole. Thus, stanza 48 contains this warning to those with evil hearts (*budhing masamang ugali*):

> ang camunting sira cundi laguiang tagpi
> pagcacara-anan nang malaquing guisi.

> if a small tear is not repaired
> a huge rent will run through.

Actually, this is not so much a warning to traitors as an admission of the fragility of that entity which has come into being.

The Ronquillo version of the awit ends right after the episode of the traitors and the sermon on envy. The final stanza simply reasserts the David-vs.-Goliath quality of the war: sticks and bladed weapons against mausers and cannon.

The main awit version continues after restating the central theme:

> Sa bilis nang bangis na di nagtitila
> cun magcatanauan ay nangagbabanga,
> sa arao at gabi tagalog castila
> patay ay nagcalat magcabicabila. (50)

> In the unabating gale of ferocity
> day and night when Tagalog and Spanish
> saw each other they collided
> dead were scattered on all sides.

In spite of many reinforcements arriving from Spain, the Tagalogs continue to be invincible because they have *tapang* (valor). The Queen of Spain is cast in grief. She finally sends to Pilipinas the very "prop" of Spain—General Polavieja. The Spanish general appears at the head of a formidable Spanish contingent, known for their "hardened bodies," expertise, courage, and daring. They are awaited in the "field of death" by Aguinaldo, who is also famous for tapang (53–54).

The awit thus states that both Polavieja's men and the Tagalogs have tapang. Is this taken to mean that they are on equal terms in the field of battle? The awit resolves this problem by calling upon the distinction between *ningning* and *liwanag*. In stanza 55, the awit explains the order of being to which the tapang of the cazadores belongs:

Cun ibabalita salamin nang lahat
na sa caningningan ualang bahid lamat,
baquit sa panahon cun ano,t, sumayad
ang linao sa labo na icababasag.

While this was heralded as the mirror of all
that glittered without stains or cracks,
why, then, when the time came
did the sparkle turn dull and the mirror break?

By associating the cazadores' tapang with the "glitter" of a shiny mirror that turns foggy and shatters under stress, the argument is translated into the distinction between ningning and liwanag. Ningning is an appealing exterior that hides impoverished being, which eventually disintegrates. The converse is implied for Aguinaldo's tapang: it belongs to the order of liwanag. His courage is a true reflection of his loób and is therefore real, just as liwanag is said to emanate from the very fullness of being.

The Polavieja offensive ends in tragedy for the Spaniards because of "fear." Polavieja is described as *matapang sa tacot*—courageous in fear: if he is such a hero, asks the awit, why doesn't he step down from his headquarters where he merely barks commands? Polavieja's distance from the "field of death" is given as the cause of the death of his field commander, Colonel Zabala. Upon learning this, Polavieja and Lachambre "left the scene in great fear with General Blanco following behind." Now this episode has little or no basis in actual events. Generals Lachambre and Polavieja were actually successful in their drive through southern Luzon, although their troops suffered immense casualties and Polavieja asked to be recalled home. However, as historians of the period have pointed out, the Spanish capture of several key towns by mid-1897 did not seriously affect the revolutionary ardor of the populace. The awit still interprets these events in terms of the idiom of chaos. In the first place, it is significant that the retreating Spanish generals are described as having *tacot* (fear) rather than being *duwag* (cowardly). The word *tacot* appears in several places in the awit, and consistently implies the type of fear one has when confronted with an incomprehensible, destructive phenomenon. The image of "the brave" Polavieja keeping at a distance and finally making a hasty retreat together with Lachambre and Blanco points not to cowardice but to their encounter with an irresistible force in the Katipunan that compels them to act in a strange manner.

The sequence of events after the retreat of the Spanish generals practically repeats the events following Blanco's earlier offensive. Having failed to destroy the Katipunan through direct assault, newly arrived Primo de Rivera alters the Spanish strategy:

Di mumunting tauo yaong nangaganyac
na manga bihasang masaquim sa pilac,
sa tanang castila sila ang nag-ulat
nagturo nang madlang mabubuting landas.

> Not a few among those accustomed
> to fill their pockets with silver were enticed back,
> these people told the Spaniards everything
> even pointing out all the good approaches.

Ang binucong yao,i, hindi rin sinapit
na pagcacanulo sa tanang capatid,
at di magagauang magbanta nang lihis
pagca,t, si Emilio,i, may magandang isip
(60–61)

> This attempt to betray and
> suppress the brotherhood failed,
> and they could not threaten wrongdoing
> for Emilio had a good mind.

The historical event corresponding to the above episode is possibly Governor-General Primo de Rivera's offer of amnesty to rebels from late April up to 17 May 1897. Among those responding to it were prominent officials of Aguinaldo's government—Minister of War Daniel Tirona, Interior Minister Jose del Rosario, and General Juan Cailles. The awit could also be referring to such nameless individuals as the townspeople of Santa Cruz de Malabon, Cavite, who quickly shifted their allegiance to Spain when the going got rough, and probably aided the Spaniards logistically as well. The awit shapes these events in terms of the pasyon, the silver-filled pockets and attempted betrayals conjuring up images of Judas.

The awit continues:

Umalis sa Imus tanang Catipunan
nagdaan sa madlang manga bayan-bayan,
pinarunan nila ay lalong mainam
sa Biac-na-bato doo,i, nagtumahan. (62)

> The whole Katipunan left Imus
> passing through a lot of towns,
> their destination was a better place
> Biak-na Bato where they settled down.

The actual reason for the transfer to Biak-na-bato was Primo de Rivera's spirited campaign against the Katipunan, forcing Aguinaldo to transfer his headquarters to different vague locations until he established himself in the secure foothills of southern Bulacan province. Mabini views the retreat from Cavite as a result of Bonifacio's execution, which had sapped the morale of the Magdiwang forces, aggravating the cleavage within the Katipunan until the Spaniards were able to harrass Aguinaldo effectively.[46] Why does the awit refuse to grapple with these events? This can only be explained by the fact that the awit's real concern is not the reconstruction of events but the articulation of meaning. The Katipunan is still seen as a whole, the events are shaped in order to highlight or bring into focus the meaningful aspects of this "whole." For example, in the stanzas that follow, the awit describes the cazadores' delight at having occupied Katipunan territory. But the point is continually emphasized that "[the Spaniards] came upon so much land / without encountering people." In stanza 64, several places are enumerated, but the reason these were taken, was that "the foe had gone." Stanza 66 describes the victory celebrations:

> Ang viva España,i, magcabi-cabila
> ualang tiguil naman tugtog nang campana,
> ibinabandilang nanalo sa digma
> Pananalong yao,i, calaban sa lupa.
>
> > Viva España was heard on all sides
> > amidst the endless ringing of church bells
> > they were proclaiming they won the war
> > a victory gained from battling the land.

By elaborating upon the emptiness of the Spanish victory a statement is made about the nature of the Katipunan. It is the union of men rather than expanse of territory that counts; the Spanish capture of some towns has made no dent in the "whole." There is also an implicit contrast between the boisterous and noisy Spanish celebrations, which signify "glitter," and the images of chaos and wild fire which are the manifestations of real victory.

After mentioning a few skirmishes that took place in the localities adjoining Manila, including Antonio Montenegro's incredible death in the battle of Barranca, the awit returns to the subject of the Katipunan in Biak-na-bato. Primo de Rivera is "in such great sorrow,"

> Ang cadahilana,i, di na masusucol
> tanang Catipunang nagca-ayon ayon,
> baga ma,t, maraming umang na patibong
> di na masisilo nila,t, macuculong. (75)

---

46. *The Philippine Revolution*, p. 48.

The reason being that the whole Katipunan
moving in unison could not be cornered,
all the traps and snares laid out
failed to catch it.

We are reminded, in this stanza, of Apolinario de la Cruz's organic conception of unity: the cofrades are the leaves of a single tree; they should also move "as one body" (*parang ysang catau-an*). Similarly the Katipunan is so unified that it moves like an agile and wily creature, evading all traps and snares.

Having again failed militarily to stamp out the Katipunan, the Spaniards resort to deceit, or daya, once more. Primo de Rivera gives the leaders and men of the Katipunan "passes to enter the towns" (76). His objective is to attract the Katipunan away from the *parang* (countryside) into towns largely controlled by the Spaniards and their principalia allies. Just as in the sequels to Blanco's and Polavieja's fruitless offensives, the awit probes into the nature of the Katipunan entity by narrating the Spanish efforts to subvert it from within. The "devious attempt" to attract Katipuneros by means of "passes" fails but Primo de Rivera has another plan: "to win over the leaders through words (*ang tanang pinuno,i, cunin sa salita*). He sends his nephew and the ilustrado Pedro Paterno, "who in reality was like an envoy" of Spain, to talk to Aguinaldo:

Na anim na buan ang hininging taning
na may manga sacsing natala sa papel,
sa pinag-usapang uicang magagaling
si guinoong Emilio naman ay umamin. (79)

A six-month truce was requested
in a treaty signed by witnesses,
to the fine language of the agreement
Don Emilio for his part acquiesced.

Immediately, the awit points to the motive of the Spaniards to deceive the Tagalogs by taking advantage of the respite to build trenches (80). It is implied that Aguinaldo has failed to see through the ruse. That is why, for the first time in the awit, the Katipunan itself is the party in grief. The image of wholeness breaks down as some leaders, obeying the terms of the truce, return home:

Nanga-alis dito ang pinunong iba
at ang nanga-iuan nalagac sa dusa,
tua nang castila,i, lubos na umasa
na ang Catipuna,i, malilicom nila. (81)

Some of the leaders left this place
and those who remained were cast in grief,
to the delight of the Spaniards who hoped
finally to dismantle the Katipunan.

The Katipunan's sadness is not really the consequence of Spanish action. It follows Aguinaldo's acceptance of the truce which can in turn be attributed to a weakness of loób that enabled it to be influenced by "fine language" (*uicang magagaling*). The overpowering role of language, especially at the hands of manipulators, continually crops up in documents related to popular politics. To understand folk perceptions of politics, it is useful to dig into the associations of common terms, like *wika-wika* (word play). In the pasyon, wika has the power to entice individuals to commit wrongdoing. Eve, for example, who is said to have a "weak mind" (*mahinang isip*), succumbs immediately upon hearing the serpent's wika (9:4). Later, she makes the excuse before God that the serpent "tricked" her, "seduced" her, and "played around with words" (*nag uica-uica*) (9:16). The pharisees use the same argument in condemning Jesus. Because the followers of Jesus are allegedly "people of weak loób" (115:13), they have succumbed to his "deceitful" teachings which are nothing but "a manipulation of language" (*gauang uica-uica*) (99:7). The point is that succumbing to wika-wika, implying failure to see the truth behind the appealing sounds of words, is a sign of a weak mind or a weak loób—a state of darkness. The awit, then, implicitly chides Aguinaldo in terms of a popular criterion of judgment. As if to stress the importance of this turn of events, Aguinaldo is no longer mentioned in the awit even though it continues for another forty-three stanzas.

Historically, Emilio Aguinaldo signed not merely a six-month truce but the so-called Pact of Biak-na-bato which called for the surrender of rebel arms in exchange for a huge sum of money to be divided among the leaders. The awit, however, cannot possibly speak in terms of a "pact" and reconciliation with Spain, from whom the separation of Pilipinas is total. After the disruption of the universe that bound Spain and Pilipinas together, the various disjointed elements within Pilipinas came together to form a new condition of wholeness, in a process that produced heat and energy. Mentioning Aguinaldo's signing of a pact with Spain would contradict the awit's basic conception. Actually, Aguinaldo himself broke the terms of the pact when he returned from exile in May 1898, six months after the pact's signing, to resume Katipunan activity. To take this into account, the awit asserts that a six-month truce (not pact) was negotiated. Thus when the gulo breaks out again, it is simply a continuation of the phenomenon of disruption after a temporary lull:

Hindi rin nangyari sa laba,i, madaig
ang tanang tagalog mahiguit sa ganid,
Primo de Rivera,i, nagbago nang isip
na ipinasamsam ang lahat nang pases.

> Even the truce did not help to subdue
> the Tagalog people more ferocious than beasts,
> Primo de Rivera changed his mind
> and had all the passes confiscated.

Sa palacad niya ay lalong nagdoop
yaong cagalitan nang tanang tagalog,
madlang bayan-bayan pilit na pinasoc
at ang cazadores canilang linusob.
(82–83)

At this turn of events, the anger of the Tagalogs
all the more burst into flames,
all the towns were forcibly entered
and the Spanish positions were stormed.

In the awit's view, the resurgence has nothing to do with Aguinaldo's return from Hongkong to direct the struggle. The reason why Aguinaldo is ignored has been hinted at already. But the awit intends not necessarily to downgrade the man. In terms of its logic, Aguinaldo breaks off from the whole when he succumbs to the "fine language" of the truce negotiators. The leader of the "revolution" is not necessarily a component of the "Katipunan" whose nature the awit articulates. It is Primo de Rivera's wrong move, not Aguinaldo's return, that "ignites" the Katipunan, and leads the awit to recall the prosodic theme:

Silacbo nang init mahiguit sa quidlat
yaong carahasang di maauat-auat (86)

Burst of heat more powerful than lightning
cannot be reduced by withdrawing fuel.

Primo de Rivera is "unable to stop the gloomy holocaust" (84). He parts from the scene and is replaced by General Agustin, who "likewise failed to turn the gulo into peace / or put a stop to the holocaust" (85). To add to the misery of the Spaniards, the Americans "burst forth in abundance" in Manila Bay (86):

Dito sa nangyari sa calunos-lunos
general Augustin ay naghihimutoc,
ang cadahilana,i, bagay sa tagalog
sa anyaya niya,i, ayao pahinuhod. (87)

In the wake of these pitiful events
General Augustin cried in sorrow
for the Tagalogs
would not respond to his appeal.

The "appeal" corresponds to Spain's actual attempt, as American warships prepared to meet the inferior Spanish Fleet in Manila Bay, to induce the Filipinos to fight on the side of "Mother Spain." The attempt failed as Aguinaldo, having arrived from Hongkong on an American warship, announced a resumption of the revolution. The awit chooses to focus upon the tears of General Agustin for they reflect Mother Spain's feelings of loss and perhaps regret for having caused her daughter's final departure. This type of scene is commonly found in Tagalog popular literature, and in daily life as well.

Since nothing further can be done, General Agustin orders the cazadores in the provinces to withdraw to the Manila district. Thus, they become "scattered" all over the place, occupying every street and alley. In stanzas 89–93, various localities in Manila and its environs are enumerated in a manner reminiscent of previous stanzas. But while the enumeration of Katipunan towns always takes place in the context of the image of a storm or conflagration that breaks boundaries, in the case of the cazadores it is an enumeration of points within a limited space. "Even the famous cemetery of Binundok" is occupied (92). The number of cazadores being crammed into Manila is termed "frightening" (91). But is this the terror that strikes one who is confronted with an uncontrollable force? As we shall see later, Manila is really empty of power and offers no resistance.

The awit continues:

Baybay nang Maynila magpahangang loob
pauang cazadores ang naguiguing tanod,
na tinadhanaan ang tanang tagalog
na di mangyayaring lumabas pumasoc.

> Manila's perimeter as well as interior
> teemed with cazadores standing guard
> all the Tagalogs were given warning
> that entering or leaving [the city] was forbidden.

Sa palacad nito,i, gumalao ang lahat,
Malabo,t, Obando bayang aliualas,
Pulo,t, Meycauayan, Marilao at Angat,
sa pagpapatayan tauo,i, nagagayac.
(94–95)

> Upon this turn of events, all started to move,
> Malabon and Obando, that spacious town,
> Pulo and Meycauayan, Marilao and Angat
> they readied themselves for the holocaust.

The enumeration of places and outstanding patriots that moved into action continues for the next twenty-four stanzas, surpassing in scale all previous enumerations. Starting from places just north of Manila, the storm or conflagration moves northeast across Bulacan to another Tagalog province, Nueva Ecija. It swings around, sweeps the towns of Pampanga (except Macabebe, where the "traitors" hail from), across more Bulacan towns, descends through Morong province east of Manila and hits Laguna province in southern Luzon. Laguna is swept completely: "the terrifying Katipunan spread even up the mountains" (105). The Katipunan touches another Tagalog province to the east—Tayabas. The unification of the towns of Batangas, south of Laguna completes the Katipunan sweep and the establishment of its new boundaries.

There is more to the awit than the listing down of those towns that joined the revolution or the glorification of heroes. More important, and consistent with what has been said so far, is what it says about the nature of "coming together" in the Katipunan. The latter part of the awit is an expression of a final burst of power. Katipunan activity had previously been limited to Manila, Cavite, and southern Bulacan. With the withdrawal of cazadores from the provinces, the final step in the process of total separation from Mother Spain, a final burst of energy takes place as the Katipunan breaks its previous boundaries.

The first line of stanza 104 states succinctly the nature of the events taking place: *sa gulong ito nang pagcacaisa* (in this gulo of becoming one). In the enumeration of places and people, it is repeatedly stated that they have prepared for the holocaust and are ready to die. Unification takes place as each element in the whole delineated by the path of the storm participates in the common struggle. Individual towns do not confront the enemy alone; they are first joined together with others and ultimately with the whole. For example, in stanza 98, one Tagalog and nine Pampangan towns are *nalancap*, or "joined together into a whole." Elements of two different ethnic groups are thus caught up in the speed of enumeration; the verse itself becomes a medium for "coming together." In stanza 101, four Bulacan towns are *nagcalaquip-laquip*, "enclosed together." As a result of their unification, which is said to take place "in the gulo," they are able to isolate the Macabebes and their Spanish allies who are described as "trapped" and "compressed in a corner." We recall that this is precisely what Primo de Rivera had tried and failed to do to the Katipunan because of the latter's swift, unified movements.

The awit also illustrates, for the last time, the powerful and terrifying force that is generated by unity:

Lahat nang hocoma,i, nagcasunod-sunod
sa pagpapatayan handa,t, naaayos,
lalo,t, cun ang bayan nila ang pinasoc
itong cazadores parang sinasalot. (117)

> All the provinces, one after the other
> were readied and ordered as they faced the holocaust,
> whenever the Spanish-held towns were entered
> the cazadores seemed to be hit by a plague.

In Batangas, the Katipunan that has "come to order" is said to be *catacot-tacot*, "most frightening." In Laguna, the Spanish commander Alberti, who is previously credited with a "serene loób" (106), breaks down before the Katipunan onrush:

Nang lumaganap na ang gulong nanabog
nitong CATIPUNAN sa tapang ay bantog,
coronel Alberti sa malaquing tacot
sumuco na siya sa tanang cahamoc. (111)

> At the height of the *gulo*
> sparked by the Catipunan famed for valor
> Colonel Alberti in great fear
> to all his opponents surrendered.

As the lengthy enumeration concludes, focus shifts to the cazadores concentrated in Manila. The final episode of the war against Spain sees the Spaniards being dealt the final blow by the Americans:

> Sa ualang magaua ang cacastilaaan
> sa americano nang paquiquilaban,
> nalis si Augusting hayag na general
> noui sa España,t, ang mando,i, iniuan

> The Spaniards having failed repeatedly
> to turn the tide of battle against the Americans,
> the famed General Augustin
> abandoned his command and returned to Spain

> General Jaudenes ang siyang nagdulot
> ng capangyarihan dahilan sa tacot,
> anoman ang gauin di macapamulos
> sa yaman at capal ng americanos.
> (120–21)

> General Jaúdenes, overcome by fear
> unleashed all his power,
> but whatever he did was useless
> against the wealth and numbers of the Americans.

The narration of the war ends here. Spain is pushed out of the scene not by her former children but by the Americans, whose power rests upon "wealth" and "numbers." Spain was a necessary presence in the process of "becoming one" as her children, the Filipinos, came into their own and defined their world in Katipunan terms. Now, Spain's departure points to a new situation for the Katipunan. In the final stanza, the awit abruptly reveals its standpoint in time—we find the "I" of the awit talking about the "youngest child" who is in hardship:

> Sucat hangang dito cayo na ang siyang
> lumingap sa bunsong na sa cahirapan,
> sila ang panganay bilang mag-aatang
> sa susunungin cong manga cahihiyan.
> (122)

> Enough to this point, now you be the ones
> to bring care and compassion to the youngest child in trouble;
> these are the first-born who will lift to my head
> the shame I will bear.

The published awit carries no date, but the statement "youngest child in trouble" indicates that the awit was first composed during the Filipino-American War. This war belongs to an order different from what the awit has narrated—no longer a separation from Mother Spain and a recovery of wholeness in the Katipunan, but a war in which the Katipunan's sacred ideals and moving spirit are threatened with extinction. On 7 August 1898, a month after the proclamation of the republic at Malolos, not long after the proclamation of independence at Kawit, President Aguinaldo declared that "there is no Katipunan today because the entire Philippines, our most dear mother country, is the true Katipunan in which all her sons are united and agreed in one desire and one wish, that is, to rescue the mother country which groans in terror."[47] Could the "nation," however, be the Katipunan if it was merely an abstract entity then led by ilustrados who had either repudiated or never experienced "katipunan" (supreme union)? Moreover, the Americans are said to have "wealth" which, to paraphrase the pasyon, has the power to "seduce" the weak of loób. The "I" of the awit seems to be situated at the point in time when the ilustrados were succumbing to the "fine language" of the Americans. This historical context is important in bringing out the significance of the final stanza and its relationship to the rest of the awit. Reflecting historical circumstances, a break with the "I" of the awit's past is signified by the sudden shift in tense (i.e., from past to present/future) and the distinction made between "youngest child" and "first born." The "youngest child" represents the revolutionaries then engaged in a difficult struggle against the Americans, the "first born" are the patriots who emerged during the war against Spain (usually referred to in Tagalog sources as the "first war"). In talking about her offspring, the "I" of the awit suggests that she is Mother Country (*Inang Bayan*) herself. The "I" must surely be a feminine person since, in the last line, she says she will carry her burden on her head (rather than shoulder), following the custom of native women.

The main point of the final stanza is that the condition of unity that the awit has described no longer exists in the present. In the first place, Mother Country appeals for "care and compassion" for her youngest child, implying that there is at present a lack or absence of these essential aspects of the Katipunan mode of struggle. Secondly, Mother Country talks about the "shame" (*kahihiyan*) that she will bear. Now *hiya*, the stem of kahihiyan, is a category of experience which among several things, denotes the individual's sensitivity to his mode of relating to others. A person without hiya is also one whose loób is hard as rock—a common Tagalog saying—and therefore has no damay or caring. A situation is *kahiya-hiya* (shameful) when an individual fails to respond to or

47. "To the Katipunan," Cavite, 15 July 1898 (in Taylor, *Philippine Insurrection,* vol. 3, p. 161).

deliberately ignores the "other" who shows him love, caring, or simply hospitality. A few passages from the pasyon episode of Peter's denial of Jesus illustrates this idea:

Tinitigan na si Pedro nitong maamong Maestro cahiya-hiya totoo, sintang hindi mamagcano at hinayang sa catoto.	This gentle teacher fixed his gaze on Peter a truly shameful situation, he had such immeasurable love and regret for his close friend.
Para nang uinica niya niyong pagtitig nang mata ?ay aba Pedro ay aba, di mo aco naquiquilala ay naquiquilala quita? (104:5–6)	As if he was saying by the look of his eyes, Alas, Peter, alas why do you not recognize me when I recognize you fully?

The appearance in the awit of the plural of *kahihiyan*, meaning "shameful things or events," implies a preoccupation with the social rather than the purely political and military dimensions of the Filipino-American War. To be specific, the awit calls the attention of the audience to "shameful events" which can only mean certain people's acting with disregard for the social whole represented by Mother Country. Bonifacio once said that all he needed in the Katipunan were people with love for Mother Country and hiya, for "only a person with such virtues can devote his whole life and love so that Mother Country may be given secure foundation."[48] Hiya, therefore, is one of the conditions of katipunan or unity; the final episode of the awit reveals that this has weakened or ceased to exist.

The awit ends in a spirit of hope. Just as, in the literature of the 1896 Katipunan, the "Lost Eden" of precolonial days will be regained when there is damay and the people interpret the struggle as a redemptive experience, so does Mother Country's gesture of bearing the kahihiyan on her head, which signifies her pasyon, herald a better future for her "youngest sons in trouble." Perhaps it is significant that her pasyon is initiated—i.e., the burden is raised to her head—by her "first-born." Since the latter represents the patriots of the "first war," it can be concluded that the awit's narration of their experiences is a way of pulling them back to the present so that the audience will understand why the struggle must go on. The awit itself, as it is recited or sung will evoke the initial conditions for the pasyon to begin.

From the analysis of a Katipunan awit, we have shown how the struggle fo independence was perceived in terms of the breaking of the relationship witl Mother Spain, the chaos that ensued, and the release of tremendous power anc

48. Kasandugo (pseud.), "Ang Katipunan" (manuscript, n.d. PNL), p. 1. Such words o Bonifacio, says Kasandugo, are "up to now remembered by veterans of the Katipunan."

energy from the masses, energy which was channeled by the Katipunan toward the reordering and unification of the masses under their true mother—Mother Filipinas. The awit reveals that during the later republican period and the war with the United States, the experience of unity through struggle was perceived, in some quarters, to be lost. The author of the awit attempted to relive it through the form and content of his work, so that anyone who heard the awit recited or sung could somehow experience that loss in himself through a juxtaposition of the poetic experience with the events of his time. Thus, there could be meaning and purpose in the continuing struggle.

During the republican period (1898–1900), katipunans continued to exist in some towns and rural areas; in most cases they simply pledged their allegiance to the republic. Generally, however, the ilustrados of the republic sensed in the continued existence of katipunans a potential threat to the atmosphere of stability and internal order that they wished to maintain. Only when the republican army had suffered defeat after defeat, and Aguinaldo himself was fleeing for his life in north-central Luzon, did the katipunans once more come to the forefront as the "approved" mode of organization for guerrilla warfare. According to Agoncillo, Aguinaldo himself, in his hideouts in the north, "came to realize that only the masses could be depended upon. It was a desperate hope, but even so he tried his best to repair the damage by recreating Bonifacio's Katipunan, the plebeian society which gave form and substance to the Filipino people's struggle for freedom and independence."[49] But Aguinaldo did not "recreate" the Katipunan in 1900; he merely acknowledged that the Katipunan mode more effectively articulated mass aspirations. Reorganizing the republican forces in 1901, Miguel Malvar, as we shall see, returned to basic Katipunan appeals in reviving the spirit of 1896. Upon his surrender in 1902, the armed struggle for independence was waged almost solely by the Katipunan and similar peasant societies.

In a Katipunan initiation document of 1900, the following statement from the leader's speech not only expresses what the Katipunan of 1896 meant to those who would continue the struggle in the twentieth century, but in the image of the beacon guiding a ship through stormy seas, recalls what Apolinario de la Cruz once said to the disoriented cofrades in 1841:

> It is indisputable that the Katipunan Society was the beacon which guided us to the shores of liberty after four centuries of navigation in the sea of slavery, and likewise was the light which illuminated the path traced out by Divine Providence, along which Filipinas, our dear country, took such gigantic steps placing her sons on the road to glory, and bringing with it that nectar of independence which we so ardently desire.[50]

---

49. Teodoro A. Agoncillo, *Malolos, the Crisis of the Republic* (Quezon City: University of the Philippines, 1960), pp. 668–69.

50. Katipunan initiation document (in translation) January 1900 (PIR-SD55.7); a portion of this document is in Taylor, *Philippine Insurrection,* vol. 1, pp. 219–20.

Leaders of the New Katipunan shortly before surrender: *from left seated* — Julian Montalan, Francisco Carreon, Macario Sakay, Leon Villafuerte; *standing* — Benito Natividad and Lucio de Vega

CHAPTER 5

The Path to Kalayaan, 1901-1910

Despite the valiant resistance of the revolutionary army in central Luzon, the defenses of the republic crumbled in the face of the superior strength of the United States Army. It was not only military weakness, however, that spelled the end of the republic. Within its *ilustrado* leadership, power struggles and opportunism caused deep demoralization that affected even the rank and file. Guerilla warfare could not be sustained except, as we shall see later, by peasant societies like the Santa Iglesia, because most of the weary Filipino elite desperately wanted peace in order to consolidate their tottering fortunes and prestige. It was the ultimate expression of their narrow conception of what the revolution was all about when they justified the new colonial order on the ground that America offered them everything they had demanded from Spain. As far as they were concerned, *kalayaan* could be attained without further bloodshed. But not everyone, particularly from the class of *pobres y ignorantes,* subscribed to this view of the path to kalayaan.

On 23 May 1901, Aguinaldo, already isolated in the mountains of Isabela, was captured by deceit and, a week later, took the oath of allegiance to the United States. On 19 April, a proclamation was issued in his name that appealed to all Filipinos to accept American sovereignty. It was on this very day that Gen. Miguel Malvar wrote to Aguinaldo inquiring about the truth of newspaper and other reports of his capture, which were received "with incredulity" by his comrades in southern Luzon. But should such reports be true, declared Malvar, not even then would they cease to continue insisting on their old ideals. Even though he continued to look up to Aguinaldo for direction and inspiration, he frankly stated that the resistance in the south would not be abandoned. In fact, when Lt. Gen. Mariano Trias, supreme commander in southern Luzon and Aguinaldo's confidante, surrendered in early April, Malvar quickly took over to halt demoralization among the troops.

Malvar's parting statement, if somewhat apologetic, reveals his unflinching commitment: "I should regret to refuse for the first time, and you would have to pardon the first proof of insubordination or lack of discipline, should you by chance order me to surrender my arms."[1]

What encouraged Malvar to continue the fight? At least part of the reason is revealed in an exchange of letters with Trias who, on 13 April, wrote informing Malvar of his decision to lay down his arms, hoping that his subordinates would follow suit. In this letter, he argued that his change of attitude was due not to the suggestion of other persons, such as the Federalistas, but to his judgment of the true sentiments of the people. He considered the revolutionary goal simply out of reach because "the evil which has caused and still causes deep loss to our revolution is to be found within itself. We did not extirpate this in time, and it would be useless and ridiculous to attempt doing so now." This "evil" was lack of unity. Leaders were fighting among themselves; leading citizens and guerilla partisans could not work in harmony. The cry heard everywhere, said Trias, was not that of revolution but of "'enough blood,' because the atmosphere of the war is asphyxiating and has destroyed not a few interests of persons and property." It was necessary to submit to "the relentless force of opinion" that the Philippines was entering upon an "era of redemption" accompanied by beneficent reforms that were welcomed by all. Unlike under Spain, Filipinos now administered their own municipalities and provinces. Public opinion had been poisoned against America, so that much energy was wasted in opposing her.[2]

Malvar remained unmoved by Trias's arguments. He replied that in his zone of operations there was "unity and harmony of action" between citizens *(principales)* and soldiers. For, unlike perhaps in other regions, the struggle in Tayabas and Batangas did not involve "personalities," and few leaders were involved in republican politics. Before the war of resistance, the guerilla leaders "had been nothing but modest landholders, who had never thought of their future as connected with the powers and honors of leadership, but in labor." Malvar, in other words, suggested that in his region the majority of the elite were medium and small landowners whose strong personal ties with the masses made them effective leaders. But in the final analysis, the resistance should be continued because the rural masses themselves were committed to it. How could Trias judge the sentiments of the people, having consulted only with principales? Concluding, Malvar reminded his superior that "not only those within the towns constitute the people; the lowest laborers are included

1. Malvar to Aguinaldo, Headquarters, 19 April 1901 (original in Spanish; in John Taylor *Philippine Insurrection Against the United States* [Pasay City: Eugenio Lopez Foundation, 1973 pp. 333–34).

2. Trias to Malvar, Silang, 13 April 1901 (original in Spanish; in Taylor, *Philippine Insurrection* vol. 5, pp. 326–27).

and they are the ones who act with greater honesty of intentions and are more sincere in their aspirations."[3]

The southern Tagalog resistance to the United States was more than just an extension of the republic's struggle for survival, and Malvar was more than just Aguinaldo's last general to surrender. True, with Aguinaldo's fall Malvar inherited the president's mantle, and was in communication with other guerilla chiefs like Lucban, Diocno, and Fullon. But what he really led was a popular guerilla war in his home region, with local leaders at the head of his forces. Even with American soldiers holding the towns and other key points, guerilla warfare could be waged successfully, unlike in central Luzon, because the lines of supply and communication between town and countryside remained open. Only the creation and brutal enforcement of "zones of concentration" destroyed this harmony. Above all, Malvar recognized that the "lowest laborers" were "more sincere in their aspirations," and he effectively harnessed this phenomenon. In Malolos, Aguinaldo's preoccupation with the forms of nationhood had forced him to curtail the energies of striking laborers and restless peasants; in Malvar's case all these energies had to be released to save the country, even if it meant the rise to prominence of precisely those societies which Aguinaldo had tried to suppress.

In order to understand why the people rallied under Malvar let us examine the proclamation *Mga Capatid at Casamasama sa Paquiquibamoc* (To our Brothers and Comrades in the Struggle), which Malvar himself drafted on 12 April 1901.[4] Certain features of its language are reminiscent of Katipunan appeals, if not of Apolinario de la Cruz himself. In fact, it is Malvar speaking in the light of the masses' perceptions of the qualities that a meaningful, popular struggle should have.

Humility and lowliness are qualities of a popular leader—this Malvar knew. Thus, in his opening lines he presents an image of himself as a humble person, a mere "soldier of the land" who does not deserve to succeed the respected Trias. But he must answer to the God of the martyrs who had love for the country. Spain and America had shown no pity for weak Filipinas; they had deceived her. Thus, she poured all her strength in order to wash with her blood the debasement of her honor. All this must not go in vain. The people must join with him; together they will take the road to kalayaan:

---

3. Malvar to Trias, Headquarters, 19 April 1901 (original in Spanish; in Taylor, *Philippine Insurrection*, vol. 5, pp. 328–29).

4. PIR-SD 692.3 (PNL). It was published on 17 April 1901. An English translation of the Spanish version is in Taylor, *Philippine Insurrection*, vol. 5, pp. 334–36. Its later date (19 April) suggests that it was based on the Tagalog original of Malvar. A comparison of the Tagalog and Spanish/English versions reveals that the latter omits certain appeals that would have been meaningful only to a Tagalog-speaking audience.

> Natatantu co ang aquing di carapatan caya nga nararamdaman cong culang aco sa lacas sa pagtupad nitong mahirap na catunculan na minamatamis cong isalin sa iba, cungdi sa pag-asa sa tulong ninyong lahat, sapagca't cung uala ito, ay ang magagaua co ay hindi lalampas sa magagaua ng cahuli-hulihang sundalo. Dito sa mahirap na calagayan ay gagauin co ang inuugali ng isang magpapalimos na masqui may saquit ay lumalacad, hangang catapusan.
>
> I am aware of my unworthiness, that's why I feel that I lack the strength to assume this difficult post, which I would willingly hand over to others, if not for the help that I hope to receive from you all, because without it, I can accomplish no more than the lowliest soldier. In these difficult straits, I will take the attitude of a beggar who, in spite of illness, walks on until the end.

All the ingredients of participation are mentioned. One must have love, generosity and concern for the people's plight. The struggle is imaged as a common journey, like that of beggars or pilgrims, along the "straight path" of the country's calling (*sa macatuiran niyang nais).* Malvar claims to acknowledge the unwavering leadership of "Generalismo" Aguinaldo, but since the latter is separated from them, the task falls on him to save the country from "drowning in the overpowering sea of greed of the rich nations." The enemy is the proverbial demon of greed, selfishness, and cruelty.

Having spoken about the need to fight the United States, Malvar, echoing Bonifacio and Mabini, reminds the people that the revolution is also an internal, cleansing process:

> Pagpilitan natin na ang *revolucion* ay maparis sa isang salaan na maglinis ng ating canicaniyang catunculan at caugalian, upang ding hindi tayo masisi ng mga hahalili sa atin at ng huag tayong matala sa Historia na may dungis.
>
> Let us strive to make the *revolution* a kind of sieve that purifies each and everyone's personal conduct and calling, so that our successors will not blame us, and history will not record a single stain in us.

Then, without interruption, he hastens to assure the people that their efforts will receive just reward. Aware of the damage to the revolution caused by the Malolos government's neglect of Katipunan veterans and the peasantry, he explains that "having knowledge" does not necessitate "being ilustrado":

> Talicdan ang cabulaanang balita na ang hindi nag aral ay ihihiualay pagcatapos, sapagcat sinomang capatid sa parang na natutong nagpaualang bahala sa mga capanganiban ng buhay sa pagtatanggol sa Patria at sa mabute niyang caugalian ay siyang cuta ng capurihan ng mga babae, buhay, carangalan at pag-aari ng mga taong tahimic, maguing tagarito o taga ibang lupa at siya'i nacatipon at nacapagturo ng isang fuerza o compania na sinoman sa ibang cababayan ay ualang ma-isurot sa caniya, iyang taong iyan ay bucal na marunong.

> Banish the rumors that the uneducated will be weeded out afterwards, because any brother in the field who has learned to ignore personal dangers in defending the country; whose good conduct has proven itself in the respect of women and of the lives, honor and property of noncombatants, native or foreign; who has organized and trained a unit or company; and who cannot be disparaged in any way by his compatriots; such a man is a well-spring of knowledge.

The idea that there is knowledge *(dunong)* in a man of true valor and uprightness who takes on hardships for the good of the whole, harks back to Apolinario's explanation of the meaning of a "good mind." It is the folk wisdom of the barrio elder or sage that Malvar draws upon and puts in the context of the anti-American struggle.

Malvar's implicit criticism of the republic does not, however, mean that he repudiates it and all that it has stood for. He manages to rationalize the absence of harmony by pointing to different ways of arriving at the common goal of *ginhawa* for the country. The "illustrious men of education *(bunying marurunong),"* like Paterno, Mabini, and the members of the Hongkong Committee, as well as the pro-American Pardo de Tavera who favors a multiparty system—all these, according to Malvar have the good of the country at heart. However, their "illustriousness" does not make them superior to the common man in arms. What the common man should guard against, cautions Malvar, is the improper use of his strength; "blind revenge" should not be a motive for his killing Americans, who also have families who will weep at home. The common people can offer to the country just as much, if not more, as the ilustrados, but only if their energies are properly directed toward obtaining independence.

The final paragraph of Malvar's proclamation rallies the populace to participate in the *pasyon* of the country. An "unseen hand" has so far protected them from serious danger because of the people's devotion to the patriarch St. Joseph. It is but fitting, declares Malvar, that St. Joseph be the patron of the guerilla columns,

> at cahiman na uari na sa caniyang pagtatanquilic ay dumating tayo sa catapusan ng pacay, pagcaualat ng manga nacahahadlang sa guitna ng linalacaran. Huag ilingon ang mata sa licod, ititig sa ating hinaharap, at paliuanaguin ang ating pinatutunguhan at calalaguian, calaquip ang pag-asa, catapangan at catiagaan, mga paraluman na nacapagpapataas sa taong na lalagay sa pagtatanquilic ng isang bagay na susog sa catuiran.

> and may it happen that with his patronage we arrive at the end of our mission, tearing down the obstacles on the path we traverse. Do not look back, fix your gaze upon what lies ahead, and cast *liwanag* upon our present state and destination, with hope, courage and perseverance, source of inspiration to the man who keeps on the 'straight path.'

That Malvar's proclamation found resonance among the masses of Laguna, Batangas, and Tayabas provinces is amply demonstrated by the tenacity with which they resisted the superior forces of the United States. But this is not the place to go into details about the war. The relevant question here is whether Malvar's belief that the poor or laboring classes had the deepest sincerity in resisting the enemy is actually borne out by the written evidence.

In late 1901, Gen. Adna Chafee, speaking before a large conference in the town of Batangas, predicted great suffering in the "reconcentrated" areas or zones if the principales did not want the total establishment of peace. To this Jose Villanueva, a pharmacist and a former town mayor replied that "the end of the war depended, not upon the principales of the towns, who desired peace, but upon the limits of Malvar's incomprehensible stubborness. Furthermore, Malvar and his troops were not dependent upon the aid of the rich, as was believed, since what they procured in the barrios was enough for them."[5] Another prominent Batangueño, Florencio Caedo, testified in February 1902 that in October of the previous year he and other principales, wishing to judge the sentiments of the people, interviewed poor laborers and concluded that the latter "were looking forward to the coming of independence, just as the Jews awaited the Messiah, and that they were mistaken with respect to the intentions of the American government."[6] In the neighboring province of Laguna, the situation was much the same. In March 1901, Lt. Col. Pedro Caballes, guerilla commander of Laguna's eastern zone, proposed to Gen. Juan Cailles that the town of Pagsanjan be razed in order to punish its treacherous principales.

> Na ito po ay sa aquing pagcanilay ay ang boong sangbayanan ay hindi na halos comiquilala sa ating Gobierno, *tangi na po lamang ang mga mahihirap*. Dito poy ang namiminuno ng pagcampi sa sinabi cong ating mga caauay ay lahat ng mayayaman, babaet lalaque at humihicayat at nagpapahina ng loób sa ating nangag sisipagtangol sa lupang tinubuan.
>
> In my judgment, sir, practically the whole town, *save for its poorer inhabitants*, no longer recognizes our government. All of the rich people here, both men and women, are the strongest supporters of the enemy, and are responsible for seducing and weakening the *loób* of us defenders of our native land.[7]

We can conclude that although recruitment into Malvar's army may have taken place along patron-client lines or, to put it simply, may have been

---

5. "Declaracíon Político-Revolucionario," Batangas, 1902 (RG 395/E2380, USNA).

6. Caedo, Testimony given at Camp McGrath, Batangas, 14 February 1902 (RG 395/E4229, USNA).

7. Caballes to Cailles, March 1901 (PIR 712.2; my italics). Caballes accuses the principales, whose names are listed down, of not having *hiya,* of being unable to empathize *(maghinayang)* with those experiencing hardship, and of enticing *(hicayat)* soldiers with promises of silver coin

motivated by personal loyalties, it appears that the masses also had a vision of the future that they were fighting for. Cooptation of the principales was not enough to stamp out the resistance. Through the principales, the Americans tried to convince the masses that kalayaan could be attained in a peaceful way; this is the "seduction" that Caballes complains about. That is why Caedo, Villanueva, and other principales sent agents to cockpits and other public places in order to convince the townfolk of "the good and sincere intentions of America," that she would grant them the kalayaan that the people had no hope of obtaining through armed struggle.[8] But the evidence indicates that, increasingly, the web of personal allegiances dominated by the *principalia* class was breaking down. Large segments of the "poor and ignorant" classes continued to hope for the fruits of struggle, often seeking new leaders or new groups to attach themselves to.

The suggestion was made in previous chapters that the stance of peasant societies toward the revolutionary "center" is a commentary on the direction that the revolution was taking. Not surprisingly, Malvar's call to arms that emphasized the values of the original Katipunan and amply recognized the contribution of each guerilla, no matter how "poor and ignorant," was heeded by the Colorum. Indeed, as early as 1898, Governor Arguelles admitted that the "antirevolutionary" Colorum enjoyed Malvar's protection in return for being his "partisans."[9] We know that in 1899 the famed Maestro Sebastian Caneo had the authority to issue passes, in Malvar's name, announcing that the bearer could pass through the lines because he was a true guerilla.[10] By 1900, Caneo held the rank of major, controlled around sixty-five rifles, and took active part in skirmishes against the Americans in the vicinity of Dolores. He was promoted to lieutenant colonel in January 1901; the number of rifles he controlled rose to ninety-five.[11] An American officer reported, in November 1901, that "hundreds of natives" were making the pilgrimage to Mount San Cristobal. There could be found a large cave which was a "rendezvous of recruits for Malvar's forces and the place of worship of the adherents of a new sect or religion" led by one "Maestro Sebastian."[12]

The role of the Colorum in the resistance during the difficult years of 1901 and 1902 is certainly more than an interesting sidelight to the events of the revolution. Toward the end of 1901, when American pressure had forced most of the principales in the towns to abandon at least their open support for the

8. Caedo, Testimony (op.cit).

9. Arguelles to Aguinaldo, Bacoor, 10 September 1898 (original in Spanish; PIR-SD 242).

10. Pass dated 1 April 1899 (RG 395/35058, USNA).

11. Testimony of Sebastian Caneo, 30 April 1903 (RG 94/Enc 2 to AGO 421607 [Gardener Inquiry], USNA).

12. CO (Commanding Officer) Sto. Tomas to CO, San Pablo, 2 November 1901 (RG 395/E5101, USNA).

struggle, Colorum chapters continued to flourish, providing an organizational structure for continued mass support of the war. In a report to Gen. J. Franklin Bell dated 12 December, Capt. C.R. Howland claimed that the Colorum had branches in all the towns and barrios of Batangas. They sustained Malvar's resistance by furnishing him with manpower. "At any moment" about thirty thousand men could be mobilized among the Colorum in Batangas, Laguna, and Tayabas provinces.[13] They also helped Malvar financially, once, in an emergency, giving him the sizable amount of ₱3000.[14] A week after receiving Howland's report, General Bell telegraphed all station commanders in Batangas to suppress the Colorum. "Do all you can," he ordered, "to discover whether such an association is in your town and to ascertain its membership, especially who is 'pator.' Arrest all members and do whatever you can to break the association up."[15]

Laguna province had its share of Colorum activity. In an "Ynforme" of 10 September 1901, presented to the American commander of the town garrison, the principales of Pagsanjan denounced as "a peril to the peace and order of this town" the "extensive society" called Colorum or Nazareno (after Jesus of Nazareth) which flourished not only in Pagsanjan nor in the province, but in the whole archipelago. They saw as the principal troublemaker one Jose Zaide, "a man of no education," who allegedly had been a thief in his youth. Zaide had been jailed several times in Manila for conspiracy. After his third release, he made Pagsanjan, his hometown, a base for the propagation of the Colorum movement. Members of his Nazareno branch traversed all the towns and barrios about Pagsanjan, predicting a great upheaval in the wake of the war and encouraging peasants to join the brotherhood in preparation for it.[16]

When General Cailles, head of all the Laguna forces, surrendered to the Americans in July 1901, Caballes refused to go along with him. Reminiscen of Malvar's break with Trias, Caballes felt that Cailles had broken his oath to rescue Mother Country, and that the people in the countryside needed leadership to continue the resistance. The attitude of Caballes's fourth regi- ment (or column) is expressed in the following excerpt from a proclamation

> Huag dadamdamin ng aming mga cababayan ang aming guinaua na mga taga 4° Columna sapagcat ito ang landas ng matouid na pinanununtunan nitong-boong mundo sapagcat ito ang aming naguing pangaco ng una at sumpa namin sa ating maning-ning na arao na nacatatag sa bandila nitong Filipino caya dapat ganapin namin ang sumpang ito cahit aming icamatay.

---

13. "Notes in Reference to the Province of Batangas," Manila, 12 December 1901 (RG 39 E2635, USNA).

14. Jose Villanueva, "Declaracíon," Batangas, 1902 (RG 395/ E2380, USNA).

15. 19 December 1901 (RG 395/E4138, USNA).

16. "Ynforme del Pueblo de Pagsanhan contra el sociedad Colorum," 10 September 1901 (395/E5160, USNA).

Tinatangap ng aming Conciencia na mga taga 4° Columna ang mamatay sa gutom puyat at pagal cailan pa man at hindi magcacaroon ng casarinlan itong ating Ynangbayan.

Ano bagang pagcasarap sarap sa loób naming mga taga 4° Columna ang mamatay sa Campo huag lamang sumoco, caya hindi dapat pagtachan ng sinomang tagalog na umi-ibig sa ating lupain.

Our compatriots, do not be upset by what we members of the 4th Regiment have done, because this is the straight path that, in fact, guides the whole world, and because this was our original promise. We vowed, before the glittering sun of our Filipino flag, to do this, and so we ought to fulfill our oath till death.

In our conscience, we members of the 4th regiment accept even death from hunger, sleeplessness and fatigue, as long as our Mother Country has not gained her independence.

How sweet it would be in our *loób* to die in the field, never to surrender, and any Tagalog who loves our land ought not to wonder at this.[17]

No one believed more in oaths and the idea of dying for Mother Country than Andres Bonifacio; these were among the ideals that shaped the Katipunan. The language of the Fourth Regiment has an added significance in that it implicitly repudiates the behavior of Cailles who, with Trias, belonged to the group that plotted Bonifacio's downfall in 1897.

Soon, Cailles and Trias would be installed as civil governors of Laguna and Cavite provinces, respectively, while Caballes, whom Malvar promoted to full colonel and made chief of all the Laguna forces, would be hunted down as a "bandit."[18] According to the Pagsanjan principales, it was the Colorum Society that "seduced" Caballes into continuing the struggle. This is most likely an exaggeration. But there is no doubt that the Colorum rallied around Caballes and provided him with manpower and financial support. One fund-raising technique of the Pagsanjan Colorum was the use of two statues called "Mahal na Ama" (Holy Father) and "Mahal na Ina" (Holy Mother), stuffed with cotton pads to make them look authentic, inside which were ventriloquists directing listeners to participate in the war, at the very least through contributions of money and kind.[19]

Clearly, Malvar, Caballes, and other guerilla leaders of principalia background pursued the war against great odds because they could rely on the wholehearted support of the poorer classes. They knew that the peasantry had pinned their hopes for a better life on the attainment of kalayaan. Interpretations of what victory would bring undoubtedly differed among the various social classes and groups that participated in the war. The Colorum Society, for

17. August 1901 (PIR-SD 752.55, PNL).

18. Around February 1902, Cailles was authorized to organize a force of volunteers from Laguna to track down Caballes (Bell to Post CO's, Laguna and Tayabas, 2 March 1902 [RG 395/3287, USNA]).

19. "Ynforme del Pueblo," 10 September 1901 (RG 395/E5160, USNA).

example, was only one of the organizations through which peasants hoped to enjoy the fruits of kalayaan. But Malvar and other patriotic principales did not hesitate to tap this popular groundswell. Nowhere in their correspondence do we find the fear of anarchy and disorder that some officials of the republic voiced in their condemnation of "fanatical" peasant societies. Malvar's formula was simple—to channel the energy of the masses toward defending Mother Country against the Americans, by stressing the Katipunan values of personal commitment to a life-and-death struggle in which each participant, especially the often-neglected peasant fighter, was assured of moral and material fulfillment. When Malvar surrendered on 16 April 1902, he did so in order to save his region and its people from total destruction. The principales in the towns either switched sides or were neutralized when General Bell's "reconcentration" and "search and destroy" policies completely disrupted economic life and freedom of movement. Famine, caused by the destruction of food supplies and the deaths of work animals from disease, and a major cholera epidemic that started around March, took a much greater toll of lives than actual warfare. Faced with the prospect of genocide, Malvar had no choice.[20]

Persistence of the Kalayaan Ideal

The surrender in 1902 of the main guerilla armies gave the populace a breathing spell during which the specters of famine and disease were tackled with United States aid. But the new colonial government found it extremely difficult to place the country, particularly the islands of Luzon, Samar and Leyte, in a condition of tranquility and order. For what the Americans had to contend with was really the mood of the populace. Notwithstanding the defeat of the revolutionary armies, the hundreds of thousands of lives lost and the desolation of the countryside, the image of kalayaan continued to pervade the consciousness particularly of the poorer and less-educated classes. American reports during the immediate postwar period constantly bemoan what they eventually term a "fanatical" attitude toward politics and independence on the part of, to the minds of the Americans, very unlikely types of people. Little children brought up the subject in conversation with American soldiers passing through the towns.[21] Even those who had made their peace with the American

---

20. See Malvar's "The Reason for my Change in Attitude" (original in Spanish), 16 April 1902 (Taylor, *Philippine Insurrection,* vol 5. pp. 358-59).

21. Andrew Haslam, *Forty Truths and Other Truths* (Manila: Philippine Publishing Co., 1900) pp. 178-79. Haslam was an American soldier who wrote about "the life and habits of the Tagalogs." After a little argument with a boy about independence, Haslam remarks: "When you see a ten-year-old boy arguing politics, what must be the feeling of the people towards the prospects of local government! They possess a strong desire for it."

occasionally revealed to their American friends their vivid memories and emotions of the struggle for self-rule. One had only to introduce the subject of the friars, or tell "tales of suffering and war," in order "to see eyes flash and cheeks burn."[22] In general, however, "the better class of people," to quote the constabulary chief, were "extremely tired of the struggle" and were willing to aid the government in stamping out further acts of resistance.[23] Doherty, in 1904, summarized the situation thus: "With the exception of a small percentage of property owners all Filipinos desire the independence of their country."[24] As late as 1907, the constabulary in southern Luzon reported that "in Sorsogon, Romblon and Tayabas the whole population seems swept off its feet by the independence idea. Only a few men of prominence have been strong enough to stand in opposition."[25]

Given the prevailing mood of the populace, many of the ilustrados and large property owners who had participated in the Malolos government continued to work for independence. But they chose to do so within the framework of the colonial order, banking on American hints that total self-rule would eventually be granted after a period of "tutelage" in which power would be shared between the Americans and the native elite. Their approach was through the formation of political parties bearing various shades of the independence platform. Not until 1907, however, did their cautious efforts bear fruit with the election of a national (Philippine) assembly dominated by the Nacionalista Party.

From around 1901, many members of the Filipino elite who had just supported the Malolos republic found it to their advantage to collaborate in the American campaign of "pacification." As a recent study has pointed out, the Filipino elite "quickly found co-operation with the United States more advantageous than their original expectations. By preserving the peace and order, they were also preserving the traditional system which gave them support."[26] This is a reference to the situation around 1907, but the study also shows that

---

22. Edith Moses, *Unofficial Letters of an Official's Wife* (New York: Appleton, 1908), pp. 349–50. Moses's husband was a member of the Philippine Commission. Her remarks were made in a letter of 15 December 1902.

23. Henry T. Allen to Adjutant General, U.S. Army, Manila, 26 December 1901 (BIA 1184-34, USNA).

24. David Doherty, "Conditions in the Philippines," U.S. Senate Document 170, 58th Congress, 2nd session, 1904 (typescript in BIA 3841-3, USNA). Doherty was a Chicago physician with an interest in the "new colony." His report challenges the official position that the threat to peace and order was caused by bandits. His travels to many unpacified areas in 1903 gave him substantial proof that the disturbances were political and geared toward independence.

25. ARPC (1907) 2, p. 301.

26. Michael Cullinane, "Implementing the New Order: The Structure and Supervision of Local Government During the Taft Era," in *Compadre Colonialism*, ed. Norman Owen (University of Michigan Center for South and Southeast Asian Studies, 1971), p. 24.

as early as 1901 members of the native elite were allowed to dominate the municipal and provincial levels of government in the "pacified" areas, thus somewhat whetting their appetite for "self-rule." This led to a situation in which prominent officers of Aguinaldo's army, as governors of their home provinces under the new order, willingly and quite ruthlessly persecuted the remaining units of guerillas fighting for independence. Gen. Juan Cailles of Laguna, Col. Pablo Tecson of Bulacan, Col. Ceferino Joven of Pampanga, Gen. Martin Delgado of Panay—these were only a few of the *revolucionarios* from prominent families whose loyalty and efficiency as provincial governors the American governor-general could hardly praise enough.[27]

These individuals could pursue their tasks with hardly any feelings of guilt or pangs of conscience because of the myth, created by the declaration of the "Bandolerismo Act" in 1902, that all remaining "troublemakers" in the new colonial order were plain bandits, or *ladrones.* This myth, initially embraced and propagated by what the Americans called the "better classes" of Philippine society, eventually came to be accepted by ever greater segments of the population as a result of its propagation in the public school system. Even today, the period from 1902 to 1910 is very little understood and, in some respects, clouded in secrecy.[28] In any case, this identification of any armed resistance with banditry provided the government and its Filipino allies with the needed justification to use harsh measures against recalcitrants. "We are getting rid of the bad men," wrote Governor Taft, "and we are not offering any terms of any sort. A number have been sentenced to be hanged, and most of the others have received long sentences. It is not quite so spectacular as to kill them in battle, but it has, I think, a better effect."[29]

It was easy for educated or propertied Filipinos to accept the bandit myth because the Katipunans that rose after 1901 were composed of "ordinary" people and led by, as one source puts it, "officers of lesser grade, men lacking in social status and intelligence."[30] Among the leaders were tailors, barbers, a cook, a blacksmith's helper, peasant farmers and vagabonds. Some, formerly cooks and servants of prominent families, had become officers in the revolu-

27. William H. Taft to the U.S. Secretary of War, Baguio, 14 April 1903 (BIA 4865-15 [extract], USNA).

28. This has given rise to several magazine articles and books attempting to dispel the bandit image of certain individuals who led movements with anti-American overtones. The books of Antonio Abad and Jose P. Santos are cited later in this chapter.

29. Taft to the Secretary of War, 14 April 1903, Baguio (BIA 4865-15, USNA). In fairness, we must point out that some of those hanged were genuine robbers, rapists, etc., who took advantage of the general turmoil to commit crimes. Some of these may even have joined the katipunan guerilla units. In general, however, the colonial government was more preoccupied with political or religiopolitical rebels.

30. "The Christmas Eve Fiasco and a Brief Outline of the Ricarte and Other Similar Movements from the Time of the Breaking Up of the Insurrection of 1899-1901" (appendix 149 in the Watson Collection and appendix N in Artemio Ricarte, *Memoirs* [Manila: National Heroes Commission, 1963], p. 171).

tionary army and refused to return to their former occupations.[31] Some were hermits and mystics, similar in most respects to Apolinario de la Cruz. Furthermore, the most able of these men were former associates of Bonifacio and among the first to initiate the Katipunan movement of 1896. James LeRoy, after a trip through the Luzon countryside in 1905, remarked that the masses still followed their leaders "practically like sheep," but because of "the turmoils incident to guerilla warfare against American authority" these masses were

> rather more at the command of new and aggressive, oft-times ignorant and mere adventurous, leaders than of the old constituted cacique class, the men of property and education, speaking generally. That the ideal of independence is disseminated among the masses, except possibly in a few of the most backward and least developed regions, is quite certain.[32]

LeRoy asserts that although new leaders had come to the fore, the masses were as passive as ever, like sheep "herded hither or thither at the command of the boss." But how do we reconcile this image of passivity with the observation that the ideal of independence was present? Why did the masses persist in flocking to these "ignorant and mere adventurous" leaders in spite of the risks involved? Our key to understanding the continuing unrest of the first decade of American rule lies in the meaning of the word *kalayaan*, the rallying cry of the different groups that appeared at this time. The new leaders gained a following because they offered a way to kalayaan that the "men of property and education" had long forsaken.

Sakay's Katipunan

In August 1901, a Nacionalista Party (not to be confused with the ilustrado-led Nacionalista Party of 1907) attempted to seek legal status, which was immediately denied by Taft because of the presence of "confirmed Katipuneros" among its leaders. Indeed, with Santiago Alvarez as one of its presidents, Andres Villanueva as vice-president and people like Macario Sakay, Aurelio Tolentino, Aguedo del Rosario, Francisco Carreon, Briccio Pantas, and Pantaleon Torres as secretaries, it seemed as if the Katipunan of Bonifacio had been resurrected. Could it be a mere coincidence that the men who believed in the sacred ideals of the Katipunan were the first to challenge the new regime constitutionally, even while many generals of the fallen republic were scampering for office and status in it? The Nacionalista Party, together with the labor union of Dominador Gomez and Bishop Gregorio Aglipay's Philippine Independent Church, attempted to form a "triple coalition" advocated by veteran Katipuneros who claimed "that sentimental consid-

---

31. ARPC (1903), 3, "Report of the Chief of the Constabulary," p. 54.
32. LeRoy Papers, folder 10 (MHC).

eration for the triangular arrangement would appeal to the secret brotherhood that they hoped to resuscitate."[33]

Taft and the Philippine Commission wasted no time in enacting, in November 1901, a "Sedition Law" which imposed grave punishment on anyone found guilty of advocating independence not only through open insurrection but also through "seditious" speeches, writings, dramas, and the display of Katipunan flags and insignias. The Nacionalista Party was thus prevented from operating legally. Despite threats and obstacles, however, the leaders of this movement who escaped imprisonment continued to wage the independence struggle through revivals of the Katipunan. The most imposing figure among them was Macario Sakay.

Sakay had been an apprentice in a *calesa* manufacturing shop, and also a tailor. He wrote and read Tagalog, and spoke a little Spanish, "but not enough to carry on a sustained conversation."[34] He knew Andres Bonifacio, both of them being residents in the Tondo district of Manila and actors in popular dramas called *komedya* or *moro-moro.* Sakay played the role of prince in the play *Principe Baldovino* and in *Rodrigo de Villas.* At other times he was Charlemagne in the komedya titled *Doce Pares de Francia* and in *Amante de la Corona.* In 1894, he joined the Katipunan and because of his good record was appointed president of the Dapitan, Manila, branch. Abad notes that, although Sakay was an active Katipunero, "the Spanish authorities failed to detect his whereabouts and activities because he participated in most komedyas held nightly in different districts in Manila. His conspicuous roles in the stage dramas disguised his real identity as a member of Andres Bonifacio's Katipunan."[35] Sakay's career as an actor in Tagalog dramas—he probably also played some parts in the *sinakulo*—likely shaped his perceptions of what revolution was all about. As an actor he participated in the unfolding of a world that belonged to the masses of Tagalog folk—a world of chivalry, loyalty and

33. ARPC (1903), 1, pp. 40–41.

34. David Doherty to the *New York Evening Post,* 2 October 1906 (BIA 4865-33, USNA).

35. Antonio Abad, *General Macario L. Sakay: Was He a Bandit or a Patriot?* (Manila: J.B. Feliciano and Sons, 1955), p. 4. Abad, as a representative of the Tagalog daily *Muling Pagsilang* (Rebirth), was able to meet Sakay who eventually turned over some personal documents to him. This book is thus a compilation of translated documents of Sakay and other leaders of the Katagalugan Republic. Abad published it in 1955 in order to dispel the bandit image of Sakay. "History," he says in the introduction, "in the hands of simpering frauds and precocious mediocrity, had lent its assistance to the perpetuation of a crude injustice." In the end, however, Abad merely notes a difference of personality between Sakay and the ilustrados who worked toward independence "through the ballot." Sakay was a romantic idealist while the Quezons, Laurels, and Osmeñas were practical enough to work within the system. Thus, Abad himself perpetuates a myth—that independence meant the same thing to all nationalists.

love, in which acts of bravery and self-control, a willingness to face death, resulted in the attainment of difficult goals.[36]

As a Katipunero, Sakay helped run the Katipunan press.[37] He also fought alongside Bonifacio in many encounters, particularly in the hills of Morong. After the downfall of Bonifacio and the Magdiwang wing of the Katipunan in 1897, Sakay's military role seems to have been curtailed. Several former generals in the revolutionary government have noted Sakay's political role, his continued commitment to the spread of Katipunan ideals among the populace. Sakay, says General Ricarte, "was one of those who went from town to town, winning the people over to the cause of the Katipunan."[38] Pio del Pilar comments that while military leaders like himself were busy conducting the war, Sakay concerned himself primarily with the formation of Katipunan chapters.[39] This preoccupation with the Katipunan was construed innocently by the leaders of the revolutionary government. In spite of the fact that Aguinaldo's ilustrado advisers were alarmed by the continued existence of Katipunan societies in many towns, they realized the importance of the Katipunan idiom in maintaining the revolutionary ardor of the populace. Men like Sakay were probably encouraged by the central government to propagate Katipunan ideals as a form of strengthening the loyalties of the rural areas to the center.

During the republican period, the term "Katipunan" was officially defined as the "nation." But very little effort, if any, was made to build the Philippine nation along Katipunan lines. Egalitarianism and mass mobilization were concepts that threatened the leadership of the ilustrados and principales. The concrete practice of Katipunan ideals thus remained confined to the local level. It is not surprising that, after the fall of the Philippine republic at the end of the century, resistance to American rule was initiated and led largely by individuals of low social status and minimal education, for it was largely this segment of society that regarded the Katipunan as a way of life constituting the essence of

---

36. Cf. Teodoro M. Kalaw, *Cinco Reglas* (Manila: Bureau of Printing, 1947), pp. 10–11, on the influence of the komedya in the making of a man of valor, the latter being "a chimera solely realized through serenity, education (knowledge) and sacrifice."

37. Gregoria de Jesus, *Mga Tala ng Aking Buhay*, in *Julio Nakpil and the Philippine Revolution,* ed. E. Alzona (Manila: Carmelo and Bauermann, 1964), p. 162. In her autobiography Gregoria, Bonifacio's widow who later married an officer in the revolutionary army, makes an impassioned plea to her countrymen to abandon the notion that Sakay was a bandit.

38. Statement of Gen. Artemio Ricarte in *Pagkakaisa* (Unity), 30 March 1930; in Abad, *Macario Sakay*, p. 33.

39. Statement of Gen. Pio del Pilar, in J.P. Santos, *Ang Tatlong Napabantog na "Tulisan" sa Pilipinas* (Gerona, Tarlac: 1936), p. 31. Santos has earned the respect of Philippine historians by collecting and publishing original Tagalog records relating to Sakay's movement. His work is all the more valuable in that he made no attempt to translate it into English, for a comparison of the Tagalog originals with Abad's translations reveals the inadequacy of common English words in capturing the nuances of certain Tagalog word-concepts.

being a true "son of Mother Country." In Sakay's case, it is clear from the records of the New Katipunan (which shall henceforth be called simply "Katipunan") that he regarded capitulation to the Americans as a deviation from the path to kalayaan. Sakay so "loved" the Katipunan, says Pio del Pilar, that he persisted in the struggle against great odds.[40] He remained active in the hills of Morong until his capture in 1901. Amnestied shortly afterwards, he promptly went underground to work for a revival of the Katipunan.[41]

Although Sakay was one of the secretaries of the short-lived Nacionalista Party of 1901, by 1902 he seems to have abandoned the "legal" approach to the independence question. In any case, the American government preferred to deal with the more malleable ilustrados in the transfer of some measure of authority to natives. Thus, to the dedicated adherents of the Katipunan, the only road to kalayaan was that traversed by Bonifacio in 1896. In 1902, we find Sakay at the head of a "Republic of Katagalugan," in the hills of southern Luzon. The ideology of his republic was in essence that of the early Katipunan. The ideas of self and society found in Jacinto's "Kartilya" of 1896 became part of the very definition of the state. Its constitution, promulgated in November 1901, expressly states that "the congress shall in no way act counter to the mode of behavior *(kaugalian)* that characterized the Katipunan ever since it was founded by the honored Gat. A. Bonifacio in the year 1892."[42]

The implications of this apparent revival of Bonifacio's Katipunan are manifold. It is not, as some historians imply, simply a continuation of the struggle for independence by an overly idealistic—and perhaps unrealistic—individual. Far from being a minor reflection of the republic at Malolos, Sakay's republic was an implicit negation of the Malolos model. As we shall see, Sakay and the group of Katipuneros around him felt that something was terribly wrong with the way the revolution had been conducted in the recent past.

One of the earliest available documents of the Republic of Katagalugan—a "War Order" of 6 May 1902—begins with an outright criticism of people's motivation during the recent war years:

> Sa paghihimagsik ng guinawa dito sa Pilipinas ay na pagmalas sa lahat ng Kababayan ang di pagcakaisang loob, gaua ng paglingap sa pilak, sa yaman at karunungan, ay uala ang pagtatanggol sa kalahatan, at itinangi ang sariling katauan. Sa ñgayon ay minarapat nitong K. Pagasiwaan itong Kautusan sa kapanahunan ng pakikidigma.[43]

---

40. Ibid.
41. ARPC (1903), 1, p. 40.
42. Part 2, section 1, "Ang Congreso," in Santos, *Tatlong Tulisan*, p. 39.
43. *Presidencia nitong Kapuluang Katagalugan*, 1, "Pamahayag" (Proclamation), 6 May 1902, in Santos, *Tatlong Tulisan*, pp. 51–53.

During the war that was fought here in Pilipinas, it became apparent to all our compatriots that unity of *loób* was absent, because all people cared for were silver, wealth, and education; thus, there was no willingness to defend the whole, as concern for one's own body was paramount. Presently, the Highest Council deems it necessary to proclaim this order for the duration of the war.

The War Order is addressed quite specifically to "those Tagalogs who are inducing the officers and men defending our Mother Country to lay down their arms and accept the jurisdiction of the United States government," and also to those actually engaged in capturing or causing the arrest of those continuing the struggle. The reference, of course, is to what American officials termed the "better classes" of society, many of them former officers of the revolutionary army, who formed a native component of the campaign against "banditry." The notion of a "better class" or "intelligent, well-to-do class" of natives is, however, part of the American colonial vocabulary. The War Order does not consider the oppressive acts of fellow Filipinos as an aspect of class conflict. Theoretically, the rich and wealthy Filipinos are not grouped into one oppressor or traitor class, as the following article from the Republic of Katagalugan's Constitution shows:

Sino mang tagalog tungkol anak dito sa Kapuluang Katagalugan, ay walang itatangi sino man tungkol sa dugo gayon din sa kulay nang balat nang isa't isa; maputi, maitim, mayaman, dukha, marunong at mangmang lahat ay magkakapantay na walang higit at kulang, dapat magkaisang loób, maaaring humigit sa dunong, sa yaman, sa ganda, dapwa't hindi mahihigitan sa pagkatao ng sino man, at sa paglilingkod ñang kahit alin.[44]

No Tagalog, born in this Tagalog archipelago, shall exalt any person above the rest because of his race or the color of his skin; fair, dark, rich, poor, educated and ignorant—all are completely equal, and should be one in *loób*. There may be differences in education, wealth or appearance, but never in essential nature *[pagkatao]* and ability to serve a cause.

In effect, there can be unity among those of different levels of wealth and education. The Katipunan viewed itself and its supporters not as a class but as the representative of the whole society confronting those who, by their conduct, subvert the very conditions for "society" to exist.[45] The ideal of unity of loób was frustrated by individuals whose actions were motivated by love for wealth,knowledge,andtheself over the whole; yet, these very same people demanded the respect of the "poor and ignorant," and reaped most of the

44. Amendments by the Junta Suprema, IV, 3 (Katungkulang Gaganapin ng Lahat. . . .), in Santos, *Tatlong Tulisan*, p. 45.

45. This is an application of an idea put forth by Karl Marx and Frederick Engels in *The German Ideology* (New York: International Publishers, 1947), p. 41, and pursued by Clive Kessler in "The Politics of Islamic Egalitarianism," *Humaniora Islamica* 2 (1974): 237–52.

benefits of the revolution. From an external viewpoint, however, the notion of "class" can be applied to the situation in which the Katipunan found itself, for the latter's enemies were no other than the "better class" that the Americans spoke proudly of. Thus, although ideas of interiority underlie the Katipunan analysis of and statements about Filipino society, there seems to be a correlation between interior state and membership in a class. This will become clearer as we delve further into the sources for the period.

The Katipunan's use of the idiom of loób is evident as we quote further from the 1902 War Order:

> Ang utos na ito ay nag buhat doon sa masamang gaui at buhalhal na asal, nagbubuhat din naman sa nagnanasa ng Kalayaan ng sariling katauan, at gayon din sa pag hahangad ng dangal at kayamanan, na di nililingap ang kapurihan ng Bayan.
>
> Kaya nga ipinatatalastas sa mga kababayang tapat na loób, manalig dito sa kautusan at tumulong sa ipagcacaisang loob ng lahat upang tamuhin sa madaling panahon ang hinahangad na Kalayaan.[46]

> The necessity for this order is due to those men of bad behavior and disorderly minds and habits. It is also due to those who seek *kalayaan* of their bodies, who hunger for honor and wealth, without showing compassionate care for the honor of the country.
>
> That is why we appeal to compatriots with upright *loób* to have faith in this and to help toward the becoming-one-in-*loób* of all, so that we may attain kalayaan as soon as possible.

As a way of expressing what has gone wrong, Sakay plays upon the alienation of words from their true meanings. In the introduction of his War Order, quoted earlier, he says that in the last war there was *paglingap* (compassionate care), not for the country as would have been proper, but for silver. Instead of paglingap for the country's honor, there was love for the self. Instead of kalayaan of the whole people, it was "kalayaan of their bodies" that many sought. The corruption of sacred Katipunan ideals along with "bad behavior and disorderly minds," manifest weakness and lack of control in the loób. The Katipunan must set things straight by mobilizing those of "upright loób" to continue the struggle for kalayaan.

For Sakay and others with him, nothing was more infuriating than the abuse of the term *kalayaan*. The word was alienated from its original, full meaning by collaborators and plain politicians who sought to justify their behavior to a populace with fresh memories of the revolution. One often finds, in documents of the period, ilustrados and principales mouthing revolutionary rhetoric in which America is magically transformed from "enemy" into liberator. A

46. Santos, *Tatlong Tulisan*, p. 53.

good illustration of this is the following excerpt from an address given by Señorita Felicia San Agustin at the festivities honoring a regiment of the United States Army that had just "liberated" her town:

> When the Filipino people aspired to free themselves from the yoke of Spain, in our weakness and impotence we raised our eyes to Heaven for help; desperate in moments of dismay we thought Japan, growing in power, might perhaps help us. At times we even thought of strong England, but we feared English pride, and we again beseeched Japan, who sympathized with us, to come to our rescue.
>
> Never once did we dream that free America would be the nation to come to help free us from Spanish domination.
>
> Thus it was before 1899 when these islands were ceded by Spain to the United States. Thoughtful people said, *it is God's will that America be the chosen one to redeem us and guide us in other paths,* to instruct and educate us. We feel that we should not have fought against her, but human passions led us into a disastrous war.
>
> Lucena is a town which is noted for its peaceful character, for its love of labor and for law and order.
>
> From the time when you first set your feet on its soil, public order has not been disturbed, and we have tried to second you in your difficult work of clearing the country surrounding of people with evil intent, *who under the false plea of patriotism imposed upon the ignorant population of the sementaries for their own profit.*[47]

This statement, given on behalf of the "genuine representatives of Lucena, proprietors, agriculturists, merchants, all industrious people," shows something of the capacity of vast segments of the Filipino elite to adapt to changing conditions. America is the savior who would lead the country along the path to kalayaan; the revolutionaries in the countryside are false patriots deceiving the people. One can imagine the surprise and disbelief of the revolutionaries at such cooptation of their language by collaborators in the towns.

Who was genuine and who was false? The Americans and their local allies certainly tried to propagate the notion that the remaining insurgents were "false patriots," nothing more than bandits. The Katipunan, on the other hand, insisted that it was the bearer of authenticity. In an undated letter to a foreign consul, the Katipunan maintains that it is fighting the United States government "in an effort to defend the genuine *(tunay)* kalayaan of the country and in an effort to pursue the genuine *katwiran.*" Furthermore, it refutes allegations of banditry by insisting that its partisans are "genuine revolutionaries in deed and in adherance to the genuine katwiran (*tunay na Revolucionario sa gawa at panununton sa tunay na katwiran*)." All in all, the word *tunay* (genuine)

47. Document attached to the official report of Col. Cornelius Gardener to the Adjutant General, Manila, 8 February 1901. Also appended to the report is a translation of a declaration of gratitude to the officers and men of the Thirtieth Regiment, U.S.V., by 326 "leading citizens of the town of Lucena, Tayabas, and Lucban (BIA 2760-65, USNA, my italics).

appears seven times in this short letter.[48] Authenticity is also the emphasis in the final lines of Sakay's Constitution:

> Kaming nanumpa sa ibaba nito, ay pawang tunay na Katipunan buhat sa unang paghihimagsik dito sa K. Katagalugan, na nagtatanggol ng Katwiran magpahanggan ngayon nitong lupang tinubuan.[49]

> The undersigned who have made the oath are a genuine Katipunan, having been so since the first war in Katagalugan, committed to defending the *katwiran* of our native land, even to this day.

All this emphasis on the "genuine" harks back to Jacinto's distinction between "genuine" light—liwanag—and the deceptive appearance of light—*ningning*, or glitter. Those who thrive on appearances not only manifest a loób that lacks sincerity and transparency, but also exploit the weak, vacillating loób of others. The War Order is addressed to such individuals, warning them of the consequences, such as confiscation of property and even death, of their treacherous acts. Moreover, in claiming that they are the genuine patriots, the Katipunan gives evidence of its commitment: it is "experiencing hardship" *(nagsusumakit)* in order to obtain independence; it has been in existence since the first war (1896). Commitment, as our analysis of the 1841 Cofradía has shown, implies a loób that has endured many trials during which it has been continually purified and strengthened. At the conclusion of the War Order, the Katipunan appeals precisely to individuals capable of genuine commitment—whose loób are "sincere"—to trust in the Katipunan and work for the attainment of "complete unity of loób," for only then will kalayaan become a reality.

Another important aspect of the idiom of loób that we discussed in previous chapters is the connection between state of loób and ability to show compassion or have *damay* for others. This dominant feature of the pasyon and the 1896 Katipunan ideology again appears in the interpretation of the 1902 situation. The War Order condemns the hardness *(katigasan)* of loób of collaborators who, rather than have compassion *(lingap)* for the country, induce *(hikayat)* guerillas to surrender.[50] A connection is posited between the state of people's loób and their relationship to the redemptive struggle being waged by the Katipunan. In familiar pasyon terms, the allusion is to serpent and Judas-like figures whose loób are harder than the hardest rock. For Katipunan fighters in difficult straits owing to American military might, receiving little or no sympathy from "leading citizens," the pasyon tradition at least provided a context of meaning in which to situate themselves.

---

48. Apparently, this letter was submitted to a Manila newspaper but never saw print owing to the newspaper's fear of prosecution under the Sedition Law (in Santos, *Tatlong Tulisan*, pp 48-49).

49. Santos, *Tatlong Tulisan*, p. 45.

50. Ibid., p. 52.

When there is hardness of loób everywhere, as the Katipunan perceived in 1902, there can be no unity and no genuine kalayaan. That is why there is an emphasis, in their documents, on the need for "purity," "sincerity," and "uprightness" of loób that results in damay, compassion and, ultimately, unity. The Constitution of the Republic of Katagalugan prescribes the ideal mode of behavior of citizens, thus:

> Ang sino mang tagalog, ay magtataglay nang magandang kaugalian, at mabuting kaisipan, huwag ilalayo sa puso ang gawang pag damay sa kapwa, at pagibig na dalisay sa kadugo, gayong din sa tinubuang lupa, lalung lalo na sa ikaaayos at ikagagaling sa kalahatan dito sa Kapuluan; kailangan ang lahat ay magtaglay nang kahihiyan at puri sa kaniyang sariling katawan, upang huwag mawala ang pagmamalasakit nang isa't isa.[51]
>
> Every Tagalog should cultivate a good manner of behavior and a good mind; he should not estrange his heart from acts of *damay* for his fellow men and from genuine love for his compatriots and his native land, especially for the benefit of all in this archipelago. It is necessary for all to have *hiya* and purity of self, so that mutual caring shall not be lost.

In order for Mother Country to be honored, continues the constitution, there should be no deviation from true katwiran, and "disorderliness of mind and habit" *(buhalhal na asal)* must be purged. Evidently, kalayaan, as the Katipunan sees it, is not merely the attainment of political sovereignty; it is a condition in which the loób of Mother Country's sons are joined together because the society's ideals of behavior have been met in the experience of the struggle.

The above ideas, found in formal Katipunan documents, also appear in a song that was popular among the rural folk who harbored and sustained the Katipunan "bandits":

Halina, halina mga kababayan
ating salubungin itong bagong datal
mga Filipinong panguloy si Sakay
siang nagmatuid nitong ating bayan

> Come, come our countrymen
> let us welcome these new arrivals
> Filipinos led by Sakay
> who set our country along the straight path.

Sa bayang Kabite doon itinawid
doon minithi ang mga matuid.
si Kareon ang Presidente
si Sakay ang komandante
si Montalan ang Jefe't
si Natividad ang Kapitan, ang sabi.

---

51. Ibid., pp. 44–45.

To the town of Kabite they transferred
there they aspired to set things straight
Kareon was made president
Sakay was the major
Montalan was the chief
and Natividad the capitan, they say.

Ang binabanig nila'y malamig na lupa.
Ang kinukumot nila'y damong mahahaba.
Mabagsik na lamok hindi maapula't
ayao magpatulog—mga kaawa-awa.
Kaya tayong lahat mag kaisa
sa pagmamalasakit ng patria.[52]

The cold earth was the mat they slept on.
The tall grass served as blanket.
The fierce mosquitos could not be driven off,
and would not let them sleep—how pitiful they are.
So let us all be one
with the suffering motherland.

The "folk" character of this song shows in the confusion of details in the second stanza. Sakay, not Kareon, was the president, while reference should have been to Kabite province, rather than town *(bayan)*. But "facts" are less what the song is about than the notion of katwiran in the first two stanzas and that of damay in the third. The Katipunan led by Sakay is said to have set the country on the straight path again, implying that previously there was disorientation, lack of firm direction. It is worthwhile to recall the image of the ship that lost its bearings in a storm, as Apolinario once described the Cofradía unguided by the light of his teachings. Is there not, perhaps, a connection between the notion of the restoration of "straightness" and the unique design on Sakay's flag—a blazing sun with the letter "K" (Kalayaan/Katipunan) in its center, its manifold rays reaching out to the very border.[53] In no other insignia of the revolutionary era do we find such an intensification of the image of light but then, never had Mother Country been in a more critical condition, having suffered not only military defeat but the acceptance, by her alleged leading men, of the path of collaboration with the new rulers. Collaboration was regarded by the Katipunan as a particularly acute manifestation of the country's deviation from the "straight path." The magnified sun in Sakay's flag can thus be regarded as a redemptive sign in a troubled era. It was the light—*liwanag*—that would show to those of upright loób the "straight path" to kalayaan.

The third and final stanza of the above song provides yet another example of the importance of damay and compassion as a social experience during the

---

52. Honesto Mariano, "Popular Songs of the Revolution" (1915) BCTE, vol. 4, no. 198.
53. Sketch in PIR-SD 1311 (PNL).

revolution. Without even entering into a discussion of the music itself, we can see how the description of the hardship encountered by the Katipuneros—the cold earth, tall grass, and fierce mosquitos that would not let them sleep—evokes the experience of compassion in the singer and listener. In the fourth line, mga *kaawa-awa,* translated as "how pitiful they are," expresses pity *(awa)* for the men in hardship. The key to the stanza's meaning is that *awa* is not merely "pity" in the sense of an emotional outpouring from the individual. It must be understood together with the succeeding lines: "And so let us all be one / with the suffering motherland." The causal connection between awa and unity is not accidental; only when there is *awa* or something related to it can there be unity among men and with the motherland who is suffering. Just as, in the pasyon, Christ is often described as *kaawa-awa* to evoke response from man, so does the song's third stanza evoke damay for the Katipunan fighters and the suffering Mother Country who are experiencing a pasyon. And where can awa or damay arise if not among those who seek to purify and strengthen their loób so that they can relate to each other? Hence we return to the fundamental meaning of unity in the Katipunan idiom.

Sakay's Katipunan, with its emphasis on keeping alive the revolutionary style of Bonifacio's Katipunan, could not have been the heir to the ilustrado-dominated revolution that preceded it. To talk of a continuum in the struggle for independence, to assume that a common meaning of "independence" existed for all, eventually leads to the conclusion that the post-1900 katipunans were superfluous because they "failed," while the ilustrados, because they expertly played the game of collaboration with the new rulers, managed to attain more and more self-rule for the country. The question has to be posed: is the "independence" that the ilustrados managed to wrest from the Americans equivalent to the condition called kalayaan? Or is it just the supreme product of the manipulation of appearances? In the Malolos republic, we recall, an emphasis on the appearance of unity to attain world recognition as a sovereign state had all but suppressed the Katipunan ideal of releasing the potentialities of loób—love, compassion, virtue—in the act of participating in the redemption of Mother Filipinas. Independence had come to be defined in a static sense as autonomy, and unity was formalized in the coming together of men of wealth, education, and social prominence in the Malolos congress. To the Katipunan, this all gave the appearance of unity, not the experience of unity. As long as gentry-revolutionaries thought in terms of maintaining vertical relationships with themselves at the top, the power of unity, of "coming together," was weak or absent.

Another perspective on the difference between the 1902 Katipunan and its republican predecessor is provided by Cenon Nicdao, a tailor and one of the leaders of the Katipunan in Baliwag, Bulacan, whom the Americans interrogated in January 1902. The Baliwag organization, which recognized Sakay as president of the republic, was headed by Alejandro Santiago, one of the members of Bonifacio's supreme council in 1896. Nicdao's replies to his captors reveal a distinction between the terms "revolucionario," or member of what he calls "Aguinaldo's revolution," and "Katipunero." According to him, "the difference between the present Katipunan and the old revolution is this: the present Katipunan men don't want to kill anybody; they want to abide by the law; they don't want to get drunk; they want to be virtuous."[54] Unfortunately, Nicdao's statements are available to us only in the interpreter's English translation. What, for example, was Nicdao's word for "law"? Could it have been "katwiran," or something akin to the notion of the "straight path"? Surely, Nicdao is not referring to the laws of the American colonial government. In contrasting "revolucionario" and "Katipunero," the state of loób—of which morality is one indicator—is his main focus. We know that Aguinaldo's "revolucionarios" could, indeed, be accused of "immoral" behavior. Says Julio Nakpil, another of Bonifacio's former associates:

> On account of the abuses and immoralities of his soldiers, such as robberies and rape of married women as well as single, many complaints were brought to E. Aguinaldo; but, instead of punishing the culprits, he would reply invariably, "Please be patient because we do not pay our soldiers."[55]

The word "virtuous" in Nicdao's last sentence is almost certainly the Tagalog *banal*. It is "virtue," or *kabanalan,* that the new Katipunan upholds. A song written in 1896 by Nakpil, who intended it to be the Philippine national anthem if Bonifacio had lived to be president, illustrates the juxtaposition of virtue and struggle:

> Mabuhay, mabuhay yaong Kalayaan, Kalayaan.
> At pasulungin ang puri't kabanalan, ang puri't kabanalan.
> Kastila'y mairing ng Katagalugan.
> at ngayo'y ipagwagi ang kahusayan.[56]
>
> Long live, long live *kalayaan, kalayaan.*
> Let honor and virtue go forward, honor and virtue.
> Let the Spaniards be mocked and disdained
> for now excellence shall triumph.

Revolutions can be judged from within as well as without. From the latter perspective it is all too easy to glorify the obvious manifestations of the continuous struggle for Philippine nationhood. But Sakay, Nicdao, and their fellow Katipuneros perceived a discontinuity. To them, "Aguinaldo's revolution" had strayed from the path that the movement of 1896 had chosen.

---

54. "Record of Examination of Cenon Nicdao," 5 January 1902 (BIA 4857-3, USNA).

55. Encarnacion Alzona, ed. *Julio Nakpil and the Philippine Revolution* (Manila: Carmelo and Bauermann, 1964), p. 50.

56. Felipe de Leon, "Poetry, Music and Social Consciousness," *Philippine Studies* 17 (April 1969): 275.

"Revolucionario" leaders, on their part, hardly recognized the post-1901 Katipunan as the legitimate continuation of their movement; joining in the American chorus of bandit accusations against Sakay and his group was simply another way of disclaiming continuity. Most of the "revolucionario" leaders acquiesced to and collaborated with the new colonial order as part of the game of flexibility and expediency which the Filipino elite has been known to play exceedingly well.[57] Unfortunately, it has been thought much too often that the rest of society simply swayed and bent together with their elite patrons, and that those who did not were really outside society, i.e., bandits or religious fanatics. It has never been pointed out how deep the Katipunan experience was, how very much alive it was after 1900, and how many from the peasantry turned to Katipunan and religio-political leaders not necessarily as a blind reaction to the turmoil and insecurity arising from the war years, but as a consequence of their view of what the revolution was all about.

From around April to August 1903, Sakay made his headquarters atop Mount San Cristobal, the site where the Cofradía de San Jose made its stand against the Spaniards in 1841. There he proclaimed himself president of the Philippine republic. Captain Grove of the constabulary and ex-revolucionario, now Laguna Governor, Juan Cailles, led various expeditions to the mountain in attempts to dislodge him. Finally, in August 1903, they forced him to transfer his base of operations to the hills of Morong.[58] Generally, Sakay's Katipunan had no trouble in securing support from the inhabitants of the hilly and mountainous areas of southern Luzon. Where the power of the town-based principales was weak, the Katipunan government provided an alternative to existing structures.

In 1906, Doherty stated with surprise that thousands of *remontados* were supporters of Sakay.[59] *Remontado*, from the Spanish meaning "to mount again" or "to take to the woods," refers not only to a group of individuals who had "fled from the bells" to live an unrestricted life, but to a whole spectrum of individual and social activities unsanctioned and often condemned by the Spanish and principalia overseers of the pueblo way of life. At an earlier stage of Spanish rule, "remontado" usually meant one who refused to accept Christianity and resettle within the orbit of a town church; eventually it could mean one who had fled to the hills to avoid the payment of tribute and forced labor, to escape from the clutches of the law, or to live as a hermit and ascetic. Some nineteenth-century observers, such as Sawyer, Jagor and even Rizal,

---

57. The elite's outlook is summed up well in David Steinberg, *Philippine Collaboration in World War II* (Ann Arbor, Michigan: University of Michigan, 1967), p. 13. Constantino's book *The Philippines: A Past Revisited* (Quezon City: Tala Publishing Co., 1975) has a similar interpretation of elite collaboration.

58. ARPC (1903), 3, "Report of the 1st District, Philippine Constabulary," p. 65; ARPC (1904) ., "Report of the Governor of Laguna," pp. 514–15; Abad, p. 124.

59. Doherty to the *New York Evening Post*, 2 October 1906 (BIA 4865-33, USNA).

seem to associate the remontado phenomenon with an innate tendency among natives in the pueblos to return to a life of freedom and "oneness with nature" in the hills.[60] In the Katipunan uprising of 1896, there is evidence of remontado support for Bonifacio's activities. One of the *supremo*'s close associates in the Balintawak uprising was an old remontado named Laóng, who wore a *salacot* hat ornamented with silver, with a knob of the same metal. Laóng is said to have "attracted, catechised and initiated out-of-hand" many peasants in the fields surrounding Balintawak. He was one of those privileged to carry a revolver, of which the Katipunan had a precious few, and was the "chief of operations" of the group of remontados and peasants that attacked the Chinese and their stores in Caloocan and other places in the vicinity of Balintawak. Perhaps it was the example of Laóng that inspired Bonifacio, having escaped to the hills of San Mateo after his defeats in Manila's suburbs, to confess that in case the Katipunan failed, he would remain an "outlaw."[61] For him, there was no thought of returning to the fold of the colonial government. Some seven years later, Sakay carried the same attitude and commitment. And the remontados were there to support him.

Kalayaan as Religion

The presence of Sakay and the Katipunan in Mount San Cristobal again puts the Colorum into the picture. We recall that the Colorum Society actively supported Malvar's resistance in 1901 and 1902. Even after his surrender, however, the provinces of Laguna, Batangas and Tayabas, with the twin peaks of Mounts San Cristobal and Banahaw straddling their boundaries, persisted in a state of rebellion and unrest. In late 1902, when practically all of the provinces had Filipino governors, an American officer, Capt. Henry Bandholtz, was appointed to the Tayabas post. Revolutionary activity in this hilly province was "specially serious" in and about the towns of Tiaong, Candelaria, Dolores, Sariaya, and Mauban, and to a lesser extent in the vicinity of Pagbilao, Tayabas, Lucban, Sampaloc and others. "In order to punish them for their deception," says Governor Bandholtz, a "thorough military reconcentration" of the towns of Dolores, Tiaong, Candelaria, and Sariaya was put into effect.[62] The significance of these place names lies in the fact that most of the members of the early Cofradía de San Jose hailed from them. Dolores, starting point for the pilgrimage to the new Jerusalem, had been totally razed during the guerilla war, yet continued to harbor "subversive" elements. It is not surprising that

60. For quotations from Sawyer and Jagor, as well as information on the *remontados*, see Generoso Maceda, "The Remontados of Rizal Province," *Philippine Journal of Science* 64 (1937) 313–21.

61. "Testimony of Pio Valenzuela," 2 September and 21 October 1896, in the *Minutes of the Katipunan* (Manila: National Heroes Commission, 1964), pp. 146–47, 154; St. Clair, *The Katipunan* (Manila, 1902), p. 137.

62. ARPC (1903), 1, "Report of the Provincial Governor, Tayabas," p. 925. The original of this report is in BIA 2760-34 (USNA).

Sakay should turn up there in 1903, to proclaim himself president of the republic.

In trying to explain the above phenomenon, Bandholtz stressed the severe economic dislocation experienced by Tayabas province. Over ninety percent of work animals had either been killed during the war or carried off by rinderpest and surra, nearly ruining agriculture and seriously crippling transportation. Poor harvests compounded Tayabas' problems, leading to the importation of rice into the province. The great hardship inflicted upon the poor people, argued Bandholtz, brought about the state of unrest.[63] But this is only part of the explanation. Economic dislocation does not automatically lead to unrest; why were many equally poor and ravaged provinces easily "pacified" by the Americans? And why did religiopolitical movements flourish just as well in relatively prosperous regions?

In 1904, David H. Doherty, an acute observer, insisted that to call the unrest in Tayabas simply "agrarian" was to ignore its Katipunan characteristics and its independence goal.[64] Peasants in the region were not reacting blindly to economic dislocation. It is a commentary on the intellectual bias of the period that peasant-based reactions to American rule were ascribed to some sort of fanaticism or irrationalism. A careful examination of the available data shows that these "messianic" or "millenarian" movements either called themselves katipunans or aided other katipunans like Sakay's in the continuing struggle for kalayaan. What ultimately bound them together was their belief that kalayaan was not mere political autonomy, but the attainment of certain possibilities of existence. Politics could not be divorced from all other aspects of life, like morality and economics. The Philippine Commission Report for 1903 notes that, at least for the Colorum, "Independence [is] a new religion opposed to the present established church, which they know is without power to punish them as of old."[65] In previous chapters, we emphasized that "religion" to the Colorum and, we might add, to the average Indio in those days, was the main organizing principle in life, inseparable from "tradition." That kalayaan became a "religion" to many Filipinos is just another way of saying that "politics" was inseparable from their daily lives.

In 1902 and 1903, the provinces of Laguna and Tayabas continued in a state of unrest largely because of the activities of Ruperto Rios y Satarain, who very much reminded the American scholar, James LeRoy, of Apolinario de la Cruz.[66] Rios or Reos as he himself spelled his name, led a movement contemporaneous with Sakay's katipunan, yet less recognized today owing to its markedly religious character. A closer look at the admittedly meager data

---

63. ARPC (1903), 3, Report of the 3rd District, Philippine Constabulary," p. 121.

64. *Conditions in the Philippines* (U.S. Senate Document 170, 58th Congress, 2nd Session, February 1904), p. 14.

65. ARPC (1903), 3, "Report of the 3rd District," p. 121.

66. *Philippine Life in Town and Country* (New York: G.P. Putnam and Sons, 1905), p. 129.

on this movement, however, reveals features of the common language that intersects through all of the popular anticolonial movements of the period.

In terms of social background, Ruperto Rios appears to have had some things in common with Sakay. Both were "town dwellers" at least partly aware of developments in the world beyond. Sakay was a barber from Tondo, while Rios was a bellowsman to the blacksmith at Atimonan. Both were, naturally, veterans of the revolution. Rios had the rank of major under the command of Lt. Col. Emilio Zurbano of the revolutionary army in Tayabas. When Zurbano, responding to General Cailles's orders, surrendered to the United States in July 1901, Rios went along and even took the oath of allegiance. But soon after Malvar and Caballes had reorganized the guerilla movement, Rios was back in the field with the rank of lieutenant colonel bestowed on him by Malvar. Just as the mantle of leadership in 1901 had passed from Trias to Malvar, and Cailles to Caballes, so did Rios inherit Zurbano's position, at least in southeastern Tayabas. In September 1901, he styled himself "political and military chief, province of Tayabas."[67] Apart from this, it is difficult to know precisely what the man was like and what his aims were, for we have to rely upon American reports which are totally unsympathetic toward this "bandit." Bandholtz's description, for example, was gathered in 1903 from captured followers of Rios and are interspersed with sarcastic remarks as to how Rios fooled and manipulated the gullible and ignorant countryfolk.[68] In interpreting his behavior, we have to keep in mind that Sakay's Tondo and Rios's Atimonan were, and still are, worlds apart in terms of urbanity and sophistication. Rios's followers were mostly poor peasants and indebted woodcutters, including some professional bandits.[69] Rather than castigate Rios for manipulating the countryfolk, we can regard his actions as a sort of mirror of popular perceptions of the revolution.

According to Bandholtz, Rios attracted a substantial following by "posing" as an inspired prophet. He managed to control "a town or two" and harassed others. Continuing a practice started under Malvar's leadership, Rios organized "exterior municipal governments" with a full complement of officials. An elaborate military command headed by a lieutenant general and a captain general was set up. Rios himself had the rank of generalissimo. He proposed to enter the town of Atimonan on 8 August 1902, to be crowned "king," but swift action by Governor Bandholtz resulted in the arrest of eighty members of Rios's group before that date. They were successful, though, in entering Unisan. As the report states, 150 of them, "nearly all barefoot and conspicuously uniformed in shirt tails," entered Unisan, whipped the municipal

67. PIR-SD 719.4 (reel 40, fr. 606; PNL).

68. ARPC (1902), 1, "Report of the Provincial Governor, Tayabas," pp. 926–27; also ARPC (1902), 1, "Annual Report of the Chief of the Philippine Constabulary," p. 38 (based largely on Bandholtz's report).

69. Statement of ex-Governor Gardener, 1902 (RG 94, Enc. 2 to 421607, p. 36, USNA).

officials and walked off with five policemen all of whom were recaptured later, unharmed.

Rios was also called "pope." He distributed *anting-anting* to all his followers. He heard confessions and granted absolution, claiming that these were more efficacious than when done by a Catholic priest. He also had the power to ascend to heaven by means of a rope. At night he would conceal himself, and then appear in the morning with announcements such as, for example, that he had talked with the emperors of Russia, Germany and France, and that these potentates would send over large fleets that would distribute 10,000 arms with the necessary ammunition on the shores of Tayabas province. Rios's state aim was to secure the independence of the country. For some time, he carried with him a chest on the cover of which was painted "Independence" and which was guarded by three "picked virgins." Quoting from Bandholtz's report:

> [Rios] stated to the ignorant barrio people that the Filipinos had for a long time been struggling for independence which he now had in his possession, and that as soon as he was convinced that his followers deserved it, he would remove the lid from the box, 'Independence' would jump out, they would catch her, and be ever afterwards happy.[70]

Independence would bring a life of ease, property would be shared, no taxes collected and jails no longer needed. When the chest was opened, it was found to contain only some old Spanish gazettes and a few hieroglyphics among which appeared the names and ranks of the officials of the organization.

American officials found the whole affair ridiculous particularly because of the "fantastic," magical notion of independence. But they also considered it dangerously subversive because this "fantastic" idea of independence seemed to imply, as Bandholtz puts it, "that each man could help himself to whatever he desired—his neighbor's pony, carabao, or property."[71] This is, of course, an exaggeration, for Rios's movement had specific "enemies"—the collaborators, who happened to be the well-to-do. What really made the movement "subversive" is that Rios's followers had an image of the future that shaped their activities. This is quite evident in the following description of a wounded guerilla captured in March 1903 near Infanta: "The fanatic rolled his glistening eyes as he drank in the thought of the approach of the millenium. 'When *independencia* flies from the box, there will be no labor, Señor, and no jails and no taxes.'"[72]

The belief that independence, or kalayaan, would jump out of a box is consistent with Katipunan images of kalayaan as a personified condition:

---

70. ARPC (1902), 1, "Annual Report of the Chief of the Constabulary," p. 926.

71. Ibid.

72. Victor Hurley, *Jungle Patrol: The Story of the Philippine Constabulary* (New York, 1938), p. 126.

Mother Filipinas or Bernardo Carpio lying in a state of limbo or sleep, awaiting the day of final liberation that would bring about prosperity, comfort, and knowledge. The popular belief in resurrection, based on traditions of ancestor worship as well as Christianity, was evidently the chord that Rios struck through his box, a symbolic coffin. There is nothing incredible about this. At around the same time in Manila, Aurelio Tolentino was staging his Katipunan-inspired drama, *Kahapon, Ngayon, at Bukas* (Past, Present, and Future), which drew upon similar images: Mother Country is ordered buried alive by Ferocious Beast (the friars), but as soon as the revolution led by Taga-ilog triumphs, Mother Country's grave opens and she comes forth, radiant as ever, a sign of the unity of her sons. The play incited the audience so much that it was promptly suppressed.[73] The fervor inspired by Rios's magical box can be understood in this light.

As a prophet, Rios could point to certain signs that a condition of kalayaan was approaching. In a sense, independence was already there in the box, just as for Apolinario de la Cruz the king was "behind the curtain," but men had to change their loób by participating in rituals and in the struggle itself, before kalayaan could be enjoyed. This is the significance of an American officer's assertion that "the followers of Rios believed that when they had proven worthy, the prophet would open the box and this mysterious thing, independence, would come forth to bless them."[74] The parallel with the interred Christ in the pasyon is too striking to be ignored: Independence, guarded by three women —the *Tatlong Maria* (Three Marys) of the pasyon—will come forth, become a social reality, only when the people, led by their "King" Rios, have fulfilled their own pasyon. Perhaps the hieroglyphics inside the chest were anting-anting, inscribed objects with the power of giving life when their prescribed rituals are accomplished with perfect control. When Independence has emerged, society will not be the same as before because man will have died to his former state. No taxes, no jails, sharing of property, brotherhood—these possibilities will have been realized in the same way that paradise is regained.

The principalia of Tayabas and Laguna feared the Rios movement not only because of the implication that their property would be threatened with independence but also because many of these "leading citizens," having participated in the revolution of 1898 and then acquiesced to the new order, were now considered by Rios traitors to a sacred cause. This explains why Rios attacked municipal officials as well as constabulary soldiers. Sizing up the situation, Governor Bandholtz came to the conclusion that "the only way to combat such an organization was through the more intelligent natives themselves." All over the province of Tayabas, Bandholtz organized compa-

---

73. E. Arsenio Manuel, *Dictionary of Philippine Biography*, vol. 2 (Quezon City: Filipiniana Publications, 1970), pp. 395-431; Amelia Lapeña-Bonifacio, *The "Seditious" Tagalog Playwrights* (Manila: Bookmark Publishing Co., 1972), pp. 177–206.

74. From a report by Capt. Murphy, March 1903 (in Hurley, *Jungle Patrol*).

nies of volunteers "composed of the higher class of natives," and armed them with guns. No doubt, a certain amount of arm-twisting was involved in getting the coöperation of all the principales; Bandholtz, for example, made town officials responsible for "bandit" activity in their jurisdiction. But, by and large, the principales were found to be more zealous than expected in combatting "banditry." "Infected barrios" were sometimes transferred by municipal governments to locations where the constabulary or local police could watch them.[75] The constabulary itself, it should be noted, was led by men of the "higher class." "Too often," remarks LeRoy, "the so-called Filipino officials of the corps are men of so large a share of Spanish blood . . . that they are decidedly hostile to the Filipinos and are hated by the people, being identified with the Spanish side of internal strife in the past." What is worse,

> many of the soldiers of the Constabulary rank and file are of the same class of informers, spies, and other former servants of the American military government who have frequently their private vengeances to pay, and do not scruple to do so under the cover of the terror which their uniform inspires.[76]

It was the combination of constabulary soldiers and principalia volunteers that broke the backs of the poorly armed and trained groups led by Rios, Destajo, Verastigui, Sakay and other veterans of the revolution.

Rios himself was captured by deceit in San Antonio, Laguna. He and his band were invited to enter the town and "make themselves at home." After "coaxing them in under the guise of friendship," the "people of San Antonio and Paete" captured the whole outfit, the constabulary reported. Later, Governor Cailles claimed he designed the capture scheme himself, and that credit should also be given to the municipal president, police, and volunteers of San Antonio—certainly not "the people," as the constabulary alleged. In a telegram of 29 May 1903, the colonial government authorized the payment of $2,000 as a reward to the individuals who had performed "an important service." "King" Rios, betrayed by principales he mistakenly trusted, was eventually hanged in Atimonan.[77]

The end of Rios did not mean an end to disturbances of the same nature in Laguna and Tayabas. In April 1904, a society called *Solo Dios* (One God), led by a certain "Francisco," was discovered on the borders of Laguna, Tayabas, and Batangas. It had a governmental structure in the town of San Pablo, Laguna, and in several barrios. Authorities eventually traced its headquarters to the barrio of San Cristobal.[78] In 1905, it was reported that the Cavite branch

---

75. Bandholtz to the Executive Secretary at Manila, Lucena, 15 January 1903 (Bandholtz Papers, MHC); ARPC (1903), 1, "Report of the Provincial Governor, Tayabas," p. 926.

76. "The Philippine Police," 14 October 1905 (LeRoy 1905 Travel Log, folder 10, MHC).

77. ARPC (1903), 1, "Report of the 1st District, Philippine Constabulary," p. 65, ARPC (1904), , "Report of the Provincial Governor, Laguna," p. 514.

78. "Christmas Eve Fiasco," in Artemio Ricarte, *Memoirs*, p. 198.

of the Colorum Society was protecting Julian Montalan and other officials of Sakay's Katipunan being hunted down by the constabulary and native volunteers.[79] Constant surveillance by the constabulary of Colorum activities, particularly in and around Mount San Cristobal, put an end to its overtly political activities. But this did not prevent the society from undergoing rapid expansion during the first decade of the century. Its principal following outside of Tayabas came from "the ignorant people of Rizal, Laguna, Bulacan, Batangas and Cavite provinces, being strongest in towns where outlawry abounds.[80] "Outlawry," of course, in those days meant primarily Katipunan and other proindependence movements.

Betrayal and Sakay's Death

The years of 1904 and 1905 saw a resurgence of Sakay's Katipunan. Except for certain highlights, the minute details of confrontations between the constabulary and the Katipunan need not be mentioned here. The overall director of military operations was Julian Montalan, who in 1904 was designated by Sakay as "lieutenant general, first chief politico-militar of southern Luzon." Described by Aguinaldo as "a valuable soldier to the revolutionary government of 1898," Montalan issued, on 10 April 1904, the so-called Montalan Law specifying the various degrees of punishment for treacherous acts against the revolutionary government.[81] Beneath Montalan in the guerilla hierarchy were Maj. Gen. Cornelio Felizardo, who operated mainly in Cavite, and Brig. Gen. Aniceto Oruga who controlled the lake towns of Batangas. On 12 November, the Philippine Scout headquarters at San Pedro Tunasan, Laguna, was attacked by Felizardo's unit. This was followed by a raid on the constabulary detachment at Parañaque on 8 December. About sunset of 15 January 1905, Montalan led a large contingent that "marched up the main street of Taal [Batangas]" and "disarmed the municipal police who made but a semblance of resistance." The municipal treasury and armory were raided while many townspeople watched approvingly.[82] On 24 January, Montalan and Felizardo teamed up in a massive attack on the old Magdiwang Katipunan stronghold of San Francisco de Malabon, Cavite. Municipal funds, arms, and ammunition were carted away and the family of Governor Trias kidnapped. Trias himself, an open enemy of the Katipunan, managed to evade capture.[83]

---

79. ARPC (1905), 3, "Report of the Philippine Constabulary, Provincial District of Cavite," p. 133.

80. ARPC (1907), 3, "Report of the 2nd District of the Philippine Constabulary," p. 301.

81. Montalan document (LeRoy 1905 Travel Log, folder 13, MHC); transcript of interrogation of Emilio Aguinaldo, 29 July 1905 (LeRoy 1905 Travel Log, folder 12, MHC).

82. "Report of Col. D.J. Baker, Ass't Chief Commanding Prov. District, Philippine Constabulary, On Work Done In That District Since Its Organization Up To 31 July 1905" (BIA 1184-60, USNA), pp. 7–8.

83. Ibid., pp. 9–10. Trias's wife and two children were eventually rescued by the constabulary

The boldness of the Katipunan, the sympathy and material support it enjoyed from the rural populace, and the inability of landlords to cultivate their lands because of the unrest, forced the colonial government, on 31 January 1905, to suspend the writ of habeas corpus in Cavite and Batangas provinces. In March, "reconcentration" or the relocation of villagers was resorted to all over Batangas and Cavite and in some parts of Laguna and Rizal.[84] This all-out colonial effort led Aguinaldo, who "in conversation with friends frequently declared against bandolerism 'as an evil,'" to complain nevertheless that there was "more fear of military and police than of ladrones among his farmers, which was apparently the case with most of the people in that region."[85] The policy worked, however. Through systematic arrests and interrogations, the guerilla units were whittled down in size and forced to seek cover elsewhere. By mid-1905 Oruga had surrendered to Governor Cailles and Felizardo had been treacherously murdered. Montalan survived the pressure only through the help of the ever-reliable Colorum Society. But suppression alone did not stamp out Sakay's Katipunan. The "supremo" himself remained entrenched in Rizal (formerly Morong) province, east of Manila. In November 1905, Constabulary Chief Bandholtz confessed that Sakay had "too many warm sympathizers in Rizal" for the government to attempt to capture him.[86] What ultimately brought about the Katipunan's surrender was the tactic of, as Bandholtz put it, "playing upon the emotional and sentimental part of the Filipino character."[87] Let us examine what he meant by this.

According to the Philippine bill (Cooper Act) which President Roosevelt signed into law on 2 July 1902, one of the conditions for the establishment of an indigenous Philippine Assembly was the complete restoration of peace and order throughout the archipelago. By 1906, it looked like this condition would not be met in time for the creation of the assembly in 1907. At least that is what Bandholtz and other American officials impressed upon aspiring Filipino politicians. "We laid great stress," says Bandholtz, "upon the fact that unless bandolerismo was extinct in Cavite and Batangas, those provinces would undoubtedly be cut off from representation in the assembly and the assembly jeopardized."[88] One aspiring ilustrado politician, Dominador Gomez, responded by appealing to Sakay, on grounds of "common cause," to surrender peacefully. He produced a letter, signed by the American governor, guaranteeing that Sakay and his men would not be punished or molested upon turning themselves in.

On the morning of 4 July 1906, the Katipunan, in full uniform, marched into Manila on a safe-conduct pass. An eyewitness reports that a brass band

84. Ibid., pp. 10, 12–13.

85. Transcript of interrogation of Emilio Aguinaldo, 29 July 1905 (LeRoy 1905 Travel Log, folder 12, MHC).

86. Bandholtz to Gen. H. Allen, Manila, 24 November 1905, (Bandholtz Papers, MHC).

87. Bandholtz to Col. J. Harbord, Manila, 8 July 1906 (Bandholtz Papers, MHC).

88. Ibid.

followed them wherever they went. "They were on foot, accompanied by hundred of townspeople. So great was their popularity that their countrymen shouted, 'Mabuhay si Sakay! Mabuhay ang mga bayani!' [Long live Sakay! Long live the patriots!]"[89] The Katipuneros attended banquets, dances, and other festive gatherings. At night, they joined bands of serenaders vying for the attention of pretty ladies. Apparently the Katipuneros, for reasons to be discussed later, perceived their surrender as an occasion to celebrate. Behind the scenes, however, a plot to apprehend the leaders had been devised. On 17 July, Sakay and his staff composed of Montalan, Leon Villafuerte, Lucio de Vega, and Benito Natividad were invited by an American officer to a dance in Cavite hosted by Acting Governor van Shaick. Just before midnight, as they were dancing in the town hall shielded from the gaze of sympathetic townsfolk, the Katipuneros were disarmed and arrested by the American officers in the crowd. Gomez, who continued to insist that he desired independence just as much, advised Sakay not to resist arrest.

"What kind of government is this!" exclaimed General Villafuerte to his Katipunan brother in their prison cell. "They invited us to celebrate our surrender, and then treacherously arrested us." Aboard a boat on the way to Manila, where he was to be tried, Villafuerte asked a Filipino officer near him: "Why are you Tagalog soldiers treating us like this? You are fighting your own kin *(kadugo)*!"[90] These statements, which echo Bonifacio's last words to his executioner on Mount Buntis, reflect a certain naiveté in Sakay's group concerning the independence struggle. Perhaps the ghost of Malolos still haunted them, dangling before them the illusion that wealthy and poor, ilustrado and *gente proletaria,* could be truly united and enjoy kalayaan by virtue of the "common blood" in their veins.

In persuading Sakay to surrender, Dominador Gomez had stated categorically that the Philippine Assembly was the "gate of kalayaan" (*Pinto ng Kalayaan*).[91] Now Sakay, as we have seen, was only too aware of the disjunction of words and meanings that wreaked havoc on the spirit of the revolution. For him to have accepted the notion that the assembly was the gate of kalayaan, as the Katipunan of Bonifacio had earlier claimed itself to be, is a tribute to Gomez's powers of speech and persuasion, his ability to play upon "the emotional and sentimental part of the Filipino character." Gomez was the quintessence of ilustrado politicians, a pure demogogue who in 1905 was found guilty by a Manila court of extortion and misappropriation of the funds

89. Abad, *Macario Sakay,* pp. 55–56. Abad himself accompanied Sakay and got to interview him. Full documentation on the circumstances of the deception is found in Abad's book.

90. Ibid., p. 114. Villafuerte was one of the more educated officers of Sakay's Katipunan. Like the famed Gen. Gregorio del Pilar, Villafuerte was very young, 24, when Sakay made him a general.

91. Gomez to Sakay, 6 July 1906, Manila (in Santos, *Tatlong Tulisan,* p. 60).

of the Union Obrero (Labor Union), and yet continued to pose as "a martyr of the poor obreros."[92] Bandholtz's description of him minces no words:

> Working with Dominador Gomez is like playing with a two-edged tool or with fire. You have to be most careful or he will get you implicated someway or other. . . . I am inclined to believe that, if he really so desired, he could at any time start a serious uprising or, if one were started, that he himself could put an end to it. Of course, he is a deep-eyed villain and absolutely unscrupulous, especially if money is concerned. Within limits, it would pay to keep him in our employ.[93]

Bandholtz claims that he bagged "Sakay and Co." through "our friend Dominador Gomez," who seems to have convinced Sakay that the Katipunan's road to kalayaan was no longer the right one. In a document signed by the Katipuneros on the night of 17 July 1906, we find the following statement:

> Na sila ay caya humarap ay dahil sa ipinalastas sa canila ng mga tauong namagitan sa canilang pagharap na ang canilang paninira sa gubat ay nacasasama at nacapapahamac sa canilang bayang tinubuan, at gayon din naman na ang canilang pagharap ay macagagaling na hindi hamac sa lupang tinubuan.[94]
>
> The undersigned declare that the reason they presented themselves is because they were informed by the intermediaries in the surrender that their holding out in the field was causing harm to and sabotaging their own country, and that their surrender would greatly benefit their native land.

No wonder the Katipuneros rejoiced upon entering Manila; they viewed themselves not as capitulating, but as helping the country gain kalayaan. Sakay is also quoted to have said: "I surrendered because fighting is an uphill game and the Filipinos will never succeed in gaining independence until they show themselves worthy of it. There is nothing to be gained by opposing the Americans."[95] Here, Sakay seems to accept the ilustrado position that cooperation with, not opposition to, America is the correct path to kalayaan. But there is more to this statement, something that brings us right back to Rios and Caneo—the idea that "worthiness," the proper state of loób, is a prerequisite to kalayaan.

During the trial of Sakay and his men, Defense Counsel Felipe Buencamino delivered a lengthy speech that attempted to illuminate the Katipuneros' actions.[96] Buencamino argued, in poetic Tagalog, that the accused were

92. "Personal and Police History of Deputies to the First Filipino Assembly," Worcester Philippine Collection, vol. 2, pt. 1, p. 8 (University of Michigan Library); Bandholtz to Carpenter, 24 July 1909 (Bandholtz Papers, MHC).

93. Bandholtz to Carson, 18 April 1907 (Bandholtz Papers, MHC).

94. Photostat in file with correspondence, 13 June 1913 (Bandholtz Papers, MHC).

95. *Springfield Republican*, 21 July 1906 (in Philippine 1900 Scrapbook, WPC).

96. *Muling Pagsilang*, 25 September 1906. The correspondent was able to pick up only portions of Buencamino's speech.

simply "gods *(dioses)* of kalayaan." He drew an analogy with Christ who "became God when he was hanging on the cross." Sakay and his men were somewhat like "gods" because they took it upon themselves to risk death itself for kalayaan's sake. Buencamino's speech took a somewhat hyperbolic turn as he described the irresistible appeal of kalayaan.

> O Kalayaan, Kalayaan, anong ganda mo at dilag! Lahat ay umiibig sa iyo at nagpapakamatay; kung mabubuhay nga lamang ang tanang nagpakamatay dahil sa iyo, marahil ay hindi magkakasiyang tumayo sa boong Sanglupalop; at kung mangyayari lamang maipon ang tanang dugong nabuhos dahil sa iyo, marahil ay hindi magkakasiyang isilid ni sa lahat ng dagat at ilog sa boong Sinukob!
>
> Oh Kalayaan, Kalayaan, how beautiful and radiant you are! Everyone falls for you, and is willing to die for you. If all who have died for you can be resurrected, not even the whole world can accommodate their numbers. And if all the blood poured for you were collected, it would overflow all the world's rivers and seas!

While admitting that Sakay and his men committed acts of violence, it was "also undeniable that the patriotism and courage of the accused deserved attention and respect." After all, they laid down their arms with tranquil *(panatag)* loób and "out of concern for the creation of the Philippine Assembly."

Buencamino also made reference to the American scheme *(política)* in effecting the Katipunan surrender. Colonel Bandholtz and Governor Ide "used the light *(ilaw)* in order to conquer darkness; their weapon was the Word *(Verbo)* of Filipinas, Doctor Gomez, so that through the influence of this sweet-talker, there would be liwanag in the clouded minds of the accused." The implication here is that Gomez used precisely the idiom of liwanag and redemption in convincing Sakay and company to surrender. Unfortunately, the accused failed to see beneath Gomez's appealing exterior. In the *awit* we analyzed in the previous chapter, Aguinaldo is depicted as succumbing to the sweet, enticing words of the Spaniards; thus his 1897 "pact" with Spain and the awit's subsequent ignoring of his later activities. Sakay's experience lends itself to a similar interpretation. However, his arrest, trial, and execution assure an unequivocal interpretation of his life pattern.

As Sakay ascended the scaffold on 13 September 1907, he paused briefly to say these parting words:

> Death comes to all of us sooner or later, so I will face the Lord Almighty calmly. But I want to tell you that we are not bandits and robbers, as the Americans have accused us, but members of the revolutionary force that defended our mother country, Filipinas! Farewell! Long live the republic and may our independence be born in the future! Farewell! Long live Filipinas![97]

---

97. Abad, *Macario Sakay*, p. 101.

Abad notes that Sakay and De Vega, the two Katipunan leaders meted the death penalty, accepted their fate "with courage." Sakay's parting words are reminiscent of the form of *paalam* (farewell) used in the poetry of the revolution to signify the beginning of a journey unto death. But every martyr's death has its expected sequel—rebirth. The juxtaposition in Sakay's last words of "farewell" and the future birth of independence explains his serenity at the scaffold; his death would take mother Filipinas a step further toward kalayaan.

In Bilibid prison, from 1906 to 1913, hundreds of prisoners most of whom were members of the Katipunan were executed without public knowledge. Certain ilustrado leaders were aware of this but did not raise their voices in protest.[98] For the ilustrados, except for a handful who sympathized with Sakay, had gotten what they wanted upon the capture of the katipunan leadership. On 30 July 1907, a month before Sakay's execution, elections for the Philippine Assembly were held peacefully. The new Nacionalista Party, running on a platform of "immediate independence," won fifty-nine seats, or seventy-two percent of the assembly's membership. Assemblyman Dominador Gomez was ecstatic. Famous Filipinos like Manuel Quezon and Sergio Osmeña would begin their long and prolific careers that would take them through the complex paths of colonial politics. The standard works on modern Philippine history are filled with this aspect of what has so often been seen as the struggle for nationhood and independence. And yet these nationalists of the 1907 assembly were chosen by an electorate comprising only three percent of the population, the same three percent who, in the waning days of Spanish rule, had comprised the native elite. A recent study reveals that the assembly delegates "were, on the whole, young, aristocratic and well-educated. Many had been to Europe for schooling."[99] Twenty-six percent had held office under the Spanish government while nearly seventy-five percent had served under the Malolos republic. It may be said that the assembly was a rebirth of the 1898 Malolos Congress.

Idiom of Protest in the"New Era"

Despite their moderate aspirations, Nacionalista party leaders were well aware that the kalayaan ideal was very much alive among the masses, and every effort was made to harness this to win popular support for the party. In the party's organ *La Independencia*, first published in 1906, there is, besides

98. Abad, *Macario Sakay*, p. 104. This information was given to Abad by Villafuerte upon his pardon in 1913. Villafuerte had no personal axe to grind against the ilustrados because the most prominent of them, Manuel Quezon, was the one who secured his pardon. The secret executions and other atrocities were later denounced by the Tagalog newspaper *Muling Pagsilang*.

99. Frank Jenista, Jr. "Conflict in the Philippine Legislature: The Commission and the Assembly from 1907 to 1913," in *Compadre Colonialism*, ed. Norman Owen, p. 82.

material in Spanish, a plethora of Tagalog articles and supplements calculated to invoke nostalgia for the revolutions of 1896 and 1898. There are few hints that ilustrado party leaders were actually little concerned with the Katipunan spirit or experience, and were merely riding on the prevailing mood of the times to establish their political careers. Occasionally, however, one finds among the Tagalog writings in *La Independencia* indirect expressions that somehow the ilustrado handling of the country's plight has run counter to the "straight path" revealed by the Katipunan. A story that appears in the 21 December 1906 issue of the newspaper illustrates this point.[100] It deals with an event that happened sometime just after the revolution, but seems to address itself to the present as its title indicates: *Hindî lahat ang natutulog* (Not Everyone Is Asleep). The title is a quotation from one of Rizal's writings, but in place of the dark night of Spanish rule we find a metaphor for the colonial politics of the present.

The narrator is a woman who, one night, finds herself unable to sleep, filled with restlessness and sadness as she thinks about the hardships and enslavement of her country and her loved ones. Lying fully awake for the better part of the night, she finally rouses her husband and asks him to "entertain" her with stories of his past experiences. Her husband is most obliging, but cautions her not to repeat his story to anyone. "My obliging and beloved husband paused for a few seconds . . . . he wiped the tears that were starting to form in his eyes, as if he remembered something bitter in the past:

> Isang gabi, anya, ng buwan ng Mayo, na aco'y nasasa Tayabas, sa pooc ng San Diego, ang langit ay nababalutan ng sapot niyang dilim, ang hangin ay umuugong casaliw sa mapanglaw na tahulan ng mga aso at sa malungcot na tunog ng isang batingaw (campana) ng calapit na simbahan na nagbabala ng isang panalangin at ala-ala patungcol sa mga camag-anac at magulang na nasa sa cabilang buhay.
>
> One night, he said, during the month of May, when I was in Tayabas, in the vicinity of San Diego, the sky was wrapped in a death-shroud of darkness, the wind was moaning in harmony with the distant barking of dogs and the melancholy ringing of church bells nearby, announcing a memorial prayer to one's parents and relatives who have passed away.

The young man has just left the house of an elder for whom he works. As he walks home in pitch darkness, the puzzling advice of his old master, who is poor and uneducated but nevertheless regarded as a sage, keeps on ringing in his head:

100. To my knowledge, the only available copy of this issue is in the newspaper collection of the U.S. Library of Congress.

Quilanlin mo muna and iyong sarili.

Huag mong papasiyahan ng padumali ang mga gawa ng tao, huag pupulaan ni pupurihin, arukin mo muna ang canyang puso bago mo pasiyahan ang canyang gawa.

Hindi mabuting panggagamot ang lasunin ang maysakit, cundi ang paginhawahin ang maysakit.

Igalang mo ang panucala, pagcat iyan ang hininga ng calolowa, at ang paghinga ng calolowa, dapat ay malaya.

Pumucol sa ala-ala na marahil anaquin, sa di catalusan ng mga bagay na ito, o tanto man caya ay di isinasagawa ng mga tao, canya di mapawi sa sangsinucob ang matandang sakit na tinatawag na pagcacaalit-alit.

Know yourself first.

Do not judge the works of another hastily. Neither criticize nor praise them; sound first the depths of his heart before you bring judgment upon his works.

It is not good medicinal practice to poison the sick. Rather, bring relief and comfort (*ginhawa*), for they are the breath of soul, and the breathing of the soul should be free.

Hammer into your mind that the reason the old illnes of the world called discord has not been cured is because men do not know or fail to accomplish what I have just said.

Suddenly the young man notices, toward the east, a "soft light," *malamlam na ilaw,* heading toward him. As the light nears, it turns out to be an old man dressed in tattered clothes, struggling with a heavy load on his shoulder. The old man asks for help in carrying his load and his request is heeded by the youth who, however, cannot get over his curiosity about the contents of the coffinlike box.

"Where are we taking this? In which feast are we going to use this? "asks the youth, guessing that it is a machine for extracting coconut juice.

"This won't be used anywhere. This contains the dregs *(tira-tirahan)."*

"And where are we taking it?'

"To the graveyard."

The youth becomes extremely frightened and confused. Can his companion be a wicked murderer, he muses. Most likely he is a poor beggar who cannot pay for a funeral. Again the youth asks,"Who is in this heavy coffin that we are carrying to the grave in a time like this?"

The stranger finally gives in: "These are the false kings who lead our projects (*naghahari-harian sa mga panucala)* and treat the country's illness with poison." At this point, the youth realizes the meaning of his sage master's advice.

The youth and the stranger together enter the graveyard in pitch darkness, the only mourners being crickets underneath the weeds and fireflies weaving about the branches of a dense *balete* tree. Having buried the coffin, the old man makes a strange request: "Let us transfer that hill over this grave, so that the ashes of those buried will never henceforth mix with the soil we tread upon and till."

The youth laughs. "Please, let us leave that matter aside. How can the two of us lift that mountain?"

"Why do you laugh? Do you not recognize me? I am the country that suffers quietly the scorns and insults heaped upon it."

"Since that is the case, sir, I humbly offer myself to you."

"Thank you. And so it is, as I have always believed fervently, that not everyone is asleep in the night of our ancestors."

At this point, says the narrator, her husband's story is cut short. And the lamp that illumines their room suddenly flickers and dies out.

The anonymous author of the *La Independencia* article obviously intended to comment upon the events of his time (1906). But to do so effectively, he needed to use an idiom of protest that was meaningful to his Tagalog audience. That the narration takes place while the couple's room is illuminated by a flickering light that dies out in the end would have reminded the reader with fresh memories of the revolution, of Jacinto's Manifesto of 1896 which is similarly framed. But even without the experience of the Katipunan behind him, the reader would have known that the story contained a revelation, that it was a moment of liwanag in a time of darkness.

Like Jacinto's Manifesto, the subject of the story is a youth's passage from darkness to light. He walks along a road in pitch darkness, which signifies a condition of ignorance and death. The "death-shrouded" sky, the moaning of the wind, barking of dogs and ringing of church bells are all signs of death. He himself manifests a loób in darkness. He cannot comprehend the teachings of his old master; he pines for a loved one who has rejected him; he talks of being lonely on the road. But most of all, he fails to recognize and is even frightened by the stranger, who is first glimpsed as a light coming from the east. Bearing a heavy load on his shoulder, the lowly stranger is no less than a figure of Christ.

It is the youth's willingness to share the stranger's burden, a willingness motivated by his own loneliness, that sets him on the road to enlightenment. His persistent questions lead the stranger to reveal the contents of the coffin they bear—"the false kings who lead our projects and who treat the country's illness with poison." This revelation enables the youth to connect the teachings of his "poor" *(dukha)* and "uneducated" *(hindi nag-aral)* master with the condition of darkness in which the country is cast. Basically these teachings "from below" state that a continuity ought to exist between the state of a man's loób and his external appearance and acts. The problem with the world is that disjunctions between "external" and "internal" are becoming widespread, making it necessary to sound the depths of a man's loób before judging his acts. The sage's statement, "it is not good medicinal practice to poison the sick," harks back to the pasyon image of Christ the Doctor to the sick (48:7), the problem being that people often fail to recognize the true intentions of a "doctor" who merely pretends at his task. The world will forever be in turmoil as long as people either fail to distinguish between reality and appearance or continue to behave outwardly in a mode that runs counter to what their loób is.

The sage states that *panucala,* i.e., human projects or programs, must be "respected" because they are the "breath of the soul which should be free" *(malaya).* Connecting the words of sage and stranger, the youth realizes that panucala should be oriented towards the country's kalayaan, only thus will her illness be cured. In this respect, the country's leaders have been playing "false kings" (*naghahari-harian*). *Hari-harian* is a popular children's game involving pretenders or pseudo kings. To play around with panucala, to treat politics as a game, is to manifest a lack of fit between loób and appearance; it is the same thing as treating the country's illness with poison. That is why these false kings and false doctors should be carried to the grave.

If the objects of criticism were the country's leading politicians, why did the author not attack them directly; why the coffin, burial and all that? It has to do less with fear of reprisal, than with situating the 1906 events in the context of popular ideas of change. The stranger in the story is several things: liwanag, Christ and, as he himself admits, the country. Unmistakably, he is undergoing a pasyon or *lakaran,* which the youth participates in, bearing the "sins" of the country on his shoulder. The box is not a coffin in the sense that we saw in Rios's case; it does not signify hope. Its contents—the remains of the "false kings"—are not to mingle with the soil tilled by man; the mountain is moved *over* the grave to signify its location at the bottom of the axis of the universe, i.e., hell. The box's contents are dregs, the *tira-tirahan,* that will be cast off like the blood and sweat of a penitent. We are reminded of the kahihiyan (shame) that Mother Country, in the awit we examined in the previous chapter, carries on her head as she, too, experiences a pasyon.

The reader of the *La Independencia* story would have found in it a way of focusing or organizing his perceptions of the politics of his time. In late 1906, with Sakay and his men safely in jail, the go-signal was given for the ambitious Filipino elite to compete for the glory and spoils of high office. The formula for success was simple: tap the masses' desire for kalayaan. Writing in October 1906, Bandholtz says this of the new game:

> Outside of Manila itself there are hardly any Federalistas, and they would probably be knocked out of business if the opposition would unite instead of splitting up into the Inmediatistas, Urgentistas, Explosivistas and N-plus-1 other kinds of ______istas. The Federals are now called the 'Poco Tiempo Independistas.'[101]

The Federalistas had always been pro-American; they had been instrumental in weaning the Filipino elite away from their support of the revolution. Now their platform was "Independence as soon as possible!" Bandholtz concluded in December that "the only thing that really distinguishes any of the parties or groups is the name, as many Federals are more radical than even the Urgen-

---

101. Bandholtz to Harbord, 7 October 1906 (Bandholtz Papers, MHC).

tistas and many of the latter are as conservative as any Federal."[102] It was a game that exploited the kalayaan ideal. For example, according again to Bandholtz, Ex-General Teodoro Sandiko became governor of Bulacan "under the impression that he would do away entirely with taxes and give the people a sort of socialistic independence. Of course, he has been unable to do so and the result is that he has lost much of the prestige that he formerly had."[103] These are some of the things that made it meaningful to talk about false kings, false doctors and the shedding of "dregs."

This form of protest would continue, often unnoticed, through the 1930s and perhaps beyond. We find the same ideas, for example, in a book titled *Pasion ng Bayan sa Kahapo't Ngay-on* (Passion of the Country in the Past and the Present), published in 1934, the eve of the Philippine Commonwealth.[104] The author, Joaquin Mañibo, draws a connection between the revolution and colonial politics in pasyon terms:

Ang unang "*Pasion ng Bayan*"	The first "*Passion of the Country*"
ay ang nangyaring digmaan	was the revolution in the past
at ang pangalawang tunay	and truly the second was
ang lumikha'y ang halalan	created by the elections
hangang ngayo'y umiiral. [105]	and still goes on today.

Interestingly enough, Mañibo extends the time of the revolution or "war" up to the first seven years of the Philippine Commission, that is, up to around the end of 1906, when the land finally "became quiet and peaceful." But then came another war that the country had to endure: "the unceasing war/ in the realm of elections (*Himagsikang walang humpay/ sa larangan ng halalan.*)[106] Why this triggered another pasyon is pretty clear:

Nang unang binabangon pa	When the two political parties
ang Lapian na dalawa	Nacionalista and Democrata
Nacionalista't Democrata	were first set up
ang binabandila nila	what they were waving
kulay ng Independencia.	was the flag of independence
Kahit ang Baya'y lumuha	Even though the Country wept
sa nagdaang pagdidigma	from the wars of the past
nagalak na at natuwa	it now was thrilled and overjoyed
sa discursong malalaya	by the uplifting speeches
ng politicong makata . . .	of the politician-poets . . .
Sila ang iisang Tawo	The two are but one person
dalawa lamang ang bautismo	there were just two baptisms

102. Bandholtz to Taft, Manila, 5 December 1906 (Bandholtz Papers, MHC)
103. Bandholtz to Carson, 18 April 1907 (Bandholtz Papers, MHC).
104. *Pasion ng Bayan sa Kahapo't Ngay-on* (Bauan, Batangas, 1934).
105. Ibid.
106. Ibid., p. 21.

ang laya'y balatkayo't	freedom (laya) was a mask
ang lihim na tinutungo'y	their secret goal was
ang libolibong sueldo.[107]	thousands in salaries.

The three most prominent politicians of the time, Quezon, Roxas, and Osmeña are called "the three false kings" *(ang tatlong hari-harian).* They have seduced the masses with talk of independence while actually violating the teachings of Rizal and Bonifacio, enriching their personal coffers and being the whip *(suplina)* with which "Tio Sam" slashes the back of the bound and helpless country.[108] But why have they been in power for so long? One of the reasons, says Mañibo, is because the masses believed that they would lead the country to kalayaan:

Sinong makatataya	How can we really judge
ng madlang potahe nila	the food they offer to us
hangang bago'y mahiwaga	full of mystery at first
saka natin nala-lasa	which we only get to taste
kapag kinakain na.	when it is already in our mouths.
Kahit lason o mapait	It may be poisonous or bitter
makalilinkag ng dib-dib	an evil cancer in our breast
linolonlon nating pilit	yet we force it down our throats
dahil sa ating nais	because of our desire
makalaya ang matuwid.[109]	for *katwiran* to triumph.

Once again we find the familiar theme of "feeding poison instead of medicine."

The cross that the country has to bear is not only that of graft and corruption, but also burdensome taxes, pitiful wages, and the general enslavement of the people. But worst of all is the senate's deceptive posture concerning kalayaan:

Itong balatkayong asal	This disguised behavior
ang unang hirap ng bayan	is the country's prime burden
Cruz na pinapasan	the cross that is borne
ng ama nating si Juan	by our father Juan
buto't balat ang katawan.[110]	whose body is skin and bones

Mañibo's *Pasion* is replete with condemnations of both the political and religious leaders of his time. Freely appropriating the form and language of the popular *Pasyon Pilapil,* Mañibo's message is simply that the "politics of in-

107. Ibid., p. 13.
108. Ibid., p. 16.
109. Ibid., p. 17.
110. Ibid., p. 19.

dependence" engaged in by the ilustrados is all deceptive glitter. The true liwanag of kalayaan had shone in the past through the selfless dedication of true sons of the country, and only those who continue the struggle of these patriots will sit beside Christ on the Day of Judgment. Evil friars, thieves, murderers, deceitful leaders, cruel soldiers, and all other oppressors will not see heaven. Furthermore,

Diya'y walang Punong lilo na nag general sa hukbo na nagpapugot ng ulo ni General Bonifacio sa Katipuna'y Supremo.	In heaven won't be found that treacherous leader who became general of the army and ordered the beheading of General Bonifacio.
Sa kay Cristong kaharian sa trono niya'y kinakanan si Del Pilar, Andres, Rizal si Mabini na lumalang ng sampung utos Bayan.	In the kingdom of Christ flanking his throne are Del Pilar, Andres [Bonifacio], Rizal and Mabini who created the country's ten commandments.
Diya'y ang mga quirubin ang madlang bayaning giting diya'y ang mga Serafin ang nag Punong matapatin nagsitupad ng tungkulin	There the cherubim are the heroic patriots all there the seraphim are the upright leaders who fulfilled their duties.
Diya'y ang mga Angeles mga dukhang anak pawis dito sa Mundo'y nagtiis ng dusa, hirap at sakit dahil sa baya'y pag-ibig.[111]	There the angels are the poor toilers who endured in this world pain, hardship, and suffering because of love for country.

It might be argued by some that the *Pasion* above reflects the perception and imagination of only one man—Joaquin Mañibo. But the author himself says that it is the "tall and leafy tree of fanaticism that protectively shelters *(kumakanlong)* the noble aspiration for independence of this country Philippines.[112] While a lot of Filipinos play the game of colonial politics, the masses preserve the sacred ideals of the Katipunan in practices and traditions usually associated with folk religion. Mañibo simply brings the folk perception of colonial politics up to date, or rather organizes such perceptions within a familiar pasyon framework. He also prescribes the "way" to be taken: if the people have damay for the suffering country, if they want true kalayaan, they must help carry the cross and join Ricarte's movement. Ricarte, the only living general of the revolution who refused to take the oath of allegiance to the United States, continued, up to the 1930s, to incite the people to rise up in arms against the United States. In 1935, shortly after Mañibo's *Pasion* was pub-

111. Ibid., pp. 29–30.
112. Ibid., p. 10.

lished, a Ricarte-inspired peasant rebellion called "Sakdal" swept central and southern Luzon. It is not surprising that one particular Sakdal doctrine had "great appeal to the masses," and "found a very fertile field in the barrio people's minds."[113] The doctrine, as quoted from the organ *Sakdal,* was the following:

> The leader of a subject country should be the first in making the sacrifice and suffer the pangs of hardship. No liberty was ever obtained happily; no success was ever attained through enriching one's self; nobody ever triumphed without passing over Golgotha and being nailed at the cross of Calvary. The leader who amasses wealth should be abhorred, should be downed, for he is not a leader but a despoiler.[114]

The Sakdal uprising of 1935 was directed as much against the Filipino elite as it was anti-American. But even in the first decade of this century there were already rumblings against the elite appropriation of the struggle for independence. Labor leaders, for one thing, knew what language to use in inspiring or manipulating the workers. During the May Day celebration in 1909, Director of Labor Ernesto del Rosario skillfully declaimed that "when the redemption of the working man was accomplished, the noble knights of labor would have another Calvary to ascend, the Calvary of a more noble, more glorious and more holy redemption, the redemption of our beloved Philippines."[115] But Bandholtz adds another insight into the significance of the same event. True, he says, ilustrado demagogues "inspire some ordinary *taos* to emulate the conduct of 'Bonifacio, Sakay & Co.'," but they themselves remain aloof. Laborers "are longing to have another Bonifacio, but most of the present day patriots are more busily engaged seeking government jobs than they are executioner's bullets."[116] It was only a matter of time before the workers found genuine leaders in their ascent of Calvary.

In the rural areas, various katipunans continued to offer an alternative to the ilustrado "way" to kalayaan. In 1905 Simeon Basa, a draftsman who had come under the influence of Ricarte, attempted to organize a katipunan in Zambales.[117] In the same year Atolio Tolentino, a cook in a Manila boarding house, mobilized a short-lived "army of independence" in Tarlac.[118] In 1907, it was reported that the katipunans of Ilocos province were expecting aid from the Japanese in the establishment of independence, for Japan's defeat of Russia had triggered hopes of a Japanese armada coming to the aid of Filipino

---

113. "The Growth of Sakdalism," *The Tribune*, 12 May 1935 (clipping in BIA 4865A93, USNA).
114. Extract from the Sakdal organ, *Sakdal* (original in Tagalog, in *The Tribune*, 12 May 1935).
115. Extract from *Los Obreros*, 3 May 1909 (in Bandholtz Papers, Box 2, MHC).
116. Bandholtz to Rethers, 4 May 1909; Bandholtz to Allen, 6 May 1909 (both in Bandholtz Papers, MHC).
117. "Christmas Eve Fiasco," p. 203.
118. ARPC (1905), 3, "Report of the 1st District, Philippine Constabulary," p. 57.

rebels.[119] In the same year, there was a revival of part of Rios's group in Atimonan, Tayabas, led by "Vice King" Marcelo Parafino and Maj. Gen. Esteban Deseo, both veterans of the revolution. Captured documents showed that this movement had had a "desultory existence" in the hills of eastern Tayabas since the destruction of Rios's group in 1903. The 1907 revival took the form of an organization called "Ejercito Libertador Nacional" (National Liberation Army). All the individual titles were military. According to American reports, "the organization was religious, but with the stated intention of rising for independence when Japan should land arms on the beach at Atimonan.[120] This liberation army was dismantled through the "active and energetic" efforts of Nacionalista Governor Manuel Quezon, who had then just been elected majority floor leader of the Philippine Assembly.[121]

The Colorum Society was also reported on the upsurge in 1907. Although its main concern was supposed to be religion, the constabulary found in its possession documents addressed to *Bathala* (Deity) in which Colorum brothers pledged "to expel all usurpers from the Filipino soil, including in this category both Americans and Spaniards, especially friars."[122] Also in 1907, Governor-General Wood reported an "extensive revival" of katipunans in Laguna province.[123] The "magical center" of the Laguna katipunans was Mount Makiling, an extinct volcano in the vicinity of Calamba, Rizal's hometown. Mount Makiling, like Mount Banahaw to the east, is considered a sacred mountain by the inhabitants of the region. Sometime in the first decade of this century Rizal, a Tagalog Christ, came to be associated with the land of paradise which is supposed to exist inside Makiling. There is a story told by the leader of a prominent Rizalist sect that Rizal once brought three peasants to Makiling's peak on a flying vessel. When they alighted,

> at once their attention was taken by the beautiful woodlands and the animals so varied and attractive around them, and Dr. Rizal took them around leisurely as if guiding them through a biological garden, until they entered a bower that led them to a descending stairway, which was bright as daylight but no lamps were visible. . . . Gradually a garden of flowers and fruit trees unfolded before them, and there were birds on the branches and luminous insects on the blossoms. "That is why Mount Makiling is so beautiful on the outside, even when far away," Dr. Rizal told them, and they believed him. "Anything that is really beautiful in the inside should be beautiful on the outside also," he emphasized.[124]

---

119. Wood to Taft, Manila, 13 April 1907 (BIA 4865, USNA).

120. ARPC (1907), 3, "Report of the 2nd District, Philippine Constabulary," p. 302.

121. Ibid. Quezon was a native of Tayabas, which has since been renamed Quezon province

122. Bandholtz (acting director of the constabulary) to Carson, 18 April 1907 (Bandholtz Papers, MHC).

123. Wood to Taft, Manila, 13 April 1907 (BIA 4865-45, USNA). Doherty believed, quite erroneously, that the Katipunan in Laguna was merely a scare rumor perpetuated by the party (Doherty to Gen. Edwards, Manila, 20 April 1907; BIA 3841-20, USNA).

124. Alfonso P. Santos, ed. *Rizal Miracle Tales* (Manila: National Bookstore, 1973), pp 123–24. The story comes from Jose Baricanosa, present head of the Watawat ng Lahi (Flag of the Race), a nationwide Rizalist church.

The last sentence of this story reiterates a theme that is familiar to us by now: true beauty is a reflection of beauty in the "inside," or loób. What Rizal tells the three peasants is that paradise is to some extent in every man whose heart is pure. But the attainment of paradise is possible only when one has taken the path traversed by Rizal. The latter's power, his mastery over a land "which was bright as daylight but no lamps were visible," is concomitant to his attainment of pure liwanag by dying a martyr's death. His revelation of paradise's beauty to the peasants is essentially what is done by persons in whom Rizal's "personality" is incarnated. As inspired prophets, they reveal an image of certain possibilities of existence which can only be attained by taking Rizal's path of dying to one's previous state.

In 1909 Arsenio de Guzman, a new Rizal, appeared in Santa Rosa claiming that he had the power to lead the peasants to the land of promise. His closest disciple, Catalino Lachica, then established a katipunan society among the "ignorant farm hands and tenants" of a hacienda in Santa Rosa owned by Dr. Zaballa, "a man of considerable wealth." At first the movement was ignored as "merely an agrarian" affair. But when it resulted in the death of Zaballa and the arrest and trial of the perpetrators, it was discovered that there was an extensive plot in the whole province to start a revolution that would establish independence from foreign rule and eliminate "oppressors" whose property would be distributed among the people. The rebels believed that arms for the revolution would come from Europe in flying machines. Arsenio de Guzman was arrested on a charge of sedition. However, the case against him was dropped when his disciple and principal witness in the trial, Catalino Lachica, refused to testify against the Rizalist leader and expressed rather his willingness to accept his fate, which was death, without implicating others.[125] De Guzman's katipunan survived, and flourishes today under the name "Watawat ng Lahi" (Flag of the Race).[126]

There were many similar movements in other parts of the archipelago which are beyond the scope of the present study. We have attempted to show thus far that independence was regarded by many people from the lower classes of Tagalog society as an imminent event to which their loób must be directed. Having experienced the turmoil and dislocation of five years of war, they expected such chaos to lead its inevitable conclusion—when society would be turned on its head, when all men would be brothers, leaders would be Christ-like, all form of oppression would end and property would be shared; in other words, when their image of kalayaan would turn into lived experience. This idea of independence differed from that of the "better classes" of Tagalog society who yearned for autonomy in the context of the stable society of the past in which they were the "natural" leaders.

125. "Christmas Eve Fiasco," in Artemio Ricarte, *Memoirs*, pp. 205–6.

126. For a detailed account of this group, see Prospero Covar's recent essay "Religious Leadership in the Iglesia Watawat ng Lahi," in L. Mercado, S.V.D., ed. *Filipino Religious Psychology* (Tacloban: Divine Word University, 1977).

Felipe Salvador after his capture in 1910 (photo from *Renacimiento Filipino*)

CHAPTER 6

The Pasyon of Felipe Salvador

From around 1894 to 1910, a religiopolitical movement called the Santa Iglesia flourished in the central Luzon provinces of Bulacan, Nueva Ecija, Tarlac, and Pampanga. These provinces are situated in the "rice bowl" of the Philippines, an immense expanse of flat land devoted to the cultivation of rice and some sugar. In the center of this region, a volcano named Mount Arayat, or Sinukuan, juts out abruptly, and is visible for many miles around. This mountain, and the swamp of Candaba which partly surrounds it, was the base area of the Santa Iglesia.

The peasants of the region believe that Arayat (derived from *Ararat)* is the highest mountain on earth. No one can ever climb to its top because of the "power" of certain relics of Noah's Ark that have remained there since the Deluge. Others believe that the cloud perpetually covering its peak during the monsoon season is a ghost of Noah's Ark sent there by the god Lakanpati as a "sign" to the faithful should the world be flooded again by the supreme god Bathala. The Ark remains there until the rainbow—the road that the soul travels on its way to heaven—appears.[1]

Mount Arayat is also known by the name of "Sinukuan," which means "to whom one has surrendered." The name is connected with the story of a beautiful and rich maiden, Marya, who lords over the peak that people describe as a kind of paradise. She lives in a large house of gold, accompanied by twelve beautiful maidens and twenty-five female Aetas who look after her needs and her gardens. In these gardens, with plentiful fruit trees and gentle animals, even the animals, birds, fishes, and snakes are adorned with jewelry of gold. When Marya goes down to the church in Candaba for the Sunday Mass, her dress of

1. T.E. Natividad, "Ang Bundok ng Arayat o Ang Sinukuan," RENFIL 2 (21 December 1911): 818-20; 2 (7 January 1912):883–84.

gold and her jewels are truly dazzling. Once, a *tikbalang*, who is king of the San Mateo mountains and a brother of Marya of Mount Makiling, falls in love with Marya of Arayat.[2] As a test, Marya tells the tikbalang to build a stone bridge that would link the peaks of Arayat and Makiling. The tikbalang works feverishly to build the bridge in one night, but the bridge does not even reach the shores of Bae lake in Laguna when dawn comes, and the sound of church bells frightens the tikbalang away. The unfinished structure collapses; the tikbalang fails to prove his love. Thus Arayat is also known as *Sinukuan*, "to whom one has surrendered."[3]

In a way the story of the tikbalang shows how, in people's minds, a connection exists between the various sacred mountains in central and southern Luzon. There is, in fact, a present-day belief that a tunnel connects the mountains of Banahaw, Makiling and Arayat.[4] All of these mountains were centers of pilgrimages, the haunts of religious sects and Katipunan-type societies. Associated with them are different personalities; around them took place events that are usually unrelated in time and specific circumstances. But, like the legend and tunnel that connect these mountains, something links together these varied men and events. We can talk about Arayat and the region north of Manila in relation to what has been examined in previous chapters because the meaning of certain events in this region points to a common mode of perceiving the world.

The pope of the Santa Iglesia—Felipe Salvador—was a deeply religious man who often walked alone in the forest of Arayat to communicate with God.[5] He claimed that his spirit took flight from Arayat's peak to visit the heavenly powers.[6] From at least 1902 to the time of his capture in 1910, his prophetic vision brought forth an image of independence inextricably linked with the millenium—there would be a great flood or fire that would wipe out unbelievers, and after the purge there would be a rain of gold and jewels for the faithful. Land and other property would be redistributed. Universal brotherhood among men would reign.[7] From the slopes of Arayat, Salvador called upon the

---

2. According to Panganiban's *Diksyunaryo-Tesauro Pilipino-Ingles* (Quezon City: Manlapaz, 1972), a tikbalang is a "folkloric creature whose supposed pastime is to get people to lose their way. He looks like an ordinary person except that he has horses' feet." The tikbalang of San Mateo is said to have caused Bernardo Carpio, the Tagalog culture hero, to lose his way and thus become imprisoned between two cliffs. Bonifacio and his Katipunan's gesture of seeking out the cave of Carpio signified the Katipunan's aim of freeing the Tagalog people (cf. chapter 3).

3. Natividad, "Ang Bundok ng Arayat."

4. Personal communication of anthropologist Robert Love (Quezon City, 1972).

5. Henry Reilly, "Filipino Bandit Terror," *The Chicago Tribune*, 2 August 1914 (BIA 4865A-1).

6. "Christmas Eve Fiasco," in Artemio Ricarte, *Memoirs* (Manila: National Heroes Commission, 1963), appendix N, p. 204. See also John Larkin, *The Pampangans: Colonial Society in a Philippine Province* (Berkeley: University of California, 1972), p. 236.

7. ARPC (1906), 2, "Report of the Director of the Constabulary," p. 226; David Doherty to the *New York Evening Post*, 2 October 1906 (BIA 4865-33). Doherty conducted his own investigation

people to join the Santa Iglesia, which he also called a "katipunan," in order to prepare for the approaching cataclysm.[8] Somehow the people who heard him seem to have known who he was and what he stood for. According to an American observer, nearly fifty thousand people, "all of the poor and densely ignorant class" responded to his call, and many more expressed sympathy for him.[9]

Salvador's Early Career

Felipe Salvador was born in Baliwag, Bulacan province, on 26 May 1870. According to an American correspondent, Felipe's father, Prudencio, was a "minor official" in the Spanish government.[10] Santos, however, claims that Prudencio held a high position in the government, and that Felipe himself once was *cabeza de barangay*.[11] It is certain, according to recent interviews of his surviving kin, that the Salvador family in the nineteenth and early twentieth centuries was relatively well-to-do. Evidence of this is the fact that the Salvador ancestral house, which used to be built of stone, stands just a block away from the old parish church of Baliwag. It also appears that the family had the means to send Felipe to Manila for some education.[12] But we must not take this to mean that, like Mabini, he joined the ranks of the ilustrados. His education must have been minimal, judging from the almost phonetic style of his autobiography and the absence of Hispanisms in it.

As a young man, Salvador already struck his relatives as being of a rebellious as well as religious nature. He insisted on going barefoot, for one thing. He also got into trouble with a lieutenant of the *guardia civil* and with the parish priest of Baliwag. He apparently had been able to persuade the vendors at the church to discontinue paying revenue to Padre Prada. This act of defiance almost caused his exile to Mindanao.[13]

---

of the Santa Iglesia and thus curbed, to a certain extent, the bandit image of the Santa Iglesia being spread by the constabulary and the local elite.

8. From a letter to one of his apostles who was captured in 1904 (ARPC [1904], 3, "Annual Report of the Philippine Constabulary," p. 64).

9. Reilly, "Filipino Bandit Terror."

10. Some of Reilly's information on Salvador's past is unreliable and must be treated with caution.

11. Jose P. Santos, *Ang Tatlong Napabantog na "Tulisan" sa Pilipinas* (Gerona, 1936), p. 8.

12. Alfredo Robles, Jr. ed., "Mga Kilusang Mesiyaniko sa Pilipinas," *Likas* (1976):66–67. In 1974, history students from the University of the Philippines, Diliman, interviewed a nephew and niece of Salvador. Their combined oral and documentary research was written up by Erlinda Marzan.

13. Santos, *Tatlong Tulisan*, p. 8. This story was confirmed by Ricardo Salvador, Felipe's nephew (Robles, "Ang Kilusang Mesiyaniko," p. 68).

In 1894, Salvador became the head of a cofradía-type society called "Gabinista," named after its founder, Gabino Cortes. Cortes himself hailed from Apalit, Pampanga, and may have been a relative to Salvador.[14] He is described as a man "of very small fortune" who in 1887 started preaching a doctrine "based on the idea that the people must seek divine protection through prayer, and thus arrive at the enjoyment of the wealth of the land and other worldly pleasures."[15] Among the stories that circulated about Cortes is that he possessed a magic ball, given to him by an old man on a mountain top, with which he could cause money, food, and male attendants to appear. He also had the power to assume many forms before his followers; he could convert wooden toothpicks into soldiers and cause other wonderful miracles to happen. Undoubtedly, the Gabinistas regarded their leader as a man of power derived from his encounter with the old man on a mountain top which, being the axis of the universe, is a channel for divine energy.[16] Like Apolinario de la Cruz and Januario Labios before him, Gabino Cortes became the focus of peasant aspirations in the region surrounding his hometown.

The Gabinistas came mainly from the towns of Apalit, San Simon, San Luis, Santo Tomas, Santa Ana, Candaba, Macabebe, Pulilan and other nearby places, but "not a few" came from Manila itself. They boasted of "considerable numbers" of adherents, "all of whom belonged to the poorest classes and thus were hoping with much anxiety for their turn to possess those riches which their present condition denies them."[17] But, although their aspirations were tantamount to an overturning of the social order, their means of obtaining their ends mirrored the style of the early Cofradía de San Jose. The Gabinistas held nightly reunions in the house of a member. They recited Christian prayers, afterwards partaking of a fraternal meal.[18] Even Spanish investigators admitted

---

14. According to Ricardo Salvador, their family had relatives in adjoining Pampanga province. It is even possible that Felipe was born in Pampanga since parish records of Baliwag fail to confirm Santos's data concerning Felipe's birthplace and birth date (Robles, "Mga Kilusang Mesiyaniko," p. 66).

15. Manuel Garcia Morales and Euprasio Munarriz, "Ynformacion sobre los sucesos de Apalit . . . el 19 del Febrero de 1898" (Madrid, Archivo Histórico Nacional, Sección de Ultramar, Legajo 5356).

16. Isabelo de los Reyes, *El Folk-lore Filipino*, vol. 1 (Manila, 1889), pp. 263-64.

17. Morales and Munarriz, "Ynformacion."

18. De los Reyes also notes that they slept on one floor without separation of sexes. This implication of sexual license practiced by such groups (including the Cofradía of 1840) may have been a rumor spread by the principales and parish priest. Sexual fertility may have been regarded as a sign of the power of certain leaders, as evidenced by reports of women surrounding these figures. (For an illuminating discussion of sex and power in traditional Java, see Anderson, "The Idea of Power in Javanese Culture," in *Culture and Politics in Indonesia*, ed. Claire Holt, Benedict Anderson, and James Siegel [Ithaca, New York: Cornell University Press, 1972], pp. 27-28.) However, these leaders also preached a doctrine of morality and control of self. In present-day societies of the same type, I have observed a strict separation of sexes during formal church services. I also note that rumors of sexual license were not corroborated by observers familiar with groups in Laguna, at least.

that "according to their doctrines one must not resort to violent methods to achieve their goals." However, Spanish authorities and native principales feared a disruption of public order, and when "the principle of authority was brought into disrepute" with the crowning of Gabino as King in 1888, the guardia civil of Bulacan, Nueva Ecija, and Pampanga were summoned to disperse the organization. As Gabino was about to be shipped off to exile in Jolo, "a great number" of people were on hand at the docks to see him off. A rumor circulated later on that the boat would not move and that Gabino disappeared.[19]

When Felipe Salvador reorganized the Gabinistas in 1894, he changed the society's name to Santa Iglesia. Significantly, the Katipunan uprising in 1896 led him to "modify the mode of action needed to realize the aspirations of the sect." Strikingly reminiscent of Apolinario de la Cruz's call for armed struggle after reading the "signs of the times," Salvador declared that "with divine protection, they would be immune to the weapons of the Spanish army and would therefore be able to take possession of the weapons in the camps with which they could assure themselves of the triumph of their cause by armed means." In a battle in San Luis, Pampanga, Salvador—styling himself "captain"— pitted a force of 300 men against 3,000 well-armed *cazadores*. Having sustained a wound in his left arm, he was forced to retreat to Biak-na-bato, where his forces linked up with Aguinaldo's.[20]

The transfer, sometime in late 1897, of Gabino Cortes to Bilibid prison in Manila occasioned another "flurry of excitement" in the Santa Iglesia which was quickly tapped by Salvador together with Guillermo Gonzales, an ex-soldier of the colonial army whose loyalty to Spain in 1896 merited from the parish priest of Apalit a recommendation for the post of "lieutenant of local volunteers." Partly owing to the loss of his wealth through gambling, Gonzales joined the Santa Iglesia in June 1897, putting his military expertise to use. During the week-long Apalit fiesta in February 1898, peasants gathered secretly to prepare for an attack on the town garrison. Success was guaranteed by Salvador not only through immunity from bullets but also because the prisoner Gabino would, at the moment of attack, appear with seven archangels. On the nineteenth, as scheduled, some 700 rebels armed with bladed weapons and just eight firearms stormed the garrison amidst shouts of "Viva Jesus Salvador!"

---

19. De los Reyes, *Folk-lore Filipino*; Morales and Munarriz, "Ynformacion." There is a well-known "King Gavino," hero of Tagalog and Kapampangan corridos. We know for certain that this character was awaited by peasants of some regions as one who would turn the tide in the revolution against Spain (*Declaration, Letter and Proclamation of Isabelo Artacho*, trans. from Spanish, 1899; PIR-DS 838). Perhaps the association with a corrido figure helped in spreading Gabino Cortes's fame.

20. Morales and Munarriz, "Ynformacion." The battle in San Luis is mentioned in Santos, *Tatlong Tulisan*, pp. 8–9.

But, like the Colorums who attacked the Tayabas garrison, the Santa Iglesia was swiftly cut down by superior Spanish firepower. A similar attack by a separate contingent on the Macabebe garrison met the same fate. Rebel casualties exceeded 100 dead or wounded. The Spanish report, to be echoed by American reports in the following decade, emphasized that the only motive of the attackers was to secure firearms. "No impositions were made upon peaceful inhabitants"; not even the stores of the Chinese were touched.[21]

To dampen the spirits of the movement, Gabino Cortes was executed shortly after. But this did not prevent the Santa Iglesia from rising again when the revolution against Spain was formally resumed with Aguinaldo's return. Felipe Salvador and his forces overran the Spanish garrison at Dagupan, capturing 100 rifles. Sometime in 1898, when Pampanga had been completely liberated by the revolutionaries, Salvador led the Santa Iglesia company in a triumphant march through the streets of Candaba.[22] He must have participated in other successful operations, for by the end of 1898 Aguinaldo had promoted him to the rank of major. Soon after this, however, Salvador was branded as "antirevolutionary" by certain prominent generals of the republic. One explanation given for this unexpected turn of events is that Salvador, having attracted so many "poor and ignorant" people into the Santa Iglesia, conspired to overthrow the government.[23] A 1906 constabulary report says that Salvador deserted his post at Marilao on the approach of the Americans and was thus branded a deserter by revolutionary officers who took this as an excuse to order his assassination. A clarification of this incident, which occurred in late 1898 or the beginning of January 1899, would not only put the aims and activities of the Santa Iglesia in proper perspective but would help explain why other similar groups, notably the Katipunan of San Cristobal and the Guardia de Honor were, at around the same time, condemned as "antirevolutionary" by the Malolos government.

Social Conflict in the Republic

Documents connected with the military trial of Salvador and the officers of the Santa Iglesia in January 1899 verify that Salvador's company indeed

---

21. Morales and Munarriz, "Ynformacion." It must be mentioned that the authors of the Spanish report consistently speak of a *Pedro*, not Felipe, Salvador. A Pedro Salvador is nowhere mentioned in other sources for the Santa Iglesia. Almost certainly they are one and the same person, although the possibility remains that Felipe Salvador had a brother, Pedro, with the same rank of captain during the revolution against Spain, who was captured and executed after the Apalit uprising of 1898.

22. Larkin, *Pampangans*, p. 235; ARPC (1906), 2, "Report of the Director of Constabulary," p. 226; Reilly, "Filipino Bandit Terror."

23. Reilly, "Filipino Bandit Terror."

withdrew without authorization from its position in Bulacan province. Salvador himself, however, argued that the Santa Iglesia, far from being disloyal to the revolution and to the Aguinaldo government, simply reacted to the oppressive acts perpetuated against it by certain "prominent" persons. Repeatedly blocked from seeing Aguinaldo in person to air grievances of his group, Salvador decided to pull back and allow his men to return to their homes. Salvador presented his side in a ten-page affidavit entitled "Narrative of the Feelings and Supplications of the Accused Major Felipe Salvador."[24] In twelve points, he enumerated his grievances as well as explained the nature of the Santa Iglesia.

The first seven points alone shatter the conventional image of unity within the army and the republic. To start with, five members of the Santa Iglesia company, including a captain and a lieutenant, had been ordered killed by then Major Maximino Hizon without proper trial and without informing their commander, Salvador. After the incident, Salvador journeyed to Cavite in order to present a written appeal. Not only was the appeal ignored, but Hizon himself, who came from a prominent Kapampangan family, was promoted to colonel. Obviously still embittered, Salvador noted in his narrative that the wives and children of the deceased were still suffering from their loss.

The next complaint brought forth was agrarian in nature. In Floridablanca, some of Salvador's followers were shown "documents"—presumably land titles—and then forcibly ejected from their ancestral lands without compensation. Ironically, the perpetrators of these crimes belonged to prominent families, some of which had supported the Santa Iglesia in the war against Spain.[25] Furthermore, these same people were detaining and punishing peasants who joined the brotherhood.

Abuses against the Santa Iglesia were particularly rampant in the town of Apalit, where the principales feared a resurgence of the Gabinista Party. Two soldiers of Salvador's company were charged with committing certain "abuses" by municipal officials, who took the law into their own hands, bound the two soldiers, threw them in the river and pumped their floating bodies with bullets. Two other Santa Iglesia members were kidnapped in the middle of the night and murdered. What further angered Salvador was that the perpetrator of this

---

24. "Kasaysayan ng mga Ipinagdamdam at Karaingan ng Comandante Felipe Salvador na Ipinagsakdal sa Mahinahong Pasia ng Kgg na Presidente ng G.R.," 14 January 1899 (PIR-SD 1284, Box 43). Attached to the manuscript is the two-page verdict of "not guilty."

25. As Majul states, "The events of the Revolution showed that the desire to own land was concomitant with the desire to get rid of the oppressive friar landlords" (*Mabini and the Philippine Revolution* [Quezon City, 1960], p. 49). Very often, however, the land titling system was manipulated by revolutionary officers and caciques in disregard of the rights of the original, though untitled, cultivators (ibid., chapter 2). See also Milagros Guerrero's doctoral dissertation, "Luzon at War: Contradictions in Philippine Society, 1898–1902" (University of Michigan, 1977), which probably constitutes the last word on the subject.

crime was a "blacksmith and drunkard" named Isidro Lugui who used to be a spy for the Spanish government but was given a municipal post in the revolutionary government. Lugui himself and others who harassed the Santa Iglesia in Apalit, however, were merely under the pay of certain prominent men who apparently never forgot the past Gabinista "disturbances" in their town. Any man found to have joined the Santa Iglesia was arrested, flogged, and even imprisoned. Wives and female relatives of Santa Iglesia soldiers passing through Apalit to visit the men on the front were apprehended and afterwards forced to walk through the center of town shouting, "Don't be like us!" There were also attempts to persuade or coerce peasants to keep distance from Salvador; the reason given was that he was "beautiful on the outside, but evil inside." At the conclusion to his seventh supplication, Salvador protested: "Why are they doing these things when they know that I am stationed at Malolos and am bound and loyal to our government?"[26]

From what has been said so far, it is clear that Salvador's loyalty to the revolution has not come in question. Although we are presented with a series of incidents in which members of the Santa Iglesia are punished for purported "crimes," we are left in the dark as to what these crimes were, other than the mere fact of joining Salvador's movement. It seems that certain powerful Kapampangans were intent upon subverting Salvador's following. By asserting that Salvador was "beautiful on the outside, but evil inside," they were, curiously enough, applying a norm that, in the *pasyon*, is applicable to wealthy, influential pharisees and town leaders, and to traitors. Such disjunction between "external" and "internal" was precisely what leaders like Salvador and Sakay found wrong in ilustrado-dominated society.

On the surface, at least, the problem was one of rivalry for the control of manpower. General Ramon Mascardo, who commanded the revolutionary forces in Pampanga province, had fallen under the influence of wealthy and educated Kapampangans who had joined the revolution only in 1898. Mascardo used to have compassion *(lingap)* for Salvador, but frequent association with these officers from prominent families caused "the eyes of his reason *(katwiran)* to be covered" and his trust in Salvador to dissolve. To Salvador, however, Mascardo was not to blame for having been "overcome" by these men, since as he reasoned out, "theirs is the advantage of education and wealth, as against my ignorance and poverty" (*palibhasa'y na sa kanila ang dunong at yaman, at sa akin ang kamangmangan at karalitaan*).[27] In other words, to Salvador the actions of Mascardo were not the products of evil intentions but the predictable effects of having been seduced by the "glitter" of wealth and education. Mascardo's loób was too weak to sustain compassion and trust in Salvador when confronted by such glitter that blinded "the eyes of his reason."

26. Salvador, "Kasaysayan," p. 3 (PIR-SD 1284).
27. Ibid., pp. 6-7.

Mascardo's subsequent action was to ask Salvador to list down the names of all Santa Iglesia members on the pretext that arms would be issued out to them. As soon as the list was made, Mascardo ordered the men arrested on the charge of forming another "party." This attempt to break up the Santa Iglesia, according to Salvador, arose from the desire of the propertied and educated officers of Mascardo to "become officials" *(mag oficial)*. They probably felt that their status and wealth gave them that right. However, they could make no headway among the thousands who had already joined the Santa Iglesia. Salvador suggested that if these notables insisted on leading men, they ought to "look for followers among the uncommitted." Since they were wealthy, perhaps they should concentrate on raising money to support the government. There were other ways in which they could further the revolution, but "they should not endanger the poor who lived peacefully."[28]

Compounding the problem was the regionalism of the elite Kapampangan officers who demanded the right to command Kapampangan troops of the army. Salvador was prejudiced not only by his identification with the poor and uneducated class but also by his being Tagalog. In his affidavit he claimed he was being persecuted because, as he puts it, "even though I am Tagalog, I was the first person to gather together many Kapampangans who helped fight in the first war (1896)."[29] In that war, the leading citizens of Pampanga largely remained loyal to Spain, even supplying the Spanish army with money, troops, laborers, horses, and medical aid. Only when it was clear that Spanish rule was on the wane did the Kapampangan elite join the revolution in mid-1898 expecting, by "natural right," to lead Kapampangan troops as well as represent them in Congress.[30] Salvador perceived things differently. With a slight tone of bitterness at those Kapampangan "revolutionaries" who forbade him to enter their towns, he asked: "Are Tagalog, Ilokanos, Pangasinanes, and Visayans different from Kapampangans in 'being Filipino'?"[31] Even the Kapampangan elite, of course, would have accepted this literal definition of nationalism. After all, the Malolos republic had been defined in these terms. But the elite thought of nationalism in terms of the unity of the "better class" which represented the "inarticulate" masses. For Salvador, nationalism brought people together regardless of their previous attachments to elites or patrons.

Because Salvador and the Santa Iglesia operated within a different framework of social relationships, the Kapampangan elite could not compete with it in their own terms. That is why the Santa Iglesia was relegated to the phenomenon of "banditry." Any disorder or bandit attack in Pampanga was,

---

28. Ibid., p. 4.

29. Ibid., p. 9.

30. For a comprehensive discussion of Kapampangan involvement in the various phases of the revolution, see Larkin, *The Pampangans*, pp. 111–19.

31. Salvador, "Kasaysayan," p. 10 (PIR-SD 1284).

according to Salvador, ascribed without evidence at all to the Santa Iglesia. By sowing this rumor, it was probably hoped that the virtuous image of Salvador would be tarnished. By being associated with banditry, the Santa Iglesia's goals of brotherhood, religious devotion, and equitable landownership could be thoroughly distorted, imbued with sinister aspects distasteful even to peasants themselves. Like their Caviteño counterparts who had sown black rumors about Bonifacio and his Katipunan among their constituents, some Kapampangan principales were using a familiar strategy to halt the growth of the Santa Iglesia. Fortunately, Aguinaldo was sympathetic to Salvador's denials of banditry, as follows:

> Even though we endured great hardship, it never occurred to us to rob the belongings of others. We survived through the begging of brothers poor like myself. In truth, even up to now I have not been able to buy a single piece of clothing; whatever I am wearing has been received through begging and I can even tell you who the persons are that gave alms. Ask the soldiers if, whenever I chanced to receive a little money, I ever failed to divide it among us, and if what I say is not true, I will gladly face the firing squad. Just do not let me hear my group being called a bandit gang.[32]

As we said previously, the impression that the root of the conflict was competition for the control of the Kapampangan peasantry, is only superficial. Salvador was not just another politician cultivating a personal following. The basis of his popularity was something else: lowliness, humility, and apparent disinterest in the material rewards and favors normally offered by a political leader. When he was stationed in Malolos, men and women came to him with tales of hardships and injustices they were forced to endure. His response was merely to "empathize" with them:

> My heart was torn with anguish, but I could do nothing except participate *(damay)* in their affliction even till death. For, in the past, my *kapatid* also participated in all of my sufferings, even though my only *puhunan* (investment) was a beautiful *(maganda)* companionship and sweet words of conversation.[33]

Damay, however, as we have noted time and again, is not a passive experience. Its presence in a group is a condition for true brotherhood. It is precisely what drew Salvador and the peasantry together.

In the above quotation, the use of the term *puhunan* (investment) is highly significant. In the idiom of *utang na loob*, "puhunan" is the set of favors or gratuitous acts that initiates a debt relationship. The hard work and depriva-

32. Ibid., p. 7.
33. Ibid., pp. 7–8.

tions of a mother who rears her children to the best of her ability is a form of puhunan which is reciprocated later on in life in the form of caring for the aged mother. Salvador emphasized the fact that his puhunan in the Santa Iglesia consisted *only* of compassion, companionship, and dialogue. He implied that he could have used other kinds of puhunan; was he, perhaps, pointing to the accumulation of wealth and attainment of education which the elite traditionally regarded as puhunan to be rewarded with social standing and loyal followers? Whether he implied this or not, Salvador unequivocally stated that his followers were bound to him, not through economic indebtedness or other vertical forms of attachment, but through mutual damay and caring. This mode of social relationships certainly contributed to the Santa Iglesia's attractiveness to the peasantry. It was an alternative to the principalia-dominated status quo which became increasingly oppressive as the elites sought to profit from the revolution or recover their losses afterwards. It was also an alternative which the peasantry was culturally prepared to accept through their experience of the pasyon. For in his lowliness and humility Salvador could have been no other than a figure of Christ. In the pasyon, it is damay that binds people to Christ, whose words bring knowledge and *ginhawa* (contentment), and the brotherhood of the "meek" that will triumph.

According to Salvador, many officers in the army accused the Santa Iglesia of devoting too much time to prayer and not enough to fighting. He vigorously denied this in this appeal, insisting upon the inseparability of prayer and warfare:

> Kun ang tawo kaya'y mawalan nang pananampalataya, paano ang pagkasulong niya sa anomang magaling na linalayon? Kun ang tawo ko'y walang guinagaua kundi ang mag dasal lamang at hindi tumatayo sa labanan, ay hindi ko nga daramdamin ang sila'y makainipan.[34]
>
> If a man is devoid of worship, how can he pursue a worthy cause? If my men do nothing but pray, if they do not also stand firm in battle, then I would not feel badly if some lose patience with them.

The same class of people that harassed the Santa Iglesia in ways previously described also attempted, he said, "to destroy our worship, forbidding prayers and other kinds of devotion." Was it simply because the Santa Iglesia was anathema to the established church? In fact, the Roman Catholic Church encouraged the suppression of this rival church with its own pope and clergy. At one point the Catholic hierarchy, alarmed by the growing popularity of the Santa Iglesia, excommunicated all its members.[35] It would not be unreason-

---

34. Ibid., p. 6.

35. Larkin, *Pampangans*, p. 236. Salvador even considered taking up the matter of religious persecution to the American authorities.

able to suppose that the Kapampangan principales exploited the religious issue to justify their suppression of the Santa Iglesia. But from Salvador's viewpoint, religious legitimacy was not at issue. As we shall see in his autobiography, his concern was with the religious experience itself. Doctrinally, his was not a radically different religion; in fact he used approved Christian forms of worship and prayer.[36] But prayer, he insisted, was not to be a "compartmentalized" activity. It was also to give direction to everyday existence, maintaining the loób in a state of full control and serenity so that in battle the Santa Iglesia soldier would make up for in courage what he lacked in arms.

As he concluded his 1899 "Supplication," Salvador explained that his life was constantly in danger from those "many and big people" from Pampanga who wished to "drown" *(lubog)* him. The image of the morally upright common tao being thrust underwater by those in power recalls Apolinario de la Cruz's message to the cofrades in 1841:

> Caya ang aming molit moling bilin ay ang malaquing pananalig sa ysang Dios na totoo, at cia ang tutulong sa Atin, macalilibong ilubog nila ang magaling ay lilitau, datapuat ang isang masama, ay madaling napaparam.[37]
>
> So let me repeat my advice that we must have great trust in the one true God, for he will help us; they may try to drown a thousand good men, but each one will rise to the surface; a single bad person quickly disappears.

In both cases, forty-eight years apart, the peasant leaders were convinced that the essential righteousness of their cause and "trust" in God would help them withstand persecution by the "big people." In Salvador's case there was the added context of the revolution. The Spaniards had been driven away, but persecution of the Santa Iglesia was as serious as ever. The irony of it all, complained Salvador, was that despite their many sacrifices for the country during the war against Spain, they were being treated like criminals by officers of the republic "who were spies for the Spaniards." He appealed to Aguinaldo, as "a youngest son to his father," to allow the Santa Iglesia to live in peace. He would always be ready to heed Aguinaldo's call to arms in order to free Mother Filipinas. If he ever disobeyed an order or acted with half-heartedness, he was willing to be shot as a traitor in the public plaza of Malolos.

Attached to Salvador's "Supplication" was the verdict of the military court dropping all charges of disloyalty and desertion of which Salvador and his men were accused. The government acknowleged that the Santa Iglesia Company fled from its post because of the injustices inflicted upon its soldiers and the impossibility of appealing directly to President Aguinaldo. Further-

---

36. "Christmas Eve Fiasco," p. 204; Robles, "Mga Kilusang Mesiyaniko," p. 70.
37. Apolinario de la Cruz to Octabio San Jorge, Manila, 15 March 1841 (PNA).

more, the Santa Iglesia was not found to be "antirevolutionary" at all; in fact, its commitment to the defense of the nation was unsullied. Satisfied with Salvador's protestations of loyalty, Aguinaldo agreed to protect the Santa Iglesia and in fact gave Salvador a sedentary job in Malolos.[38] But among the ilustrados, a fear or distrust of Salvador seemed to linger. Mabini even denounced him publicly as one "sharp enough to show an apparent interest in a solicitude for the poor fools and amuse them with stories of wonderful miracles and prophecies . . . so as not to give his victims time to think of their injured pocket books."[39]

Santa Iglesia Struggle, 1899–1906

Given the ilustrado attitude toward Salvador, it may seem odd that he was promoted to colonel sometime in 1899. But this was the year of the American military thrust against the republic in central Luzon. Salvador had the commitment and following—lacking in many generals of the regular army—to sustain a guerilla war against the Americans. To tap this source of support, the least Aguinaldo could do was recognize Salvador in rank. When Malolos fell in March, Salvador returned to Baliwag and began to expand his own armed force and network of support. Eventually he chose the barrio of Camias, near Apalit, as his "capital." Refusing to surrender along with the bulk of the revolutionary army in November 1899, he engaged in guerilla warfare until his capture in early 1900. He spent some months in prison before taking the oath of allegiance to the United States in August 1900. Upon his release, he rejoined his men in the field and thus qualified as an "outlaw" to the Americans.[40]

The Santa Iglesia differed in many ways from the other guerilla forces in the region. Camias, for one thing, was also a "holy diocese" run by Salvador as "highest pontiff," who advised his soldiers to pray constantly and conduct elaborate rituals especially just before going to battle.[41] There is also evidence that Santa Iglesia leaders went about their usual practice of seeking alms *(limos)*—in the form of rice, clothing and cigarettes—from the heads of barrios they passed through.[42] In some instances, Santa Iglesia detachments,

---

38. Aguinaldo's commissioner, Gregorio Ramos, promised to bring to his superior's attention the oppressions suffered by the Santa Iglesia (verdict in Salvador, "Kasaysayan," p. 13). See also Robles, "Mga Kilusang Mesiyaniko," p. 69.

39. *El Comercio*, 1 February 1900 (BIA 2291-96).

40. This reconstruction of Salvador's activities in 1900 is the best that can be made from the fragmentary data in Reilly, "Filipino Bandit Terror"; ARPC (1906), 2, p. 226; "Christmas Eve Fiasco," p. 204; and Robles, "Mga Kilusang Mesiyaniko," pp. 68-69, which makes use of the *Manila Times*. See also Guerrero, "Luzon at War," pp. 183–84.

41. Robles, "Mga Kilusang Mesiyaniko," p. 69; Guerrero, "Luzon at War," p. 184.

42. Valentin de Guzman to Juan Eusebio, *cabeza* of Barrio San Agustin, Paombong, 7 August and 19 September 1900 (in Tagalog; PIR-SD 546.3). De Guzman was captured by the constabulary in August 1906 (see detailed account in *Muling Pagsilang*, 10 August 1906).

owing to lack of firearms, joined up with larger brigades in the guerilla zones. But the fact that they maintained a separate identity was a source of friction within guerilla ranks. For example, barrio officials in the Hagonoy-Paombong area of Bulacan complained that Severo Rodriguez and Manuel Garcia (alias Comandante Tui or Capitan Tui)—Santa Iglesia leaders attached to the Third Zone Brigade—were recruiting right and left among the barrio folk, to the extent that some disruption of barrio life was being felt by the *cabezas.* The military hierarchy was also somehow upset. While trying to mobilize his forces in August 1900, the military commander at Hagonoy found out to his dismay that many soldiers "belonged" to a motley of other officials, among them Comandante Tui of the Santa Iglesia.[43]

By the end of 1901, only the Santa Iglesia and similar organizations like the Guardia de Honor were left to harass the Americans and their local allies in central Luzon. The other guerilla units had heeded Aguinaldo's proclamation in April calling for the acceptance of American sovereignty. As the conquering army shifted its attention to Malvar's resistance in the South, the constabulary inherited the task of tracking down Salvador, the main threat to the "peace and order" of the region. In 1902, the police finally caught up with him in the province of Nueva Ecija.

Salvador's career, however, merely entered its second phase in 1902. Convicted of sedition, the Santa Iglesia leader was being brought to Bilibid prison in Manila when he managed to elude his guards and flee to his old base on Mount Arayat. Claiming that from the mountain's peak his spirit had travelled to heaven and conversed with God, Salvador announced the coming of independence. Before this new era would begin, the world would be ravaged by a great flood and conflagration, for which the people must prepare themselves by joining his katipunan. They must raid the various constabulary camps in order to secure weapons for the great battle to come. But even without weapons, he said, the people could join the struggle armed with bolos and clubs, which would turn to rifles if they fought bravely. What mattered most was their commitment to the Santa Iglesia katipunan and its goals, their adherence to its rules of constant prayer and religious exercises to purify the loób and render it serene in the face of certain danger. The reward for their faith and willingness to die was quite explicit: a rain of gold and jewels, and a redistribution of land and other property as soon as Salvador's sovereign government was installed.[44]

The central Luzon peasantry responded enthusiastically to Salvador's call. Constabulary reports from 1903 to 1906 make no secret of the Santa Iglesia's

43. A. Angeles, Comandante Militar of Hagonoy, to the Politico-Military Governor of Bulacan, 6 September 1900 (in Spanish; PIR-SD 546.3).

44. "Christmas Eve Fiasco," p. 204; ARPC (1903), 3, p. 66; ARPC (1906), 2, p. 226.

firm hold over the rural population. In 1904, for example, the district inspector at Nueva Ecija admitted that in his province "all the population are in sympathy and the majority in some way connected with the movement." Furthermore, he said, in a single group of raiders were men not only from Nueva Ecija but from Pampanga, Pangasinan, Bulacan, and Tarlac—provinces comprising at least three different linguistic groups.[45] Obviously, provincial and linguistic boundaries were no impediment to the movement's rapid expansion from 1903 to 1905. Even in Manila and the southern Tagalog provinces of Cavite and Laguna, the Santa Iglesia could count on numerous members.[46] In fact, the Pangasinan-based Guardia de Honor movement recognized the supreme authority of Salvador and experienced an upsurge in 1905.[47] In the "crisis" of 1910, which will be treated in detail later, the Colorum and Sagrada Familia brotherhoods, as well as veterans of the Katipunan, put their sectarian interests aside and heeded Salvador's call for a renewed independence struggle. With a broad peasant base that shared the Santa Iglesia's sentiment, Salvador and his core of about two hundred armed men were able to move about central Luzon freely. They were like fish in water, despite the "hundreds of thousands of pesos" and the horde of secret service agents poured in by the government to secure their capture.

The Santa Iglesia drive to capture firearms and ammunition in preparation for a "great war" reached a peak in 1906. The constabulary camps at Malolos and San Rafael, Bulacan province, and smaller camps elsewhere, were attacked "with fanatical determination" by predominantly bolo-armed men. In the Easter Sunday attack on Malolos, the provincial capital, Salvador stayed at a distance to direct movements while offering prayers for the operation's success. Leading the Santa Iglesia into Malolos was General Manuel Garcia—"Capitan Tui" to his men—who strode fearlessly with chest bared and a bronze medal of the Holy Trinity prominently affixed to his forehead.[48] Caught by surprise, the constabulary detachment was overwhelmed long enough for Capitan Tui and his men to run off with its arms and ammunition. Meanwhile, panic broke loose throughout the center of the town. Governor Teodoro Sandiko, himself a former revolutionary general, was allegedly forced to flee the capital.[49]

---

45. ARPC (1904), 3, p. 72.

46. Reilly, "Filipino Bandit Terror." In 1906, Camp Hayson, midway between Manila and Cavite province, was attacked presumably by southern Tagalog followers of Salvador since there were simultaneous operations north of Manila (George Coats, "The Philippine Constabulary, 1901–1917" [Ph.D. dissertation, Ohio State University, 1968], pp. 209–10). Coats's data on the Santa Iglesia is culled mainly from the *Manila Times.*

47. Coats, "Philippine Constabulary," p. 207.

48. Ibid., pp. 201, 208. The original account is in Ignacio Villamor, *Criminality in the Philippine Islands: 1903–1908* (Manila, 1909), pp. 51–52.

49. Santos, *Tatlong Tulisan*, p. 37.

Now Sandiko himself was no conservative. History has given him due credit for his contribution to the patriotic cause. As a revolutionary general, he had proven himself by organizing a resistance movement and sympathy labor strikes in American-occupied Manila in 1898. When he assumed office as Nacionalista governor of Bulacan, he promised to do away with taxes and implement a "socialistic" administration.[50] But he was committed to the independence struggle as the ilustrados basically conceived it, working within the rules set down by the Americans. Sandiko must have found himself in the same predicament as other politicians who regarded Sakay's new Katipunan as a major obstacle to the formation of the 1907 national assembly. Sandiko could not have failed to note the Santa Iglesia's vision of independence. But because this vision entailed a period of armed struggle and a possible disruption of the existing social order, he had no choice but to suppress the organization.

After the 15 April debacle at Malolos, Governor Sandiko "made a desperate effort to gain the native support of the people in order to destroy Salvador's force."[51] One of his first moves was to call a meeting, in early May, of all the town mayors specifically to thresh out the Santa Iglesia issue. After much discussion and debate regarding the activities and aims of the movement, the local officials concluded that Salvador and his followers deserved to be called *tulisanes* (bandits) because they were "against *katwiran* (righteousness)" and "moreover were feared by the people." They also resolved to petition the Philippine Commission to publicly declare the Santa Iglesia an "enemy of *katwiran*" and that its members, after a certain grace period, be hunted down as bandits.[52]

Although we have evidence only of the Pampanga and Bulacan principalia closing ranks against the Santa Iglesia, it is likely that this occurred also in Pangasinan, Nueva Ecija, and other provinces where Salvador's influence was felt. The relative success of the constabulary's counteroffensive in mid-1906 must be seen in this light. Sandiko, for example, threatened to reconcentrate the rural populace (a tactic also used against Sakay's mass base) in case they refused to aid the constabulary.[53] The local gentry had their own sources of information, plus the traditional ability to influence public opinion. The Santa Iglesia's failure to establish a foothold in the Tagalog province of Bataan must be attributed to this. Having sailed across Manila Bay in small boats, a contingent led by Capitan Tui could not obtain assistance from the Bataan populace, who had apparently been "prepared" by the principalia and secret-

50. See chapter 5 above, pp. 250.

51. Coats, "Philippine Constabulary," p. 250.

52. *Muling Pagsilang*, 8 May 1906.

53. Coats, "Philippine Constabulary," p. 210; Constantino, *The Philippines: A Past Revisited* (Quezon City: Tala Publishing Co., 1975), p. 269.

service agents to repel an invasion of "bandits." Chased up and down the coast by the constabulary, Capitan Tui and his men had no choice but to sail back to Bulacan in early July. A few days later, they engaged the constabulary in a fierce battle near Hagonoy which left twenty of them, including Capitan Tui, dead.[54]

The loss of General Manuel Garcia, alias Capitan Tui, somewhat diminished further armed action on the part of the Santa Iglesia. Apparently, a near-successful attempt was made to negotiate Salvador's surrender. No doubt the government approach was similar to that used successfully with Sakay. Salvador, however, wisely decided to await the outcome of Sakay's trial.[55] From that time on, successive efforts to track down his whereabouts failed dismally owing to the pertinacity of the rural folk who protected him. The near absence of any mention of the Santa Iglesia in constabulary sources from 1907 to 1909 had led scholars to regard 1906 as a turning point for the movement. Despite an upsurge in 1910, of which little is said, the Santa Iglesia is seen in progressive decline until Salvador is finally captured in July 1910. The notion of a "turning point" in 1906, and the gap or discontinuity between 1906 and 1910, is due to our reliance on constabulary sources for much of the Santa Iglesia's story. As we shall see, Salvador himself never perceived a gap.

Meaning and Autobiography

In 1936 Jose P. Santos, a relative of the fiscal who prosecuted Salvador, published "without any corrections" Salvador's account of his escape from detention and his activities up to his recapture in 1910.[56] In this narrative of his experiences up to 2 August 1910, only three events can be verified against other sources: the escape of 1902 and return to Mount Arayat, the celebrated entry into Arayat town in 1910, and his capture that same year. There is a remarkable absence of any mention of raids and skirmishes which fill the constabulary reports. Except perhaps for the three events mentioned above, there is hardly anything in the account that matches the drama and narrative progression usually found in autobiographies of political leaders. What we find is a rather repetitive and "unexciting" story of Salvador's day-to-day activities as a wanderer in the swamps and forests about Mount Arayat (Sinukuan).

The absence of new "facts" about Salvador and the Santa Iglesia is most likely the reason why scholars have not made use of Salvador's autobiography. But as explained in the first chapter, documents "from below" are useful not because they are repositories of "solid facts," but because they point to

54. ARPC (1906), 2, p. 240; Coats, "Philippine Constabulary," pp. 212–13.

55. ARPC (1906), 1, p. 32.

56. In Jose P. Santos, *Tatlong Tulisan*, p. 11–21. All quotations from Salvador's first-person account are from Santos's book. English translations are mine.

underlying meanings and perceptions of events. Salvador's account is significant precisely because he wrote about what he felt were important to him rather than to an imaginary interrogator. The very repetitiveness and factual "incompleteness" of the account indicate that Salvador did not self-consciously dissociate himself from the events in order to view his account as a whole, as a novelist or historian might have done. He wrote as if he were speaking. For us who are trying to understand his experience, the task is to discover the units of meaning that shape the narrative. We must take seriously Salvador's final sentence: "This . . . is truly what I did and what happened to me."

The account begins with a narration of how Salvador manages to obtain his freedom and return to Mount Arayat:

> Nang acoi manggaling sa NoEvacija at cami natatauag dito sa Maynila pag dating namin sa Cabiao ang aquing casamahang manga capua co preso ay nag sang usapan na sila ay tumanan sinabi sa aquin. Ang sagot co sa canila ay ayao co gusto conang maluas dito sa maynila pagcat acoi ualang naqui quilalang casalanan co pag ca acoi na Jusgado ay acoi pirmeng macauauala ang sinabi sa aquin ng ibang manga Preso icao ang bajala cong icao ay matira rian ay icao ay babarilin ng manga sundalo acopoi natacot cayat ng silay mag si alis ay acoi sumunod ng acopoi lumalacad na acoi nagtago sa tabi ng pantalan ng mag daan ang manga sundalong humahabol sa nagsipag puga acoi nag tauid sa ibayo ng ilog at acopoi nagtungo sa Bundoc ng sinucuan. (p. 11)

> When I arrived in Nueva Ecija on the way to Manila where we were being summoned, when we reached Cabiao my fellow prisoners agreed among themselves to escape and they informed me of this. I answered them with a refusal: I want to go to Manila because I am unaware of wrongdoing on my part; when I am tried I will certainly be released. The other prisoners said, it's up to you; if you are left here you will be shot by the soldiers. I became afraid so I followed behind when they had left; and while I was walking I hid behind a pier. As the pursuing soldiers passed by, I crossed to the far side of the river and I headed for the mountain of Sinukuan.

As Salvador is walking by the side of the river, he comes upon a banca with people in it. He asks for rice, and is given some. After eating, he crosses to the other side of the river and continues toward the mountain. Then he goes to a forested place called Kabalatukan, where he sees a hut inhabited by a man named Vicente. Again he asks for some rice. "I was given some and when I had eaten we got to talking, I told him about my experiences since the escape from Cabiao. The man had *awa* (pity) for me, hence his reply to what we had talked about was, thanks to to the Lord God I was not harmed." (p. 12) Salvador then asks Vicente if soldiers ever reconnoiter in the area. Rarely, is the reply. He asks if Vicente would "take him under his care" *(ampon)*. Vicente is willing, and so Salvador settles there for two months.

He next goes to a place called "buntoc babi," which is by the side of the river, where he meets a friend named Juan who makes a living by gathering buri-palm shoots (*tulod ng bule*) which are sold in the towns. Salvador is taken in Juan's banca to some kind of a rest camp.

> When we reached there we cooked rice and after cooking we ate and after eating we talked. I told him about my experiences while fleeing from Cabiao. It was because the man had *awa* for me that he replied that only God was responsible for my being unhurt; yes, I said, and we talked about many other things concerning life. (p12.)

They agree that Salvador is to help cut buri-palm shoots. Their harvests will be combined and the income from the sale will go toward purchasing the necessities of life: rice, salt, and other foodstuffs or cigarettes. Salvador spends some time with Juan,because of "their good relationship." When Juan is away for two weeks or more, Salvador approaches houses at night and asks for rice. He writes, " I was given some little by little, as much as they wished to give. This was the kind of life I led for many days."

In the narrative above, there are very few facts that can be verified in other sources. Salvador and other prisoners from Nueva Ecija indeed escaped as they were being transferred to Manila in 1902. And "Vicente," the first of several names mentioned by Salvador, is most likely a certain Vicente Francia identified by the constabulary in 1910 as a constant companion of Salvador in the environs of San Luis, Pampanga.[57] But the other names and events cannot be identified, confirmed, or located in time. Not that this is crucial in making use of the narrative. The fact that Salvador's narrative is reduced to a series of encounters with strangers points to certain ideas shaping the account. Note that Salvador does not talk about feelings of loneliness or pain as he wanders about the foothills and forests of Sinukuan. He encounters strangers, asks for food, and is given some. In the first instance, he asks for cooked rice. In the second instance he asks, in addition, for extra provisions like milled rice. In the third instance, he asks Vicente to care for him; the same is true with Juan. In all cases, there is never a possibility of refusal, no tension involved. Contrary to insinuations in constabulary reports, Salvador is not a fugitive living off the toil of others. In his view of society, it is perfectly natural to ask (or to beg), to give and to receive among perfect strangers.[58]

One pattern that emerges is that the sharing and partaking of food paves the way for brotherly relationships. "Conversation" *(usap-usap)* always follows a meal. Salvador talks about his experience of the escape, and then his

57. Philippine Constabulary Reports (henceforth, PCR), 2 June 1910 (vol. 2, p. 463; MHC).

58. Only one American observer seems to have noted this. In a letter to the *New York Evening Post* (2 October 1906), David Doherty insisted that Salvador and his followers could not be bandits because they only asked for alms and usually received some, practiced brotherhood among men, fasted and prayed (clipping in BIA 4865-33).

companions are said to have awa. Concomitant with awa is the realization that God has preserved Salvador from harm. Both Vicente and Juan have exactly the same reaction: "It was because the man had *awa* for me that he replied that only God was responsible for my being unhurt." We can take this statement to mean that Vicente and Juan attributed Salvador's experience to God's will. In fact, while Salvador was in jail, he told his followers that his confinement was a voluntary expiation of his sins on earth. He was merely heeding God's wish, he said, and at any time he should decide to leave jail he would merely walk out of the place. And so when he did manage to escape, his followers believed that it was a fulfillment of a prophecy.[59] But Salvador, in his narrative, seems to be saying more than this. The recognition of God's intervention is always preceded by the experience of awa. As we saw in previous chapters, awa is not just "pity" in the sense of an individual emotional outpouring. In Salvador's idiom, awa has a social meaning similar to damay in pasyon and Katipunan rituals. When there is awa, people can attune themselves to Salvador's experience. They can situate it in a framework of meaning with which they are familiar. Only then can they really grasp why Salvador has been preserved from harm.

Let us continue with the narrative. Salvador encounters another person, named Damaso. They become friends while cutting buri-palm shoots together. "Since our companionship was good," says Salvador "he would regularly bring me the necessities of life: rice, *tuyo,* salt, *bagoong* and cigarettes." Each time Salvador learns that soldiers are conducting one of their rare operations in the area, he leaves his hut and hides in the nearby forest.

Eventually he transfers to another forest bordering the town of Zaragosa, spending quite a bit of time there because of a friendship he has struck with one Epifanio de la Cruz. Like him, Epifanio lacks a *cedula personal* (a tax receipt also serving as an identity card) and thus cannot enter the town. He takes care of Salvador in the swampy forest of Zaragosa. After several says, Salvador decides to return to the riverbank, where he stays for another extended period because it is "such a good place." Then he decides to "go home" to Camias. Damaso takes him there and, for two weeks, takes care of Salvador.

Apparently, Epifanio has rejoined Salvador and Damaso. Together they board Damaso's banca and head for a place called Santa Cruz in the territory of Concepcion. As they are walking they meet a man who is Damaso's acquaintance. He takes the group to his shelter in the forest and offers them food. After the meal they engage in conversation. Salvador asks if soldiers frequent the area. Receiving an affirmative reply, Salvador induces the group to leave immediately. Their host shows them the road to Camanse.

59. Coats, "Philippine Constabulary," pp. 202–3; Villamor, *Criminality,* p. 51.

In Camanse they proceed to a place called Quilem, where they remain for about a week. In order to survive they have to ask for food from passing boatmen. There is never a refusal to share food with them. Only when bancas fail to appear in the river or do not carry provisions do they have to endure "a little hunger." Finally, they leave the place in a banca laden with palm shoots, disembarking before a place called Santol.

In the forest of Santol they meet two men who, Salvador observes, seem to recognize him. During the customary greetings the two men ask where the travelers have come from; from Quilem, they reply. Upon learning that the group has not yet eaten, the two men suddenly disappear, returning later with some rice. After eating they engage in conversation:

> We talked about the kind of life I led in the recent past. They asked me what the aim of the Santa Iglesia was. I answered: to pray, to ask the Lord God for *awa,* and I said that the Santa Iglesia trusts in the Lord God and engages in firm *(matibay)* acts of worship, repentance, and obedience to the commands of the Lord God. (p. 14)

They talk about "many other related matters." After the conversation the two men leave to procure more rice.

As we noted earlier, Salvador's narrative is structured as a series of encounters with people. That is why he does not talk about his activities during his long stay at "buntoc babi" with Juan, except to note that they had a good relationship, and that when Juan was away for long periods he approached strange houses to beg for food. Neither does he tell us what he did during his long stay in the forest near Zaragosa, except to note that Epifanio cared for him there. His two-week stay at Camias, which he calls his "home," is not described. We know from other sources that there was a church at Camias where Salvador performed religious services. But all he says is that Damaso cared for him there. Obviously, the time spent in fixed locations is compressed; it has little "value" in the scheme of the narrative. It may be argued that this was the only way Salvador could summarize some eight years of his life. But what are the criteria by which he states some facts and omits others?

The manner in which events are strung together in the narrative gives the reader the impression that Salvador is constantly on the move. In each place he meets new people who invariably offer him food, care, and awa. In these episodes there is a recurring pattern. Movement stops as the meeting or encounter is described in some detail. For example, we find variations of the following passage: "When we reached Juan's camp we cooked rice and after cooking we ate and after eating we talked." When people bring gifts and provisions, these are enumerated one by one: cooked rice, milled rice, salt, *bagoong,* cigarettes, and so forth. The sense of movement punctuated by human encounters perfectly describes the *lakaran,* the term in the pasyon for Christ's basic activity among men, and the term Apolinario de la Cruz used for the proselytizing journeys of the cofrades.

Many persons become attached to Salvador in the course of his wanderings. Damaso and Epifanio, for example, henceforth accompany him from place to place. In the course of the narrative the number of his "followers" increases. What is it that binds them to Salvador? What is the basis of the man's "attractiveness"? Obviously it cannot be wealth or status. They all belong to the same social category. They gather buri-palm shoots together. Some, like Epifanio, are also fugitives. Moreover, Salvador is fed, sheltered, and otherwise "cared for" by the people he meets. They give him provisions and gifts *(regalo)* and yet never receive anything material in return. The traditional "patron-client" type of relationship surely cannot be the basis of the bonds between Salvador and his "followers" because it is the "leader" who is indebted. But the absence of "patron-client" ties does not mean that Salvador's society lacks a traditional basis. This becomes clear when we look into the meaning of *utang ng loób*, or "debt of loób."

The current sociological definition of utang na loób implies that the imbalance inherent in a debt relationship must always tend toward equilibrium; that is, the debtor must forever be bound to the giver while the debt is being repayed. This definition of human relationships is often used to explain political behavior. The utang na loób relationship, says Agpalo, "is an asymmetrical and hierarchical one between two entities—the superordinate and the subordinate. The superordinate is the creditor, the person who gives a favor; the subordinate is the debtor who receives a favor." Political leaders, therefore, tend to come from the propertied class because they are able to "give" and thus bind the common *tao* to them through utang na loób.[60] But if this is always the case, why not simply use the term *utang* (debt)? The presence of the word loób points to something other than the simple economic relationship between lender and debtor, giver and receiver. In Salvador's idiom, the gift is a mode of strengthening the bonds among the loób of men. Begging and the acceptance of food, shelter and protective care create, not a subordinate-superordinate relationship, but a horizontal one akin to love. Consistent with his 1899 appeal to Aguinaldo, Salvador presents in his 1910 account an image of society without the pervasive influence of an elite; where things are, in fact, turned upside down—the debtor is the man of power.

According to news reports, Salvador claimed to be a "great disciple of Christ" and able to speak with him whenever he wished. He and his followers wore long hair and robes of coarse cloth in imitation of figures in the pasyon.[61] In Salvador's narrative, however, there are no such direct allusions to the pasyon. We are not told what he looked like; there is not a single mention of

60. Remigio Agpalo, *Pandanggo-sa-Ilaw: The Politics of Occidental Mindoro* (Athens, Ohio Ohio University Center for International Studies, 1969), pp. 4–5. Agpalo's views are typical of social scientists who have discussed Philippine political culture.

61. Reilly, "Filipino Bandit Terror"; Coats, "Philippine Constabulary," p. 201 (from *Manila Times*, 28 March 1905).

Christ or other pasyon characters. Salvador does not step outside the flow of events to make reference to an external form. The pasyon idiom is imbedded in the narrative itself.

One of the important aspects of the pasyon is the imagery of the suffering Christ which evokes the experience of awa in the reader or listener. But no amount of awa can alter the course of the pasyon because Christ is merely enacting what has been foretold and what the Father has designed for the world. The experience of awa induced by the language and music of the pasyon can only put the audience in a state of receptivity for meanings that are usually hidden, such as the connections between the pasyon and life. Now in the case of Salvador, the telling of his story to the people he meets likewise evokes awa and at that point they see the connection between person and figure. In the first two instances of this, narration of his past life evokes awa and the realization that God has saved him from harm. In the third instance the two fishermen who hear his story, instead of replying that God has saved Salvador from harm, inquire about the Santa Iglesia. This increased awareness is possible because the experience of awa makes them see connections. Salvador's story becomes a sign of Christ's presence in the world. That is why, having heard him speak, the two fishermen rush off to spread the word and Salvador's "following" multiplies quickly.

The spontaneous growth of the Santa Iglesia is described in the continuation of the narrative. When the fisherman return they bring cooked and uncooked rice, a kettle, salt, fish, and other kinds of food. They are also accompanied by ten people who all decide to remain with the group. As Salvador puts it, "they joined us in their desire to participate in devotions to the Lord God." They then break camp and walk in the direction of Candaba.

Along the way they meet a fisherman who inquires where they are going. In the direction of Pinac, they reply. The fisherman follows them until they stop to set up camp and rest:

> We started talking about things pertaining to the Lord God. My companions cooked rice; after cooking the rice we ate, and the man I was talking to shared our meal. (p. 15)

After the meal the fisherman departs. Two days later, he returns with other men and women. They bring "gifts, rice, viands, and cigarettes." They ask how Salvador is and he replies, "I am fine, thanks to the mercy of God." After the exchange of greetings, they engage in conversation:

> We talked about the things in life *(buhay-buhay)* that each and every man must lead in relation to seeking God's *awa;* I told them to pray the Rosary morning, noon, and before retiring at night, and that in the context of good acts of worship we should trust in God that we may be placed in even greater tranquility *(catahimican).* (p. 15)

They talk about "other matters related to the Lord God." Later, they partake of a fraternal meal. After eating and resting, the guests bid farewell saying they will return to their homes.

After about a week in the same location, they see five men carrying big baskets who claim they are fish-trappers from San Miguel. After discussing matters concerning "life" and things related to the Lord God, the fish-trappers bid goodbye. Several days later they return accompanied by more people. Salvador asks them where they are going; they reply that they have come to visit, bringing "gifts, rice, viands and cigarettes."

> We talked about life and some of the things we discussed concerned the Lord God and the good things that man can do in his daily life; I told them that man while still alive has to endure all kinds of hardship that come from the intensity of faith *(lalong pananalig)* and that he has to pray the Most Holy Rosary morning, noon and before retiring; and I also said that man has to inflict penitence *(penitente)* upon himself; they asked me what sort of penitence should be made and I said: first, prayer; and second, abstinence *(pagcocolacion),* the endurance of hardship and the forceful effort not to commit wrongdoing against the Lord God; we talked about many other things of the same nature. (p. 16)

When the time comes to eat, they all together partake of a meal. Having rested, the visitors bid farewell, saying they will return to their homes.

Several days later, "all of a sudden" the same people return (*pihit:* to turn or twist around), bringing bundles of clothing. What are all those clothes for, asks Salvador. They reply that "it was decided in their loób ever since they left their homes" that they would join him. Salvador, remarking that they did well *(mabute)* asks them the precise reason for their joining him. They reply that "they wish to know the things related to the Lord God that each and every man should do while still living." The new arrivals total thirty persons. They transfer to a new location not far away. There, says Salvador, they "did nothing but pray the Most Holy Rosary in the morning, at noon before eating, and in the afternoon."

Again, several days later, more men and women arrive bringing "gifts, rice, and other kinds of food." Salvador thinks that they are relatives of his companions. They engage in conversation "about things pertaining to the Lord God that should well be done by each and every person in his household:

> I told them that they should pray the Most Holy Rosary morning, noon and in the afternoon so that the Lord God may grant us His holy grace, because to my belief the Lord God's anger at us is already great, that is why men today have shorter lives, and perhaps death is just around the corner.

After the conversation they eat; after resting, the visitors depart for home. Other groups of men and women visit them in the succeeding days. They bring "gifts which we accept because they are offered to us." With them

Salvador discusses matters "pertaining to the Lord God." The guests are always offered food and rest before they return to their homes.

Since the time Salvador spoke to two fishermen about the aims of the Santa Iglesia, the group around him has grown from two to around forty-five people. Moreover, they are visited regularly by men and women who participate in discussions and meals but eventually have to return home. To pursue a question asked earlier, what was it that made people flock to Salvador?

In March 1905, the *Manila Times* described the pattern in which Salvador obtained money and recruits for his movement: claiming to be a pope, he would enter a town with some of his followers, all dressed like pasyon characters. A bamboo cross was planted in the center of the plaza. Exhortations and speeches "quickly worked the population into a frenzy to the point where the people willingly turned over money and many joined his force."[62] The reader of this account quickly gets the impression that propaganda and the manipulation of gullible minds were key weapons of the Santa Iglesia leadership. The problem with such a news report as this is that it stops short of describing the language of the propaganda and the effect it had on the loób of the audience. In Salvador's narrative it is clear that the leader, far from being manipulative, remains a poor and humble figure who evokes awa and damay from the people he encounters. We are reminded of the Katipunan leader who, during initiation rites, utters the lament of old, suffering *Kalayaan* in order to evoke damay and patriotism.

The remarkable thing about Salvador's account is that it shows him in a state of being unaware of the effect or "power" of his words and presence. When a group of men and women return with bundles of clothing, intending to stay with him, he is quite surprised and questions them about their intent and motive. Their answer is revealing: when they first met Salvador, they decided *in their loób* that they should remain with him. They have returned in order "to know" how to orient their beings to the Lord God. In the pasyon, we recall, awa and damay are manifestations of a "turning" in one's loób. It is the state of loób that makes people follow Christ or the "way" that must be lived. When peasants left their homes to live with Salvador in the swamps and forests, they were experiencing, consciously or unconsciously, the ideal form of behavior suggested by the pasyon. Salvador was their teacher, the one who showed them the "way."

Salvador's account repeatedly mentions prayer as an essential activity in everyday life. At first glance, it appears that prayer is merely an outpouring of emotions and requests. For example, the Santa Iglesia version of the "Our Father" *(Ang Ama Namin)* practically pleads for divine compassion as well as the nourishment of body and soul:

---

62. Cited in Coats, "Philippine Constabulary," p. 201.

Ama namin sumasalangit ka po sumasalupa ang iyong ginawa lingapin mo po ang aming pagluha.	Our Father thou art in heaven thy creatures are on earth look with compassion on our weeping.
Ikaw po ang aming sinasampalatayanan at ikaw rin ang aming inaasahan panggagalingan kakasangkapanin ng aming kalolowa at katawan.	Thou art the object of our faith and worship and Thou art also our hope the source of nourishment for our bodies and souls.
Amen Jesus.[63]	Amen Jesus.

But it is significant that the "Our Father" and the "Hail Mary"—of which the Santa Iglesia also had a version—are recited in the context of the Holy Rosary. The latter, as pointed out earlier, encapsulates in its fifteen mysteries the basic themes of the pasyon. Salvador's teaching that the Rosary be prayed thrice daily—morning, noon, and evening—can be interpreted as a mode of situating everyday life in the context of the pasyon. Prayer, far from being just an emotional outpouring, becomes a positive act of giving meaning to the totality of existence.

Ultimately, prayer is inseparable from the other activities—endurance of hardship, penitence, abstinence, and so forth—that serve to purify, control, and give direction to the loób. Intense prayer, says Salvador, leads to hardships which must be endured. This does not mean a resignation to things as they are (e.g., a life of hardship) because the world is static and unchanging. If this were so then it would be impossible for the Santa Iglesia to have fought in the revolution and engaged the constabulary in armed battle. The world is changing, in the sense that God's plan for mankind is unfolding itself. Through the proper interpretation of signs, man anticipates change and prepares for it in the loób as well as externally through the gathering of men and weapons.

The preoccupation with the state of the loób stands out clearly in the notion of penitence. *Penitente,* according to Salvador, is first of all prayer, and secondly abstinence, endurance of hardship and the "forceful effort" not to commit wrongdoing. Notice how little penitence has to do with just being sorry for one's sins. It involves self-disciplining through the proper performance of prayers. It involves a choice not to partake of certain kinds of foods

63. This prayer was found, together with a version of the "Hail Mary" (*Aba Ginoong Maria*) and various scapulars and *anting-anting,* in the possession of captured Santa Iglesia members (*Muling Pagsilang,* 10 August 1906).

or comforts. The very mention of "forceful effort" implies not merely a passive avoidance of sin but a disciplined effort to live in accordance with certain rules and precepts. The ultimate form of penitence, as we have seen, is when one traverses the "Way of the Cross" during Holy Week. At the end of the road, the penitent is usually half-dead of exhaustion, pain and loss of blood, but he emerges a "new man" whose loób has been renewed, ready to face squarely the challenges of this world.

Prayer and other forms of penitence are ways of purifying and steadying the loób. But this transformation of loób also means an accumulation of power. As pointed out in previous chapters, folk religious ideas and practices must also be seen in the context of "animistic" belief in a divine substance or power permeating the universe. This power can be concentrated in certain objects and persons, and is imaged as a sun, lamp, or other source of *liwanag*. This idea of power renders intelligible several details about Salvador's career. To understand his emphasis on prayer, for example, is much like seeing the connection between Holy Week rituals and anting-anting.

According to a *Manila Times* article of July 1906, Salvador was constantly accompanied by some twenty disciples, who also seemed to function as bodyguards. When not on the move, he was surrounded by an inner group of six who knelt in a circle, face outward, eyes closed, and continuously praying. The remainder formed another circle several meters from the inner one and also prayed, but with their eyes open. On one hand, it can be said that concentric circles meant maximum security; those in the outer ring kept their eyes open in order to spot any danger that might befall their leader.[64] On the other hand, the same formation can be interpreted as an image of liwanag radiating outward from their source in Salvador, who was in a state of intense prayer. The men in the outer circle stared outward much as statues and portraits of the saints do—in order to reach others through their glance, to diffuse the concentrated power of the center.

In the pasyon, Christ's disciples are armed with special powers to better able them to spread the message to all men. It makes sense, then, that such powers should be ascribed to a man like Salvador who not only claimed to be Christ's disciple but actually attempted to live out the pasyon. The following account is typical:

> His adorers, among whom are not a few men of apparent culture and some of them of high position, assert that no one can deny Salvador's mysterious power. He has been able to go everywhere freely without being seen, move rapidly from one place to another, with the desired velocity, and has the property of being able to be in several places at the time.[65]

---

64. This is how Coats ("Philippine Constabulary," pp. 201-2) interprets it.
65. PCR, 29 July 1910 (vol. 2, p. 577; MHC).

When Salvador was captured in 1910, people believed that escape was only a matter of time. "When they think him safest," the belief was, "he will disappear from the presence of his enemies. He will go through walls, and will appear glorious and full of divine grace, confronting his pursuers."[66]

The striking fact about Salvador's powers described above is that they are attributes of a possessor of anting-anting. The pasyon not so much explains as legitimizes or confirms indigenous notions of power. The image of Salvador "full of divine grace," going through walls and "confronting his pursuers" with his radiance, is reminiscent of the pasyon resurrection scene. But a Javanese prince or rebel could be described in roughly the same terms.[67] To pursue the analogy, in traditional Javanese thought there is "the idea that the human seed, and specially the seed of a man of Power, is itself a concentration of Power and a means of its transmission."[68] To the ordinary Javanese, sexual potency in a leader is a sign of political strength. This is made possible in the first place by intermittent periods of sexual abstinence and asceticism during which power is accumulated. Perhaps this is the context in which we should interpret the report that every month Salvador "had a virgin presented to him in the hope that from this union there would be born a Redeemer, a Saviour of the Philippine Islands."[69] It is significant that women are presented to Salvador rather than sought by him. The motives of people have less to do with sex in itself than with recognition of Salvador's power and hopes of liberation.

We began this discussion by asking how, in the narrative, Salvador's group could have grown so quickly from two to around forty-five people. The answers are to be found basically within the narrative itself—the way events are strung together, the idiom of awa, and Salvador's own teachings about prayer, penitence, and the expectation of change because of "God's anger." We can conclude that people flocked to him because they recognized him as a man of exemplary loób, a man of extraordinary power, and a figure of Christ the Redeemer. He more or less conformed to popular conceptions of a leader in a time of imminent change. For those who believed that independence was just around the corner, Salvador was the focus of their hopes. In 1910 a peddler from Pampanga was overheard saying:

> I have confidence in Apong Ipe. He will save us as he has saved himself with his miracles. He is a good man; he does not hurt good Filipinos. But let the bad ones look out; when we win we shall not leave one alive. The Americans are afraid

---

66. Ibid.
67. See Benedict R. O'G. Anderson, "Power in Javanese Culture," p. 39 and passim.
68. Ibid., p. 27.
69. *Manila Times*, 20 July 1906 (in Coats, "Philippine Constabulary," p. 200).

of him and do not dare to catch him because the whole Philippines will rise to defend our only true Saviour.[70]

We can also conclude from the narrative that people were attracted to Salvador, not merely because of his individual traits, but because through their association with him certain possibilities of existence were realized. In 1904 Salvador in passing referred to the Santa Iglesia as a katipunan. In the narrative, Salvador talks about what "katipunan," or brotherhood, is all about. The minute descriptions of the bringing of gifts and food, the cooking and sharing of meals, and the conversations; the sharing of work and earnings; the pervading atmosphere of damay—all these point to how the katipunan ideal is being realized. In each of Salvador's encounters with people, "katipunan" is experienced. Many stay on with him or, having left, return to stay on because they wish to make this experience permanent. What makes this possible, in Salvador's view, is constant prayer, an activity which keeps the loób of the brothers pure, controlled, and steadfast in the commitment to the katipunan's goal.

The People's Rising of 1910

Returning to Salvador's narrative of his past, we arrive upon an event that is described in constabulary records—the Santa Iglesia entry into the town of Arayat in April 1910. Here is Salvador's version of the event: after several days of devotions, Salvador decides to subject his companions to a test. He wants to know, he says, "if what we were doing was authentic (*tunay*) or if their association *(paquiquisama)* with me was authentic." He suggests that they enter the town and pray publicly there. His companions are enthusiastic. That is good, they say, so that people will know that the aims of the Santa Iglesia are not bad. In Salvador's mind, it is good that the entry into the town be publicized so that people will not be "mistaken" regarding the many "crimes" he has been accused of.

At four in the afternoon they begin their trek to the town of Arayat. They carry no weapons, just wooden poles and bamboo sticks. Travelling along the road they pass through the barrios of Candating, Santa Cruz, Gemasan, and Batasan. Presumably having walked through hilly terrain they "descend," cross a river, and head toward the town. They come upon the road that leads to the town church. Upon reaching the church they all kneel before it. "We all prayed," narrates Salvador, "and we managed to complete three parts of the Rosary before we stood up and when we had stood up I suggested to my companions that we leave." They travel along the same route out of town and

70. PCR, 17 June 1910 (vol. 2, p. 492; MHC).

across the river. Finally they stop to rest in Sapang Batasan, where an encounter with the constabulary—the only one ever mentioned by Salvador—takes place:

> We were there the whole afternoon; it was there that we cooked rice and after cooking we ate; no one came to visit us there because . . . people had such great fear of approaching us; when nightfall came we were praying; the soldiers arrived shooting at us; my companions became afraid; I do not know where they fled; in that shooting there still remained fifteen who had not run away, but when we had regrouped some of them bade leave saying they would go home first; and so remaining with me were my two original companions, Epifanio de la Cruz and Damaso Clarin. (p. 18)

The story of the entry into Arayat followed by the encounter with the soldiers is in many respects central to Salvador's account. But before we explain its significance in the context of the narrative, let us situate the story in a wider historical context. What Salvador narrates is merely an episode in a countrywide outburst of proindependence sentiments that reached a peak in 1910. The causes of this phenomenon are varied and complex, and need not be discussed here fully. Peter Stanley has recently described in detail the circumstances leading to the break-up in 1910 of the alliance between the Philippine Commission and the Nacionalista majority in the Assembly. The Payne bill of 1909 that sought reciprocal free trade was opposed by the Nacionalistas on the grounds that this would cause dislocations in parts of the Philippine economy and allow American trusts and monopolies to invade the country. With some qualifications, the bill became law in August as part of the Payne-Aldrich Tariff. During the next few years, says Stanley, "relations between Filipinos and the American government were worse than any other time between the official end of the insurrection in 1902 and the outbreak of the cabinet crisis under Leonard Wood in 1923." The problem was not that the Filipino politicians opposed the entry of American capital, but that they wanted a parallel assurance of their political control of the country. The independence issue was thus brought to the forefront of politics in the latter part of 1909.[71]

The Nacionalista victory in the Assembly elections of November 1909 was an indication of the people's proindependence sentiments. Other parties could not but veer to the left, even exceeding the Nacionalistas in their radical stance. In actual fact, few Filipino politicians ever supposed that independence could be gained immediately; what they wanted was immediate definition of American intentions before "tutelage and development" were furthered.[72] However, in their desire to obtain popular support, perhaps to serve

---

71. Peter Stanley, *A Nation in the Making: the Philippines and the United States, 1899–1921* (Cambridge, Massachusetts: Harvard University, 1974), pp. 148–57.

72. Ibid., p. 154.

as leverage in bargaining with the Commission, Filipino politicians helped create an atmosphere of imminent independence in 1910. In any political meeting, reports an informer, "it is sufficient for the orator to speak of independence, of the spilling of blood, of violent acts against the present state of things, no matter if his language is uncultured, and they applaud him with delirious enthusiasm."[73] Scattered news from the outside world—the petition for Philippine independence by American Democrats, the censure by an American congressman of the sale of friar estates to large syndicates, and the growing tension between the United States and emergent Japan over dominance in the Pacific—became topics not only of speeches but of daily conversation. It was reported in mid-1910 that rumors of such events had "spread to the populace in an exaggerated form." The barrage of speeches and news articles pertaining to the country's future had the effect of making "all or nearly all believe that national independence [was] only a step distant from [them], and there [was] no reason capable of convincing them of the contrary."[74]

Contributing significantly to the state of excitement and expectation among the masses in 1910 was the rumor that the appearance of Halley's coment meant war, and that this war might possibly be the prelude to independence. The "general belief of the ignorant popular masses," adds the constabulary report, was that "it was this Halley comet which announced the birth of the Son of God to the Wise Men, and that today it announces to the Filipino people the proximity of the day of their independence."[75] The comet was a clear sign *(tanda)* which various politicians and peasant leaders pointed to in order to further convince the people that 1910 was the year to rise in arms. In fact, the other events previously mentioned—particularly the rise of Japan—were regarded as so many other signs pointing to war and a change of *panahon* (era).

The first evidence of heightened unrest in 1910 is a constabulary report of 29 January that the Colorum, Sagrada Familia, and Santa Iglesia organizations in central and southern Luzon were making unusually heavy contributions toward the support of Salvador's men in the field. Salvador had recently prophesied that war would break out between Japan and America, and that arms would soon arrive from Japan. The three distinct organizations all recognized the supreme leadership of Salvador whom they addressed, significantly, as "King of the Philippines."[76]

By March, the constabulary realized that a general uprising was in the making. One agent reported that even in the smallest barrios of Pampanga, "inquietude and agitation" were caused by rumors of approaching war. The presence of Salvador "wandering through some towns in Pampanga, Tarlac,

---

73. PCR, 23 May 1910 (vol. 2, p. 440; MHC).
74. Ibid.
75. PCR, 12 May 1910 (vol. 2, pp. 423–24; MHC).
76. PCR, 29 January 1910 (vol. 2, p. 211; MHC).

and Nueva Ecija" made the situation there critical "since among those people they talk only of war and the approaching revolution which will be begun by Felipe and his partisans."[77] Another agent reported that such rumors were widespread "from Polo, Bulacan, to Malabon, Rizal, and from San Mateo to Pasig, Rizal." Mount Arayat seemed to be the focus of a perceptible movement of people; in fact, eight men from Laguna, Cavite, and Batangas en route to Arayat had already been arrested.[78] From Cabiao, Nueva Ecija, came a report that two Santa Iglesia leaders had gathered several hundred people to pray on the nearby slopes of Arayat because, through some Japanese agents, "they had received word that Salvador was daily expected to arrive, bringing arms and the independence of the Philippines."[79]

Pangasinan and Zambales provinces also had Santa Iglesia chapters which appeared to be "greatly excited." In the southern Luzon provinces of Batangas, Cavite, Laguna and Tayabas, Colorum chapters were no less agitated. Their preparations for Holy Week seemed to be more fervent and active than usual. Perhaps it is not entirely coincidental that Holy Thursday and Good Friday, 24 and 25 March, were the days chosen for a large meeting of all Colorum members from Manila, Rizal, and Cavite. They assembled in a barrio of Pasay, a suburb of Manila, "to wait for instructions or orders from Felipe Salvador."[80]

In the previous chapter we noted that as the principalia-led resistance to the United States began to disintegrate in 1901, the Colorum and other religiopolitical groups gained correspondingly in adherents. Peasants who never lost hope in the arrival of independence were able to join organizations whose language, form, and goals sustained the Katipunan spirit throughout what Agoncillo has called "the period of suppressed nationalism." At times, like in 1910, when independence seemed imminent and arms were at least promised, such organizations quickly moved into action. But, as one observer pointed out, the people gathered on Mount Arayat were not all members of "fanatical sects." Many were simply ex-Katipuneros, veterans of the revolution. For example, 300 armed men who passed through a barrio of Cabiao on the way to Mount Arayat said they were soldiers of ex-General Mariano Llanera. In a sense, what they were doing was familiar to them; the revolution had come alive. These veterans were about to relive the past as they trekked to Camanse, one of the foothills of Arayat celebrated as a Katipunan strong-

77. PCR, 22 March 1910 (vol. 2, p. 349; MHC).

78. PCR, 9 March 1910 (vol. 2, p. 291; MHC).

79. PCR, 17 March 1910 (vol. 2, p. 313; MHC). Most people, including the constabulary, were convinced that Salvador had gone to Japan and was returning with a Japanese fleet. Careful investigation after Salvador's capture proved this rumor false (PCR, 31 August 1910 [vol. 2, p. 586); MHC]). There is a remarkable consistency in Filipino beliefs about a returning liberator. Aguinaldo, Rizal, Salvador, Ricarte, and MacArthur are prominent examples.

80. PCR, 15 March 1910 and 29 March 1910 (vol. 2, pp. 310, 359; MHC).

hold in 1896. The agent—a veteran himself—who spied on the group notes in his report: "It cost the Spanish army many lives to take [Camanse], for which reason the enemies of America wish to do the same as was done to Spain."[81]

The revolution sparked by the Katipunan uprising, we recall, eventually came under the direct control of the principales and ilustrados. The republic then had to cope with internal problems, particularly the opposition of so-called fanatical groups. These groups felt that the ilustrados had fallen short of fulfilling the promises of kalayaan; in turn, they were branded as "antirevolutionary." By 1910, however, it was obvious to everybody that only a figure like Felipe Salvador was capable of leading a mass uprising or revolution. In the first place, socially prominent Filipinos had discovered a patriotic role for themselves as members of the Assembly and the various *independista* parties. When an armed uprising became a distinct possibility in 1910, radical ilustrados like Artemio Ricarte, Mariano Ponce, and some Nacionalista politicians discovered that Salvador was "the only man available to lead the movement." Thus they designated him general-in-chief of the revolutionary forces from Nueva Ecija to Bulacan. At least, one experienced observer noted wryly, "the revolutionists need not bear the attacks which the fanatics might make on them as occurred during the past revolution."[82] The overall assessment of the constabulary was simply that Salvador had great influence over the masses. A summary report of August 1910 states:

> It is corroborated by recent facts that at present he is the only man with sufficient power over the masses to call to the mountains at any given moment the number of men which he might desire for any contingency, men who would respond without discussion or hesitation and who would do all he might order them.[83]

Another ironic twist of events is that one of Salvador's subordinate lieutenants—Anselmo Alejandrino—was a scion of a landed Pampanga clan. Alejandrino had been a major during the revolution. His brothers, ex-General Jose and ex-Colonel Joaquin Alejandrino, had transferred residence to Batangas, leaving him in Pampanga as a councilor of the town of Arayat and owner of a large plantation with many tenants. Whether it was because all of the tenants happened to be Santa Iglesia members or because of the family's deep involvement in the revolution, Salvador was allowed to roam freely through the Alejandrino estates. The constabulary eventually found this out and,

---

81. PCR, 22 March 1910 (vol. 2, p. 349; MHC). The author of this report seems to have been a high-ranking officer in Aguinaldo's army. He wrote in Spanish, periodically alluding to events in the revolution with which he was intimately familiar.

82. PCR, 24 March 1910 (vol. 2, p. 386; MHC).

83. Memorandum for the Director, Information Division, PCR, 25 August 1910 (vol. 2, pp. 616–18; MHC).

during the start of the "panic" in March, arrested the "agitator" Anselmo for the illegal possession of two rifles. As he was being brought to the justice of the peace at Arayat, he managed to escape, taking with him the revolver of his guard. The story of this thin and "very feeble" man's escape from his burly American guard "served as a stimulus" for others—his tenants included—to follow him to the mountain, where he had offered his services to Salvador.[84] This must have been a triumph of sorts for the Santa Iglesia leader who had been hounded throughout his career by the gentry of Pampanga. The story goes that "the same day Alejandrino arrived, Salvador said: 'Just as soon as the comet shines in all its splendor, the era of the happy emancipation of the Philippines will be born.'"[85]

The celebrated entry into Arayat took place on 17 April. According to the constabulary, some eighty "Salvadoristas" simply walked through the center of the town, making purchases of food and other provisions, until about noon when "they were pleased to depart." The local officials, police, and all the residents knew from the first moment what was occurring, but nothing was done about it. In fact, some townspeople were friendly toward the visitors, who were able to collect money and other donations. It was only the following day that the constabulary and the governor were notified of the event by the town mayor, who had remained silent the previous day in order to avoid shots being fired in his town. Without further delay, a detachment from neighboring Santa Ana left in pursuit of the "Salvadoristas," finding some three hundred of them with sixty rifles camped in a place called El Pinac. After some resistance, the "Salvadoristas" fled, some in the direction of Cabiao, others toward Mount Arayat.

Returning to Salvador's account, the obvious question comes to mind: why does he drastically reduce the events of 1910 to the entry into Arayat and a few other episodes? If we look at the autobiography as an articulation of meaning, the answer is pretty clear. All along, Salvador has been talking about the rise of a katipunan—the Santa Iglesia. The entry into Arayat, as Salvador himself says, is a test of this katipunan's authenticity or "genuineness." True brotherhood, according to Apolinario de la Cruz, exists only when the loób of the individual members have been "converted," and this can only be revealed when the loób is confronted with the imminence of death. Now Salvador and his group have always avoided places reconnoitered by government soldiers. For they know that, if captured, they will be punished severely or even executed. To walk right into the center of town, where the power of the

84. PCR, 22 March 1910, 23 April 1910, 24 April 1910 (vol. 2, pp. 350, 381, 387; MHC). There was some suspicion that Anselmo was a government spy, but the constabulary records make it clear that the Alejandrino family had always protected Salvador, and refused to reveal his whereabouts.

85. PCR, 30 April 1910 (vol. 2, p. 403; MHC).

government is most strongly felt, is thus tantamount to risking death itself.

Salvador has a motive for his suggestion—to prove to the townspeople that they are mistaken in associating his figure with banditry. Why do the townspeople think this way, in the first place? One striking fact about Salvador's account of the Santa Iglesia is that everything takes place in the countryside. Salvador draws people away from their homes and settled social life and they join him in his wanderings about the swamps and forests around Mount Arayat. Towns, he says, are to be avoided because he lacks a cedula personal. But more than that, towns represent a mode of social relationships quite alien to the Santa Iglesia. They are held together by extensive kinship networks and dominated by a hierarchy determined largely by wealth. The top principalia families live precisely in the town centers. We know from constabulary sources that these families often allied with the colonial government in attempting to suppress the Santa Iglesia. They spread ugly rumors of bandit activity, attempting to instill a false image of Salvador in the minds of townspeople. "Our rich people," commented a sympathizer of Salvador in 1910, "are the ones who denounce us to the authorities and the courts, making themselves feared in that way, and making us serve them almost for nothing."[86] The Alejandrino family must have been an exception.

The meaning of the entry into Arayat becomes clearer when this episode is juxtaposed with its analogue in the pasyon. Even before Jesus is born, certain events already point to a distinction between town and countryside. It is clearly stated that the town proper of Bethlehem ignored Mary and Joseph as they looked for a place to stay:

Sa pagca tauong mahirap	And because the loving couple
ang mag-asauang sing liyag,	were such poor people,
ng manuluya,t, tumauag,	whenever they knocked and called,
uala isa mang tumangap,	not one person received them,
hinlog man o camag-anac	not even kinsmen and relatives. . .
Ng uala ngang matuluyan	Since no one took them in
ualang maauang sino man,	since no one had *awa*
sa canilang pagcalagay,	for the state they were in,
doon na sila tumahan,	they finally settled down,
sa uacas loual ng bayan.	in the outskirts of town. (20:8, 21:3)

The distinction becomes even sharper during the lifetime of Jesus. Those who follow him are either plain country people or town dwellers who reject

86. From a dialogue among peddlers from Pampanga overhead by a government agent (PCR, 17 June 1910 [vol. 2, p. 492; MHC]).

the dominance of the town elite. "Town," in fact, is associated with the pharisees and *pinunong bayan* (town authorities), to whom wealth, education, and social status are ascribed. One manifestation of their influence is the confusion that reigns among townspeople regarding the real identity of Jesus. At one point Jesus asks his disciples: "What is the talk about town . . . who do the townspeople think I really am?"

Ay ang sagot sa caniya	And they answered him
icao rao po,i, dili iba	they say you are no other
yaong si Juan Bautista,	than John the Baptist,
anang iba, i, Elias ca,	others claim you are Elias
Jeremias na profeta.	or Jeremias the Prophet.
(54:10)	

What is worse, the town notables are spreading rumors that Jesus is a bad man, a traitor, a troublemaker. The continued ignorance of the townspeople can be attributed to the machinations of their envious and threatened leaders. The parallel here with Salvador's account is not accidental. Of all the available facts about the Santa Iglesia in 1910, Salvador chose certain details of the entry into Arayat to illustrate the identity of pasyon and experience.

Salvador says that he and his men knelt in front of the town church and prayed. This is not mentioned in the constabulary records. Did Salvador fabricate the story in order to divert attention from the more "political" acts of the Santa Iglesia? Possibly. But the more crucial question is whether in fact a distinction was perceived between "political" and "religious" acts. One of the root causes of the Santa Iglesia "schism" was the fact that the Roman Catholic clergy had become entangled in the web of allegiances of the towns. The clergy as well as the principalia perceived the Santa Iglesia as a threat, and often took concerted action against it. As Guerrero has pointed out, many churches in Pampanga prohibited the entrance of those who attended Santa Iglesia functions. The church at Betis, for example, authorized any parishioner to bodily expel any "Salvadorista" who attempted to enter the church.[87] The Santa Iglesia's gesture of kneeling and praying the Holy Rosary before the church was to reveal to the watching townsfolk (and perhaps to the parish priest) the nature of their association. They wanted their misinformed audience to understand that, far from being bandits, they were a brotherhood that attempted to transform into lived experience certain ideals which the church and town notables preferred to confine to the realm of prescribed rituals and private devotions.

Perhaps it is not entirely coincidental that when Jesus entered Jerusalem, he headed for the church or synagogue. The people greeted him with great

87. Guerrero, "Luzon at War," p. 184.

rejoicing, for by that time many had come to know him. The pharisees, however, were burning with hatred for the man:

Saca yaong manga lilo mainguiting fariseo pinagbaualan ang tauo ang magpatuloy cay Cristo parurusahang totoo.	And so those traitors the envious pharisees under threat of punishment prevented the people from inviting Christ in.
Maghapon ang Poong Ama, nangangaral sa lahat na, doon ipaquiquilala, ang linamnam at ang lasa nang mahal niyang Doctrina.	All day long the Lord Father, was teaching the multitude, introducing to them, the taste and deliciousness of his holy doctrine.
Nang lulubog na,i, ang arao manga tauo,i, nagsipanao noui sa canilang bahay, at ang Poong nangangaral na sa loob ng Simbahan.	As the sun was about to set the people disappeared returning to their homes, and the Lord Teacher was inside the church.
Uala isa mang pumiguing cay Jesus na Poon natin maghapong hindi cumain, binata ang pagcaalipin ito,i, aral din sa atin.	Not one offered a meal to Jesus our Lord who did not eat the whole day, enduring such servility as another lesson for us.
Lumabas na sa Simbahan itong Dios na maalam sampuong discipulong abay, at nagtuloy capagcouan doon sa Betaniang bayan. (69:16, 70:1–4)	And so this learned God emerged from the church escorted by his disciples, and then proceeded toward the town of Betania.

The passages above show that no one offered Jesus and his disciples a meal; in the end, there was no awa. It is clear, however, that such behavior of the townspeople was the result of intimidation on the part of the ecclesiastical and civil authorities.

Since the pasyon is a matrix of meaning in Salvador's account, it is understandable that certain details present in constabulary records are ignored. These records insinuate that Salvador had sympathizers among the town elite. And there is little doubt that the "Salvadoristas" spent a lot of time in Arayat procuring food and supplies. But Salvador does not mention this. In other episodes, he carefully enumerates the kinds of food and provisions people bring to him in the countryside. Conspicuously absent in the town episode is a meal or a conversation. The group simply prays in front of the church, managing to complete three parts of the Rosary before they stand and leave abruptly. Why, we are not told. But, significantly, no one visits them as they are camped in the outskirts of town, because people have "such great fear" of approaching them. Since the Santa Iglesia has revealed to the townspeople its true nature, such great fear can only be the result of the propaganda or threats of the authorities.

The only people who "visit" the Santa Iglesia camp are government soldiers. They arrive shooting at the brethren who are in the midst of a prayer session. Physical violence, a manifestation of the power of the government and the town leaders, manages to overcome the self-control of many who flee into the night. Those who manage to stand fast eventually ask to be allowed to return home. At the episode's end, Salvador is left with his two original companions.

There is a certain matter-of-factness about the way Salvador narrates these developments. Perhaps it is because there is something in the experience of "katipunan" that makes such an outcome natural. Perhaps it is related to Apolinario de la Cruz's acceptance of the turning away of the cofrades because union can only be evoked, not forged. Salvador's men, in a way, have failed the test. But in the pasyon, we recall, even the closest disciples of Jesus lose control of their loób at the critical hour. While walking in the Mount of Olives, Jesus tells them that their companionship will fall apart when the soldiers arrive that evening:

Oh manga Apostoles co pili cong manga catoto, ay ngayon ding gabing ito, ualang pagsalang totoo aco,i, papanauan ninyo.	Oh my apostles my chosen companions on this very night truly without fail you will abandon me.
Cayo rin nga,i, iilag magpapabaya,t, dorouag loob ninyo,i, maalapaap, malilimutang di hamac itong ating paghaharap. (91:6, 92:1)	You yourselves will retreat turn cowardly, neglecting me your loob will waver forgetting completely our present dialogue.

Three months intervened between the Arayat incident and Salvador's capture. According to constabulary records, in mid-May Salvador led a large group of men across the Zambales mountains in expectation of a landing of arms on the western coast. Some two weeks later, they returned to central Luzon empty-handed. The failure to provide firearms may have led to a dispersion of some of the groups on Mount Arayat. However, it is clear that popular expectations of an imminent upheaval did not diminish. For some, it was a question of waiting for the comet to pass through. Salvador, while abandoning his haunts near Arayat town because of government surveillance, continued to be the focal point of the movement while hiding out in the vicinity of Floridablanca and San Luis.[88]

In Salvador's autobiography, we get a different picture of developments after the Arayat episode. Salvador, together with Damaso Clarin and Epifanio de la Cruz, have resumed the *lakaran*. They come upon a hut by the roadside. They ask for rice; they eat, and rest in a "peaceful place." They walk on until they reach their former camp by the river Munte. They lie down and sleep. After awakening, they sit by the riverbank and ask for some rice from a passing boatman. After eating, they continue on to Zaragosa. Having reached that place, Epifanio goes off to ask for rice and other food from former benefactors. After three days rest, they resume the cutting of buri-palm shoots in order to have money to buy the necessities of life.

One day, Salvador, accompanied by Damaso, heads for his "home" in Camias. Epifanio decides to stay behind in Munte. On the way to Camias they pass through many familiar barrios, avoiding towns like Candaba and San Luis. The names of these places are enumerated as if Salvador is making a former journey in reverse. Indeed, if in previous episodes the movement through various localities resulted in the augmentation of his following, the present return to Camias leaves him, in the end, alone. One day, while in Camias, Damaso says that he would like to visit his family in San Nicolas. He departs, taking with him the remaining unspent income from the sale of palm shoots. But Damaso never returns. Salvador later receives the news of Damaso's death from cholera. "From the time Damaso died," he says, "there was no one to care for or watch over me."

At this point, Salvador is back where he started—an escaped convict alone in the forest. Without any break in the narrative, however, events begin to repeat themselves. Because he lacks provisions, Salvador approaches a house one night and asks for food, which is given to him. He bids leave from his kind benefactors and returns to his "place of hiding." As the afternoon is passing, "all of a sudden" he sees a man who has wandered nearby. This man runs off to inform others of Salvador's presence. According to the account, "When the news had spread around, a number of people began to arrive; as soon as they arrived we got to talking about matters related to the Lord God." After the conversation the visitors bid leave to return to their homes. But "all of a sudden," more people arrive. "How are you?" they ask, and Salvador replies "Fine, thanks to the will and *awa* of the Lord God." In turn, Salvador asks how they are, to which they reply that they are "fine," and have not been ill, thanks to the awa of God. The visitors then suggest that he build himself a hut where he can rest, for, having discovered him sheltered beneath a

88. PCR, 27 May 1910, 2 June 1910, 10 June 1910, 25 August 1910 (vol. 2, pp. 450, 463, 478, and 616 ff.; MHC).

bamboo grove, they have awa. After talking about these desultory matters, he tells them "what each and every man must do while he is alive in this world":

> First I told them that they must ask awa from the Lord God, engage in proper devotion and prayer, follow the commands of the Lord God, love God above all things and love their fellowmen as they love themselves, not to think about anything dishonorable *(di macararangal)* to the Lord God. (p. 20)

When he has finished speaking, they bid goodbye and return to their homes. Salvador, meanwhile, starts to construct a hut.

Passion, Death, and . . .

Salvador gives the precise date of his capture—Sunday, 24 July 1910. He has just completed the hut, when "all of a sudden" someone comes along. It is the man who later will lead the authorities to him. Having foretold his end, Salvador narrates the events of the day: a woman arrives, followed not much later by Salvador's son and a woman companion. Then comes an old woman accompanied by a niece, a nephew, and two children. Three more people arrive. They all start to pray as nightfall approaches. After prayers, "all of a sudden" the police, led by the informer, arrive. Salvador is bound and brought to the governor's house. There his ropes are cut; he is handcuffed and fed. Having rested a bit, he is put on a train bound for Manila. At this point, the narrative ends.

Most likely, the man who led the soldiers to Salvador was Eusebio Clarin, a relative or possibly brother of Damaso, Salvador's closest companion. We know for certain that Governor Arnedo of Pampanga twice persuaded Clarin to declare that he was his personal agent.[89] That a traitor, or former disciple even, should be the immediate cause of Salvador's capture, was not predetermined. Yet how well it fits the scenario of his life.

While the Americans and most local politicians heaved a sigh of relief over Salvador's capture, grief and shock swept the areas of Santa Iglesia influence. A memo to the constabulary director states: "Everywhere one hears lamentations because of Salvador's capture and hopes for his escape." Some nationalist politicians were "saddened" because "they hoped to use him in the struggle for independence."[90] Salvador's peasant followers, overcoming their initial shock, believed that he allowed himself to be caught to demonstrate his power, for he could escape anytime he wanted to. Even as far as south as

89. PCR, 2 August 1910 (vol. 2, p. 589; MHC).

90. PCR, 25 August 1910 (vol. 2, pp. 616–18; MHC). Buencamino, in particular, is mentioned.

Cavite, the talk was that Salvador would soon escape and take command of the "redeeming forces" which would drive out the Americans and proclaim independence. Fearing that such an escape might trigger another wave of mass unrest, the government watched Salvador carefully. Even his guards were screened lest there be sympathizers among them.[91]

Salvador was convicted of sedition and sentenced to be hanged on 15 April 1912. On the eve of the execution, a reporter from the Tagalog daily *Taliba* was in Bilibid prison and witnessed the final meeting between Salvador and his family. This is how he described the scene: all of the visitors were choked with anguish, eyes filled with tears, feeling nothing but pain and sorrow. The wife and children were "bursting inside with grief . . . as if they saw their beloved Felipe gasping for breath and presently laboring in the final throes of death." Actually, he was very much alive and in good spirits:

> Felipe Salvador did not reveal the slightest fear or loss of fervor. He was as he had always been: smiling, gentle, speaking with a clear voice. Not a tear fell from his eyes; he was not sad; in fact, he was as animated *(masigla)* as one nearing the fulfillment of his hopes.[92]

It was "with a perfectly calm loób" that Salvador said these parting words to his family:

> Huwag kayong umiyak. At sa pagka't ito'y huling oras na, ipagdasal ninyo ako. Kayo ang bahala sa inyong buhay. Kayo na ang bahala sa kanilang magiina. Ako ay tatanggap ng kamatayang matamis sa aking loób.

> Do not weep. And because this is my final hour, say some prayers for me. Take care of yourselves. Take care of the mother and her children. I am about to embrace death which is sweet to my loób.

Having bade their last farewells, "the visitors went home with tightness in their loób, and Felipe Salvador was left in high spirits, strong and without a frown on his forehead."

Nothing reveals as dramatically as the parting scene above—reported by an outsider—that Salvador lived and died in damay for the hero of the pasyon. Faced with the certainty of death, Salvador and countless other patriots before him could live out their final moments in joyful expectation because they had been culturally prepared for it. They could be completely serene in loób while around them reigned the anguish and emotional outpourings of those who

---

91. PCR, 29 July 1910, 14 September 1910 (vol. 2, pp. 577, 647; MHC).

92. The *Taliba* accounts of Salvador's execution, wake, and funeral are published in Santos, *Tatlong Tulisan*, pp. 21–27.

failed to see beyond the loss of a human life. The contrast between Salvador and his family recalls that between Jesus and his mother Mary. On the day of the Pasch, as Jesus is about to leave home, he tells his tearful mother to endure the pain because he is doing God's will. Like Salvador's final request to his relatives, Jesus tells his cousin John (the Evangelist) to take good care of his mother. Several stanzas describe the sorrowful parting, in which Mary's emotional outpouring contrasts with the calmness of her son. In another scene, after Jesus has fallen under the weight of the cross, he calls out to his mother to show him awa, to turn her loving gaze on him. "As if by a miracle," Mary hears her son's request and rushes to him with tears in her eyes and her heart rent with anguish. In some ten stanzas of the pasyon Mary pours out her feelings and begs that she be allowed to carry the cross. But Jesus replies that there is no other "way"; she must wipe her tears and God will take care of her:

Ang sagot ni Cristong mahal oh Ina cong nalulumbay suca na,t, iyong itahan, pagdaing, pananambitan sa Anac mong mamamatay.	The holy Christ replied oh my sorrowful Mother it is time you ceased the cries and supplications for your Son who will die . . .
Aco,i, hindi nasisinsay nitong aquing cagagauan ang loób cong iningatan, sa dibdib di napaparam pagsacop co nga sa tanan. (144:9, 13)	I am undaunted by this act of mine my loób was prepared for it, the task of redeeming mankind does not vanish in emotions.

Like Apolinario de la Cruz, Jose Rizal, Macario Sakay, and many other Filipinos who were executed by the colonial authorities, Felipe Salvador met his fate with serenity and joy. We know that death, for Rizal, was the culmination of his pasyon. For Salvador, we can only guess at the meaning he saw in his final moments. Here is the *Taliba* reporter's description of the event:

Outside the room where [Salvador] was confined, waited some twenty to thirty people who would be witnesses to a very sad death. Meanwhile, two American officials entered his room...

Several seconds elapsed, and the condemned man was brought out by two officials. Following behind were two priests, one American and the other Filipino.

The condemned man showed not a trace of weakness, paleness or fear. In fact, he looked as he was before—his face radiant with joy, his manner of walking firm even as he ascended the scaffold. Even as he stood in the middle of the platform, not the slightest weakening was noticed. He stood very erect and straight, adjusting his bodily position to ease the strain of the leather strips that bound his hands and feet.

From the time his face was covered with a black shroud similar to his garments and his neck tied, to the time he was swept off the platform and the renowned Felipe

Salvador bade farewell to this life, some half an hour elapsed.

All, the two priests included, were filled with deep sadness as they gazed at the body of the man who for a long time led the Santa Iglesia.

And everyone, even only in his heart, prayed with total sorrow.

There was twenty minutes of silence . . . heads bared . . . bowed before the lifeless body.

We are reminded of Rizal's Christ-like death in Bagumbayan in 1896, when the friars and officials who wanted Rizal dead could not immediately shout "Viva España!" and a solemn silence reigned for some minutes as they gazed at the victim lying face up, a rosary wound about his wrist. A similar condition must have gripped the crowd that saw the way in which the "bandit" Salvador met his death. Did they, perhaps, for a brief moment perceive the connection between Salvador and the pasyon?

When the *Taliba* reporter visited the wake in Tondo, he noticed that Salvador's face had changed little in appearance since the previous morning, when he was still alive. In fact, the reporter heard many remark that Salvador "seemed only to be asleep, happy, his complexion not darkening as is usually expected of someone like him who has died of unnatural causes." One would almost expect people to say this of a man like Salvador. In the pasyon, when Mary dies, the comment is made that she "is as if only asleep" and her face seems to radiate light. In fact, she had assured the apostles that she would remain with them:

Aniya aco,i, patay man	I may be dead, she said
totoo rin acong buhay	but I will also be alive
cayo,i, di malilimutan,	I will never forget you
iaadya,t, tutulungan	and will always help you
sa pangambang ano pa man.	in any kind of danger.
(195:4)	

To be sure, then, Salvador's physical features in death were perceived as signs that he was truly alive and would always be with them. During the funeral on 16 April, *Taliba* reported, a large crowd turned out to pay their last respects. Among them was an association, the Lingap Kapatid (Brotherly Compassion), whose banner led the cortege to the cemetery of Paang Bundok (Foot of this Mountain.)

Lapiang Malaya praying before encounter with the constabulary

Epilog

In October 1906, an American investigator suggested that "if Salvador himself could be disposed of, it would be the beginning of the end." The active followers—perhaps three or four hundred—would scatter and the members of the Santa Iglesia would be left subject to the influence of the pulpit, school, press, and railroad.[1] It may be true that, after 1912, the Santa Iglesia seems to have "quickly disappeared."[2] However, the ethos which it represented continued to live on, manifesting itself in such uprisings as the Colorum and Sakdal and in the continued popularity of katipunan-type brotherhoods among the common masses. Felipe Salvado Did not really die in 1912. Many of his followers, according to Sturtevant, refused to accept his death.[3] In 1966, an old Colorum leader named Pedro Calosa, who as a youth had heard all about Salvador, told Sturtevant during an interview:

> Salvador tried to destroy the sources of hate. He tried to show people the beauty of love. More than 3,000 people followed him. It is true, he was captured by the Constabulary and he was hanged. But he did not die. His personality lived on and took different forms. I knew him in Honolulu. In Hawaii he was called Felipe Santiago. When I was in prison he was a crazy man in the next cell. I talked with him and he told me many things. He was Felipe Salvador. You understand.[4]

To paraphrase Calosa, Salvador did not die because his "personality" lived on in others. It makes little difference whether we speak of a De la Cruz or a Sakay,

1. Doherty to *New York Evening Post,* 2 October 1906 (BIA 4865-33).
2. Larkin, *Pampangans*, p. 237.
3. David R. Sturtevant, "Philippine Social Structure and Its Relation to Agrarian Unrest" Ph.D. dissertation, Stanford University, 1958), p. 120.
4. "Epilog for an Old 'Colorum,'" *Solidarity* 3 (August 1968): 15.

a Rios or a Caneo, a Bonifacio or a De Guzman, a Labios or a Salvador. All of these leaders and their movements are, to use Calosa's phrase, "part of the same tree." We can include among them the martyrs Gomez, Burgos, Zamora and Rizal—all educated men whose mode of dying was nevertheless perceived as signs of the pasyon's reenactment in the Philippine landscape.

The continuity in form between the Cofradía in 1841, the Katipunan revolt of 1896, the Santa Iglesia and other movements we have examined can be traced to the persistence of the pasyon in shaping the perceptions of particularly the poor and uneducated segments of the populace. Through the text and associated rituals, people were made aware of a pattern of universal history. They also became aware of ideal forms of behavior and social relationships, and a way to attain these through suffering, death, and rebirth. And so in times of crisis—economic, political, real or imagined—there was available a set of ideas and images with which even the rural masses could make sense out of their condition. Popular movements and revolts were far from being blind reactions to oppression. They became popular precisely because leaders were able to tap existing notions of change; the pasyon was freed from its officially sanctioned moorings in Holy Week and allowed to give form and meaning to the people's struggles for liberation.

Felipe Salvador's mode of death was identical to that of Apolinario de la Cruz in 1841, and this is not surprising. We began this study with the Cofradía de San Jose because it is perhaps the earliest, documented example of a movement which attempted to make the pasyon and everyday worlds coincide in a distinctly Filipino manner. The brotherhood's prayers and hymns and the leader's correspondence reveal a world outlook dominated by ideas of liwanag, transformation, and control of loób, commitment in the face of suffering, and paradise. Significantly, paradise was not confined to an otherworldly condition; it included freedom from taxes and forced labor, and the birth of a native church (*Yglesia*). Under the leadership of De la Cruz, who was a figure of Christ, a man of *anting-anting*, and eventually king of the Tagalogs, the Cofradía expanded swiftly, making confrontation with the Spaniards inevitable. Even with the dismantling of the Cofradía, its ethos lived on after 1841 and other charismatic leaders followed De la Cruz's footsteps.

In 1897, the Colorum Society interpreted the Katipunan revolt as a sign of an approaching cataclysm. We examined their participation not as a curious sidelight to the revolution but as a revelation of folk perceptions of events. In fact, the Katipunan itself attained such a massive following because ideas of nationalism and independence were expressed in the idiom of the pasyon. The history of the Filipino people was seen in terms of a lost Eden, the recovery o which demanded the people's participation in the pasyon of Mother Country Initiation rituals involved a transformation of loób, a rebirth in the brotherhood a passage from darkness to light. And paradise became *kalayaan*—not only independence from Spain but enlightenment, prosperity, and true brotherhood. The split within the leadership of the Katipunan manifested, among other things, a tension between the "sacred" ideals of the Katipunan upheld by Bonifacio and a limited notion of kalayaan to which Aguinaldo and most of the *principalia* were attracted.

Ilustrados and principales ultimately had their way with the founding of the republic in 1898. If the revolution was experienced by some as a rebirth, a fulfillment of hopes, this quickly faded away as the leaders' efforts were directed toward stabilizing the infant nation-state. Attempts by some groups to effect social and economic changes in the name of the revolution were termed subversive and promptly suppressed. The republican phase of the revolution was perceived to be quite different from the "first war" of 1896, particularly as American armed might proved to be too formidable. In the face of increasing disunity, people longed for the spirit of 1896. The breaking off from Spain was recalled as an apocalyptic event, when the loób of all the sons of Mother Country became one in the Katipunan and an invincible force arose which no one could resist. Military defeats and the capitulation of republican leaders in 1899 were signs of the decline of the Katipunan ethos in the revolution.

Could the pasyon of Mother Country be halted; could there be a turning back on the path to kalayaan? This question apparently did not bother the lot of republican politicians and generals who found a niche for themselves in the American "New Order." But there were some like Sakay who insisted that genuine kalayaan was possible only through the Katipunan mode of struggle. In the meantime large numbers of peasants flocked to religiopolitical brotherhoods for whom kalayaan had become a sacred goal; Malvar's continued resistance owed much to them. It was the pasyon outlook which enabled these groups to organize their experience of the New Order and continue the struggle meaningfully. Ilustrados who ostensibly fought for independence through legal means were regarded as inauthentic because of their preoccupation with personal wealth and status rather than Christ-like suffering and the transformation of loób.

Although such movements continue to exist, there is a reason for culminating this study with the Santa Iglesia. It began very much as a Cofradía in the 1880s, actively participated in both phases of the revolution, and ended up in 1910 at the helm of the popular anticolonial struggle. With Felipe Salvador talking about Katipunan and independence, as well as *awa, damay*, prayer, *anting-anting* and control of loób, it becomes difficult to adhere to the distinctions other scholars have made between religious and secular, agrarian and nationalist, little-tradition and great-tradition movements. The Santa Iglesia was all of these. Religion to the "Salvadoristas" was not just devotion to God and concern with the supernatural, but a way of organizing their daily lives. Appropriated from the friars, religion gave form to peasant hopes for brotherhood and more equitable economic relationships. And by the first decade of this century, it had merged with the nationalist and revolutionary ideologies originating from the urban elite to become the driving force of the peasant-based anticolonial movement. At that time, given the masses' experience of the "long dark night" of Spanish rule, there was no other way in which the revolt of the masses could have taken shape.

There is a well-known saying that "men make their history upon the basis of prior conditions." But what determines human behavior must include not only real and present factors but also a certain object, a certain future, that is to be actualized. We have seen that even the poor and unlettered masses in the nineteenth century had the ability to go beyond their situation, to determine what its meaning would be instead of merely being determined by it. Not that the aspirations of the masses always were of a revolutionary nature or went beyond limited, private demands. Nonetheless, only those movements were successful that built upon the masses' conceptions of the future as well as social and economic conditions. The subjects of this book have at one time or another been called bandits, ignoramuses, heretics, lunatics, fanatics, and, in particular, failures. Not only has this been a way in which the "better classes" keep these people in oblivion; worse, this signifies a failure or a refusal to view them in the light of *their* world. Oddly enough, such epithets are found in the pasyon; popular culture itself anticipates such attitudes on the part of the elite. But as we move forward on the path to kalayaan, we can hardly ignore the voices from below.

Appendix 1

Dalit sa Caluwalhatian sa Langit na Cararatnan ng mga Banal

1 Arao nacapitapita
lalong caligaligaya
cun ang macaguiguinhawa
matingnan ng ating mata.

2 Catao an lupa mang hamac
mamahal ding diualas
at ang Dios ang nag aatas
at nagbibigay ng Palad.

3 Saca cun aling buhayin
ang banal namasunorin
laloring pagpapalain
sa sucat nating sabihin.

4 Dili ngani maysip
ang galing namasasapit
mapapanolos ang ybig
mauaualan ng ligalig.

5 Dili masabi ang licsi
para ng Dios nacasi
caniya ding pasarili
sa catotong guinaganti.

6 Con bagai sila'y lalacad
toling ibong lomilipad
malayo ma'y natatangbad
dili magaabut quisap.

7 Magaan ualading bigat
lumacbay man sa dipalac
pababababama't pay-taas
yto't yao'i cagyat cagyat.

8 Ang liuanag ang sabihin
catilitiling tanghalin
ualaring macatitingin
ang sila'y masisilao din.

9 Ang capouaman catao-an
matataos mararaman
dili nga macalalaban
Espiritung pagcaasal.

10 Lima sa catao ang sangcap
matatalim pauang tatas
ualaring maca liuag
pauang pauang aliualas.

11 Ang dilan panga ngataoan
maguiguing isaring pisan
mamomuchang pagcalagui
catao-an ni Jesus, namahal.

12 Niyong siya ang dirito
ng taong maycapat tatlo
ang lahat nanganing tauo
bata't matanda'y ganito.

13 Icaycapat tatlo ngang taon
ang pag catauo ng Poon
tayo nga'y maguiguin gayon
mauauangis maoocol.

14 Baguntauo ma't dalaga
manga tauo mang naona
magulang caya't batapa
mag cacasing parapara.

15 Ang mahal ma't ang mababa
ang mayaman ma't ang ducha
mag sising musing mucha
ang Dios din ang may panata.

16 Ualang gaby't pisang arao
ualang init, ualang guinao
ualangotom, ualan ohao
ualan lumbay, ualan panglao.

17 Ualan tacot, ualan sindac
ualang tolog, ualang poyat
ualan balisang paghanap
at ang dila'y sadyat sangcad.

18 Ualan capanaghilian
ualaman capalaloan
ang silang lahat ay banal
nag cacaybig ybigan.

19 Ang Dios namang maycapal
pinag cacaybiganan
asal nila'y casantosan
ualan bacas casalanan.

20 Ualan tamad ualan galit
ang calibogay napatid
caramita'y nanga alis
sampon cayamo at ynip.

21 Ang canilang guinacamtan
ang lalaquing cabanalan
pararatihing ingatan
ng Panginoong may caual.

22 Dios ang pagcarongsolan
titingnang pagcaraniuan
siyang mata't titigan
ualang humpay ualang hoyang.

23 Doon sila nabobosog
nanapopono ang loob
ng niig napag calogod
ualang sauang panonood.

24 Ano man dito sa lupa
dapat ding ualing bahala
sinongaling salopica
buticaya't malic mata.

25 Ang magaling at ang totoo
na sundin sundin ng tauo
ang yamang dimacabuyo
sa langit matotoo.

26 Ang sa arao naliuanag
at ang sa bouang banaag
culang liuanag, at hamac
con sa canila'y harap.

27 Sa langit, napag catahan
dilocloc ang ualang pagal
tindig din ang pagcalagay
di nag papangimbolohan.

28 Dilima cocotya cotya
hobo mang sa hihilata
con ualaman salat sama
ualan sucat ycahiya.

29 Dilan sala sa catao-an
ng sila'y manga bubuhay
pilay, cayat, cabulagan
bacas sugat, cabongian.

30 Pilat at ano anoman
pauang ualana't nabahao
ang ticas ng pagcaasal
boong cataong posacal.

31 Ang lalong naca y ygui
palad nayaoi darati
ualang masamang halili
lumbay caya't douahagui.

32 Ualan sala salauahan
budhi ualang calabcaban
di macapag bagong lagay
mag pa sa cailan mang arao.

33 Cun ang Ama mo't ang Ina
sa infierno'y maquita
di mabauasang ligaya
asal di mangongolila.

34 Dios ang canilang Ama
at catoto't cabihasa
siya yna alaala
iba'y ina alintana.

35 Ang loob ay malologdin
sa Dios nanag aangquin
ang ysip nila'y matalim
ang ala ala'y gayondin.

36 Talos mangamaroronong
mga mumunting sanggol
sa manga binsang lauan
hangan salupa domuon.

37 Doon nga sa cadiosan
dilan buti matitingnan
doon din maquiquinabang
carunongang dilan bagay.

38 Maguin patas at paham
diman nagaral napagal
ysip nila'y susubuan
ng mataas na aral.

39 Ang cacasa casamahin
Angeles nama niningning
silay cacapanayamin
at cacao caosapin.

40 Marteres cacabatiin
Virgenes cacatotohin
Confesores cacasihin
pauang nag aaloningning.

41 Ang Dios nga'y natitingnan
matan ysip macacamtan
si Maria'y calologdan
at pag ca caronsulanan.

42 Sila'y mag sisicatoua
pasalamat sa may katha
at ang sila'y ynilisya
gayong arao namasama.

Appendix 2

Ang Paghihimagsik Laban sa Espanya: The Ronquillo Transcription

1 Oh! inang Espanyang pinagkautangan
ng balabalaking mga karunungan
kami'y naghahandog, kung sa nag aalay,
ng lubhang maraming kapasalamatan.

2 Totoo po't kami'y nangakong matibay
di ka lilimutin at paglilingkuran
sa tubig, sa kati, ipagsasanggalang
sa magsisidigma na morong kaaway.

3 Kung kaya gayon po ang naipangako
sa iyo'y guguli't ibuhos and dugo,
isip namin ina ay mahal sa puso,
taguring tawag mo, palayaw na bunso.

4 Hindi pala ina't kami ay *animal*
kung laging murahin ng kakastilaan
at walang katwirang maipagtagumpay
at kung dumunong pa'y destierro at
bitay.

5 Ang mga tagalog paanong pagdunong
kung may katwiran ma'y hindi maitutol?
Kung ito'y *kumontra* dili ka aayon
panganganlan mo pang tulisan at mason.

6 Ito baga ina ang iyong pagkasi
na kami'y lunurin sa luhang marami,
sa maraming hampas ng mga prayle?
Diwa'y binigyan ka ng kuwaltang
marami!

7 Di nagpagawa ka ng mga kolehio
na pag-aaralan ng hangal at bobo?
Saka ngayon ina na sila'y matuto'y
ipabibilanggo't ipadedestierro.

8 Sa prayle galing ang lahat ng hirap
tinitiis ina ng lahat mong anak,
siya nang pagtangis nitong Pilipinas
sa suhol sa iyo na maraming pilak.

9 Lumalaganap na nga ang kapangyarihan
ng mga prayle sa lahat ng bayan,
sila po ang hari, sila ang kapitan,
sila ang direktor na nagdidiusdiusan.

10 At ang lupa nami'y pinagsukat na nga,
hiningan na nila buwis na sagana,
mga inkilino ay parang alila
sa kanila are ng pagpapagawa.

11 At ang mga bukid ay pinabuwisan
palay po ang sulong sa kapanahunan
malaking bodega ang pinagsisidlan
niyong asenderong malalaking tiyan.

12 Ang mga kahoy po'y pinabuwisang lahat
sa mangga'y kahate, sa kuwaya'y sikapat
sa bawa't palumpong kung ikaw'y tatawad
mukha'y mamumula, mata'y mandidilat.

13 Ang gutom na hayop ang nakakahambing
kapag tumamad ka bigla kang sikmatin
at pag lumaban ka'y narito ang sibil
at gagapusin ka't dadalhin sa kuartel.

14 Sa pinuno nila ikaw'y ihahatid
yari ang causa, gapos ay mahigpit;
at bago dadalhin doon sa Bilibid
sabihin ang hirap na dili maisip!

15 Sa mga eleksion ay sila rin naman
sa lahat nang ito ang nakaaalam,
kung di nila gusto ang magkakapitan
papalitan ng kahima't mangmang.

16 Kahiman at mangmang ilalagay nila
kapagka sumuyo at kapag nagtsapa,
itong punong ito'y siya ring bugaw nila
sa naiibigang magandang dalaga.

17 Mahabaging langit, iyong natitiis,
pinanununghan mo kaming na sa hapis.
Kaya nga sa antak ng maraming sakit
ay kusang nagbalak ng panghihimagsik.

18 At sumikat na nga sa Kasilanganan
ang araw ng puut ng ating si Rizal,
tatlong daang taong laging iningatan
sa dagat ng dusa at karalitaan.

19 Mula nang isuhay kaming iyong anak
sa bagyong masasal ng dalita't hirap,
iisa ang puso nitong Pilipinas
na ikaw ay di na ina naming lahat.

20 Sa kapuwa ina'y wala kang kaparis
ang layaw ng anak ay dalita't sakit
nagpapatirapa't sa iyo'y ninibik
ang lunas na ganti ay kalaitlait.

21 Gapusing mahigpit ang mga tagalog
lamugin sa sikad, kulata at dagok,
taguring madalas na kami ay hayop
ito baga ina ang iyong pag-irog?

22 Masdan mo init ng nasasakupan
malabay na pakpak ng Katagalugan
ay kusang nag-isip na sila'y lumaban
sa inang Espanyang walang pagmamahal.

23 Hukumang Kabite siya nang pagkilos:
Nobeleta't Kawit, Binakaya't Imus,
Mendez, Amadeo, ay pawang sumunod,
katulad ng Silang at saka Bakood.

24 Bayang Dasmarinyas at sampu Indang
at Malabon grande na pinagsimulan,
Naik, Marigundong ay hindi mabilang
ang sumamang tao sa pagpapatayan.

25 Sampung taga Barra, at taga Alfonso
pawang nagsiayon sa nasabing gulo,
Tansa at Salinas, marami ring tao
ang nangagsisamat sa laba'y dumalo.

26 Sa Imus na bayan doon nagkapisan
ang mga bayani, malakas, matapang
pinakapangulong sinusunod bilang
bunying Aguinaldong sa tapang ay
sakdal.

27 Na sa gulong ito ay siyang paglitaw
ng bunying Jimenez taga Bagungbayan(?)
saka si Licerio na taong Montalban,
ito'y pinuno rin na maraming kawal.

28 Lumitaw ang Luis, saka Eusebio,
Antoniong balita bunying Montenegro,
at ang tatlong itong ngalang sinabi ko
ay parang may kawal na parepareho.

29 Lumitaw ang Juliang sa tapang ay bantog
taong Marikina(?) na magandang loob
at yaong sarhento(?) na taga Sampalok,
sila'y may kawal ding mga bukodbukod.

30 Na sa gulong ito'y siya ring paglitaw
ng taga Malibay na si Pio del Pilar,
ito'y pinuno rin na maraming kawal
na natatalaga sa pagpapatayan.

31 Sila bagang lahat ngalang sinabi ko
may kanikanila na mga sundalo,
at siyang lumaban noong magkagulo
buhat nang magpuno si General Blanco.

32 Sa pagpapahirap na sa taong madla
natanyag sa tanang iba't ibang lupa
magmula na noon hindi na tumila
ang pagpapatayan tagalog kastila.

33 At ang gulong ito na lumalagablab
matay mang sugpui'y di maampat-ampat,
nang magkagayon na'y nagpadalang sulat
ang General Blanco't ipinatalastas.

34 Sa dakilang Reyna ang nangyaring gulo
na di magkahusay ang maraming tao,
at dahil sa gayo'y nagsirating dito
mga cazadores, may limangpung libo.

35 Isinabog na nga ng bunying General
sa mga hukuma't mga bayanbayan,
nang sa Katipunang ito ay malaman
hindi na huminto ng paglusob naman.

36 Halos araw-gabi walang bigong kilos
mga cazadores parang sinasalot,
lalo na ang mga sa Sapote'y tanod
ay hindi mabilang kastilang inubos.

37 Nang mabalitaan ng General Blanco
lubhang mahirap nang mahusay ang gulo
agad nagpadala ng malaking hukbo
na pawang kastila't Imus ang tinungo.

38 Bukod pa sa rito ay may mga bapor,
may Caballeria pang abay sa escuadron,
ang utos ni Blanco sa lahat ng kampon
ang Imus na baya'y lansagin sa kanyon.

39 Nang ilang buwan nang hindi rin
magtigil
ang putok ng kanyon at mga mauser,
ang bala sa Imus doon kung dumating
ay nangababaon lamang sa buhangin.

40 Ano pa't ang guerra ay pinagtatakhan
ng ingles at pranses, hapon at aleman,
sa kanyo't mauser ang inilalaban
ay ang sa tagalog na itak na pangal.

41 Lahat nang pinuno niyong cazadores
sa labanang ito'y nagsisipagngitngit
dahilan sa kapal ng almas na gamit
ang katagalugan ay hindi magahis.

42 Sa di pagtitigil niyong paghahamok
ng mga kastila at mga tagalog
di naman mangyaring dayaing mapasok
ang gaya ng Imus sila'y natatakot.

43 Ang lahat ng kanyon ay walang magawa
dahil sa trincherang matibay na kuta,
di naman mangyaring bumaba sa lupa
pagka't pag umahon sila'y mapupuksa.

44 Lahat nang pinuno ay nagsipanginig
dahil sa kalaban nilang mababangis
di naman nangyaring dayaing malupig
pagka't si Emilio'y may magandang
isip.

45 Ang labanang ito ay katakataka
sa tanang labanan sa mga provincia
pinuno, sundalo at saka ang kura
ay di pinapatay, binibihag nila.

46 Sa magkagayon na'y ang bunying general
malaki ang lumbay na di ano lamang
at kung kaya lamang naawas-awasan
dahil sa ilonggong dito'y nagsidatal.

47 At ang makabebeng taong salanggapang
nangakong matibay sa bunying General
sila ang wawalat sa kutang matibay
bago si Emilio'y gagapusing buhay.

48 Nanalig sa gayon ang bunying General
kaya nagpagawa isang holang bakal
na itinalaga sa paglululanan
dito kay Emilio na kahambalhambal.

49 Hindi rin nangyari ang tangka sa loob
niyong manglulupig na may asal hayop,
ang pinagnasaa'y niligtas ng Dios
at itong nagnasa'y buhay ay natapos.

50 Kaya ang wika ko sa sino ma't alin
huwag magmalaki sa tapang na angkin
mahaba't maiksi, tsinelas ma't tsapin
ay may mga paang nakakasukat din.

51 Balita man lamang mapagtatalastas
may kanyo't mauser sa kastilang almas
taglay ng tagalog na ibinababag
ang sibat na kuwayan at pangal na itak.

52 Hanggang dito na po't akin nang tigilan
yaring sinabi kong pinag-ugnay-ugnay
kung sakali't kapos sa letra ay kulang
husto ninyong bait siyang karagdagan.

Appendix 3

Kantahing Pulube: The Estrella Transcription

1 Ang paghihimagsik laban sa Espanya
ng bunying Jimenez taga Bagumbayan
saka si Licerio na taong Montalban,
itoy' pinuno rin ng maraming kawal.

2 Lumitao ang Luis, saka Eusebio.
Antoniong balita bunying Montenegro,
at ang tatlong itong ngalang sinabi ko
ay parang may kawal na parepareho.

3 Lumitao ang Juliang sa tapang ay bantog
Taong Marikina na magandang loób
Ay yaong sarhento na taga Sampalok,
sila'y may kawal di nga bukod bukod.

4 Na sa gulong ito'y siya ring paglitaw
ng taga Malibay na si Pio del Pilar
ito'y pinuno rin ng maraming kawal
na tatalaga sa pagpapatayan.

5 Sila bagang lahat ngalan sinabi ko
may kanikanila na mga sundalo,
at siyang lumaban noong nagkagulo
buhat ng magpuno si General Blanco.

6 Sa pagpapahirap sa taong madla
natanyag sa tanang iba't ibang lupa
magmula na noon hind na tumila
ang pagpapatayan tagalog kastila.

7 At ang gulong ito na lumalagablab
matay man sugpui'y di maampat ampat,
ng magkayon nay nagpadalang sulat
ang General Blanco't ipinatalastas.

8 Sa dakilang Reyna ang nangyaring gulo
na di magkahusay ang maraming tao
at dahil sa gayo'y nagsirating dito
mga cazadores, may limampung libo.

9 Isinabog na nga ng bunying General
sa mga hukuma't mga bayanbayan,
nang sa katipunang ito ay malaman
hindi na huminto ng palusob naman.

10 Halos araw-gabi walang bigong kilos
mga cazadores, parang sinasalot
lalo na ang mga sa sapote'y tanod
ay hindi mabilang kastilang inubos.

11 Nang mabalitaan ng General Blanco
Lubhang mahirap nang mahusay ang gulo
agad nagpadala ng malaking hukbo
na pawang kastila'y Imus ang tinungo.

12 Bukod pa sa rito ay may mga bapor,
May "Caballeria" pang abay sa escuadron,
Ang utos ni Blanco sa lahat ng kampon
Ang Imus na baya'y lansagin sa kanyon.

13 Nang ilang buwan nang hindi rin magtigil
ang putok ng kanyon at mga mauser,
ang bala sa Imus doon kung dumating
ay nanga babaon lamang sa buhangin.

14 Ano pa't ang guerra ay pinagtatakhan
Ng ingles at pranses, hapon at aleman,
Sa kanyo't mauser ang inilalaban
Ay ang sa tagalog na itak na pangal.

15 Lahat ng pinuno niyong "cazadores"
Sa labanang ito'y nagsisipagngitngit
Dahilan sa kapal ng almas na gamit
Ang katagalugan ay hindi magahis.

16 Sa di pagtitigil niyong paghahamok
Ng mga kastila at mga tagalog
di naman mangyaring dayang mapasok
Ang gaya ng Imus sila'y natatakot.

17 Ang lahat ng kanyon ay walang magawa
Dahil sa trencherang matibay na kuta
Di naman mangyaring bumaba sa lupa
Pagka't pag umahon sila'y mapupuksa.

18 Lahat ng pinuno ay nagupanginig
Dahil sa kalaban nilang mabàbangis
di naman nangyaring dayaing malupig
Pagka't si Emilio'y may magandang isip.

19 Ang labanang ito ay katakataka
Sa tanang labanan sa mga provincia
Pinuno, sundalo at saka mga kura
Ay hindi pinapatay, binibihag nila.

20 Sa mag kagayon ma'y ang bunying
General
Malaki ang lumbay na di ano lamang
At kung kaya lamang naawas-awasan
Dahil sa ilonggong dito'y nagsidatal.

21 At ang makabebeng taong salanggapang
Nangakong matibay sa bunying General,
Sila ang wawalat sa kutang matibay
Bago'y si Emilio'y gagapusing buhay.

22 Nanalig sa gayon ang bunying General
Kaya nagpagawa isang holang bakal,
Na itinalaga na paglulanan
Dito kay Emilio na kahambalhambal.

23 Hindi rin nangyari ang tangka sa loób
Niyong manglulupig na may asal hayop
Ang pinagnasaa'y niligtas ang Dios
At itong nagnasa'y buhay ay natapos.

24 Kaya ang wika ko sa sino ma't alin
Huwag magmalaki sa tapang na angkin
Mahaba't maiksi, tsinelas, ma't tsapin
Ay may mga paang na kakasukat din.

25 Balita man lamang mapagtatalastas
May kanyo't mauser sa kastilang almas
taglay ng tagalog na ibinababag
Ang sibat na kawayan at pangal na itak.

26 Hanggang dito na po't akin nang tigilan
Yaring sinasabi kong pinagugnayugnay
Kung sakali't kapos sa letra ay kulang
Husto ninyong bait siyang karagdagan.

Appendix 4

Casunod nang buhay na Pinagdaanan ng Ating manga Capatid

1 Sa dahas ng unos na di magpatantan
na bumabagabag sa nangangalacal,
siyang di itiguil sa puyat at pagal
ng manga bihasa sa pagpapatayan.

2 Buhat sa clerigong manga mababait
at sa manga tauong biniguiang pasaquit,
boong Filipinas di na natahimic
magpahangan ngayon palaguing ligalig.

3 Di lihim at hayag ang gulong nangyari
dito't sa provincia nagbuhat sa fraile
at saca sa curang Gil na maigui
na alinsunod ng gobiernong pipe.

4 Na ang fraileng ito nagcura sa Tundo
paguiguing cura na,i, natanyag sa tauo
na sa cabutihan maraming totoo
ang ipina-baril, ipina-destierro.

5 Sa napanganyayang buhay na nauala
niyong manga tauong biniguiang dalita,
ang gobierno naman sa malaquing tua
biniguian ng dangal ang curang daquila.

6 Tusong caballero,i, ipinagcaloob
ng gobierno dito sa curang na bantog
na sa paraan niya,t, magagandang ayos
hanggang sa España ngalan niya,i,
nasabog.

7 Nang panahong yaon ang lahat nang cura
parang nagtiyapan sa tanang provincia,
mayama't marunong binibiguiang sala
nitong magagaling at dito ang hanga.

8 Caya nga,t, walanang dapat paglulanan
nitong ualang sala na pinaratangan,
Castillo,t, Bilibid nangag-pupunuan
macapal na tauong hindi na mabilang.

9 Na cun caya lamang parang lumuluag
sa siquip ang madla na nasasa-hirap,
cun binabaril na o caya ipatpat
sa manga destierro ang cahabaghabag.

10 Ipagpalagay cong may dalauang libo
ang nasasa-carcel at na sa castillo,
cun baril ng baril saan patutungo
mababauasan din ang bilang ng tauo.

11 Bagama't, sa carcel nama,i, naiiuan
na di nararamay sa pinarusahan,
di maglipad buan bubugso na naman
macapal na tauong taga ibang bayan.

12 Ano pa,t, ang lagay carcel nang Bilibid
na gripong mistula nag nacacaparis,
maguing arao gabi ang balang umiguib
hindi nagcuculang ang nasabing tubig.

13 Naganap na lahat ang balang ibiguin
sa aming tagalog lunuri,t, barilin,
saan man itungo nila,t, ihumaling
tumutol at hindi icao,i, papatayin.

14 Ang bilis nang dusa na di magpatantan
nang tanang pinunong na sa bayan-bayan,
doon sa pahirap ay lalong naglatang
ang init nang loob nitong CATIPUNAN.

15 Na sa Balintauag maligayang barrio
doo,i, nagcatipon ang maraming tauo,
ang punong sinunod pinacapang-ulo
ay ang matalinon Andres Bonifacio.

16 Valentin de la Cruz siyang icalaua
na taga Santolan maraming casama,
at ito ang tunay at uala nang iba
gumulo nang una na sa Santa Mesa.

17 Cay D. Ramon Blanco sa mabalitaan
ang lumilipanang manga Catipunan,
manga guardia civil biglang inutusan
na pinaparoon labasin ang parang.

18 Uala ring nangyari tanang inacala
nitong manga punong mabuting castila,
hangang linalabas lalong lumalala
yaong Catipunan na lumilipana.

19 Hocomang Cavite nama,i, nagsiquilos
Noveleta,t, Cauit, Binacaya,t, Imus,
Pasay at Palanyag, Las Piñas umayos
Zapote at Silang at taga Bacood.

20 Bayang Dasmariñas sampong taga Indang
at Malabon Grande nanga lahoc naman,
Naic, Marigondong, ay dili mabilang
ang sumamang tauo sa pagpapatayan.

21 Sampong taga Barra,t, manga maldiqueño
cumilos din naman sa nasabing gulo,
Tansa at Salinas marami ring tauo
ang nangagsi-sama sa laba,i, dumalo.

22 At doon sa Imus nagcatipon lahat
ang manga bayaning pauang mararahas,
na inalinsunod magpahangang uacas
bunying Aguinaldong punong nag-aatas.

23 Na sa gulong yaon lumitao ang ngalan
bayaning Jimenez taga Bagong-Bayan,
saca si Licerio na tauong Montalban
may sari-sarili silang manga caual.

24 Saca si Julian sa tapang ay bantog
tauong Mariquina na magandang loób
at yaong sargento na taga Sampaloc
may manga caual din silang bucod-bucod.

25 Lumitao ang Luis saca si Eusebio
Antoniong bayaning bunying Montenegro
na ang tatlong itong ngalang sinabi co
may sari-sarili na manga vasallo.

26 Na sa gulong ito siyang pagcatanghal
nang taga Malibay na Pio del Pilar,
ito,i, pinuno rin na maraming caual
na natatalaga sa cacastilaan.

27 Silang lahat bagang ngalang sinabi co
may canicaniya na manga sundalo,
ito ang lumaban niyong unang gulo
buhat mag-general si D. Ramon Blanco.

28 Sa pagpapahirap na sa tauong madla
matanyag sa tanang iba,t, ibang lupa,
magmula na niyon hindi na tumila
ang pagpapatayan tagalog castila.

29 Na ang gulong yaon na lumalagablab
matay mang pugnauin di maampat-ampat,
sa nangyaring ito,i, nagpadalang sulat
ang general Blanco,t, ipinatalastas.

30 Sa daquilang reina ang nangyaring gulo
na di magcahusay ang maraming tauo,
Caya nga't, sa gayon nagsidating dito
manga cazadores may limang puong libo.

31 Isinabog nitong bantog na general
sa madlang hucuma,t, manga bayan-bayan,
nang sa Catipunan sila,i, matanauan
di na tiniguilan ang pagpapatayan.

32 Maguing arao gabi,i, ualang bigong quilos
manga cazadores parang sinasalot,
lalo na,t, ang tauong manga taga Imus
castilang pinatay ay catacot-tacot.

33 Sa mabalitaan nang general Blanco
na di magcahusay ang nangyaring gulo,
agad pinalacad ang nasabing hocbo
na pauang castila, Imus ang tinungo.

34 Bucod pa sa roon ay may manga vapor
may caballerong acbay sa escuadron,
ang utos ni Blanco sa lahat nang campon
ang Imus na baya,i, lansaguin sa cañon.

35 Nang may ilang buan na di nagtitiguil
silagbo nang cañon at putoc nang mauser,
ang bala sa Imus doo,i,cun dumating
ay nangababaon lamang sa buhangin.

36 Ano,t, itong guerra ay pinagtatachan
nang ingles at frances, japon at aleman,
sa cañon at mauser ang inilalaban
nitong Catipunan ay itac na pangal.

37 Lahat nang pinuno nitong cazadores
ang labanang tao,i, nagsisipagngitngit,
dahilan sa capal armas nilang gamit
ang catagalugan ay hindi magahis.

38 Sa di pagtitiguil niyong paghahamoc
nang tanang castila at manga tagalog,
di naman mangyaring dayaing macupcop
ang bayan nang Imus sila,i, natatacot.

39 Ang lahat nang cañon ualang nagagaua
dahil sa trincherong matibay na cuta,
di naman magauang sumampa nang lupa
na cun maglabanan sila,i, napupugsa.

40 Sa ualang mangyari tanang cazadores
sa manga calabang pauang mababangis,
di naman madaya nila at maguipit
pagca,t, si Emilio,i, may magandang isip.

41 Ang labanang ito ay catacataca
niyong Catipunan sa tanang provincia,
pinuno,t, sundalo at ang manga cura
hindi pinapatay binibihag nila.

42 Dito sa nangyaring manga pagca-amis
nang cura,t, castila, balita,i, sumapit
ang general Blanco,i, malaqui ang hapis
sa lahat nang yao,i, halos magcasaquit.

43 Na cun caya lamang na auas-auasan
dahil sa ilongong dito,i, nagsidatal,
at ang macabeong tauong salangapang
nangacong matibay sa bunying general.

44 Sila ang lalacad na doo,i, lalacbay
sa Imus na bayan bilang sasalacay,
ipa-uauasacan ang cutang matibay
saca si Emilio,i, gagapusing buhay.

45 Nanalig sa gayon ang bunying general
caya,t, nagpagaua isang jaulang bacal,
na natatalaga na paglululanan
na sa cay Emilio na cahambalhambal.

46 Hindi rin naganap binanta sa loób
nitong manlililo na may asal hayop,
ang pinagnasaa,i, niligtas nang Dios
at itong nagnasa buhay ang natapos.

47 Caya ang sinoma,i, di dapat mangahas
na sa catapangan at dunong na ingat,
mahaba,t, maicsi, chapin ma,t, chinelas
ay may manga paang naguiguing casucat.

48 Ang sinalita co,i, dapat mapag-uari
nang may manga budhing masamang ugali,
ang camunting sira cundi laguing tagpi
pagcacara-anan nang malaquing guisi.

49 Balita man lamang mapagtatalastas
may mauser at canon sa castilang armas
taglay mang tagalog na ibinababag
cauayang matulis at pangal na itac.

50 Sa bilis nang bangis na di nagtitila
cun magcatanauan ay nangagbabanga,
sa arao at gabi tagalog castila
patay ay nagcalat magcabicabila.

51 Di maglipat buan dito,i, dumarating
daming cazadores sa España,i, galing
ualang nangyayari at ayao pasupil
ang catagalugan sa tapang na angquin.

52 Caya nga,t, sa gayon ang daquilang reina
sa hapis na lamang ay doon nanira,
siya nang pagdating nitong Polavieja
na pinacatucod nang boong España.

53 Pagdating na rito balita,i, cumalat
sa nasasacupan nitong Filipinas,
na dili umano cataua,i, may cunat
sa guerra,i, bihasa,t, matapang marahas

54 Ito pala naman ay inaabangan
niyong si Emiliong hayag din sa tapang,
nang mapapagquilala ang ayos nang laban
inaantay niya sa campong patayan.

55 Cun ibabalita salamin nang lahat
na sa caningningan ualang bahid lamat,
baquit sa panahon cun ano,t, sumayad
ang linao sa labo na icababasag.

56 Sa bayang Palanyag ay doon na suboc
itong Polaviejang matapang sa tacot,
cun ito,i, bayani baquit di manaog
na sa campanario utos lang nang utos.

57 Sa panucala niya ay napalamara
ang puno nang tropang coronel Zabala,
tulay nang Zapote doon nga humanga
ang ingat na buhay sa tama nang bala.

58 Nang mabalitaan ang tanang nangyari
nitong Polavieja saca ni Lachambre,
sa malaquing tacot nagsi-alis dine
ang general Blanco sumunod sa huli.

59 Dito ang pagdating Primo de Rivera
nangacong matibay sa daquilang reina,
ang nangyaring gulo na sa Filipina
sa pagcacagayon ang huhusay siya.

60 Di mumunting tauo yaong nangaganyac
na manga bihasang masquim sa pilac,
sa tanang castila sila ang nag-ulat
nagturo nang madlang mabubuting landas.

61 Ang binucong yao,i, hindi rin sinapit
na pagcacanulo sa tanang capatid,
at di magagauang magbanta nang lihis
pagca,t, si Emilio,i, may magandang isip.

62 Umalis sa Imus tanang Catipunan
nagdaan sa madlang manga bayan-bayan,
pinarunan nila ay lalong mainam,
sa Biac-na-bato doo,i, nagtumahan.

63. Doon sa nangyari pinunong castila
madlang cazadores malaqui ang tua,
at nasapit nila ang maraming lupa
uala namang tauo silang nacabanga.

64 Napasoc ang Imus hangang Noveleta
Naic, Marigondong, dinating nila,
ang Malabong Grande,t, bayang iba,t, iba
cun caya nahuca,i, uala ang cabaca.

65 Dito sa nangyaring manga cabagayan
nang sila,i, naroon sa nasabing bayan,
magpahangang dito balita,i, dumatal
tanang cazadores nagsisipagdiuang.

66 Ang Viva España,i, magcabi-cabila
ualang tiguil naman tugtog nang
campana,
ibinabandilang nanalo sa digma
Pananalong yao,i, calaban sa lupa.

67 Pagcatiguil nila na sa bayan-bayan
di rin napayapa sa caligayahan,
dahil sa malimit dalaui,t, parunan
niyong nalalabing munting Catipunan.

68 Siyang pagcatanyag nang general Luis
nang paronan nila bayang Novaliches,
tatlong puo,t, pito caual na calaquip
na ang nacalaba,i, daming cazadores.

69 Tatlong puo,t, ualo silang magcasama
aanim ang baril nilang dala-dala,
pauang manga itac ang taglay nang iba
na inilalaba,t, may reventador pa.

70 Manga tanod doon sangdaang mahiguit
na taga pag-ingat bayang Novaliches,
sa putoc at tunog nang reventadores
nagsipagtacbuhan tanang cazadores.

71 Yaong Montenegrong Antoniong masigla
napalaban naman sa lupang Barranca,
ipinamarali nang tanang cabaca
ang bayaning ito ay napatay nila.

72 Jimenez, Licerio at Pio del Pilar
ito,i, parapara na manga general,
di mumunting hirap ang pinagdaanan
sa manga castila sa pagpapatayan.

73 Ang general Panta naman ay natanyag
sa lupang Caloocan siya ang nag-atas,
na ang tanang caual na umaalagad
manga parapara namang mararahas.

74 Lisanin co yaon salit,i, ipunta
cay ginoong Emilio ay tanang casama,
sa Biac-na-bato niyong pagcatira
malaqui ang lumbay Primo de Rivera.

75 Ang cadahilana,i, di na masusucol
tanang Catipunang nagca-ayon ayon,
baga ma,t, maraming umang na patibong
di na masisilo nila,t, macuculong.

76 Sa ualang magaua naisip-isipan
Primo de Rivera nag-iba nang lalang,
pinuno,t, sundalo tungcol Catipunan
binibiguiang pases pumasoc nang bayan.

77 Hindi rin mangyari tanang inacala
na manga palacad nila,t, gauang daya,
ay ang naisipan at minagaling nga
ang tanang pinuno,i, cunin sa salita.

78 At pinaparoon sa Biac-na-bato
ang pamanquin niya saca si Paterno,
na ang catutura,i, parang sugo ito
namaqui pag-usap cay guinoong Emilio.

79 Na anim na buan ang hininging taning
na may manga sacsing natala sa papel,
sa pinag-usapang uicang magagaling
si guinoong Emilio naman ay umamin.

80 Caya pala gayon ang dayang hinangad
nang macapaglaan sila nang balangcas,
trincherang matibay cublihan nang lahat
niyong cazadores nang di mapahamac.

81 Nanga-alis dito ang pinunong iba
at ang nanga-iuan nagalac sa dusa,
tua nang castila,i, lubos na umasa
na ang Catipuna,i, malilicom nila.

82 Hindi rin nangyari sa laba,i, madaig
ang tanang tagalog mahiguit sa ganid,
Primo de Rivera,i, nagbago nang isip
na ipinasamsam ang lahat nang pases.

83 Sa palacad niya ay lalong nagdoop
yaong cagalitan nang tanang tagalog,
madlang bayan-bayan pilit na pinasoc
at ang cazadores canilang nilusob.

84 Sa di maapula ang calaguim-laguim
na pagpapatayan at di nagti-tiguil,
Primo de Rivera,i, umalis na tambing
at ang nahalili,i, general Augustin.

85 Anoman ang gauin nang bagong general
di rin mapayapa tanang kaguluhan,
at di nagtitiguil ang pagpapatayan
dito,t, sa iba pa na manga hucuman.

86 Silacbo nang init mahiguit sa quidlat
yaong carahasang di maauat-auat,
at sa gulong ito,i, siyang pagcatanyag
nang americanong dumagsa sa dagat.

87 Dito sa nangyari na calunos-lunos
general Augustin ay naghihimutoc,
ang cadahilana,i, bagay sa tagalog
sa anyaya niya,i, ayao pahinuhod.

88 Sa ualang magaua na isip-isipan
nitong si Augusting hayag na general
iniutos niyang dito,i, magsidatal
tanang cazadores na sa bayan-bayan.

89 Sa boong Mainila,i, isinabog niya
at may manga puno na natatalaga,
Pineda,t, Concepcion, Malate,t, Ermita
Singalong at Paco hangang Santa Ana.

90 Nacalatang lahat nitong cazadores
baya,t, manga nayon na dito,i, caratig
S. Juan, Santa Mesa, at labas nang buquid
linaguian nang tanod ang linibid-libid.

91 Lahat nang daana,t, manga suloc-suloc
ay may cazadores doo,i, natatanod
ang daang Malalim hangang Paang-Bundoc
natatayo roon ay catacot-tacot.

92 At ang cementeriong hayag na libingan
nang taga Binundoc ay marami namang
boong Gagalangin nangalaganapan
nitong cazadores na pauang matapang.

93 At sa Caloocang nasabing convento
marami ang tanod hangang campanario,
doon sa Maypajo at sa bayang Tundo
di mo mabibilang pinuno,t, sundalo.

94 Baybay nang Maynila magpahangang loób
pauang cazadores ang naguiguing tanod,
na tinadhanaan ang tanang tagalog
na di mangyayaring lumabas pumasoc.

95 Sa palacad nito,i, gumalao ang lahat,
Malabo,t, Obando bayang aliualas.
Pulo,t, Meycauayan, Marilao at Angat,
sa pagpapatayan tauo,i, nagagayac.

96 Bucaue,t, Bigaa, Guiguinto,t, Pulilan,
Paombong, Hagunoy at iba pang bayan,
Factoria,t Santol at Cabanatuan,
Cabiao, Peñaranda, Bungabong at Gapan.

97 Ang namuno dito sa bayang lahat na
capitan Mariano bantog na Llanera,
mahiguit sanglibo ang tauong casama
sa cacastilaan maquiquipag baca.

98 Calumpit, Apalit at ang Santo Tomas,
sampong S. Fernando naman ay nalangcap,
Mexico,t, Santa Ana saca ang Arayat,
San Luis, S. Simon at Candabang hayag.

99 Santa Rita,t, Coliat nangahaua naman
saca ang Baculod balitang hucuman,
Betis at ang Uaua, saca ang Sexmoan
at ang taga Lubao umayon sa laban.

100 Bulacan at Quiñgua nama,i, nagsiquilos
Baliuag at Busto,i, nagca-ayos-ayos,
ito,i, paraparang sa guerra,i, lumahoc
at ang manga tauo na taga Malolos.

101 Na sa gulong ito,i, nagcalaquip-laquip
S. Miguel, S. Rafael, Garay at S. Josef,
siyang pagsucol sa laba,i, guinipit
tauong macabeos at ang cazadores.

102 Tañgi ang Baliuag doo,i, may sumibol
Mariano Yoyongcong hugot sa panahon,
marami ang armas mauser ang nalicom
na sa cazadores sa laba,i, guinahol.

103 Cun caya nacuha hocomang Bulacan
dahil cay Gregoriong hayag na del Pilar
at saca cay Prigong balita sa tapang
sila ang namunong cumubcob sa bayan.

104 At sa gulong ito nang pagcacaisa
sa Pulo,i, naglagay naman nang trinchera,
Tambobong, Calaocan nang macuha nila
ay siyang pagquilos nang Santa Maria.

105 Taga Lalaguna nama,i, nagsisunod
Luciano Taleon ang punong nag-utos,
at sa catipunan na catacot-tacot
siyang lumaganap magpahangang bundoc.

106 Manga cazadores nang dumating doon
sa bayang Santa Cruz nagca-tipon-tipon,
punong sinusunod nang soldadong campon
coronel Alberting loob na hinahon.

107 Nang naroroon na silang calahatan
uala nang tigatig nangasasayahan,
dapua,t, hindi rin naman nagtumagal
dahilan sa capal nitong Catipunan.

108 Tanang bayan-bayan ay nangagsiquilos
Pagsanghan at Lumbang, S. Antoniong
bantog,
Paite at Paquil nagca-ayos-ayos
Siniloan, Pangil at ang bayang Lungos.

109 Saca ang mabitac, at Santa Maria,
Cavinti,t, Nagcarlang at ang Magdalena,
Majayjay at Lilio, S. Pablo at Pila,
Calauang at Bay at ang Los Baños pa.

110 Calamba,t, Cabuyao, Santa Rosa,t, Biñang,
saca ang Carmona,t, San Pedro Tunasan
ang namuno rito na naguing general
ang lubhang bayaning si Ponciano Rizal.

111 Nang lumaganap na ang gulong nanabog
nitong CATIPUNAN sa tapang ay bantog,
coronel Alberti sa malaquing tacot,
sumuco na siya sa tanang cahamoc.

112 Ang lahat nang armas na inilalaban
nitong cazadores pauang inialay,
ipinagcaloob kay Ponciano Rizal
at sa matatapang niyang manga caual.

113 Sa lubhang masidhi catapangang ingat
nang bayaning Taleon sa tanang calamas,
manga bayan-bayan pinasoc na lahat
siya,i, nacarating hangang sa Tayabas.

114 At hindi rin naman siya,i, nalaunan
na sa cazadores ng paquiquilaban,
sapagca,t, sumuco ang tanang dinatnan
manga tanod doon na cacastilaan.

115 Provinciang Batangas nama,i, nagsi-ayos
tanang catipunan na catacot-tacot,
at ang puno roon bilang sinusunod
ang bayaning Malvar sa tapang ay bantog.

116 Ito ay natangi sa ibang may tapang
baquit marunong na marami pang yaman
na di natatacot sa manga calaban
cataua,i, talaga sa pagpapatayan.

117 Lahat nang hocoma,i, nagcasunod-sunod
sa pagpapatayan handa,t, naaayos,
lalo,t, cun ang bayan nila ang pinasoc
itong cazadores parang sinasalot.

118 Si Pio del Pilar at Mariano Noriel
Julian de Ocampo at si Leon Juanching,
at si Isidoro Carmonang magaling
sa paquiquibaca naman ay hayag din.

119 Si Juan Gutierrez nama,i, naqui-ayos
sampong pamunuan na taga Bacood;
buhay na nasapit aquing ititiclop
saca sa huli na nila matatalos.

120 Sa ualang magaua ang cacastilaanan
sa americano nang paquiquilaban,
nalis si Augusting hayag na general
naui sa España,t, ang mando,i, iniwan.

121 General Jaudenes ang siyang nagdulot
ng capangyarihan dahilan sa tacot,
anoman ang gauin di macapamulos
sa yaman at capal ng americanos.

122 Sucat hangang dito cayo na ang siyang
lumingap sa bunsong na sa cahirapan,
sila ang panganay bilang mag-aatang
sa susunungin cong manga cahihiyan.

Glossary

Anting-anting	Amulet or potion that gives special powers, such as protection from injury and ability to pass through walls
Awa	Mercy, pity
Awit	Native song or metrical romance
Cabecilla	Spanish term for local leader or headman
Cazadores	Spanish troops (lit., "hunters")
Colorum	Derived from the Latin *per omnia saecula saeculorum*; popular term for "fanatical" members of cofradías, especially in southern Luzon
Damay	Empathy; participation in another's experience
Daya	Deceit; trickery
Dunong	Knowledge, sometimes with reference to secret lore
Ginhawa	Prosperity; ease of life; relief from pain
Gobernadorcillo	Filipino petty governor of a municipality
Gulo	Chaos; turmoil
Guardia civil	Civil guard organized in the Philippines in 1868
Hiya	Sensitivity to reciprocal obligations (lit. "shame")
Ilustrado	The "enlightened"; the educated segment of the native population
Indio	Spanish term for native Filipino, with a derogatory connotation in nineteenth-century usage
Inang Bayan	Mother Country; personification of the Philippine motherland
Kaginhawaan	See *ginhawa*
Kalayaan	Liberty; freedom (see *layaw*)
Kapatid	Sibling, member of a brotherhood
Kasaganaan	See *sagana*
Katwiran	Reason, the "straight path"; (r.w. *tuwid*: straight)
Katipunan	(Lit. "a gathering together") Revolutionary secret society founded by Bonifacio in 1892
Komedya	Popular Tagalog drama, also called *moro-moro* because of the preponderance of the Muslim-vs.-Christian theme
Lakaran	Traditionally referred to a pilgrimage with biblical connotations; (lit. "a journey on foot")
Layaw	Pampering treatment by parents; satisfaction of wants; freedom from parental control
Lingap	Compassionate care
Liwanag	Light, illumination
Loób	The "inside" of something; the inner being
Maginoo	The Tagalog equivalent of *datu*; a gèntleman of rank in the nineteenth century
Ningning	Glitter; the apppearance of light; empty exteriority
Panahon	Time; season; era
Pinunong bayan	The ruling elite in the towns
Principalia	Class composed of *pinunong bayan*, leading citizens, and in general, people of means
Pobres y ignorantes	"Poor and ignorant"; phrase commonly used by Spaniards and upper-class Filipinos to refer to the native masses
Puhunan	Investment (in social terms, related to *utang na loób)*
Sagana	Abundance (of food, crops, etc.)
Sinakulo	Passion play in Tagalog
Talinhaga	Metaphor; mystery to be reflected upon
Tanda	Sign; omen
Utang na loób	Debt of gratitude (lit. "inner debt")

Bibliography

Manuscript Collections

Archivo Histórico Nacional, Madrid. Pertinent to the study was Legajo 5356, Sección de Ultramar, "Sucesos contra el orden publico independientes de la rebelión." The most relevant document in the file was Manuel Garcia Morales and Euprasio Munarriz, "Ynformación sobre los sucesos de Apalit. . . el 19 de Febrero de 1898."

Archivo de la Provincia del Santisimo Rosario (The Dominican Archives) Quezon City.

Canseco, Telesforo. "Historia de la insurrección filipina en Cavite." 1897. A typed copy is available in the Ateneo de Manila Rizal Library, Quezon City.

Australian National Library, Canberra.

Beyer Collection of Tagalog Ethnography. The core of this collection are the bound and unbound volumes of ethnographic materials, mostly research papers by Professor H. Otley Beyer's students at the University of the Philippines. The following papers in the Tagalog ethnography series were particularly useful for the present study:

Arriola, Asuncion. "How 'Holy Week' is celebrated in Gasan Marinduque." 1916. Vol. 1, no. 6.

Atienza, Aquilino. "The Kolorum." 1915. Vol. 1, no. 39.

Caluag, Hermogenes. "Some Tagalog Beliefs and Maxims." 1915. Vol. 1, no. 156.

Estrella, Jose Dal. "Old Tagalog Songs." 1921. Vol. 10, no. 352.

Fernandez, Dominador. "Superstitious Beliefs of the People of Lilio." 1918. Vol. 2, no. 81.

Gonzales, Mariano. "Stories about *Anting-Anting*." 1915. Vol 4, no. 183.

Guzman, Paz de. "Tagalog Songs." 1915. Vol 4, no. 167.

Lopez, Julian. "Social Customs and Beliefs in Lipa, Batangas." 1915. Vol. 1, no. 64.

Magpantay, Severo. "Kabal." 1915. Vol. 1, no. 57.

Malabanan, Tarcila. "Social Functions among the Peasants of Lipa, Batangas." 1917. Vol. 2, no. 59.

Mariano, Honesto. "Popular Songs of the Revolution of '96." 1915. Vol. 4, no. 198.

Mascardo, Serviliano. "Ceremonies for Dying and Dead Persons in Lopez (Tayabas)." 1916. Vol. 1, no. 12.

Morente, Amanda. "Social Customs of the People of Pinamalayan." 1916. Vol. 1, no. 2.

Pagaspas, Juan. "Native Amusements in the Province of Batangas." 1916. Vol. 2, no. 66.

Penson, Maximo. "Superstitious Beliefs in our Town (San Miguel, Bulacan)." 1917. Vol. 3, no. 147.

Reyes, Benito. "Lenten Fiestas in Manila and Neighboring Towns." 1937. Unbound ms.

Silva, Paz. "Some Interesting Customs in Laguna Province." 1915. Vol. 2, no. 86.

Tirona, Ramona. "The Kolorum and the Spiritismo." 1916. Vol. 1, no. 41.

Michigan Historical Collections, Bentley Library, University of Michigan.

H.H. Bandholtz Papers. Harry Hill Bandholtz served as governor of Tayabas province in 1902 and 1903. He then became assistant chief of the Philippine Constabulary. From 1907 to 1913, he was brigadier general and chief of the constabulary. Owing to his key position, his letters contain information and assessments not found elsewhere. Included in Bandholtz's papers are two bound volumes of carbon copies of Philippine Constabulary Reports spanning the period from 1909 to 1913.

LeRoy Papers. James Alfred LeRoy accompanied Taft in 1901 as assistant secretary of the Philippine Commission. In 1905, he was back in the Philippines as private secretary to Secretary of War Taft. The accounts of both trips, plus related news clippings and articles, were consulted for this study.

Philippine National Archives, Manila.

Apolinario de la Cruz Papers. Lodged in the director's office is a bundle of uncatalogued documents relating to the Cofradía of 1840–41 and Labios's revival of the Cofradía in 1870. Among the documents are captured correspondence between Apolinario and the Cofradía, miscellaneous letters by the parish priests of Lucban, Majayjay, and Tayabas, Governor-General Oraá's reports to the home government, and interrogation records of captured cofrades in 1870. Of interest also are an oath of submission to the Cofradía's Patron, St. Joseph, and a forty-three stanza hymn titled *Dalit sa Caluwalhatian sa Langit na Cararatnan ng mga Banal* (19 Feb., 1840).

Philippine National Library, Manila.

Historical Data Papers, 1952–53. This compilation by schoolteachers of the "history and cultural life" of all the towns of the Philippines was useful to the extent that it contained old songs and stories about *anting-anting* and other unusual occurrences associated with the revolutionary period.

Philippine Insurgent Records (Revolutionary Records). These captured papers of the revolutionary government were transferred from the U.S. to the Philippine National Library in 1958 and are presently being rearranged. While working in this collection, I found the following boxes of documents particularly interesting and useful: Box I-19 (Public Instruction), I-25 (Religion), VII (Newspapers), IX (Katipunan), P-9 (Poems and Hymns).

Before the documents were transferred to the Philippines, a complete microfilm copy was made and lodged in the U.S. National Archives as Microcopy no. 254. Microfilm copies of this 643-reel set have been obtained by the National Libraries of Australia and the Philippines, among others. I was able to examine completely only the 80 or so reels comprising the "Selected Documents" (SD). Reel 4 lists the contents of 1306 folders in the "Selected Documents" but this guide is unreliable.

Miscellaneous Bound Manuscripts. The following items in the Filipiniana Section of the library contained immensely useful information about the Katipunan: Alvarez, Santiago, "Ang Katipunan at Paghihimagsik" (25 July 1927, 426 pp., typescript); Kasandugo (pseud.), "Ang Katipunan at si Gat Andres Bonifacio (n.d., 947 pp., typescript); and *Documentos de la Revolución Filipina* (Kalaw collection, 1952[?], 2 vols., typescript).

U.S. National Archives, Washington, D.C.

Correspondence of the Office of the Adjutant General (AGO), Record Group 94. The activities of Sebastian Caneo, Ruperto Rios, and other resistance leaders are often alluded to in the papers relating to the military investigation of Col. Cornelius Gardener, U.S.V., first civil governor of Tayabas province (AGO 421607).

Records of the Bureau of Insular Affairs (BIA), Record Group 350. The following files were particularly useful: 1184 (Philippine Constabulary) 2291(Insurgent Records), 2760 (Tayabas: government, officials, etc.), 3841 (Doherty file), 4587 (Katipunan Society), 4865 (Pacification).

U.S. Army Operations and Commands, 1898–1942, Record Group 395. A few reports from U.S. garrisons in Laguna and Batangas refer to the Colorum support given to Malvar in 1901–1902. Letters by principales to American commanders, "confessions" of arrested or captured guerillas and sympathizers, and various assessments by intelligence officers, all provide data of some sort about popular participation in the Malvar-led resistance.

Worcester Philippine Collection, Harlan Hatcher Library, University of Michigan.

Documents and Papers, 1834–1915. These volumes were useful for this study: vol. 4 (American occupation and Philippine independence); vol. 6 (Philippine insurrection); vol. 21 (Philippine government and politics).

The University of the Philippines Library, Diliman, Quezon City.
Carlos Ronquillo, "Ilang talata tungkol sa paghihimagsik ng 1896–97." MS., Hongkong, 1898.

Newspapers and Periodicals

Ang Bayang Kabapisbapis. San Francisco de Malabon, Cavite, 1899. In PIR Box 7.

La Independencia, 1906–1907. Library of Congress, Washington, D.C.

Ang Kaibigan ng Bayan, 1898–1899. Scattered copies in PIR and Library of Congress, Washington, D.C.

Kalayaan, January 1896. Spanish translation in W. Retana, *Archivo del Bibliófilo Filipino.* Vol. 3 Pp. 52–64.

La Política de España en Filipinas, 1891–1892.

Renacimiento Filipino, 1910–1912.

El Renacimiento/Muling Pagsilang, 1906–1907.

Unpublished Theses and Articles

Cauayani, Consejo V. "Some Popular Songs of the Spanish Period and Their Possible Use in the Music Program of Our Schools." M.A. thesis, University of the Philippines, 1954.

Coats, George Y. "The Philippine Constabulary: 1901–1917." Ph.D. dissertation, Ohio State University, 1968.

Eugenio, Damiana L. "*Awit* and *Korrido*: A Study of Fifty Philippine Metrical Romances in Relation to Their Sources and Analogues." Ph.D. dissertation, University of California at Los Angeles, 1965.

Guerrero, Milagros C. "Luzon at War: Contradictions in Philippine Society, 1898–1902." Ph.D. dissertation, University of Michigan, 1977.

Lumbera, Bienvenido L. "Tradition and Influences in the Development of Tagalog Poetry (1570–1898)." Ph.D. dissertation, Indiana University, 1967.

Sturtevant, David R. "Philippine Structure and Its Relation to Agrarian Unrest. Ph.D. dissertation, Stanford University, 1958. Since the writing of this book, Sturtevant's revised thesis has been published as *Popular Uprisings in the Philippines, 1840–1940.* Ithaca, Cornell University Press, 1976.

_____ "Rural Discord: The Peasantry and Nationalism." Paper for a symposium on Philippine Nationalism, Ithaca, 1969.

Published Sources in Tagalog

Aglipay, Gregorio. *Pagsisiyam sa Virgen sa Balintawak: Ang Virgen sa Balintawak ay ang Inang Bayan* (orig. in Spanish). Manila: I. de los Reyes, 1925.

Aguinaldo, Emilio. *Mga Gunita ng Himagsikan.* Manila: N.p., 1964.

Anak-bayani (pseud.). "Anting-anting." RENFIL 3 (1913): 1369.

Aranas, Simeon. *Kaligaligayang Bundok ng Banahaw (awit).* 2 vols. Manila: P. Sayo, 1927.

Azagra, Gregorio. *Maicling Casaysayan nang Catipunan nang Laguing Pag-eestacion.* Manila, 1894.

"Bagumbayan." RENFIL 2 (14 July 1913): 189.

Casaysayan nang Pasiong Mabal ni Jesucristong Panginoon Natin. Manila: J. Martinez, 1925 (first published in 1814).

"Mga Dahon ng Kasaysayan: Sa Kalupi ng Isang Babaing Naanib sa Katipunan." RENFIL 2 (28 Sept., 7 Oct. 1911): 388, 454–56.

Flores, Hermenigildo. *Hibik ng Filipinas sa Ynang España* (poem). N.p., 1888.

Francisco, Gabriel B. *Kasaysayan ni Apolinario de la Cruz na may Pamagat na Hermano Pule.* N.p., 1915.

_____. *Ang Katipunan: Aliwan na may Dalawang Babagui.* Manila, 1899. 2d. printing.

Gala, Severino. *Dasala't Dalit ng Kolorum.* Manila, J. Fajardo, 1912.
Herrera, Pedro de. *Meditaciones, cun manga Mahal na Pagninilay na Sadia sa Santong Pageexercicios.* Manila, 1645.
Historia Famosa ni Bernardo Carpio (awit). Manila: J. Martinez, 1919 (orig. published in 1860).
Iglesia Watawat ng Lahi. *Bagong Liwanag: Ang Tinig ng Katotohanan.* Calamba: F. Salazar, 1970.
Mahalagang Kasulatan; Alaala sa Magiting na Dr. Jose Rizal. Barasoain, 30 December 1898.
Mañibo, Joaquin. *Pasion ng Bayan sa Kahapo't Ngay-on.* Bauan, Batangas: Javier Press, 1934.
Mariano, Antonio, O.S.B. *Patres Patriae (Mga Ama ng Bayan).* Manila: Institute of National Language, 1950.
Merced, Aniceto de la. *El Libro de la Vida. . . .* Manila: J. Martinez, 1906.
_____. *Manga puna . . .* Manila: Fajardo y Cia, 1907.
Mojica, Diego. "Pasiong Bagong Katha." RENFIL 1 (21 March 1911): 34.
Molina, Antonio J. *Ang Kundiman ng Himagsikan.* Manila: Institute of National Language, 1940.
Natividad, T.E. "Ang Bundok ng Arayat o ang Sinukuan." RENFIL 2 (21 Dec. 1911): 818–20; 2 (7 Jan. 1912): 883–84.
Poblete, Pascual. *Caguilaguilalas na Buhay ni Juan Soldado* (verse). Manila, 1899.
Quezon Province. *Dahong Pang-alaala sa Bayan Tayabas.* 1928.
Ricarte, Artemio. *Himagsikan nang manga Pilipino Laban sa Kastila.* Yokohama, 1927.
Robles, Alfredo Jr., ed. "Mga Kilusang Mesiyaniko sa Pilipinas." In *Likas.* Quezon City: University of the Philippines, 1976. Pp. 50–113.
Ronquillo, Carlos, ed. "Mga Kantahing Bayan." RENFIL 1 (28 August 1910): 23.
_____. ed. "Ang Paghihimagsik Laban sa Espanya" (Kantahing Pulube). RENFIL 1 (7 June 1911): 34; 1 (14 June 1911): 33.
_____. "Ang Tagalog: Kung Bakit Mahiligin sa Tula." RENFIL 1 (21 August 1910): 24–26.
Santos, Jose P. *Si Andres Bonifacio at ang Himagsikan.* 2d. printing. N.p., 1935.
_____. *Buhay at mga Sinulat ni Emilio Jacinto.* Manila: Published by author, 1935.
_____. *Buhay at mga Sinulat ni Plaridel.* Manila: Dalaga, 1931.
_____. *Ang Tatlong Napabantog na "Tulisan" sa Pilipinas.* Gerona: Tarlac, 1936.
Sequera, Mariano. *Justicia ng Dios: Mga Ilang Bagay na Inasal dito sa Filipinas nang manga Fraile* (verse). Manila, 1899.
Tandiama Eulogio, Julian de. *Ang Cahabaghabag na Buhay na Napagsapit nang ating manga Capatid (awit).* N.p., n.d.
_____. *Casunod nang Buhay na Pinagdaanan ng Ating manga Capatid (awit).* N.p., n.d.
Tiongson, Nicanor. *Kasaysayan at Estetika ng Sinakulo at Ibang Dulang Panrelihiyon sa Malolos.* Quezon City: Ateneo de Manila University Press, 1975.

Published Sources in Spanish

"Amuletos Guerreros de la Pasada Revolución." RENFIL 1 (7 Oct. 1910): 17-18.
Caro y Mora, Juan. *La Situación del País.* 2d. ed. Manila, 1897.
Chamorro, Pedro. *Memoria Histórica de la Conducta Militar y Política del Teniente General D. Marcelino Oraa.* Madrid, 1851.
Cruz, Apolinario de la. "Declaración de Apolinario de la Cruz." *La Política de España en Filipinas,* Vol. 2. Madrid, 1892. No. 32, pp. 113–14; no. 33, pp. 130–31; no. 34, p. 155.
Dolendo, Teodorico T. "Los sucesos del Mag-Puli." RENFIL 2, (21 Aug. 1911): 220–23; (21 Sept. 1911): 367–69.
Guerra, Juan A. *De Manila á Tayabas.* 2d. ed. Madrid: Fortanet, 1887.
Kalaw, Teodoro. *Cinco Reglas de Nuestra Moral Antigua; Una Interpretación.* Manila Bureau of Printing, 1947 (first published in 1935).
Mas, Sinibaldo de. *Informe sobre el Estado de las Islas Filipinas en 1842.* 2 vols., Madrid, 1843.
Miranda, Claudio. *Costumbres Populares.* Manila: Imprenta "Cultura-Filipina," 1911.

Noceda, P. Juan de, and P. Pedro de Sanlucar. *Vocabulario de la Lengua Tagala*. Manila, 1860 (first published in 1754).

Retana, Wenceslao. *Archivo del Bibliófilo Filipino*. 5 vols. Madrid,1895–1905.

_____. *Supersticiones de los Indios Filipinos: Un Libro de Aniterias*. Madrid, 1894.

Reyes, Isabelo de los. *Apuntes para un Ensayo de Teodicea Filipina: La Religión del "Katipunan"*... Madrid, 1899.

_____. *El Folk-lore Filipino*. 2 vols. Manila, 1889. 1890.

Sancho, Fr. Manuel. "Relación Espresiva de los Principales Acontecimientos de la Titulada Cofradía del Señor San Jose...," *La Politica de España en Filipinas,* vol. 1, 21 (1891): 250–51; vol. 1, 23 (1891):289–91; vol. 2, 25 (1892): 18–19; vol. 2, 26 (1892): 30–32; vol. 2, 29 (1892): 74–75; vol. 2, 31 (1892): 99–101.

Venegas, Paco. "El anting-anting." RENFIL 2 (from 21 Sept. to 28 Nov. 1911).

Published Sources in English

Abad, Antonio K. *General Macario L. Sakay: Was He a Bandit or a Patriot?* Manila: J.B. Feliciano & Sons, 1955.

Achútegui, Pedro S. de, S.J., and Miguel A. Bernad, S.J. *Aguinaldo and the Revolution of 1896: A Documentary History*. Quezon City: Ateneo de Manila, 1972.

Agoncillo, Teodoro A. *The Revolt of the Masses*. Quezon City: University of the Philippines, 1956.

_____. *Malolos: The Crisis of the Republic*. Quezon City: University of the Philippines, 1960.

_____. *The Writings and Trial of Andres Bonifacio*. Manila: Bonifacio Centennial Commission, 1963.

_____. and Milagros Guerrero. *History of the Filipino People*. 5th ed. Quezon City: R.P. Garcia, 1977.

Agpalo, Remigio. *Pandanggo-Sa-Ilaw: The Politics of Occidental Mindoro*. Ohio University Center for International Studies, 1969.

Alip, Eufronio. "The Mystic Lure of Mount Banahao." *Philippine Magazine* 34 (1937): 542–43, 561–62.

Alzona, Encarnacion. *Julio Nakpil and the Philippine Revolution*. Manila: Carmelo and Bauermann, 1964.

Anderson, Benedict R. O'G. "The Idea of Power in Javanese Culture." In *Culture and Politics in Indonesia,* ed. by Claire Holt, Benedict R.O.G. Anderson, and James Siegel. Ithaca: Cornell University, 1972. Pp. 1–70.

Auerbach, Erich. *Mimesis: The Representation of Reality in Western Literature*. Princeton, N.J.: Princeton University, 1953.

Benda, Harry. "Peasant Movements in Southeast Asia." *Asian Studies* 3 (1965): 420–34.

Bernad, Miguel A., S.J. *Philippine Literature: A Twofold Renaissance*. Manila: Bookmark, 1963.

Blair, Emma H. and Alexander Robertson, eds. *The Philippine Islands, 1493–1898*. 50 vols. Mandaluyong, Metro Manila: Cacho Hermanos, 1973.

Bloch, Marc. *The Historian's Craft*. New York: Vintage Books, 1953.

"The Christmas Eve Fiasco and a Brief Outline of the Ricarte and Other Similar Movements from the Time of the Breaking up of the Insurrection of 1899-1901." In Artemio Ricarte, *Memoirs*, Manila: National Heroes Commission, 1963. Appendix N. pp. 157-216.

Bonifacio, Amelia Lapeña, *The "Seditious" Tagalog Playwrights*. Manila: Bookmark, 1972.

Constantino, Renato. *The Philippines: A Past Revisited*. Quezon City: Tala Publishing, 1975.

Corpuz, Onofre D. *The Philippines*. Englewood Cliffs, New Jersey: Prentice-Hall, 1965.

Costa, Horacio de la. *Readings in Philippine History*. Manila: Bookmark, 1965.

Covar, Prospero. "Religious Leadership in the Iglesia Watawat ng Lahi." In *Filipino Religious Psychology*, ed. by L. Mercado, S.V.D. Tacloban, Leyte: Divine Word University, 1977.

Dichoso, Fermin. "Some Superstitious Beliefs and Practices in Laguna, Philippines." *Anthropos* 62 (1967): 61–67.

Doherty, David H. *Conditions in the Philippines.* U.S. Senate Doc. 170, 58th Congress, 2nd Session, February 1904.

Foronda, Marcelino. *Cults Honoring Rizal.* Manila: R.P. Garcia, 1961.

Friend, Theodore. *Between Two Empires: The Ordeal of the Philippines, 1929–1946.* New Haven: Yale University, 1965.

Guerrero, Milagros C. "The Colorum Uprisings: 1924-1931," *Asian Studies* 5 (1967): 65–78.

Haslam, Andres J. *Forty Truths and Other Truths.* Manila: Philippine Publishing Co., 1900.

Hobsbawm, Eric. *Primitive Rebels: Studies in Archaic Forms of Social Movement in the 19th and 20th Centuries.* New York: Norton, 1963.

Hurley, Victor. *Jungle Patrol: The Story of the Philippine Constabulary.* New York, 1938.

Ileto, Reynaldo C. "Tagalog Poetry and Perception of the Past in the War Against Spain." In *Perceptions of the Past in Southeast Asia,* ed. by A. Reid and D. Marr. Singapore: Heinemann, 1979.

Kessler, Clive. "The Politics of Islamic Egalitarianism," *Humaniora Islamica* 2 (1974): 237–52.

Kiefer, Thomas. *The Tausug: Violence and Law in a Philippine Muslim Society.* New York: Holt, Rinehart & Winston, 1972.

Larkin, John A. *The Pampangans: Colonial Society in a Philippine Province.* Berkeley: University of California, 1972.

Leon, Felipe P. de. "Poetry, Music and Social Consciousness." *Philippine Studies* 17 (1969): 266–82.

LeRoy, James A. *Philippine Life in Town and Country.* New York: G.P. Putnam & Sons, 1905.

Lumbera, Bienvenido. "Assimilation and Synthesis (1700–1800): Tagalog Poetry in the Eighteenth Century." *Philippine Studies* 16 (1968): 622–62.

_____. "Consolidation of Tradition in Nineteenth-Century Tagalog Poetry." *Philippine Studies* 17 (1969): 377–411.

Lynch, Frank, S.J., comp. *Four Readings on Philippine Values.* Quezon City, Ateneo de Manila Institute of Philippine Culture, 1962.

Mabini, Apolinario. *The Philippine Revolution* (Guerrero translation). Manila: National Historical Commission, 1969 (orig. Spanish version was published in 1931).

Maceda, Generoso. "The Remontados of Rizal Province," *Philippine Journal of Science* 64 (Nov. 1937): 313–21.

Majul, Cesar A. *Apolinario Mabini, Revolutionary.* Manila: National Historical Commission, 1964.

_____. *The Political and Constitutional Ideas of the Philippine Revolution.* Quezon City: University of the Philippines, 1957.

Manuel, E. Arsenio. *Dictionary of Philippine Biography.* 2 vols. Quezon City: Filipinina Publications, 1955, 1970.

Marche, Alfred. *Luzon and Palawan,* trans. by C. Ojeda and J. Castro. Manila: Filipiniana Book Guild, 1970. (French original was published in 1887).

Marx, Karl and Friedrich Engels. *Basic Writings on Politics and Philosophy,* ed. by Lewis Feuer. New York: Doubleday Anchor, 1959.

Mayo, Katherine. *The Isles of Fear: Truth about the Philippines.* New York: Harcourt, Brace & Co., 1925.

Minutes of the Katipunan. Manila: National Heroes Commission, 1964.

Moses, Edith. *Unofficial Letters of an Official's Wife.* New York: Appleton, 1908.

Owen, Norman G. *Compadre Colonialism.* University of Michigan, Center for South and Southeast Asian Studies, 1971.

Panganiban, Jose V. *Diksyunaryo-Tesauro Pilipino-Ingles.* Quezon City: Manlapaz, 1972.

Pastores, Elizabeth. "Religious Leadership in the *Lapiang Malaya:* A Historical Note." In *Filipino Religious Psychology,* ed. by L. Mercado, S.V.D. Tacloban: Divine Word University, 1977.

Phelan, John L. *The Hispanization of the Philippines.* Madison: University of Wisconsin, 1959.

Quirino, Carlos. "Historical Introduction." In *The Trial of Andres Bonifacio.* Manila: Ateneo de Manila, 1963.

Ricarte, Artemio. *Memoirs*. Manila: National Heroes Commission, 1963.

Rizal, Jose. *The Subversive* (El Filibusterismo). Trans. by Leon Ma. Guerrero. New York: Norton, 1968.

_____. *Noli Me Tangere*. Trans. by Leon Ma. Guerrero. London: Longmans, 1961.

St. Clair, Francis (pseud.) *The Katipunan; or the Rise and Fall of the Filipino Commune*... Manila: n.p., 1902.

San Juan, Epifanio, Jr. *A Preface to Pilipino Literature*. Quezon City: Alemar's, 1971.

Santos, Alfonso P., ed. *Rizal Miracle Tales*. Manila: National Bookstore, 1973.

Santos, Epifanio de los. *The Revolutionalists: Aguinaldo, Bonifacio, Jacinto*. Manila: National Historical Commission, 1955.

Sanz, Leandro Tormo. *Lucban (A Town the Franciscans Built)*. Manila: Historical Conservation Society, 1971. (orig. in Spanish).

Schumacher, John N., S.J. *The Propaganda Movement*, 1880–1895. Manila: Solidaridad, 1972.

_____. "The Religious Character of the Revolution in Cavite, 1896–1897." *Philippine Studies* 24 (1976): 399–416.

Siegel, James T. *The Rope of God*. Berkeley: University of California, 1969.

Stanley, Peter. *A Nation in the Making: The Philippines and the United States, 1899–1921*. Cambridge, Mass.: Harvard University, 1974.

Steinberg, David J. "An Ambiguous Legacy: Years at War in the Philippines," *Pacific Affairs* 45 (1972): 165–90.

_____. *Philippine Collaboration in World War II*. Ann Arbor: University of Michigan, 1967.

Sturtevant, David R. *Agrarian Unrest in the Philippines*. Ohio University: Center for International Studies, 1969.

_____. "Epilog for an Old Colorum,'" *Solidarity* 3 (1968): 10–18.

_____. "Guardia de Honor: Revitalization within the Revolution." *Asian Studies* 4(1966):342—52.

_____. *Popular Uprisings in the Philippines, 1840-1940*. Ithaca: Cornell University Press, 1976.

Sweet, David. "The Proto-Political Peasant Movement in the Spanish Philippines: The Cofradia de San Jose and the Tayabas Rebellion of 1841," *Asian Studies* 8 (1970): 94–119.

Taylor, John R.M. *The Philippine Insurrection against the United States: A Compilation of Documents with Notes and Introduction*. 5 vols. Pasay City: Eugenio Lopez Foundation, 1971–73 (based on 1906 galleys).

U.S. Philippine Commission. *Annual Reports of the Philippine Commission* (various titles). Washington, D.C.: Government Printing Office, 1901–1910.

Villamor, Ignacio. *Criminality in the Philippine Islands: 1903–1908*. Manila, 1909.

Woods, Robert G. "Origin of the Colorum," *Philippine Magazine* 16 (December 1929): 428–29; (Jan. 1930): 506, 514, 516–17.

_____. "The Strange Story of the Colorum Sect," *Asia* 32 (1932): 450–54, 459-60.

Zaide, Gregorio F. *History of the Katipunan*. Manila: Loyal Press, 1939.

_____. *The Philippine Revolution*. Rev. ed. Manila: Modern Book Co., 1968.

Index

PASYON AND REVOLUTION, unlike earlier Philippine historical writings that use largely the Filipino educated elite's categories of meaning, seeks to interpret Philippine popular movements in terms of the perceptions of the masses themselves. Ileto submits to varied kinds of analyses standard documents as well as such previously ignored sources as folk songs, poems, and religious traditions, in order to articulate hidden or suppressed features of the thinking of the masses. Paramount among the conclusions of the book is that the pasyon, or native account of Christ's life, death, and resurrection, provided the cultural framework of movements for change. The book places the Philippine revolution in the context of native traditions, and explains the persistence of radical peasant brotherhoods in this century. Seen as continuous attempts by the masses to transform the world in their terms are the various movements that the book analyzes—Apolinario de la Cruz's Cofradía de San Jose, Andres Bonifacio's Katipunan, Macario Sakay's Katipunan, Felipe Salvador's Santa Iglesia, the Colorum Society, and other popular movements during the Spanish, revolutionary, and American colonial periods.